EURO♥ISION
SONG CONTEST

The EUROVISION SONG CONTEST

THE OFFICIAL HISTORY

John Kennedy O'Connor

CARLTON
BOOKS

1977

DEDICATED TO MY FATHER AND SON:
Martin John and James Edward O'Connor.
Not exactly Eurovision's greatest fans.

A former record executive in the UK, John Kennedy O'Connor lived in California for thirteen years where, apart from producing international events all over the world, he contributes music and film reviews to many American publications and websites as well as writing regular travel journals and city and venue guides. Born into a political Anglo-Irish family in North London at the peak of Beatlemania, it was the Eurovision Song Contest that diversified his musical interests into European and International pop and gave him a wanderlust to discover other countries and cultures. His teenage son continues the same passion for music but, sensibly, holds no interest in Eurovision at all.

This updated edition published in Great Britain by
Carlton Books Limited 2010
20 Mortimer Street
London W1T 3JW

First published by Carlton Books Limited 2005

ISBN: 978-1-84732-521-1

Printed in Dubai

Editorial Manager: Lorna Russell
Picture research: Sarah Edwards
Art Director: Clare Baggaley
Design: Simon Wilder
Cover design: Alison Tutton
Production: Lisa Moore

www.eurovision.tv

The publishers would like to thank the following sources for their kind permission to reproduce the pictures in this book. The page numbers for each of the photographs are listed below, giving the page on which they appear in the book and any location indicator (c-centre, t-top, b-bottom, l-left, r-right).

Associated Press: /Dave Caulkin: 148bc.
BBC Photo Library: 2tc, 3tr, 7, 16l, 16bl, 22, 23, 24l, 24br, 32, 33tr, 34, 35, 36l, 36br, 37, 38, 40l, 42-43, 48, 49, 54-55, 56l, 58, 60br, 62-63, 66, 68, 69, 70, 72, 76b, 88bc, 90, 92l, 114tl, 120l, 122.
Robert Bengston: 2l.
Empics: /ANP: 10-11, 14-15, 44br, 52, 55, 74, 96l, 98, 104bc, 109, 116bc, 128, 132b, 144l, 146, 146-147, 160b, 215; /DPA: 3bl, 24bl, 86, 92bc, 95, 96bc, 96-97, 100, 101, 116l, 116-117, 117bc, 119, 156b, 206; /EPA: 3tl, 28-29, 160l, 161, 162, 164bc, 164-165, 168l, 168-169, 170, 205, 213; /David Jones: 152, 153, 154; /Martin McCullough: 132l, 134tr; /PA: 16br, 44bl, 84br; /Polfoto: 164l, 166.
Getty Images: 173, 174br; /Frank Barratt/Keystone: 50; /Central Press: 60l, 63r, 76l, 79; /Larry Ellis/Express: 30; /Evening Standard: 64; /Express: 5; /Sean Gallup: 180br, 184l, 186l, 186r; /Keystone/Hulton Archive: 8, 9, 12, 13, 14l, 14bl, 18-19, 26, 27, 36tr, 46br, 73, 80b, 83, 84l, 86-87; /Aris Messinis/AFP: 184r; /Bendt K. Rasmussen/Keystone/Hulton Archive: 2bl, 80l, 81, 209; /Janek Skarzynski/AFP: 172b; /Sergei Supinsky/AFP: 180bl; /Wilds/Keystone/Hulton Archive: 44l, 45, 46l.
IBL Bildbyra: /Charles Hammarsten: 92-93, 102.
NRK: /Barbara Halden: 110br, 124; /Tore Halden: 104-105.
RTE Stills Library: 133, 134tl, 136-137, 138, 140, 142-143, 148l, 149, 150-151.
Redferns: /Gems: 59.
Rex Features: 28l, 28bl, 56-57, 182; /Action Press: 165br, 168bl, 172l, 174bl, 176l, 178bl, 218; /Allover Norway: 196-197; /Andre Brutmann: 156l, 158; /Araldo di Crollalanza: 40-41; /Sari Gustafsson: 192l, 193, 194-195; /Juha Jormanainen: 210; /Lehtikuva OY: 144b, 189, 190; /Jarmo Matilainen: 202; /Pat Maxwell: 85, 112, 113, 114tr; /Picture Perfect: 196l, 198l, 198r; /Sten Rosenlund: 2br, 88l, 88-89, 89, 200; /Heikki Saukkomaa: 188l; /Sipa Press: 104l, 106, 108, 110bc, 129, 130, 157, 176b, 178br, 194, 217.
SVT Bild: /Allan Olofsson: 126, 141.
Topfoto.co.uk: 20-21, 31, 33tl, 120.
Mark Weeks: back cover b.

Every effort has been made to acknowledge correctly and contact the source and/or copyright holder of each picture and Carlton Books Limited apologises for any unintentional errors or omissions that will be corrected in future editions of this book.

1980

1982

Contents

Foreword by Svante Stockselius   4

Introduction   6

The Eurovision Song Contest 1956-2006   8

Eurostats   200

Semi-finals Results   219

Foreword

One of the most enjoyed TV shows in the world for over fifty years, the Eurovision Song Contest is now bigger, better and more popular than ever.

This is definitely not your everyday, ordinary TV show. It is a magical event every year for millions and millions of fans worldwide. A glittering extravaganza showcasing pop music from all over Europe and beyond, glamorous, fun and exciting in equal measure – no wonder Eurovision Song Contest has lasted so long.

This book celebrates the history of the competition. You will find many wonderful stories from the past 50 years, and all the facts and figures. But it is also a tribute to the future of this very special entertainment phenomena.

In today's fast-moving world of TV entertainment it cannot be taken for granted that any show will survive for more than one year, let alone fifty. But I am totally convinced that the popularity of the Eurovision Song Contest will yet remain sky high for many, many years to come. Maybe even to celebrate its 100th birthday?

And finally, I wish that Mr Marcel Besançon (1907–1981) could have lived to see his brilliant idea of a European contest with songs celebrate it's 50th anniversary. The European Broadcasting Union (EBU) is proud to be the founder and organiser of this very special and unique event.

Svante Stockselius
EXECUTIVE SUPERVISOR OF THE EUROVISION SONG CONTEST
EBU

The scoreboard shows:

1	UNITED KINGDOM	SAY WONDERFUL THINGS
2	NETHERLANDS	EEN SPEELDOOS
3	GERMANY	MARCEL
4	AUSTRIA	VIELLEICHT GESCHIENT EIN WUNDER
5	NORWAY	SOLHVERV
6	ITALY	UNO PER TUTTE
7	FINLAND	MUISTOJENI LAULU
8	DENMARK	DANSEVISE
9	YUGOSLAVIA	BRODOVI
10	SWITZERLAND	T'EN VA PAS
11	FRANCE	ELLE ETAIT SI JOLIE
	SPAIN	ALGO PRODIGIOSO

Part of the great legacy of Eurovision, all the competitors in the 1963 contest, staged in London, gather for a photograph beneath the scoreboard.

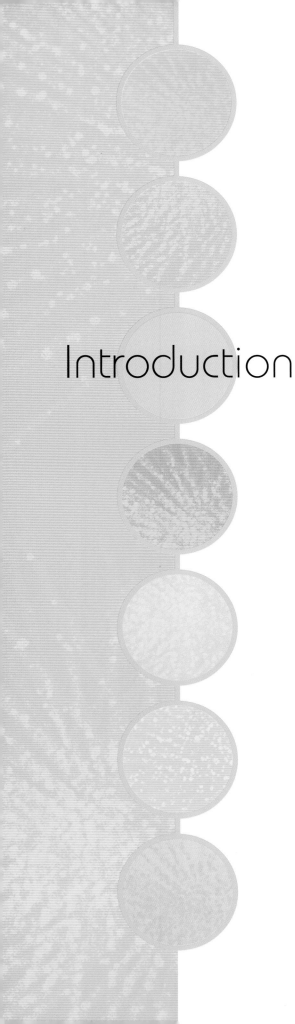

Introduction

I first became interested in the Eurovision Song Contest in 1970. I first became obsessed with it in 1971! I had developed something of an infatuation with the British representative in Dublin, Clodagh Rodgers, and I was so taken with her song 'Jack In The Box,' that it became the first record I ever owned. I didn't see the contest, but when my father told me that Clodagh had not won, I was devastated. When I saw the contest itself for the very first time in 1972, I tipped the Dutch song to win (they came in fourth), but above all I wanted The New Seekers to triumph for the UK. They finished second – an appropriate introduction to the contest for me: the British being the perennial runners up!

In these pages you'll discover who sang about the mysterious ladies: Marie-Blanche; Jennifer Jennings; Mrs Thompson and Mrs Caroline Robinson. And the equally beguiling men: Marcel; Johnny Blue; Giorgio; Fernando and Philippo. You'll also discover who sang odes to Socrates, Charlie Chaplin, Marlene Dietrich, Rudolf Valentino, Ghengis Khan and Walt Disney. The majority of the entries deal with the subject of love, but you'll also find songs about the sun, moon, stars, heavens, comets and other celestial bodies. Puppets, dolls, clowns and merry-go-rounds play a large part in Eurovision history, as do songs about European places as well as such far-flung destinations as Colorado, San Francisco, Brazil and Lusitania. Particularly watch out for hearts going boom, boom boom, boom, boom, badadoum and boom bang-a-bang. There are countless songs about music itself, including references to such great composers as Purcel, Puccini, Offenbach, Debussy, Gershwin, Chopin and Beethoven, and that's just the Austrian entry from 1980! Perhaps most surprisingly of all, you'll even find one song about Eurovision itself.

Both Gary Speirs and David Elder have been invaluable in sharing their vast knowledge of the contest with me. Gary provided me with the details of entries and voting records for the first quarter century of the contest and David (possibly Eurovision's biggest fan) has always given me monumental encouragement. Nick King and Richard Swales provided many hours of video and audio support for which, many thanks. *Baby Baby Eurovision* by Jan A. Gotz was an invaluable source of reference for the recordings and international chart history of songs from the contest. Alan Stuart also deserves thanks for founding the Internet site 'EuroActive' that brought me

Eurovision veteran Katie Boyle presented the contest four times.

back into the Eurovision fold after my move to the USA in 1992. I'd most of all like to thank my mother for giving me the idea of writing this book in the first place. I'm only sorry my father, who always feigned interest in the show in a paternal display of support, did not live to see it completed.

I have checked and re-checked all of the facts contained herein, but I have included conjecture where it is appropriate, always noting it as such. The voting records are taken from the EBU's own records. Often the results have been amended after the contest transmission, and these officially amended scores have been used for the results with appropriate annotation. The translation of song titles has proved something of a headache. I have used the English versions of songs given in the commentary or in the official programme where this is available, even if these translations bear no resemblance to the original title of the song. Where this information was not available, I have used literal translations of the song's titles.

If you've ever wondered what the world-wide phenomenon that is The Eurovision Song Contest is all about and who has sung what over the past fifty years, here's your chance to find out everything that you've ever wanted to know!

John Kennedy O' Connor

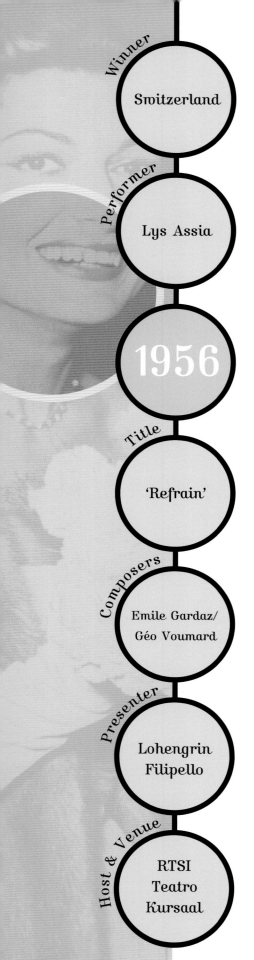

Winner

Switzerland

Performer

Lys Assia

1956

Title

'Refrain'

Composers

Emile Gardaz/
Géo Voumard

Presenter

Lohengrin
Filipello

Host & Venue

RTSI
Teatro
Kursaal

Lugano
Switzerland

Lys Assia, winner of the inaugural contest, told the UK's Channel Four in an interview recorded in 2000 that she had the best song, the best orchestra and was the best singer in the contest – hence her victory. It is hard to argue with confidence of that nature.

The Eurovision Song Contest is an annual television show that is broadcast across Europe, and is designed to 'stimulate the output of original, high-quality songs in the field of popular music by encouraging competition between authors and composers through the international comparison of their works.' Risible as that statement may appear, it is, in truth, the stated objective of what is possibly the most controversial and maligned television show ever broadcast in the world. But, way back at the start, it's foremost objective was to promote television.

In 1954 the recently formed cartel of public service broadcasters, the European Broadcasting Union (EBU), was charged to come up with new joint-broadcast ideas, and its Italian members proposed a one-off 'Grand Prix of European Song' to be broadcast in the spring of 1956.

Only seven of the founding EBU nations participated in the inaugural event – Switzerland, Luxembourg, The Netherlands, Belgium, West Germany, Italy and France. Denmark, Austria and the UK registered too late to take part and had to sit out the first year, although they did screen the final. With Marcel Besançon, the Director General of Swiss television, behind it, the Swiss hosted the inaugural competition. It took place in the tiny Teatro Kursaal in the city of Lugano, part of Switzerland's Italian-speaking region, on Thursday 24th May 1956. Each of the seven competing nations was permitted to select two songs to compete in the final, the only time multiple entries have ever been allowed. All countries competing were asked to organise a nationally televised heat to select their entry.

The very first song ever performed in the contest was the first Dutch entry, 'De Vogels Van Holland' ('The Birds Of Holland'), which was sung by **Jetty Paerl**. Today, little remains of Jetty's performance or those of any of the other seven competing nations. A soundtrack recording of the show has survived, but no confirmed videotape of this landmark broadcast appears to exist. Also left unclear was how the winner was determined. What is recorded is that each country was allowed to appoint just two judges to cast votes on their behalf – for some obscure reason, two Swiss nationals were invited to represent Luxembourg. It was no surprise, then, that Switzerland won the very first Eurovision Song Contest. Of **Lys Assia**'s two songs 'Refrain' was chosen as the winner. Afterwards, she set a precedent for the competition when she performed a reprise of the winning

country	song	performer	place	score	draw
Netherlands	De Vogels Van Holland	**Jetty Paerl**	NK	NK	1
Switzerland	Das Alte Karussel	**Lys Assia**	NK	NK	2
Belgium	Messieurs Les Noyés De La Seine	**Fud Leclerc**	NK	NK	3
Germany	Das Lied Vom Grossen Glück	**Walter A. Schwarz**	NK	NK	4
France	Le Temps Perdu	**Mathé Altéry**	NK	NK	5
Luxembourg	Ne Crois Pas	**Michèle Arnaud**	NK	NK	6
Italy	Aprite Le Finestre	**Franca Raimondi**	NK	NK	7
Netherlands	Voorgoed Voor Bij	**Corry Brokken**	NK	NK	8
Switzerland	Refrain	**Lys Assia**	1	NK	9
Belgium	Le Plus Beau Jour De Ma Vie	**Mony Marc**	NK	NK	10
Germany	So Geht Das Jede Nacht	**Freddy Quinn**	NK	NK	11
France	Il Est Là	**Dany Dauberson**	NK	NK	12
Luxembourg	Les Amants De Minuit	**Michèle Arnaud**	NK	NK	13
Italy	Amami Se Vuoi	**Tonina Torrielli**	NK	NK	14

NK = Not known

'Refrain' was released around the continent with little remembered success, with branding on the sleeve indicating it as the Grand Prix winner, as required by the rules of the contest.

melody at the close of the show. Overcome with emotion, she lost concentration and improvised with a few verses of 'la la la', a lyrically challenging theme that would haunt the contest for decades to come.

Some basic rules to the contest have remained over time. Live singing is mandatory and back in 1956 live music was, too. For the first contest, there was no limit to the number of performers on stage, and the song could be sung in any language. In subsequent years, a maximum of two singers was allowed to perform a song, and it had to be in one of the recognised official languages of the competing nations. The songs could not have been published, recorded or performed prior to being submitted to the national heat. Each country has its own internal method of selecting their entry, but essentially they all adhere to the same regulations. Over the years, as performance techniques have become more sophisticated, so have the rules. Supporting musicians first appeared in 1957, and dancers began to appear in the early 1960s. A pre-recorded backing track was first used in 1973 by the UK entry, and in 1999 these replaced the orchestra completely. Vocals remain live, although with the advent of backing singers, dancers and musicians, there have been many instances when the 'lead' singer has barely sung at all. Today, no song can last more than three minutes, but in the first contest there was no time limit, and in 1957 an official time limit of three and half minutes was first introduced. Many songs broke this rule early on, something that would not be tolerated today.

Winner

Netherlands

Performer

Corry Brokken

1957

Title

'Net Als Toen'

Composers

Willy van Hemert/ Guus Janssen

Presenter

Anaïd Iplikjan

Host & Venue

HR/ARD Grosser Sendesaal des Hessisches Rundfunk

Frankfurt
Germany

On Sunday 3rd March 1957, the second Eurovision Song Contest was staged in Frankfurt, West Germany. Rather than a theatre, the German broadcaster chose their own TV studio to host the event, building a set that featured a staircase for the entrances of the performers and a giant harp-shaped backdrop. The centre of the backdrop contained a different graphic for each nation, and the orchestra sat opposite it.

Ten nations entered this year, with the Danes, Austrians and British lining up for the first time. Unlike the competition at Lugano everyone was limited to a single song, performed by one or two performers with no vocal backing. The voting was new, too – impressed by the regional voting that was used to pick the UK's entry the EBU instigated the same method for the Eurovision final. Ten individuals from each country sat on a jury, following the live transmission from their own country. Each judge was then to be invited to cast a single vote for the song they liked the best, although they could not vote for their own nation.

The lounge-suited Belgian **Bobbejaan Schoepen** opened the show, punctuating his song 'Straatdeuntje' ('A Hit') with a whistled melody and bursts of 'la la la' – already a Eurovision standby. It was a pleasant opener and was rewarded by five of the 90 judges, who picked it as their favourite, resulting in a shared eighth place for Schoepen.

After an impassioned performance by Luxembourg's **Daniele Dupré** it was time for the United Kingdom's first

Bottom left: Writer Willy van Hemert congratulates Corry Brokken, while the head of German television looks on.

Bottom right: The winning team smile for the camera.

entry into Eurovision. Like everyone else performing that night, **Patricia Bredin**'s operatics hardly reflected the rock'n'roll sounds that dominated the European pop charts of the time. From the outset Eurovision seemed to be in a world of its own but, even so, Bredin seemed very out of place. This wasn't helped by her conductor, **Eric Robinson**. Their relationship was apparently very hostile and, although this was not apparent from their on-screen appearance together, Robinson didn't wait for his singer to take her position before starting the song. In addition, the UK opted for the shortest song ever heard in the contest. At just one minute and fifty seconds long, it was well short of the three-and-a-half-minute time limit. However, at over five minutes long, the Italian entry, 'Corde Della Mia Chitarra', ('The Strings Of My Guitar') which was performed by **Nunzio Gallo**, is the longest Eurovision entry ever. From 1958, the time-limit was to be 'strictly observed' by all participants.

The Dutch singer **Corry Brokken** had already gained some Eurovision experience, as she had appeared in the first contest the year before. She seemed ridiculously tall towering over her diminutive accompanist **Sem Nijveen**, who had come along to perform the violin solo in the middle of her song. The judges managed to overlook their odd appearance and Brokken and Nijveen were the runaway leaders from the start of the voting, which almost got off to a calamitous start, when stagehands carrying a table onto the stage nearly bowled over the hostess for the evening, **Anaïd Iplikjan**.

The Dutch may have triumphed, but Germany holds the dubious honour of being the first nation to use a prop

Commercially at least, the entries from this year's contest do not appear to have achieved much more success than the songs from the first competition. Corry Brokken, however, took advantage of the international possibilities by recording French and German versions of **'Net Als Toen'**, alongside the original Dutch.

during Eurovision. **Margot Hielscher**, who had experienced difficulties negotiating the staircase entrance due to the volume of her gown, enhanced her performance with ringing sound effects and a white telephone that had been placed next to her – well, the song was called 'Telefon, Telefon' ('Telephone, Telephone'). At the climax, the phone rang for one last time. As the singer lifted the receiver, viewers were no doubt wondering if she would respond, 'Not now, I'm singing in the Eurovision Song Contest.' Sadly, she did not.

There was more groundbreaking novelty from Austria who combined whistling with an already familiar 'la la la' chorus, and Denmark's **Birthe Wilke and Gustav Winckler** who wore costumes to illustrate their lyrics about a naval captain saying farewell to his sweetheart. Many viewers around the continent were reputedly offended by the amorous clinch that ended their performance but they achieved third place with ten votes in a very impressive debut. Not until 1994 would any country better their placing with a first attempt.

country	song	performer	place	score	draw
Netherlands	Net Als Toen	**Corry Brokken**	1	31	6
France	La Belle Amour	**Paule Desjardins**	2	17	8
Denmark	Skibet Skal Sejle I Nat	**Birthe Wilke & Gustav Winckler**	3	10	9
Luxembourg	Tant De Peine	**Danièle Dupré**	4=	8	2
Germany	Telefon, Telefon	**Margot Hielscher**	4=	8	7
Italy	Corde Della Mia Chitarra	**Nunzio Gallo**	6	7	4
United Kingdom	All	**Patricia Bredin**	7	6	3
Belgium	Straatdeuntje	**Bobbejaan Schoepen**	8=	5	1
Switzerland	L' Enfant Que J'Etais	**Lys Assia**	8=	5	10
Austria	Wohin, Kleines Pony	**Bob Martin**	10	3	5

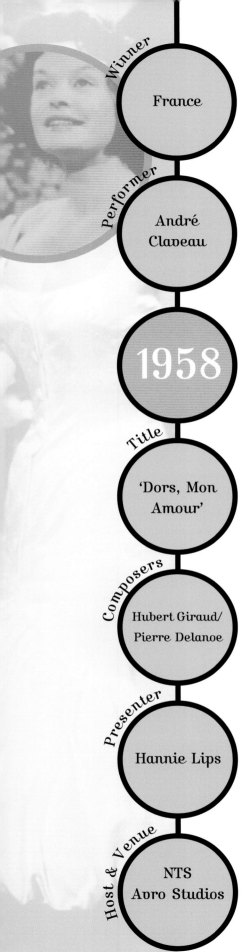

Winner

France

Performer

André
Claveau

1958

Title

'Dors, Mon
Amour'

Composers

Hubert Giraud/
Pierre Delanoe

Presenter

Hannie Lips

Host & Venue

NTS
Avro Studios

Hilversum
The Netherlands

The third Eurovision Song Contest, which was broadcast on Wednesday 12th March 1958, was the first to be staged by the country that had won the previous year. The contest had been growing in popularity across the continent, except in the United Kingdom. The British were miffed that their first foray into the competition had fared so badly and decided not to compete in Hilversum, but Sweden eagerly stepped into the vacant slot. There were also rumblings about the lack of commercial success for any of the Eurovision songs. All that was set to change. For the first time, a truly enormous hit song emerged from the show and became one of the most successful songs of the year, if not of all time. However, not for the last time, this international hit was not the winning song.

Italy's entry was a rousing opener, which the large and ebullient **Domenico Modugno** performed with tremendous gusto. Waving his arms around his head, he belted out the sing-a-long chorus 'Volare, oh, oh/Cantare, oh, oh, oh, oh'. It finished in third place with support from 13 of the 90 available judges, but bigger things were destined for Italy's song elsewhere. Modugno hit number one in the American Billboard charts, becoming the first Eurovision entry to register there at all, and it remains the most successful across the Atlantic. In the UK, despite the British not having taken part in the contest, the song became the first Eurovision song to chart here, making the top ten. Modugno also found much success in the Netherlands, spending four months in their chart and reaching number four. In Italy he was number one for 16 weeks. The song became the most recorded and possibly the most successful Eurovision song

Right: Margot Hielscher rehearses her song. For the actual performance, she dressed as a beauty queen and dismissed the idea of being a national title-holder, preferring instead to spin records. To illustrate this, she had brought along three 7" singles which she 'played' on an imaginary record player throughout the song.

country	song	performer	place	score	draw
France	Dors, Mon Amour	**André Claveau**	1	27	3
Switzerland	Giorgio	**Lys Assia**	2	24	10
Italy	Nel Blu Dipinto Di Blu	**Domenico Modugno**	3	13	1
Sweden	Lilla Stjärna	**Alice Babs**	4	10	5
Belgium	Ma Petite Chatte	**Fud Leclerc**	5=	8	7
Austria	Die Ganze Welt Braucht Liebe	**Liane Augustin**	5=	8	9
Germany	Für Zwei Groschen Musik	**Margot Hielscher**	7	5	8
Denmark	Jeg Rev Et Blad Ud Af Min Dagbog	**Raquel Rastenni**	8	3	6
Netherlands	Heel De Wereld	**Corry Brokken**	9=	1	2
Luxembourg	Un Grand Amour	**Solange Berry**	9=	1	4

of all time – and yet it had not won. The Italian did, however, get to sing his song twice. At the end of the presentation of the songs **Hannie Lips**, the mistress of ceremonies, swept onscreen in a voluminous gown and explained in Dutch, English and French that due to technical difficulties the Italian song had not been seen and heard in a number of countries and would therefore be performed again.

Earlier that night, **Corry Brokken**, returning to the competition with a song that was very similar to her winner from the year before and wearing what looked remarkably like the same dress, became the first victim of what has since become known as 'the curse of number two' – the position in the draw in which strongly fancied entries have done exceptionally badly. Having entered wanting to repeat her success, the Dutch singer became the only artist ever to have finished both first and last in the competition. The other fast-emerging Eurovision trend was acting. Prior to performing 'Jeg Rev Et Blad Ud Af Min Dagbog' ('I Tore A Page From My Diary'), Denmark's **Raquel Rastenni** sat on a stool as she thoughtfully made an entry into a diary. Clearly unhappy with her efforts, she ripped out the page and discarded it, rising from her stool to sing the song. She kept her diary clasped to her breast for the remainder of her winsome ballad.

A closely fought contest with Switzerland's former winner **Lys Assia**, competing for the third time, saw the French triumph with a very gentle ballad, 'Dors, Mon Amour' ('Sleep, My Love'), that was much in the Chevalier mode of French music, sung by the dapper 42-year-old **André Claveau**.

But the main talking point was the debut Swedish entry. While everyone else appeared in tuxedos or elaborate evening dresses, **Alice Babs** la-la-la-ed her way through her song, 'Lilla Stjärna' ('Little Star'), wearing traditional national costume. Looking very winsome, Babs provided a unique sight for the viewers, and one that the judges did not entirely dismiss.

The importance of this third Eurovision should not be underestimated. Although it did not win, the commercial success of 'Nel Blu Di Pinto Di Blu' ('The Blue Painted In Blue') or 'Volare' as it became known, woke many up to the potential of the contest and from this year forward the show's possibilities were more greatly exploited. The British were clearly impressed, as they returned to the contest the next year and began the longest uninterrupted run of entries in the competition to date. The contest had made its breakthrough and would begin to dominate the television calendar for forty-plus years.

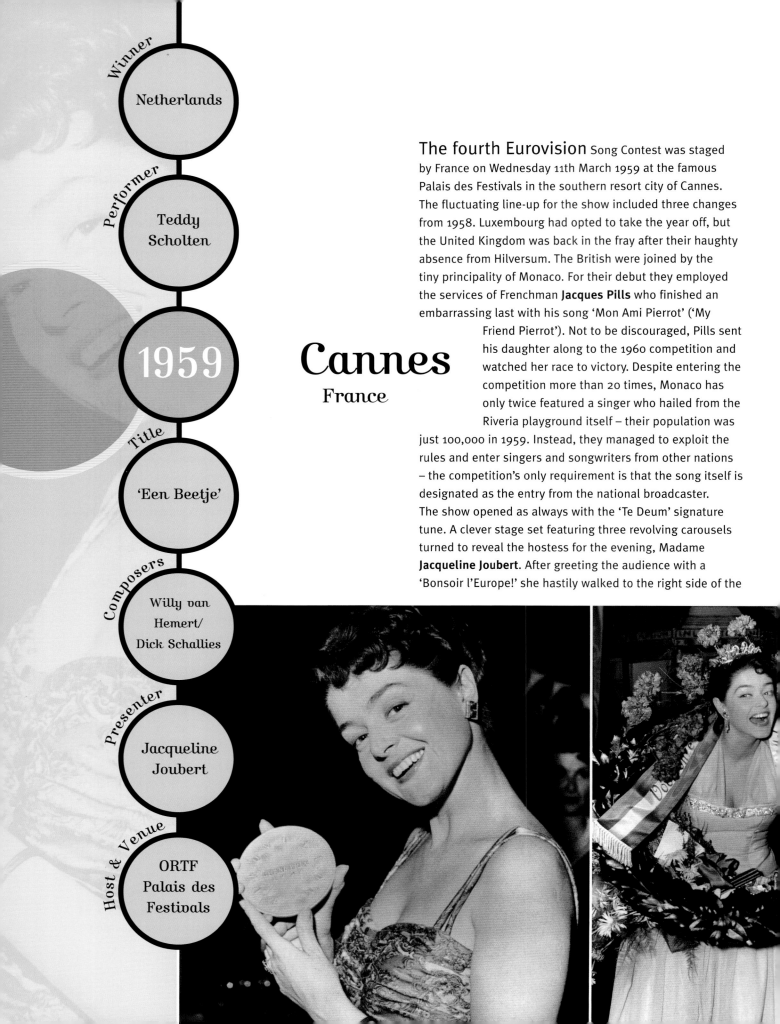

Winner	Netherlands
Performer	Teddy Scholten

1959

Title	'Een Beetje'
Composers	Willy van Hemert/ Dick Schallies
Presenter	Jacqueline Joubert
Host & Venue	ORTF Palais des Festivals

Cannes
France

The fourth Eurovision Song Contest was staged by France on Wednesday 11th March 1959 at the famous Palais des Festivals in the southern resort city of Cannes. The fluctuating line-up for the show included three changes from 1958. Luxembourg had opted to take the year off, but the United Kingdom was back in the fray after their haughty absence from Hilversum. The British were joined by the tiny principality of Monaco. For their debut they employed the services of Frenchman **Jacques Pills** who finished an embarrassing last with his song 'Mon Ami Pierrot' ('My Friend Pierrot'). Not to be discouraged, Pills sent his daughter along to the 1960 competition and watched her race to victory. Despite entering the competition more than 20 times, Monaco has only twice featured a singer who hailed from the Riveria playground itself – their population was just 100,000 in 1959. Instead, they managed to exploit the rules and enter singers and songwriters from other nations – the competition's only requirement is that the song itself is designated as the entry from the national broadcaster. The show opened as always with the 'Te Deum' signature tune. A clever stage set featuring three revolving carousels turned to reveal the hostess for the evening, Madame **Jacqueline Joubert**. After greeting the audience with a 'Bonsoir l'Europe!' she hastily walked to the right side of the

Teddy Scholten recorded two different Dutch versions of 'Een Beetje', taking it to No. 4 in the Dutch chart. She also made German, French and Italian recordings, the latter making it to No. 13 in Italy. In addition, she performed an English version of the song, but never recorded it.

stage where the scoreboard was located. Picking up a giant stick, she began to point to each of the countries, which were listed with their song titles. As she did so, the stage revolved to reveal each of the singers who took a bow to the applause from the audience. This spectacular opening gave the show an added air of theatricality.

The contest began with hosts France, who slipped in lyrical references to many familiar places such as Capri and Hawaii to give their song a more universal appeal. It didn't work on this occasion, but it has not stopped anyone else from trying the formula repeatedly over the years. The French ended the night in the top three for the third year running, finishing in third place with 15 votes.

The Italian singer **Domenico Modugno** returned, flushed with the worldwide fame and fortune he had achieved from his losing entry the year before. He once again had come

up with a song for Italy that garnered global commercial success, but again had to miss out on the Grand Prix. 'Piove' ('It's Raining') was very similar in structure to 'Volare', using the orchestra to dramatic effect by recreating the sound of rainfall in the first verse. As before, Modugno was disappointed with the judges' decision. He needn't have worried; renaming the song 'Ciao, Ciao Bambina', he went on to achieve another global hit.

The Austrian entry was the bizarre 'Der K Und K Calypso Aus Wien' ('The K And K Calypso From Vienna'), which was performed by the laid-back **Ferry Graf**. Singing in tones that fluctuated from very high to very low and including yodelling in addition to the calypso beat, the song was all over the place and finished in equal ninth place.

After their disappointing appearance in the 1957 contest, the British came to Cannes with a song that would give them the first of an unparalleled 27 finishes in the top five and 15 in second place. 'Sing Little Birdie' bore no resemblance at all to the type of music that was successful in the UK at the time, but the husband and wife team of **Pearl Carr and Teddy Johnson** were popular TV and radio stars who employed a finger puppet to represent the little bird in the song title. Although they led for large parts of the voting, the British pair was pipped by **Teddy Scholten** from The Netherlands. Not only did the Dutch became the first country ever to win the contest twice, but Willy van Hemert became the first songwriter to pen two winners, a distinction he held alone until 1972.

Despite having won, the Dutch broadcaster NTS declined the opportunity to host their second contest the next year, citing the high production costs as their reason for passing the job to the runner-up. Eurovision was going to the UK.

Far left: Teddy Scholten holds up her Grand Prix medal. 'Een Beetje' was not the best song on show, but the charm of the presentation and quirky nature of the music and lyric won the judges over.

Left: Teddy celebrates her triumph.

country	song	performer	place	score	draw
Netherlands	Een Beetje	**Teddy Scholten**	1	21	5
United Kingdom	Sing Little Birdie	**Pearl Carr & Teddy Johnson**	2	16	10
France	Oui, Oui, Oui, Oui	**Jean Philippe**	3	15	1
Switzerland	Irgendwoher	**Christa Williams**	4	14	8
Denmark	Uh-Jeg Ville Ønske Jeg Var Dig	**Birthe Wilke**	5	12	2
Italy	Piove	**Domenico Modugno**	6=	9	3
Belgium	Hou Toch Van Mij	**Bob Benny**	6=	9	11
Germany	Heute Abend Wollen Wir Tanzen Geh'n	**Alice & Ellen Kessler**	8	5	6
Sweden	Augustin	**Brita Borg**	9=	4	7
Austria	Der K Und K Calypso Aus Wien	**Ferry Graf**	9=	4	9
Monaco	Mon Ami Pierrot	**Jacques Pills**	11	1	4

Winner

France

Performer

Jacqueline
Boyer

1960

Title

'Tom Pillibi'

Composers

Pierre Cour/
André Popp

Presenter

Katie Boyle

Host & Venue

BBC
Royal Festival
Hall

With the birth of the Swinging Sixties, the Eurovision Song Contest came to the city that was the heart of the new era – London, the British capital. Not that there was anything particularly 'swinging' about the 13 songs competing for this year's Grand Prix. The setting was the grandiose Royal Festival Hall, built for the Festival of Britain nine years earlier. With seating for two thousand, it was by far the largest venue used for the contest so far. The broadcast date was Tuesday 29th March 1960, and it was the last contest to be held midweek.

London
United Kingdom

Thirteen nations took part, a new record. Luxembourg returned after their year away and Norway made their debut. Considering how badly the Norwegians have fared over the years, their first effort was very well received by comparison. In a Sámi-inspired outfit, **Nora Brockstedt** sang 'Voi Voi', a lively tale of a young Sámi girl singing for her boyfriend who was far away.

For the second year in succession, the hosts had been drawn to sing first. 'Looking High, High, High', written by schoolteacher John Watson, told the story of a man's search for his true love over land, air and sea. It had a strong melody and the pleasing baritone voice of **Bryan Johnson** (the brother of the UK's 1959 representative Teddy) ensured

Jacqueline Boyer was seen one last time clutching the silver gilt vase as the credits rolled. Before her Eurovision win, Jacqueline had already found success in France, and went on to achieve popularity around the whole continent.

In rehearsal (left to right): Anita Traversi for Switzerland; Siw Malmkvist for Sweden; Katy Bodtger for Denmark, whose Victorian outfit did not impress the judges, and Nora Brockstedt for Norway.

it was well performed. Dressed in a black tuxedo and appearing in front of a backdrop that featured an unpleasant-looking sky scene, so indicative of British weather, the song built to a rousing finish and earned Bryan huge applause from the partisan audience.

Siw Malmkvist took the dreaded second slot for Sweden this year and could only muster four votes, ending the night in a shared tenth place. That was better than Luxembourg who ended the night last with a single vote – their entry was sung in Luxembourgian, rather than the more typical French that the Grand Duchy favoured.

Fud Leclerc returned to sing for Belgium for the third time, representing the French-speaking part of the nation with a typically mournful ballad. Austria added a touch of gravitas when the world-famous operetta composer Robert Stoltz took the baton to conduct his own composition, 'Du Hast Mich So Fasziniert' ('You Have Fascinated Me So'), which was sung by **Harry Winter**. It was a surprisingly conservative and stiff piece. Austria had yet to grasp the knack of Eurovision. Lightening the mood, Germany submitted a song with a French title, 'Bonne Nuit, Ma Chérie' ('Good Night, My Dear'), which was sung in German by the large and imposing **Wyn Hoop**. Adding to its continental appeal the tune had a bolero rhythm. The obvious attempt to curry international favour largely paid off – the Germans ended the show in fourth place, matching their best-known result to date.

The final song of the evening came from France. **Jacqueline Boyer**, the daughter of Jacques Pills who had

'Tom Pillibi' was commercially very popular, reaching No. 33 in the UK, No. 11 in the Netherlands and No. 6 in Sweden. Jacqueline Boyer recorded a German version, but allowed stage star Julie Andrews to release an English version. In 1991 Ms Boyer re-recorded the song for inclusion in a CD retrospective of her biggest hits.

finished last the previous year when singing for Monaco, gave a charming and winsome performance that won over the majority of judges. It was nonetheless another closely fought battle for the top honour and for the second time the British entry was narrowly defeated. Frustratingly, their 25 votes was actually a higher total than 1959's winning song.

The voting was not without its hitches. Austria's five votes for France were registered as seven on the scoreboard, and with the audience cheering each vote for the United Kingdom, the irritated mistress of ceremonies, **Katie Boyle**, snapped that if they continued to applaud each score she would not be able to hear. They dutifully shut up! Boyle eventually hosted the contest four times and is today widely regarded as the 'Grand Dame' of all things Eurovision.

To award the Grand Prix to Jacqueline Boyer was the winner of the last contest, Teddy Scholten. It was the first time that the previous year's winner was invited to appear at the ceremony and, although the idea did not immediately catch on, by the mid-1960s it had become a tradition.

	country	song	performer	place =	score	draw
	France	Tom Pillibi	**Jacqueline Boyer**	1	32	13
	United Kingdom	Looking High, High, High	**Bryan Johnson**	2	25	1
	Monaco	Ce Soir-là	**François Deguelt**	3	15	8
	Norway	Voi Voi	**Nora Brockstedt**	4=	11	6
	Germany	Bonne Nuit, Ma Chérie	**Wyn Hoop**	4=	11	11
	Belgium	Mon Amour Pour Toi	**Fud Leclerc**	6	9	5
	Austria	Du Hast Mich So Fasziniert	**Harry Winter**	7	6	7
	Switzerland	Cielo E Terra	**Anita Traversi**	8=	5	9
	Italy	Romantica	**Renato Rascel**	8=	5	12
	Sweden	Alla Andra Får Varann	**Siw Malmkvist**	10=	4	2
	Denmark	Det Var En Yndig Tid	**Katy Bødtger**	10=	4	4
	Netherlands	Wat Een Geluk	**Rudi Carrell**	12	2	10
	Luxembourg	So Laang We's Du Do Bast	**Camillo Felgen**	13	1	3

Winner

Luxembourg

Performer

Jean-Claude Pascal

1961

Title

'Nous Les Amoureux'

Composers

Jacques Datin/ Maurice Vidalin

Presenter

Jacqueline Joubert

Host & Venue

ORTF Palais des Festivals

Cannes
France

On 18th March 1961, the French Riviera's Palais des Festivals in Cannes was once again the auditorium chosen to play host to the Eurovision Song Contest. For the first time the competition was being held on a Saturday night and there were a record 16 entrants. Finland, Spain and Yugoslavia all joined the Eurovision family this year. For the Finns, it wasn't to be their most successful relationship with the contest. It took over 40 years to not only score a victory, but just to finish in the top five.

The stage area was covered by a drawn curtain, which swept back to reveal the 'garden' set. A lavish Hollywood-style staircase covered in flowers, trees and shrubs dominated the stage and an outdoor scene was painted across the backdrop. But much else seemed very similar to the 1959 contest – even the scoreboard was recycled. **Jacqueline Joubert** was given the invitation to act as the mistress of ceremonies, becoming the first person ever to do to the job twice. Alongside Katie Boyle, she remains one of only two people ever asked back to do the job for a second time.

Below: Jean-Claude Pascal with Tessa Beaumont, who performed the interval act.
Below right: The Allisons' song started before they had even entered the garden set or Ms Joubert had finished her introduction. Hearing the music, they rushed down the steps, arriving just in time to sing the first line. Despite this, they gave a relaxed and professional performance.

Jean-Claude Pascal enjoyed limited success with **'Nous Les Amoureaux',** largely confined to French-speaking markets. He re-recorded the song in 1966 and cut an Italian version, which failed to hit the charts. But his career as a performer thrived for decades.

Conchita Bautista became the very first Spanish artist to sing in the contest. With her frilled gown swirling around her, Bautista sang in a powerful flamenco style, adding some dance steps in the instrumental breaks. It was the first song of its style heard in the contest to date, but it was perhaps a bit too avant-garde for the judges, who awarded it only eight votes, leaving Spain in ninth place.

The Austrians only managed a single point with their song, 'Sehnsucht' ('Longing'), which was performed by Athens-born Jimmy Makulis, the first Greek ever to sing in the contest. But they were not alone at the bottom of the pile. Bob Benny's lengthy, bongo-powered entry for Belgium, 'Septembre, Gouden Roos' ('Golden Rose Of September') had a similarly wilting effect on the judges.

Sweden entered 'April, April', one of many songs that dealt with the subject of seasons and time in this year's contest. France also sang about springtime, and Jean-Paul Mauric bouncing across the stage crooning 'bing-a-bong' is the lasting memory of 'Printemps, Avril Carillonne' ('Springtime, April Ringing'). Norway's Nora Brockstedt, meanwhile, was keen on summertime in Palma.

The biggest star of the night was Germany's Lale Andersen, formerly forces' sweetheart Lili Marleen of the Desert War, but her trademark speak-singing left her in thirteenth place.

The suave, French boulevardier Jean-Claude Pascal had been invited to cross the border to sing for Luxembourg this year, and with 'Nous Les Amoureux' ('We Who Love Each Other') he presented a strong ballad with a slow jazz tempo. A successful actor, having appeared in several movies, he stood almost motionless on the stage, but using some almost imperceptible facial movements and an enigmatic smile, he had no problems translating the smouldering passion of the song as he built to a crescendo climax. Two years after withdrawing temporarily from the contest, the small Grand Duchy became the fourth country to take the Eurovision title, winning with the fourth French song to capture the judges' approval.

Perhaps spurred on by the commercial success of the Italian entries, the United Kingdom had selected a song that successfully straddled both the current pop scene and the preferences of the Eurovision judges, but once again the Italians' entry ('Al Di La' by Betty Curtis) was the biggest international hit. Although they weren't related, The Allisons – John Alford and Bob Day – based their act on the hugely popular American duo The Everly Brothers. The song, 'Are You Sure?', was riding high in the UK charts and they were confident of Eurovision glory. However, for the third year in succession the UK finished in second place.

The 1961 contest was another success for the producers and, in terms of ratings, with the general public. Although France did not win for a third time an all-French effort had triumphed anyway. The French themselves only had to wait one more year for win number three to come their way, when the contest travelled to Luxembourg.

country	song	performer	place	score	draw
Luxembourg	Nous Les Amoureux	Jean-Claude Pascal	1	31	14
United Kingdom	Are You Sure?	The Allisons	2	24	15
Switzerland	Nous Aurons Demain	Franca di Rienzo	3	16	10
France	Printemps (Avril Carillonne)	Jean-Paul Mauric	4	13	9
Denmark	Angelique	Dario Campeotto	5=	12	13
Italy	Al Di Là	Betty Curtis	5=	12	16
Norway	Sommer I Palma	Nora Brockstedt	7	10	12
Yugoslavia	Neke Davne Zvezde	Ljiljana Petrović	8	9	5
Spain	Estando Contigo	Conchita Bautista	9	8	1
Monaco	Allons, Allons Les Enfants	Colette Deréal	10=	6	2
Finland	Valoa Ikkunassa	Laila Kinnunen	10=	6	4
Netherlands	Wat Een Dag	Greetje Kauffeld	10=	6	6
Germany	Einmal Sehen Wir Uns Wieder	Lale Andersen	13	3	8
Sweden	April, April	Barbro Svensson (Lill-Babs)	14	2	7
Austria	Sehnsucht	Jimmy Makulis	15=	1	3
Belgium	September, Gouden Roos	Bob Benny	15=	1	11

Winner

France

Performer

Isabelle Aubret

1962

Title

'Un Premier Amour'

Composers

Rolande Valade/ Claude-Henri Vice

Presenter

Mireille Delanoy

Host & Venue

CLT Grand Auditorium de RTL

There were no new countries taking part in the seventh Eurovision Song Contest. For the very first time, the line-up remained exactly the same as it had been the year before, with the 16 nations who had attended the Cannes contest all returning to the competition. Broadcast from the Grand Auditorium de RTL on Sunday 18th March, this was the last contest that was not held on a Saturday night. Many of the artists taking part had been to the contest before or would come back to the contest again later. To add to the routine of hearing 16 songs from the same 16 countries as the year before, the winning nation, France, won the prize for the third time in five years, singing in a language

Luxembourg

and style that had won five of the first seven contests.

The European Broadcasting Union decided that for the first time the juries should rank the songs and award points to their three favourites, rather than simply asking each judge to select one single favourite. It was a good idea in theory, but it led to a very dull climax with France leading from start to finish. Each jury was again made up of ten judges, and juries would give three, two and one point only to their first, second and third ranked choices. With 15 songs competing for each jury's favours, 12 songs would have to be left out in the cold by each nation. Inevitably, all the juries left some of these songs off their lists completely, and four songs finished the night without a single point between them. The era of the dreaded 'nul points' had begun.

Left to right, seated: Austria's Eleonore Schwarz, whose operatic opus for Austria was a consummate tour de force, but destined for failure; Marion Rung (Finland); Victor Balaguer (Spain); Ellen Winther (Denmark).

Left to right, standing: Camillo Felgen (Luxembourg), whose spoken asides during the verse perhaps helped him to earn eleven marks and end in third place; Ronnie Carroll (UK); winner Isabelle Aubret (France); Jean Phillipe (Switzerland).

country	song	performer	place	score	draw
France	Un Premier Amour	**Isabelle Aubret**	1	26	9
Monaco	Dis Rien	**François Deguelt**	2	13	16
Luxembourg	Petit Bonhomme	**Camillo Felgen**	3	11	14
Yugoslavia	Ne Pali Svetla U Sumrak	**Lola Novaković**	4=	10	12
United Kingdom	Ring-A-Ding Girl	**Ronnie Carroll**	4=	10	13
Germany	Zwei Kleiner Italiener	**Conny Froboess**	6	9	7
Finland	Tipi-Tii	**Marion Rung**	7=	4	1
Sweden	Sol Och Vår	**Inger Berggren**	7=	4	6
Italy	Addio, Addio	**Claudio Villa**	9	3	15
Denmark	Vuggevise	**Ellen Winther**	10=	2	5
Norway	Kom Sol, Kom Regn	**Inger Jacobsen**	10=	2	10
Switzerland	Le Retour	**Jean Philippe**	10=	2	11
Belgium	Ton Nom	**Fud Leclerc**	13=	0	2
Spain	Llamame	**Victor Balaguer**	13=	0	3
Austria	Nur In Der Wiener Luft	**Eleonore Schwarz**	13=	0	4
Netherlands	Katinka	**De Spelbrekers**	13=	0	8

'Un Premier Amour' did not do well outside its home nation. Frida Boccara also recorded a version of this year's winner, seven years before she herself would take top honours in Madrid. The conductor of the winning entry, Franck Pourcel, released an instrumental version, but with little success.

Finland's second entry into the contest was the first song of the show. 'Tipi-Tii' ('Tweet Tweet') became the first of two entries that **Marion Rung** would perform for her country and both of her songs would open contests staged in Luxembourg. For consistency, no other singer can match that feat. The song itself was very repetitive, but somewhat jolly, with Rung even miming the flute accompaniment at one stage to imitate birdsong. This cheerful opener ended the night with just four points. The next three songs, however, suffered the ultimate Eurovision indignity.

'Ton Nom' ('Your Name') was the fourth song that **Fud Leclerc** had sung for Belgium, and it was the entry that put his name in the Eurovision record books – or at least the hall of shame. The judges were so unimpressed that they could not be persuaded to give it a single mark, and Fud went down in history as the first singer ever to receive the dreaded 'nul points' in the contest. In fairness, he takes this dubious honour merely from the luck of the draw – Spain, The Netherlands and an operatic Austrian entry also failed to win any support.

With so many songs from the first half of the draw faring so disastrously, France, the most successful country in the contest to date, had little to live up to when **Isabelle Aubret** took to the stage of the Villa Louvigny auditorium. Accompanied by conductor Franck Pourcel, her hypnotic ballad, 'Un Premier Amour' ('A First Love'), had a mesmerising effect on the audience as well as the judges.

After a breakdown in transmission following the French song, the contest resumed and the Yugoslavs at least brought some originality to their song, using the theme of two cigarettes glowing in the dark as a metaphor for romance. Glamorising smoking in this way would probably raise some eyebrows today!

Many critics thought the 1962 contest was a particularly drab affair. French TV opted not to stage the contest for the third time in five years, passing the baton to the United Kingdom, who produced a show that shook up the contest and created possibly the most controversial result in the competition's entire history.

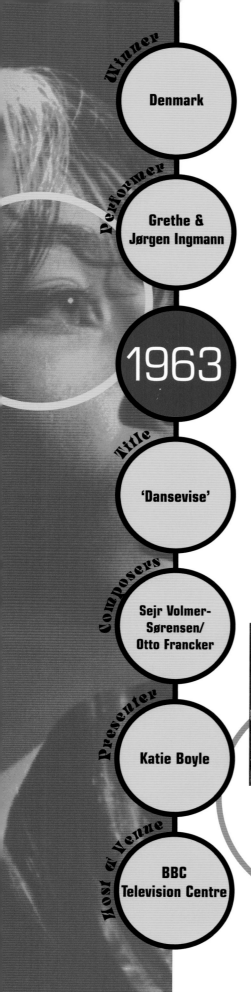

Winner

Denmark

Performer

**Grethe &
Jørgen Ingmann**

1963

Title

'Dansevise'

Composers

**Sejr Volmer-
Sørensen/
Otto Francker**

Presenter

Katie Boyle

Host & Venue

**BBC
Television Centre**

London
United Kingdom

Dashing Jacques Raymond (Belgium) in rehearsal. On the night he performed 'Waarom?' ('Why?') standing under a variety of inverted funnels. It was a gentle piece with a contemporary flair, but only amassed four points to end tenth. Still, it was an improvement upon the previous year's 'nul'.

Despite the fact that the United Kingdom was still without a Eurovision victory, the eighth contest was staged at the new BBC Television Centre in Shepherd's Bush, London. The British were offered the opportunity to host the contest after the top three nations from 1962 had declined.

Anxious to show off their new facility, the broadcast, which was transmitted on Saturday 23rd March 1963, was spread between two separate studios. The audience, hostess and scoreboard were housed in one, while the orchestra and performers performed in another studio that was stark, white and scattered with props. Rumours have spread in the subsequent years that much of the show was either pre-recorded or at the very least pre-arranged, but both the BBC and the EBU have consistently denied this. Either way, a cloud of suspicion still hangs over this contest more than 40 years later. It is scepticism fuelled by Britain's own entry, again by **Ronnie Carroll**, which featured backing singers who were very obviously lip-syncing their vocals. But this was just part of the controversy that continues to haunt this particular Eurovision Song Contest.

After a quarter of the entries failed to win any support under the voting system introduced the year before, the EBU expanded the number of points awarded this year to cover the top five songs chosen by each nation, and increased the

Grethe and Jørgen enjoyed moderate success with **'Dansevise'**, topping their own chart and making the Top 30 in the Netherlands, but failed to excite elsewhere.

number of judges from ten to twenty, and then back to ten after protests that it was going to take too much time. This change in number was made rather late in the day and apparently not communicated to some juries.

The same 16 nations competed in London that had competed in the previous two years but, unlike 1962's contest, there was a distinct variety of music on show this time. One country breaking with tradition was the previously stilted Austria, who employed the services of the Israeli-born **Carmela Corren**, who performed her entry, 'Vielleicht Geschieht Ein Wunder' ('Maybe A Miracle Will Happen'), resplendent in a sparkling, dark Lurex, halter-neck gown. Midway through her jazz-inspired ballad she switched languages to English – a radical new step.

Denmark offered a sophisticated ballad that was performed by the husband and wife team of singer **Grethe** and her guitar accompanist **Jørgen Ingmann**. The hypnotic tune was helped by the visual effects in the studio as a spinning vortex of whirling shapes spun around the screen, adding to the dream-like effect of the music. It was the only song that relied entirely on visual rather than physical props and this helped it to stand out. In the closest fought contest to date, Denmark triumphed, although initially this did not appear to be the case.

The whole voting process was conducted in total silence, with the audience, who were unseen throughout the entire transmission, remaining deathly quiet. Several odd things happened. The process clipped along speedily until it came for the votes from the Norwegian jury. The spokesman in Oslo failed to give the correct numerical identity of each song, which confused the presenter Katie Boyle, who asked him to start all over again, stressing that the number on the board needed to be stated. There was an uncomfortable pause while the spokesman rustled his notes. Could he come back later? There were further slip-ups as the Monaco jury gave one point to two countries, the UK and Luxembourg, although no official noticed and the scoreboard changed before scores were announced. With the result hanging in the balance, and Switzerland leading Denmark by two points, Katie called Norway again.

Norway had not received the word from the EBU that there should be only ten judges on their jury and not twenty, and at fifth down the list, had not been ready to give their verdict when Katie first called. Now fully prepared, four went to their Danish neighbours, twice the number originally awarded. Three went to Italy, one less than before, two points were given to Germany, and one was left for Switzerland, who had earned three earlier in the evening. This neatly switched the top two scores, leaving the Danes ahead with 42 to Switzerland's 40 points. Ever since, the Swiss have considered 1963 the year they were robbed of victory.

Katie Boyle making her second appearance as the show's hostess.

country	song	performer	place	score	draw
Denmark	Dansevise	Grethe & Jørgen Ingmann	1	42	8
Switzerland	T'En Vas Pas	Ester Ofarim	2	40	10
Italy	Uno Per Tutte	Emilio Pericoli	3	37	6
United Kingdom	Say Wonderful Things	Ronnie Carroll	4	28	1
France	Elle Etait Si Jolie	Alain Barrière	5=	25	11
Monaco	L'Amour S'En Va	Françoise Hardy	5=	25	15
Austria	Vielleicht Geschieht Ein Wunder	Carmela Corren	7	16	4
Luxembourg	A Force De Prier	Nana Mouskouri	8	13	16
Germany	Marcel	Heidi Brühl	9	5	3
Belgium	Waarom	Jacques Raymond	10	4	14
Yugoslavia	Brodovi	Vice Vukov	11	3	9
Spain	Algo Prodigioso	José Guardiola	12	2	12
Netherlands	Een Speeldoos	Annie Palmen	13=	0	2
Norway	Solhverv	Anita Thallaug	13=	0	5
Finland	Muistejeni Laulu	Laila Halme	13=	0	7
Sweden	En Gång I Stockholm	Monica Zetterlund	13=	0	13

Winner

Italy

Performer

Gigliola Cinquetti

1964

Title

'Non Ho L'Etá'

Composers

Mario Panzeri/ Nicola Salerno

Presenter

Lotte Wæver

Host & Venue

DR Tivolis Koncertsal

Copenhagen
Denmark

Sixteen nations came to Copenhagen to compete at the Tivoli Garden concert hall on Saturday, 21st March 1964, although there was one change to the final line-up. Industrial action by their musicians' union meant that Sweden was unable to compete. Portugal took their place. Since the Portuguese finished the evening as one of four competitors with 'nul points', it's surprising that they went on to become regular Eurovision competitors.

The voting system also underwent another reform in 1964: the juries were asked to rank the songs in order of preference but, as with 1962, they were only asked to pick their top three favourites. Five points would be given to the song the jury liked the best, three to the second and one to the third. If all ten judges in each country favoured the same song, then it would be awarded nine points.

Unfortunately, as seemingly with the inaugural 1956 contest, there is no archive film recording of the 1964 Eurovision Song Contest. This is a great shame as this was the first and only broadcast to be interrupted by a protester. After the Swiss entry had performed, a man who had been hiding backstage disguised as a stagehand dramatically walked on carrying a banner bearing the legend 'Boycott Franco and Salazar', referring to the dictactors governing Spain and Portugal at the time. He only managed a few brief moments in front of the cameras before the director cut to a shot of the scoreboard, but at least he made his mark.

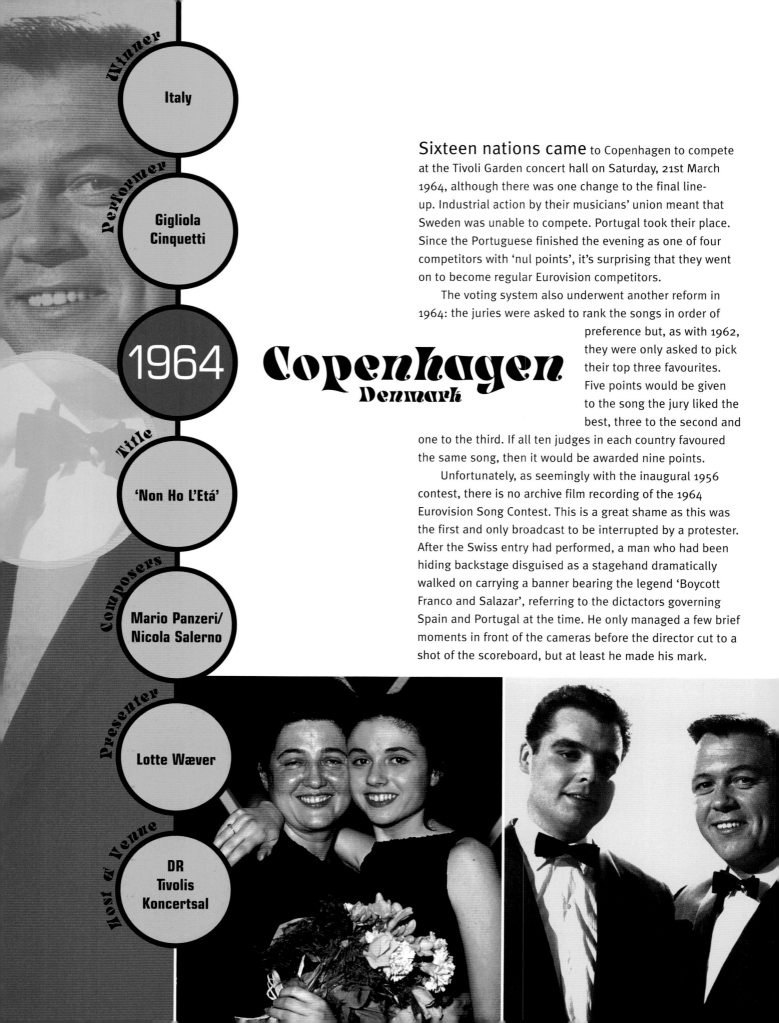

country	song	performer	place	score	draw
Italy	Non Ho L'Etá	**Gigliola Cinquetti**	1	49	12
United Kingdom	I Love The Little Things	**Matt Monro**	2	17	8
Monaco	Où Sont-Elles Passées?	**Romuald**	3	15	10
Luxembourg	Dès Que Le Printemps Revient	**Hugues Aufrey**	4=	14	1
France	Le Chant De Mallory	**Rachel**	4=	14	7
Austria	Warum Nur Warum?	**Udo Jürgens**	6	11	6
Finland	Laiskotellen	**Lasse Mårtenson**	7	9	5
Norway	Spiral	**Arne Bendiksen**	8	6	3
Denmark	Sangen Om Dig	**Bjørn Tidmand**	9	4	4
Netherlands	Jij Bent Mijn Leven	**Anneke Grönloh**	10=	2	2
Belgium	Près De Ma Rivière	**Robert Cogoi**	10=	2	15
Spain	Caracola	**Nelly, Tim & Tony**	12	1	16
Germany	Man Gewöhnt Sich So Schnell An Das Schöne	**Nora Nova**	13=	0	9
Portugal	Oração	**Antonio Calvario**	13=	0	11
Yugoslavia	Život Je Sklopio Krug	**Sabahudin Kurt**	13=	0	13
Switzerland	I Miei Pensieri	**Anita Traversi**	13=	0	14

There were a number of familiar faces on show, some making the first of several attempts at the title and others returning for another stab at the prize. **Udo Jürgens** made the first of three consecutive appearances in the contest for Austria, Switzerland was represented for a second time by **Anita Traversi**, while Monaco fielded the French male vocalist **Romuald**, who went on to sing for Luxembourg in 1969, before returning to represent Monaco in 1974.

France sang seventh with the interestingly titled 'Le Chant De Mallory' ('The Song of Mallory'), performed by a young woman known only as **Rachel**. Winning female singers opting to be identified by a single name through the years include Massiel, Lulu, Salome, Dana, Séverine, Nicole, Carola, Katrina and Ruslana.

Popular crooner **Matt Monro** represented the United Kingdom with a song written by Tony Hatch – a man responsible for many hits, including Petula Clark's 'Downtown'. Despite an excellent performance with the only English-language song of the night, Monro finished a distant runner-up.

The song that won the contest so convincingly came from Italy. 'Non Ho L' Eta' ('I Am Too Young') was a plea from the 16-year-old **Gigliola Cinquetti** to allow her time, as she was too young to love anyone right now. It was an emotion that struck the right chord with the juries, agreeing for once with the general public that the Italians not only had the most commercial song, but the best on the night.

Norway, Denmark and Finland all voted for each other, even though no one else appeared to rate their entries. But it didn't matter as Italy's score of 49 represented 65 per cent of the available votes cast – the highest yet recorded. Cinquetti also became the youngest winner of the contest to date, an honour she held until 1986, when a singer three years younger than her 16 years triumphed. In 1974 Cinquetti returned to the contest for a second time, and would have won easily, had she not faced the might of the super Swedes Abba in the Brighton final. In 1991, she acted as the hostess of the contest in Rome.

Far left: Gigliola Cinquetti with her mother. The judges were swept away by 16-year-old Gigliola's beautiful singing voice and powerful understated emotion. Her song led in the voting from start to finish.

Left: Composer Tony Hatch with Matt Monro. Seen by many as Britain's answer to Frank Sinatra, Monro amassed 14 hits over a lengthy career and spent nearly 130 weeks in the UK Top 50. He made something of a name for himself singing the themes to a string of successful movies, including *From Russia With Love* and *Born Free*.

Gigliola Cinquetti recorded Spanish, German, Japanese and French versions of 'Non Ho L'Etá'. She took her Italian version to No. 17 in the UK. In the Netherlands she made it to No. 3 and followed this with No. 8 in Sweden.

Winner

Luxembourg

Performer

France Gall

1965

Title

'Poupée de Cire, Poupée de Son'

Composer

Serge Gainsbourg

Presenter

Renata Mauro

Host & Venue

Sala di Concerto della RAI

Naples
Italy

The tenth anniversary edition of the Eurovision Song Contest was staged on 20th March 1965 in the grandly named Sala di Concerto della RAI. It was the biggest to date, reaching new television audiences in Eastern Europe and beyond. It was estimated that about 150 million viewers watched the show around the globe.

The same countries that had competed in Copenhagen were all back on the starting grid with two additions. Swedish television, which had finally sorted its industrial relations the day before the 1964 contest, was back in the fold this year, and the country that would go on to win the title more times than any other nation, Ireland, made its debut.

A far more contemporary musical mix was led by the United Kingdom's entrant, **Kathy Kirby**, a huge star in her homeland with her own TV show and a string of hits. A magazine poll the previous year had named her 'Top British Female Singer', ahead of Cilla Black, Dusty Springfield and Petula Clark. In Naples, Kirby took to the stage in a sparkling, form-fitting black gown, with her trademark blonde hair and red lipstick cementing her image as a young Marilyn Monroe lookalike. 'I Belong' reflected current musical tastes more than any previous British entry, but it paled in comparison with the song that really brought Eurovision screaming up to date.

country	song	performer
Luxembourg	Poupée De Cire, Poupée De Son	**France Gall**
United Kingdom	I Belong	**Kathy Kirby**
France	N'Avoue Jamais	**Guy Mardel**
Austria	Sag Ihr, Ich Lass Sie Grüssen	**Udo Jürgens**
Italy	Se Piangi, Se Ridi	**Bobby Solo**
Ireland	I'm Walking The Streets In The Rain	**Butch Moore**
Denmark	For Din Skyld	**Birgit Brüel**
Switzerland	Non A Jamais Sans Toi	**Yovanna**
Monaco	Va Dire A L'Amour	**Marjorie Noel**
Sweden	Annorstädes Vals	**Ingvar Wixell**
Netherlands	'T Het Is Genoeg	**Conny van den Bos**
Yugoslavia	Čeznja	**Vice Vukov**
Norway	Karusell	**Kirsti Sparboe**
Portugal	Sol De Inverno	**Simone de Oliveira**
Spain	Que Bueno, Que Bueno	**Conchita Bautista**
Germany	Paradies, Wo Bist Du?	**Ulla Wiesner**
Belgium	Als Het Weer Lente Is	**Lize Marke**
Finland	Aurinko Laskee Länteen	**Viktor Klimenko**

Representing Luxembourg, **France Gall** was a 17-year-old Parisian whose look was as trendy as her sound. Her song 'Poupée De Cire, Poupée De Son' ('Wax Doll, Singing Doll'), was written by her musical mentor Serge Gainsbourg. It related how she was tired of simply being a musical doll and longed to feel emotion and experience aspects of life outside the recording studio, as the lyrics to her songs had become engraved on her heart. It was pretty strong stuff, which is not really surprising as Gainsbourg already had a reputation for controversial lyrics. Years later his steamy 'Je T'Aime', which he performed with his wife Jane Birkin, scandalised the world and was publicly denounced by the Pope. France Gall's pert performance was enough to conquer all comers and prove that there was a place for the hip and trendy in the contest after all. Impressed by what they saw she became the judges' clear favourite.

Other highlights of the contest included **Conchita Bautista**, who had performed Spain's very first Eurovision entry back in 1961. Dressed in a sleeveless gown that had a tiered, swirling skirt, which she used to great effect, Bautista did her best to imitate a flamenco dancer in the limited space. However, like many others who've tried, she was to learn that if at first you don't succeed at Eurovision it's probably best not to try again. Her song became the first of only two Spanish entries ever to fail to score.

France Gall found further success in France, Germany and Japan, but she became the first Grand Prix winner who seemed determined to shake off the Eurovision tag at the earliest opportunity and refuses to discuss the contest today, or perform 'Wax Doll, Singing Doll' in public.

place	score	draw
1	32	15
2	26	2
3	22	11
4	16	6
5	15	13
6	11	4
7	10	14
8	8	18
9	7	9
10	6	10
11	5	1
12	2	17
13=	1	7
13=	1	12
15=	0	3
15=	0	5
15=	0	8
15=	0	16

POUPEE DE CIRE, POUPEE DE SON

France Gall shot to the top of the French charts with 'Poupée De Cire, Poupée De Son' and made it to the Top 10 in Sweden, the Netherlands, Germany and Italy. She severed links with Gainsbourg two years after the contest when she tired of his suggestive lyrics, and broke into a new realm of recording more sophisticated tunes.

Unlike Spain, Ireland did very well in their first contest with a mournful ballad that was performed by the lead singer of the Capital Showband, **Butch Moore**. It was the first time that any country other than the UK had submitted a song performed entirely in English (although Sweden performed in English also this year), and from the outset it was clear that the Irish would challenge the British for supremacy in the contest. Although it was a strong debut, Moore's old-fashioned style owed more to the 1950s than the 1960s and did not carry him higher than sixth place, with eleven points from three nations.

Representing the home nation, heart-throb **Bobby Solo** attempted to emulate the success of Gigliola Cinquetti with his song 'Se Piangi, Se Ridi' ('If You Cry, If You Laugh'). Solo had not been able to perform the song at rehearsals in Naples due to a throat problem, but had saved himself for the big night, bringing along the only backing group seen in the contest this year, a trio of young ladies who performed the harmonies. Solo's low-key crooning style was a very effective interpretation of the song, but when compared to the up-tempo numbers from Luxembourg and the UK, it was always bound to be less successful.

What was becoming the usual neighbourly support from some countries occurred again this year. Ireland and the UK started a trend of ignoring each other's songs, which has largely continued ever since, while Monaco reliably gave their top mark to their French neighbours, with Sweden doing the same for the Danes.

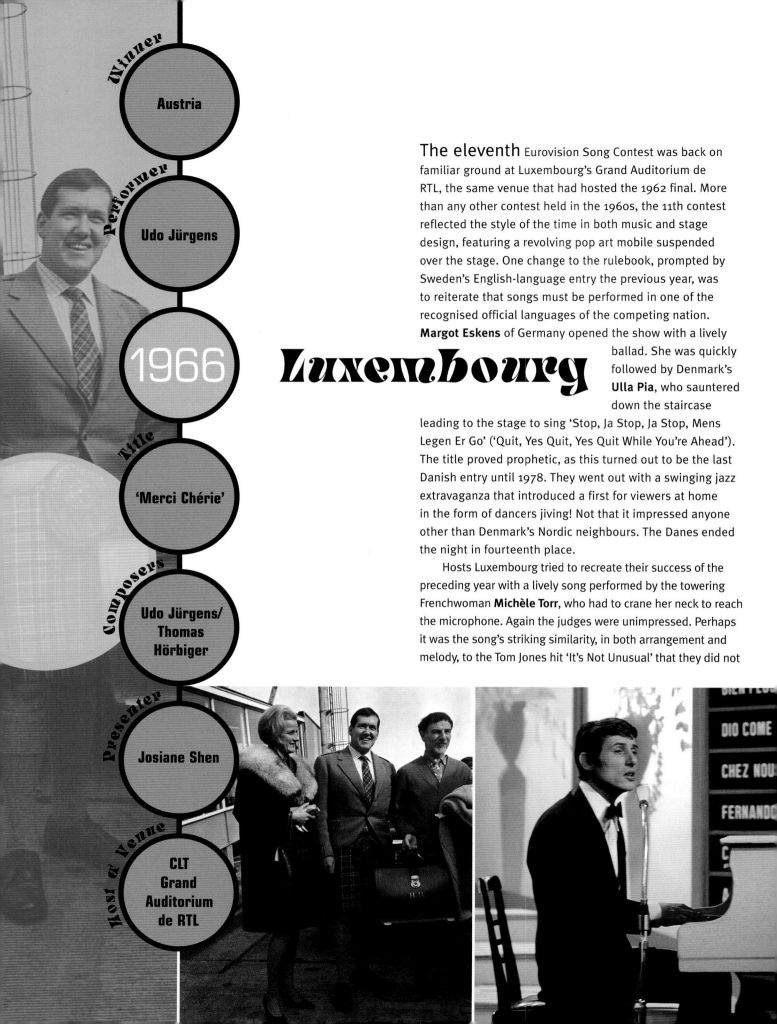

Winner

Austria

Performer

Udo Jürgens

1966

Title

'Merci Chérie'

Composers

Udo Jürgens/
Thomas
Hörbiger

Presenter

Josiane Shen

Host & Venue

CLT
Grand
Auditorium
de RTL

Luxembourg

The eleventh Eurovision Song Contest was back on familiar ground at Luxembourg's Grand Auditorium de RTL, the same venue that had hosted the 1962 final. More than any other contest held in the 1960s, the 11th contest reflected the style of the time in both music and stage design, featuring a revolving pop art mobile suspended over the stage. One change to the rulebook, prompted by Sweden's English-language entry the previous year, was to reiterate that songs must be performed in one of the recognised official languages of the competing nation. **Margot Eskens** of Germany opened the show with a lively ballad. She was quickly followed by Denmark's **Ulla Pia**, who sauntered down the staircase leading to the stage to sing 'Stop, Ja Stop, Ja Stop, Mens Legen Er Go' ('Quit, Yes Quit, Yes Quit While You're Ahead'). The title proved prophetic, as this turned out to be the last Danish entry until 1978. They went out with a swinging jazz extravaganza that introduced a first for viewers at home in the form of dancers jiving! Not that it impressed anyone other than Denmark's Nordic neighbours. The Danes ended the night in fourteenth place.

Hosts Luxembourg tried to recreate their success of the preceding year with a lively song performed by the towering Frenchwoman **Michèle Torr**, who had to crane her neck to reach the microphone. Again the judges were unimpressed. Perhaps it was the song's striking similarity, in both arrangement and melody, to the Tom Jones hit 'It's Not Unusual' that they did not

country	song	performer	place	score	draw
Austria	Merci Chérie	**Udo Jürgens**	1	31	9
Sweden	Nygammal Vals Eller Hip Man Svinaherde	**Lill Lindfors & Svante Thuresson**	2	16	10
Norway	Intet Er Nytt Under Solen	**Åse Kleveland**	3	15	6
Belgium	Un Peu De Poivre, Un Peu De Sel	**Tonia**	4=	14	3
Ireland	Come Back To Stay	**Dickie Rock**	4=	14	17
Switzerland	Ne Vois-Tu Pas?	**Madeleine Pascal**	6	12	12
Yugoslavia	Brez Besed	**Berta Ambrož**	7=	9	5
Spain	Yo Soy Aquel	**Raphael**	7=	9	11
United Kingdom	A Man Without Love	**Kenneth McKellar**	9	8	18
Germany	Die Zeiger Der Uhr	**Margot Eskens**	10=	7	1
Luxembourg	Ce Soir Je T'Attendais	**Michèle Torr**	10=	7	4
Finland	Playboy	**Ann Christine Nyström**	10=	7	7
Portugal	Ele E Ela	**Madalena Iglesias**	13	6	8
Denmark	Stop, Mens Legen Er Go	**Ulla Pia**	14	4	2
Netherlands	Fernando En Philippo	**Milly Scott**	15	2	16
France	Chez Nous	**Dominique Walter**	16	1	15
Monaco	Bien Plus Fort	**Tereza**	17=	0	13
Italy	Dio, Come Te Amo	**Domenico Modugno**	17=	0	14

approve of. Like Germany, the hosts won only seven marks to share a disappointing tenth place.

Only one singer has ever won the contest at their third attempt, and that was Udo Jürgens this year. Udo had been placed sixth in Copenhagen in 1964, and finished fourth in Naples. 'Merci Chérie' ('Thank You, Dear') may have had a French title, but it became the first German-language song to clinch the Eurovision prize, and it remains one of only two German-sung compositions to have done so.

Far left: Kenneth McKellar leaves for Luxembourg, with wife Hedy. The Scottish tenor drew gasps from the audience when he appeared on stage in traditional costume, complete with kilt, sporran and ruffled shirt.
Left: Winner on his third attempt, Udo Jürgens.

'Merci Chérie' charted in Netherlands, Belgium, Switzerland, Austria and Germany. Udo Jürgens wrote hits for a slew of international stars, including a No. 1 in the UK for Shirley Bassey, 'Reach For The Stars'. In 1981, he cut a new version of his contest winner, which he performed at the winners' gala in Oslo.

Black artists did not fare particularly well at Eurovision until Dave Benton broke through the barrier and won for Estonia in 2001. **Milly Scott** could not have imagined that it would take 35 years after she had become the first black singer to appear in the contest, before another finally took the Grand Prix. Performing for the Netherlands, Milly's entry was a sing-a-long number with more than a hint of Mexico about it. Milly also made a minor piece of technical history by becoming the very first artist to perform at Eurovision using a hand microphone. The freedom it gave her to bounce around the stage was obviously not the envy of all the other contestants, as the following year only one other singer emulated the concept, although that singer went on to win.

Both the Irish and the British entered male singers. The Irish entrant, **Dickie Rock,** was a dinner-suited artist who sang a gentle ballad that had the indelible stamp of what became the 'Irish formula' all over it. The UK had made the unlikely selection of **Kenneth McKellar**, a Scottish tenor who had as little a connection with the pop charts as his conservative stage appearance had with current trends. The maudlin ballad saw Britain suffer their worst result in their first 20 years of participation, despite being one of only two UK entries to ever receive top marks from their Irish neighbours.

Winner

United Kingdom

Performer

Sandie Shaw

1967

Title

'Puppet On
A String'

Composers

Bill Martin/
Phil Coulter

Presenter

Erika Vaal

Host & Venue

ORF
Wiener Hofburg
Palace

Vienna
Austria

In the year that the Beatles produced their landmark album *Sergeant Pepper's Lonely Hearts' Club Band* and the Summer of Love took place, the Eurovision Song Contest plodded along, blissfully unaware of the outside world. But even in the cosy world of the contest, things were changing.

The ornate and grandiose grand ballroom of the historic Wiener Hofburg Palace in the Austrian capital Vienna was chosen as the venue for the twelfth contest. The broadcast date was 8th April 1967. For the first time there were fewer countries participating than the year before, with Danish TV, DR, deciding to opt out of the competition.

Among the innovations at this year's contest – which included shots of the contestants backstage, reacting to the tense voting process – were on-screen translations of each song title into German, English and French. Not that it was needed for the opening song, which was the Dutch entry. Performed by **Thérèse Steinmetz**, 'Ringe-Dinge' is essentially nonsense in any language.

Having allowed Udo Jürgens to reign over the contest for three consecutive years, Austria now turned to **Peter Horten** to sing 'Warum Es 100,000 Sterne Gibt', which according to the on-screen English translation simply meant 'Why?'; more accurately, it means 'Why Are There 100,000 Stars?'. Wearing a black tuxedo, Horten sang well, but the tune was perhaps

country	song	performer	place	score	draw
United Kingdom	Puppet On A String	Sandie Shaw	1	47	11
Ireland	If I Could Choose	Sean Dunphy	2	22	17
France	Il Doit Faire Beau Là-Bas	Noëlle Cordier	3	20	4
Luxembourg	L'Amour Est Bleu	Vicky Leandros	4	17	2
Monaco	Boum-Badaboum	Minouche Barelli	5	10	14
Spain	Hablemos Del Amor	Raphael	6	9	12
Belgium	Ik Heb Zorgen	Louis Neefs	7	8	10
Sweden	Som En Dröm	Östen Warnerbring	8=	7	7
Germany	Anouschka	Inge Bruck	8=	7	9
Yugoslavia	Vse Rože Sveta	Lado Leskovar	8=	7	15
Italy	Non Andare Piu Lontano	Claudio Villa	11	4	16
Portugal	O Vento Mudou	Eduardo Nascimento	12=	3	5
Finland	Varjoon-Suojaan	Fredi	12=	3	8
Netherlands	Ringe-dinge	Thérèse Steinmetz	14=	2	1
Austria	Warum Es Hundert-Tausend Sterne Gibt	Peter Horten	14=	2	3
Norway	Dukkemann	Kirsti Sparboe	14=	2	13
Switzerland	Quel Coeur Vas-Tu Briser?	Géraldine	17	0	6

Ms Shaw claims to have despised 'Puppet On A String'. Nevertheless, the song went to No. 1 all over the continent, and she recorded German, French, Italian and Spanish versions that did well too. She outsold all other singles in the UK and Germany in 1967.

too similar to the winning song of the previous year to stand out in the crowd. Like the Dutch, the Austrians could only muster two votes from the juries.

Portugal fielded **Eduardo Nascimento**, the first black male singer to appear at Eurovision, only a year after the first black female had taken part.

Sweden had the trendy and bespectacled **Oesten Warnerbring** singing 'Som En Dröm', ('As A Dream'). The song started very quietly with just a drum and guitar playing, but built to a fuller sound at its climax. It was an unusual effort for the Swedes, but did not do as well as their 1966 runner-up, ending in eighth place with seven votes. Sweden's neighbours, Finland, were also well down the field with their song, which was performed by the very large **Fredi**. His enormous height and wide girth disguised a very quiet voice, which had something of a rasping quality, but it didn't help the Finns attract any more than three votes.

The UK had taken a long hard look at the contest and their approach to it after their relatively dismal showing in Luxembourg. The hugely popular singer **Sandie Shaw** was persuaded to perform the British entry. Shaw had shot to fame in 1964 when '(There's) Always Something There To Remind Me' topped the British charts. She amassed six top ten hits, including two chart toppers over the next 18 months and was a by-word for all that was cool about Swinging London. She had a very modern look and always appeared barefoot on stage, a gimmick that quickly became her trademark.

She gave a stellar performance on the night of the quirky, yet instantly appealing song, despite it having what she called a 'stupid cuckoo clock tune'. As she started to sing, her hand microphone, the only one in use all night, failed and the first note of the song was not heard. It made no difference. Sandie later admitted she knew she had won before she opened her mouth. It had taken the UK a decade to achieve their first Eurovision victory and they did so in unparalleled style. It broke the mould of the style of songs that had been heard in the contest to date.

The voting process was not without its problems for hostess **Erika Vaal**. When Yugoslavia awarded Austria one vote, the total was shown as 12 instead of 2, while for much of the process Ireland's score read as 2 when it should have been 22. While all this was going on, the UK was in fact notching up the third biggest win in the contest to date. 'Puppet On A String' earned a total of 47 votes, over 29 per cent of the total score available to all the songs, leading the Irish song by a 53 per cent margin.

Sandie Shaw's win was the catalyst for a new approach to the contest. Unfortunately, inferior imitations of her song flooded the competition, lowering the standard of entries for many years to come. Despite this, the ratings across the continent were now beginning to rocket, and for the next decade the contest was continually amongst the most watched programmes of the entire year. Things were looking up and the contest was about to enter a new era of colour television.

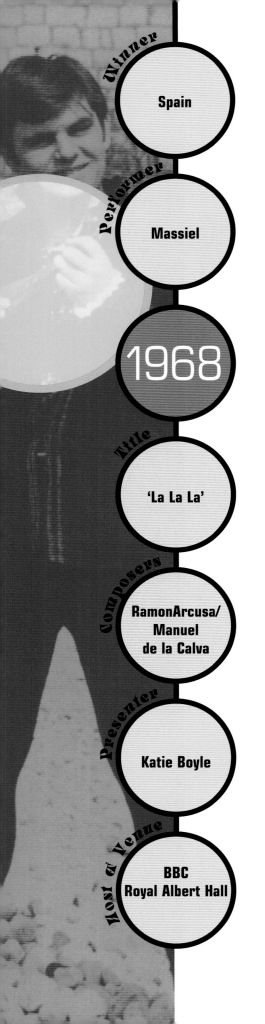

Winner

Spain

Performer

Massiel

1968

Title

'La La La'

Composers

RamonArcusa/ Manuel de la Calva

Presenter

Katie Boyle

Host & Venue

BBC Royal Albert Hall

Only twelve months separated the 1967 contest in Vienna and the 1968 contest in London, but to look at the two shows today, they appear to be decades apart. Not that the format of the show or the quality of the songs was noticeably different, what transformed the contest was that the transmission was in colour.

The same 17 nations that had competed in Vienna assembled in London to compete once again for a show that was to be broadcast from the Royal Albert Hall on 6th April 1968. There was briefly an eighteenth nation in the frame, as a delegation of disguised BBC pranksters arrived at the Royal Albert Hall in a limousine on the day of the rehearsal claiming to be the Albanian entry!

London
United Kingdom

The honour of opening the thirteenth Eurovision Song Contest fell to **Carlos Mendes** of Portugal. 'Verão' ('Summer') was a catchy number that was more in line with current musical trends than much of what came after it. **Ronnie Tober** had tried to get to the Eurovision final on a number of prior occasions. He finally made it in 1968 when 'Morgen' ('Tomorrow') won the Dutch heat and took him to London to sing for the Netherlands. Tober sang with great charm and looked very confident, if a little stiff. But the 'curse of number two' was to strike yet again and Ronnie only managed one vote in the final countdown, ending in equal last place.

Monaco was represented by a French couple, **Line and Willy,** and Luxembourg fielded a trendy young duo, **Sophie Garel and Chris Baldo,** to sing 'Nous Vivrons D'Amour' ('We Will Live Our Love'). Baldo sang the verse of the song in a very deep tone, almost speaking the words à la Maurice Chevalier, while Sophie joined in for the slightly more upbeat chorus. Their voices did not entirely compliment each other and their costumes were very disparate indeed. Sophie wore

A host of orchestral and vocal versions of 'La, La, La', flooded on to the market after Massiel's victory, including one from former winner Jørgen Ingmann. It's possible that sales of Massiel's own version suffered as a result. Massiel returned from the contest a national hero and remains a legend in Spain. She recently recorded a rap version of her winner.

Above: Katie Boyle retained her composure throughout, but has since revealed that her marriage was going through some troubles at the time. She'd been crying so much that she spent the last few hours before the broadcast lying down, with shredded raw potato on her eyes to reduce their puffiness.
Left: Massiel shows her trophy to Cliff Richard.

a long, white and shapeless knitted dress, covered in odd black and red markings, while Chris adopted a more formal look in a very pale blue suit and tie. Most of the men in this year's contest contrasted starkly with the women, who had seized the opportunity of the colour broadcast to don bright costumes. **Gianni Mascolo**, the Italian representing Switzerland, was the main exception wearing an ill-fitting suit of bright orange with a matching tie and spectacles. With its lilting melody, he had one of the more pleasant sounding songs of the year, but the judges must have been unable see beyond his clothes as he managed to squeeze just two points out of the very last jury and thus avoided total embarrassment.

France's **Isabelle Aubret**, who had won Eurovision in 1962, was the only returning artist to feature in the 1968 line-up. Her song 'La Source' ('The Source') benefited from an excellent arrangement and a gentle yet catchy melody, but she was not able to take the title for a second time, despite the fact that for a long time during the voting, it looked as if she would be the runaway winner. Also in the running in the early stages of the scoring was Ireland,

represented by **Pat McGuigan,** or as he liked to be known then, Pat McGeegan. His son Barry, watching at home, went on to become an Irish folk hero when he became a world boxing champion in 1984. He always opened his fights by inviting his father into the ring to perform 'Danny Boy', and, until his premature death, Pat always obliged.

By far the biggest cheer of the 1968 contest went out to the artist singing for the home team. **Cliff Richard** was the undisputed king of British pop, with a string of hit songs dating back to 1957's 'Move It' and successful movies such as *Summer Holiday*. His Eurovision song 'Congratulations', which was penned by the previous year's triumphant songwriters, Bill Martin and Phil Coulter, was already riding high in the British charts and no one in Britain thought it could possibly lose.

For his big night Richard wore a blue, double-breasted suit with a white ruffled shirt in something of a Regency style and eased himself around the stage with a stellar performance. The screams that greeted his arrival on stage continued after he had finished singing, and anyone watching would have assumed that the top prize was his.

Anyone, that is, except the judges.

During the mock voting at the dress rehearsal, Cliff had been dismayed to see his song losing. Feeling the tension, he realised he couldn't sit through the real thing, so, when he left the stage, he headed straight to the toilets where he locked himself away.

Odd Børre may have had the strangest name of anyone singing in the Albert Hall, and he certainly had the oddest song. The gangly, bespectacled Norwegian sang the staccato free-form jazz number, 'Stress'. The writers had asked him to appear anxious on stage, and he did not let them down. The song's lyrics were somewhat bizarre too: 'Hjem, hjem. hjem … Må, må, må, (or ha, ha ha)' It made what Spain had to offer next sound like a lyrical masterpiece.

If the lyrics to the Norwegian song had been somewhat bizarre, the lyrics for the Spanish entry 'La, La, La' were just plain bad. **Massiel** was a dark-haired beauty who had been approached by Spanish TV after the original singer, Joan Manuel Serrat, pulled out because he was not allowed to sing in Catalan. Massiel was on tour in Mexico at the time, but agreed to represent Spain. And much to everyone's surprise – and the disgust of many – she won. The most repetitious song ever heard in the contest, 'La, La, La' has become a byword for everything that is wrong with the Eurovision contest, and gets more criticism than any other winner.

Another Norwegian took to the stage next, to sing for Germany. **Wencke Myrhe** had tried to represent her native country several times, but had always fallen at the first hurdle. She interspersed the German lyric with 'Three cheers for love/Viva l' amour', and added a chorus of 'la la la', as was becoming the pattern. Myrhe did well with this up-tempo number, finishing in sixth place. However, the Germans are better remembered for the votes they gave, rather than the votes they received in 1968.

As the voting neared its climax the UK led with 26 points, with Spain trailing on 23 and France on 20. Germany cast the penultimate marks and when they awarded Britain two votes, huge cheers and screams echoed around the Hall. When they followed this with six for Spain, the cheers turned to gasps of shock. With only Yugoslavia left to vote, the Germans had put Spain one point ahead.

Katie Boyle was as anxious to get to the final result as the primarily British audience, which was now on the edge

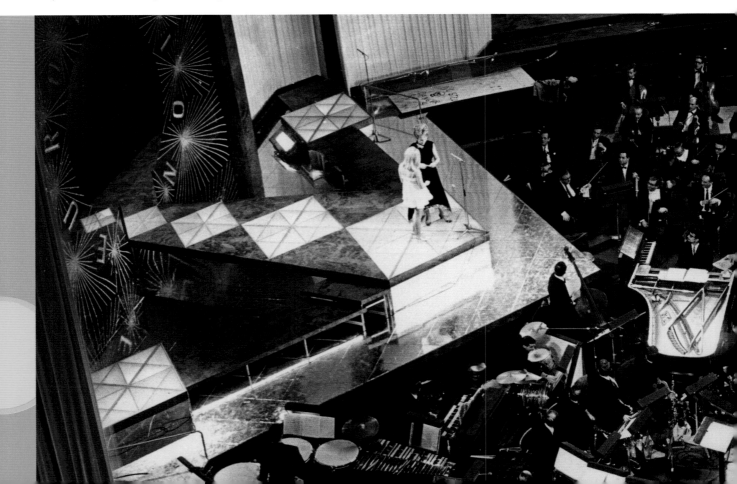

of its seats. Not since 1963 had the outcome hinged on the final country's scores. Katie called Skopje in Yugoslavia who chose to award neither the UK nor Spain any points at all. There were stunned gasps from the audience and the reprise of the winning entry was met with a muted response.

Backstage, locked in the toilets, Cliff Richard heard from his manager that he had lost, while the TV credits rolled over a final look at the disappointed audience leaving their seats. Over the subsequent few days, the British media were particularly scathing about the show, or more explicitly the result. Meanwhile, Massiel returned to Spain a national hero. She was greeted at Madrid airport by thousands of fans, carrying placards bearing messages of congratulations. Cliff Richard may have been joking, but during a live concert at London's Talk of the Town later that year, he vented some frustration at the whole contest, stating that after the show he walked over to Massiel and 'shook her warmly by the throat'.

The first colour contest was a triumph for the BBC production team, but the result a disappointment for the millions watching in the UK and elsewhere. For the first time the show's credibility was seriously being called to account.

Above: Yugoslavia's Luci Kapurso and Hamo Hajdarhodzić, who were backed by three more singers. It was a totally unique presentation with all five performers dressed in doublet and hose, in shades of maroon, brown and purple.

Left: Dress rehearsal at this year's venue, the Royal Albert Hall.

country	song	performer	place	score	draw
Spain	La La La	Massiel	1	29	15
United Kingdom	Congratulations	Cliff Richard	2	28	12
France	La Source	Isabelle Aubret	3	20	10
Ireland	Chance Of A Lifetime	Pat McGuigan	4	18	14
Sweden	Det Börjar Verka Kärlek Banne Mej	Claes-Göran Hederström	5	15	8
Germany	Ein Hoch Der Liebe	Wenche Myrhe	6	11	16
Belgium	Quand Tu Reviendras	Claude Lombard	7=	8	3
Monaco	A Chacun Sa Chanson	Line & Willy	7=	8	7
Yugoslavia	Jedan Dan	Luci Kapurso & Hamo Hajdarhodzić	7=	8	17
Italy	Marianne	Sergio Endrigo	10	7	11
Portugal	Verão	Carlos Mendes	11=	5	1
Luxembourg	Nous Vivrons D'Amour	Chris Baldo & Sophie Garel	11=	5	5
Austria	Tausend Fenster	Karel Gott	12=	2	4
Switzerland	Guardando Il Sole	Gianni Mascolo	12=	2	6
Norway	Stress	Odd Børre	12=	2	13
Netherlands	Morgen	Ronnie Tober	16=	1	2
Finland	Kun Kello Käy	Kristina Hautala	16=	1	9

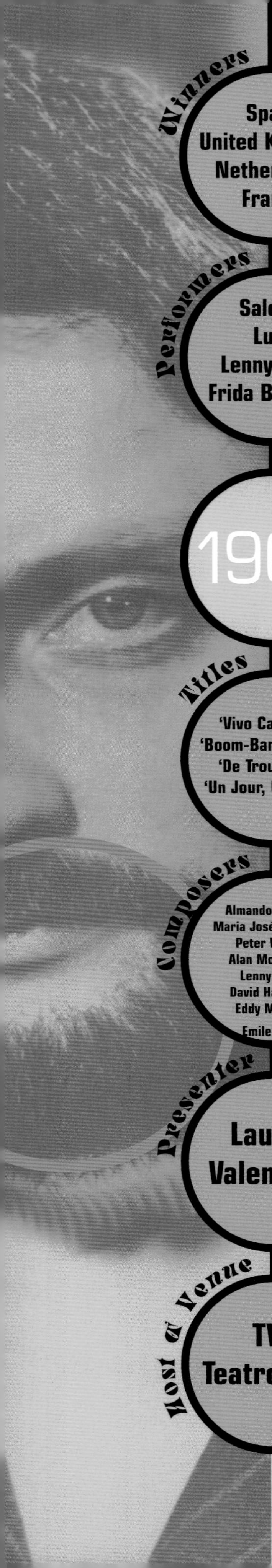

Winners

Spain
United Kingdom
Netherlands
France

Performers

Salomé
Lulu
Lenny Kuhr
Frida Boccara

1969

Titles

'Vivo Cantando'
'Boom-Bang-A-Bang'
'De Troubadour'
'Un Jour, Un Enfant'

Composers

Almando Alcalde/
Maria José de Cerato
Peter Warne/
Alan Moorhouse
Lenny Kuhr/
David Hartsema
Eddy Marnay/
Emile Stern

Presenter

Laurita Valenzuela

Host & Venue

TVE
Teatro Real

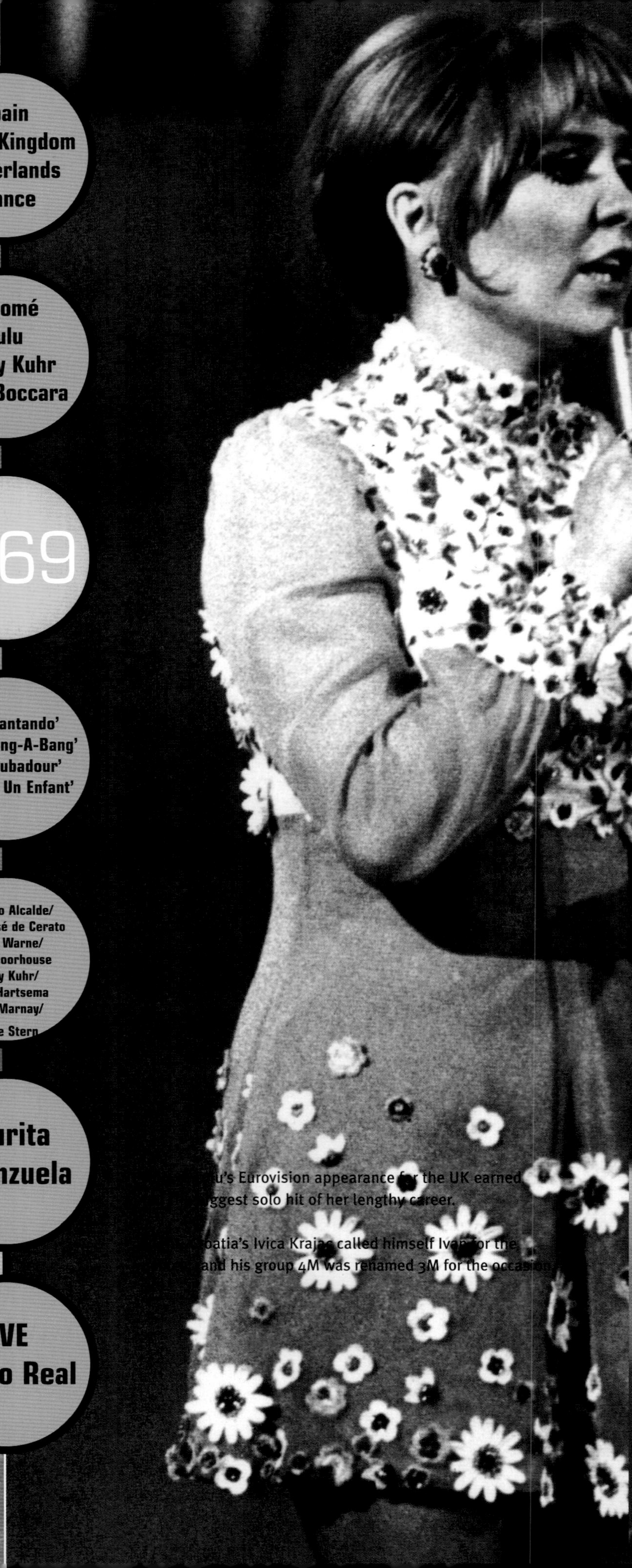

u's Eurovision appearance f r the UK earned ggest solo hit of her lengthy career.

oatia's Ivica Kraja called himself Ivan for the and his group 4M was renamed 3M for the occas

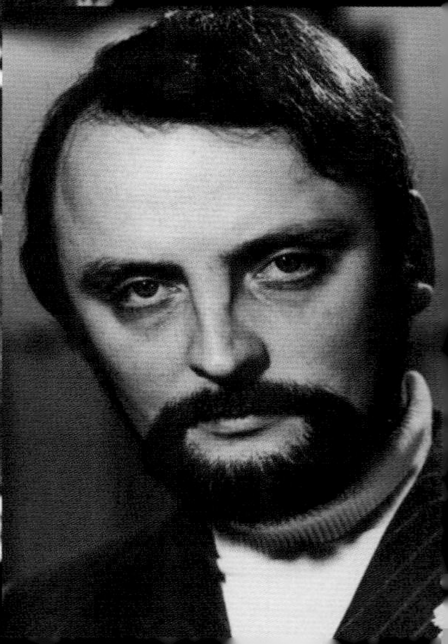

The second contest to be produced in colour was staged at Madrid's Teatro Real Opera House on Saturday 29th March 1969. Austria took a political stance and refused to take part, objecting to participating in a show staged under the regime of General Franco. This was noble, although as Austria had given Spain two votes in 1968, they could be considered partially responsible for having sent the contest there in the first place. The political overtones of the Spanish regime did not overtly cloud the competition, but the show itself still ended up embroiled

Madrid
Spain

in a controversy that almost brought the Eurovision Song Contest to an ignominious end.

Several competitors were making return visits to the contest; indeed a quarter of the 16 entrants had been there before, including the Frenchman **Romuald**, who had represented Monaco five years previously, but was now singing for Luxembourg. The show opened with the orchestra playing the Eurovision theme, 'Te Deum'. As that ended, an unusual Eurovision logo filled the screen. Salvador Dali, the legendary Spanish surrealist, had been commissioned to design the logo, which he painted as a large poster, including many of his famous trademarks, such as melting clock faces and a large pair of red lips. As viewers took in this remarkable piece of art, the orchestra launched into a reprise of the previous year's winner, 'La, La, La'.

Having closed the show in London, Yugoslavia now opened it in Madrid. **Ivan**, a demonic-looking Croatian,

sporting jet-black hair, a pointed beard and a black tuxedo, sang 'Pozdrav Svijetu' ('Greetings To The World'). He had an unusual habit of rolling his eyes into the back of his head as he sang, which was strangely compelling to watch, though the song itself was more forgettable. It was a ballad based around greetings in various languages, and included English, German, French and Italian salutations.

No country had yet won the contest two years in a row, and only the Swiss had ever managed to win on home ground back in 1956. Spain's entrant, **Salomé**, or Maria Rosa Marco as she was also known, was undaunted by this poor form and wrote herself into the record books with 'Vivo Cantando' ('I Live My Life Singing'). Salomé had male trio Los Valldemosa in tow as she took to the stage to a thunderous reception, dressed in a one-piece pantsuit in a shimmering pale blue fringe. As the tempo of her entry increased, she became more and more excited in her movements. Even though she was singing alone into a stand-mike, she had put together some very bizarre choreography, which resembled the movements of one of the puppets from *Thunderbirds*.

Other strange sights included a 12-year-old boy, **Jean Jacques**, singing about his mother for Monaco; Sweden's **Tommy Körberg** getting his microphone lead tangled on something backstage and having to yank it free; and three Portuguese backing singers, whose floor-length chiffon gowns made it look as if they were gliding on air. Best of all was **Louis Neefs** for Belgium, making a second run at the title. He had perfected an odd presentation that consisted of sudden unexpected bursts of movement, which involved him throwing his arms straight up over his head.

The Irish press made great capital of the seemingly irrelevant fact that Ireland was to be represented by a Protestant singer for the first time. 'The Wages of Love', sung by

Far left: Northern Ireland's Muriel Day. For the event itself she wore a striking green bat-wing mini dress, and was backed by three ladies who were collectively known as The Lindsays, all of whom wore clashing purple and green floral floor-length gowns.

Left: Portugal's Simone de Oliviera. Simone chose to perform wearing a floor-length green chiffon gown, with sleeves that also reached the ground. Her three backing singers were similarly dressed in red. As they entered the stage, they appeared to be gliding on air, as their feet were not visible to the audience.

Northern Ireland's **Muriel Day**, was a very upbeat number, and the first entry from Ireland that was in the bouncy, Euro-song mode. Day leapt about the stage, swinging her hand mike with reckless abandon. She got huge cheers from the audience and was clearly enjoying herself – much more so than the judges listening. Although the Irish song finished in seventh place with ten votes, it was their worst placing to date.

After the disappointment of the result in London, the United Kingdom chose another of their leading stars to try and correct that perceived miscarriage of justice. Unfortunately for Scots singer **Lulu**, she was given the lyrically challenged 'Boom Bang-A-Bang' as her entry by BBC TV viewers. Lulu had shot to fame at the age of 15 in 1964, with her recording of the Isley Brothers song 'Shout'. In 1967 she released the biggest-selling single of the year in America with the theme tune for the movie *To Sir With Love*. Just days before she flew to Madrid she married Maurice Gibb, a member of the Bee Gees, in a much-publicised wedding.

Lulu arrived in Madrid as the hot favourite, despite her own misgivings about the song. She preferred another tune, 'I Can't Go On Living Without You', which was written by the then unknown partnership of Elton John and Bernie Taupin, but it had failed to win votes from the British TV viewers. On the night, Lulu arguably gave the best performance of any artist in the contest.

country	song	performer	place	score	draw
Spain	Vivo Cantando	**Salomé**	1=	18	3
United Kingdom	Boom Bang-A-Bang	**Lulu**	1=	18	7
Netherlands	De Troubadour	**Lenny Kuhr**	1=	18	8
France	Un Jour, Un Enfant	**Frida Boccara**	1=	18	14
Switzerland	Bonjour, Bonjour	**Paola del Medico**	5	13	11
Monaco	Maman	**Jean-Jacques**	6	11	4
Ireland	The Wages Of Love	**Muriel Day & The Lindsays**	7=	10	5
Belgium	Jennifer Jennings	**Louis Neefs**	7=	10	10
Sweden	Judy, Min Vän	**Tommy Körberg**	9=	8	9
Germany	Prima Ballerina	**Siw Malmkvist**	9=	8	13
Luxembourg	Cathérine	**Romuald**	11	7	2
Finland	Kuin Silloin Ennen	**Jarkko & Laura**	12	6	16
Yugoslavia	Pozdrav-Svijetu	**Ivan**	13=	5	1
Italy	Due Grosse Lacrime Bianche	**Iva Zanicchi**	13=	5	6
Portugal	Desfolhada Portuguesa	**Simone de Oliveira**	15	4	15
Norway	Oj, Oj, Oj, Sä Glad, Jeg Skal Bli	**Kirsti Sparboe**	16	1	12

Her resident musical director, Johnny Harris, was conducting, and as Lulu ended the song with an impromptu 'Olé', the audience gave it a huge reception.

Next, **Lenny Kuhr** performed 'De Troubadour' ('The Troubadour') for the Netherlands. She had written the lyrics of the song, alongside composer David Hartsema, and also accompanied herself on the guitar, making her the first female to pen a Eurovision winner and the first female winner of the contest to play an instrument on stage. It had a very gentle tone, yet the many bursts of 'Li, li, li, la', were hardly a highly original innovation.

The most emotional and dramatic performance of the night came from France. 'Un Jour, Un Enfant' ('One Day A Child') was the delicate ballad sung by **Frida Boccara**, which she performed alone in a black gown, topped with a beaded golden bodice. The song was augmented with an orchestra, unlike the recorded version, which relied largely on just strings and piano, and had a very simple and lilting tune. Most pundits and observers have often cited this song as the clear winner of the night, even though it was not so in reality.

For the juries there seemed to be little to choose between the competitors. As the voting neared its close the UK, Netherlands, France and Spain all vied for the top slot. Portugal levelled the field, giving two votes to both Spain and France, tying them with the Dutch on 18 votes. Their single point for the UK held the British at 17 votes. With only Finland left, things were certainly very tense.

Finland gave one vote to the UK, which was greeted with shocked gasps, levelling all four countries. Their remaining nine votes were spread between Ireland, Italy, Sweden and Switzerland. When Helsinki finished voting, the audience gave rapturous applause, but then fell into stunned silence. Nobody seemed to know what this result meant, least of all the mistress of ceremonies, Laurita Valenzuela, who was decidedly flustered by the outcome. She asked Eurovision's scrutineer, Clifford Brown, for his adjudication, yet when he confirmed that there were four equal winners, she did not initially believe him. She twice asked him again to clarify the confusion and he twice reiterated that the result was a four-way tie. As Laurita announced each of the winners in turn, she remained incredulous that such an incident could occur and the audience seemed equally baffled.

Clifford Brown admitted to a BBC documentary in 1992 that the result caused disgust among many people, not least the Scandinavian countries. The media were universally scathing of the result and, in every country, news reports condemned the four-way tie. Adding another layer of conspiracy, it was claimed that Norway's **Kirsti Sparboe** had been made a scapegoat for the country's unpopular seal culling – although her songs trite lyrics featuring 'Oy, oy, oy' may have been a bigger factor.

After mounting public and media discontent following the two results that ended the 1960s, the Eurovision Song Contest was not looking too healthy. The 1970 edition was threatened by a mass walkout of nations and, despite continued mammoth ratings, things certainly did not look promising for the show as it headed into the new decade.

Lulu recorded her winner in five languages. She reached No. 2 in Britain, No. 3 in Sweden, No. 19 in the Netherlands and also charted in several other countries. Frida also recorded five versions of hers, with Agnetha Faltskog cutting it in Swedish. Lenny Kuhr made six versions of 'De Troubadour', reaching No. 12 in the Dutch chart. Salomé (above) topped the Spanish chart, but failed to hit elsewhere with her seven versions.

Winner

Performer

1970

Title

Composers

Presenter

Host & Venue

Ireland

Dana

'All Kinds of Everything'

Derry Lindsay/ Jackie Smith

Willy Dobbe

NOS RAI Congrescentrum

amsterdam
The Netherlands

After the debacle of 1969, the future of the Eurovision Song Contest was in the balance. The controversial tied result had led to a storm of protests and the EBU were obliged to re-examine the entire competition. After much lobbying from the member broadcasters, it was decided that a mechanism would be put in place to break a tie should it occur. Other than that, the voting system of ten judges with one vote each remained the same, although it was still under review. Nevertheless, many of the participating countries took the view that the contest was dying anyway, and Norway, Sweden, Finland, Portugal and Austria all refused to take part in the fifteenth edition.

Despite the dark cloud over Eurovision, all four of 1969's winning nations applied to host the 1970 event – the Netherlands producing the event after winning a ballot. But with only 12 nations participating, it was difficult to envisage a particularly hopeful future.

Willy Dobbe was selected to act as presenter for the contest, even though her role was somewhat reduced from many of her predecessors. Willy has become synonymous with Eurovision in the Netherlands, and indeed in future years hosted the Dutch heat on many occasions. For her big night, she wore a long, pale blue gown, decorated liberally with rhinestones around the bodice. Her blond hair swept high above her head, she seemed a little stiff and somewhat nervous throughout the evening.

The overall production of the 1970 show, which was broadcast on 21st March, acquired a much more modern look, possibly to reflect the start of the new decade. The set was very dramatic, and lighting was used to very clever effect for the first time in the colour era. **Roland de Groot** was in charge of the set design and he created a simple, yet very effective mobile set. Five half rings, of varying size were suspended over the performing area, with a cluster of golden spheres suspended in the centre, over a curved ramp-way that allowed the singers to enter and exit the stage. The spheres were continually lowered and raised and rearranged

Dana topped the charts in the UK and all over the continent with **'All Kinds Of Everything'**, an extremely simple and effective ballad, not unlike 'My Favourite Things' from *The Sound of Music*. Dana was mobbed by reporters and TV cameras on her arrival back in Belfast, and she sang the song from the steps of the aeroplane.

throughout the evening, while the concentric half rings could be adjusted to form different patterns. Added to this, the entire backdrop of the stage was illuminated in different colours for each country. It was a big step forward in terms of stage design and, although it did not immediately catch on, in later years it became a benchmark for future contests.

The broadcast opened with another innovation; after the 'Te Deum' and titles, viewers were treated to a lengthy travelogue featuring the Dutch countryside and landscape and highlighting many of the small nation's famous landmarks. The film ended with establishing shots of the ultra-modern RAI Congrescentrum. In a welcoming gesture, two young ladies opened the doors to the auditorium and beckoned the cameras inside. And this year saw filmed 'postcards' for the first time, introducing each song for the TV audience. In most cases, the performers were filmed in the countries they represented, but in the case of Monaco and Luxembourg, their artists were actually seen wandering around Paris. Sadly, this made it rather obvious that neither singer was actually from the country that they were to perform for, a pretty standard occurrence in both cases.

The host nation was drawn to sing in the opening slot. The Maessen sisters, Patricia, Stella and Bianca, had been selected to sing 'Waterman'. The sisters were known collectively as The Hearts of Soul, but it was still not permitted for groups of three or more to sing in the contest. To overcome this problem, the sisters were billed as **'Patricia and the Hearts of Soul'**, thus appearing as one performer with two backing singers. The song told the story of a man born under the sign of Aquarius, and certainly had all the elements of the successful hit-making girl groups of the day. Patricia wore purple, while her sisters were in brown, although all three had heavy gold sequins and embroidery around the bodices of their knee-length frocks. While Patricia sang, her sisters provided some rather

In the postcard introduction, Dana was seen skipping and cycling around Dublin in a number of trend-setting outfits, but for her appearance on stage she had opted for this rather childish-looking, plain, off-white mini-dress, with Irish symbols embroidered on the skirt.

eccentric choreography, and the whole effect was somewhat mesmerising. Not surprisingly, the Dutch audience gave them a warm reception.

Switzerland had a very typical Euro-song lined up for 1970 and **Henri Dès** seemed almost uncomfortable performing the nonsense lyrics of 'Retour' ('Return'). Sound effects from the orchestra added to the trite nature of the entry, while Henri himself made sounds mimicking brass instruments. It was a very stiff performance and not helped by some 'unusual' leg movements from the performer, which seemed to have no relevance to the melody at all. It is not at all unfair to suggest that this was the weakest song in the field, but the judges were clearly impressed. Henri surprised everyone by scoring well enough to secure equal fourth place.

Another male artist, **Gianni Morandi** was representing Italy with the song 'Occhi Di Ragazza', ('Eyes Of A Girl'), an up-tempo ballad he delivered with great enthusiasm. Gianni was one of the most popular male stars in Italy at the time, and was known not only as a singer but as a movie actor too. For his 'postcard' he was seen wandering the ruins in Rome around the Coliseum. On stage, he wore a traditional black tuxedo for his performance and appeared entirely alone on stage. It was a far superior song to Switzerland's effort, although the judges did not agree.

Eva Srsen was seen in the bleak snow of her homeland Slovenia before making her way on stage to sing for Yugoslavia. Dressed in a short orange frock, with her blond hair loose around her shoulders, she gave a tuneless performance of 'Pridi Dala Ti Bom Cvet' ('Come, I Give You My Bloom'). The BBC commentary claimed, somewhat kindly, that she was 'a newcomer on the pop scene'.

France's **Guy Bonnet** made his debut as a Eurovision performer in 1970, although this was in fact the second of three entries for France that he penned. His 1968 offering, 'La Source', had done very well, finishing third for Isabelle Aubret. This year he performed his composition himself. 'Marie Blanche' was a slow ballad, which Bonnet sang alone at his grand piano. It never seemed likely that he would make it two victories in a row for the French, but he did score well enough to finish equal fourth.

Not for the first time, the UK was represented by the biggest star of the night, in this case, **Mary Hopkin**. A Welsh singer, Hopkin had rocketed to fame in 1968 after winning the TV talent show 'Opportunity Knocks'. The model and actress Twiggy recommended her to Paul McCartney and

Mary Hopkin was filmed walking around London in the postcard introducing the UK song. It was the only film that actually featured the cameraman, who was seen lying on the ground to get a clearer shot of his subject.

she was signed to the Beatles' Apple label. Her Eurovision song 'Knock Knock (Who's There?)' was the clear favourite to take this year's prize. David Gell, who was providing the commentary for the UK broadcaster BBC1, mused that the song bore such similarity to 'Puppet On A String', 'Congratulations' and 'Boom Bang-A-Bang' that it may have been written by a computer. For the first time though, the UK had added a chorus of 'la la las' just for good measure. Two male singers provided the backing vocals, the only act of the night to do so. Hopkin sang confidently in her crystal-clear voice, and seemed very comfortable with her performance.

David Alexandre Winter was a Dutch DJ who had spent time working for Luxembourg's television station, RTL, giving him a stronger link to the Grand Duchy than many previous singers could claim. 'Je Suis Tombé Du Ciel' ('I Fell From The Sky') was a well-sung dramatic French ballad; however, it failed to impress a single judge. Luxembourg was destined to score their first and only zero in the history of the competition. It also marked the last time any song failed to garner a score until 1978.

Although Mary Hopkin was the biggest name in the show, the Spanish had sent a singer who would outstrip her achievements a hundred-fold over the subsequent decades. At this point, **Julio Iglesias** was little known outside of Spain, where he was rapidly becoming a very popular artist. His self-penned entry, 'Gwendolyne', could not have contrasted more starkly with the two songs that had brought victory for Spain in the last two years. It was an impressive ballad, but

country	song	performer	place	score	draw
Ireland	All Kinds Of Everything	**Dana**	1	32	12
United Kingdom	Knock Knock (Who's There?)	**Mary Hopkin**	2	26	7
Germany	Wunder Gibt Es Immer Wieder	**Katja Ebstein**	3	12	11
Switzerland	Retour	**Henri Dès**	4=	8	2
France	Marie Blanche	**Guy Bonnet**	4=	8	6
Spain	Gwendolyne	**Julio Iglesias**	4=	8	9
Netherlands	Waterman	**Patricia & The Hearts Of Soul**	7	7	1
Italy	Occhi Di Ragazza	**Gianni Morandi**	8=	5	3
Belgium	Viens L'Oublier	**Jean Vallée**	8=	5	5
Monaco	Marlène	**Dominique Dussault**	8=	5	10
Yugoslavia	Pridi, Dala Ti Bom Cvet	**Eva Srsen**	11	4	4
Luxembourg	Je Suis Tombé Du Ciel	**David Alexandre Winter**	12	0	8

the anxiety of trying to win Spain a third consecutive contest proved too much – a mis-timed ending being one of several errors that marred an otherwise slick performance.

Once again, Monaco fielded an all-French entry for their effort. Performed in a Cabaret style by **Dominique Dussault**, 'Marlène' was a tribute to the legendary German icon Marlène Dietrich. The song told of how the singer wished she had the attributes of the star and included lines in both German and English as the performer imitated her idol, ending her performance by turning her back on the audience and walking away; it was certainly the most theatrical presentation of the night, even if it was not the most popular.

After a sultry performance by Germany's **Katja Ebstein**, the final entry came from Ireland. **Dana** was billed as a fresh-faced 17-year-old hailing from the notorious Bogside of Northern Ireland, which actually made her a British citizen. In reality, her name was Rosemary Brown and she was closer to 19, but this did not emerge until after the contest. Her song 'All Kinds Of Everything' was an extremely simple and effective ballad, not unlike 'My Favourite Things' from *The Sound of Music* in sentiment. To sing the winsome song, Dana appeared on stage alone and perched on a cylinder, something she later complained about, as it meant there was nowhere for her heels and she feared she would slip off! Excluding accompanying musicians, Dana is one of only five principal winners of the contest to win sitting down; the other four are Udo Jürgens in 1966, Johnny Logan in 1980, Nicole in 1982 and Harrington & McGettigan in 1994.

After the scoring complications in Madrid, the EBU had decided on a new way of settling a drawn contest. If another tie occurred, the songs involved would be performed again, and all the juries – with the exception of the countries involved in the tie – would give one casting vote. Thankfully, such measures were not necessary, as Ireland's victory was pretty conclusive from the start, racing to a big lead, attracting 11 votes out of a possible 20 from the first two juries alone and nine out of ten from Belgium.

Dana went on to top the charts all over Europe with her winner. She spent two weeks at number one in the UK, holding off Mary Hopkin's song at number two, just as in the contest. Hopkin's single also did phenomenally well, but it marked something of a swansong for her recording career. Of course, Dana and Mary Hopkin were not the only success stories from 1970. Julio Iglesias was later topping the charts and setting female hearts a-fluttering all over the world. Katja Ebstein also proved very popular in Germany, and returned to Eurovision the next year to sing again for her country.

The 1970 competition was something of a landmark for the Eurovision Song Contest. The production set a standard and format that has been retained pretty much ever since, and the winning song and performer became one of the most successful in the competition's history. Eurovision was back on track and, with the return of the boycotting nations, and indeed the emergence of new contestants, it was about to enter its most prolific and successful period.

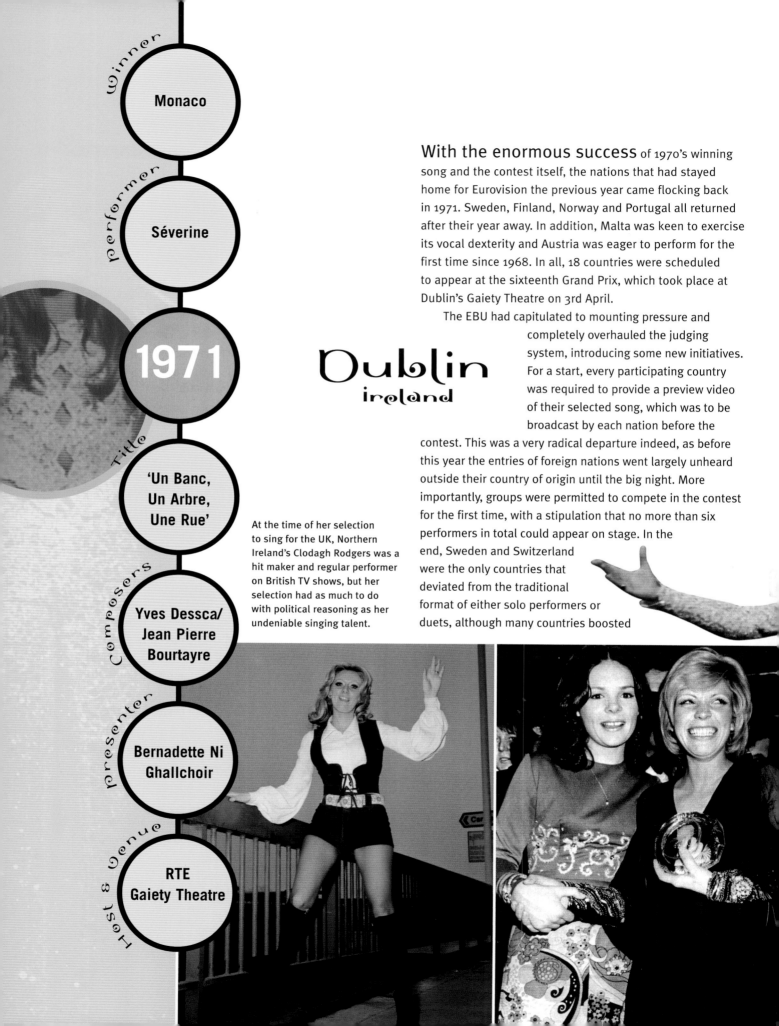

Winner

Monaco

Performer

Séverine

1971

Dublin
ireland

Title

'Un Banc,
Un Arbre,
Une Rue'

Composers

Yves Dessca/
Jean Pierre
Bourtayre

Presenter

Bernadette Ni
Ghallchoir

Host & Venue

RTE
Gaiety Theatre

With the enormous success of 1970's winning song and the contest itself, the nations that had stayed home for Eurovision the previous year came flocking back in 1971. Sweden, Finland, Norway and Portugal all returned after their year away. In addition, Malta was keen to exercise its vocal dexterity and Austria was eager to perform for the first time since 1968. In all, 18 countries were scheduled to appear at the sixteenth Grand Prix, which took place at Dublin's Gaiety Theatre on 3rd April.

The EBU had capitulated to mounting pressure and completely overhauled the judging system, introducing some new initiatives. For a start, every participating country was required to provide a preview video of their selected song, which was to be broadcast by each nation before the contest. This was a very radical departure indeed, as before this year the entries of foreign nations went largely unheard outside their country of origin until the big night. More importantly, groups were permitted to compete in the contest for the first time, with a stipulation that no more than six performers in total could appear on stage. In the end, Sweden and Switzerland were the only countries that deviated from the traditional format of either solo performers or duets, although many countries boosted

At the time of her selection to sing for the UK, Northern Ireland's Clodagh Rodgers was a hit maker and regular performer on British TV shows, but her selection had as much to do with political reasoning as her undeniable singing talent.

the number of backing singers for their artists.

Peter, Sue and Marc became the first group ever to appear at the contest when they sang for Switzerland. This was the first of four entries for the trio, each of which was sung in a different language – French in 1971, English in 1976, German in 1979 and Italian in 1981. Their debut effort was their least appreciated entry, though, and they ended in twelfth position. The other group in Dublin were the Swedish entrants **The Family Four** who finished six places ahead.

Austria was drawn to sing first with 'Musik', which was performed by **Marianne Mendt**. The Austrian began confidently, but by the time she reached the chorus she was wavering off key. Singing in a local Viennese-German dialect, Mendt was clearly anxious at having to perform at the top of the show. With Austria back in the fold, a new member of the Eurovision family followed to sing second – Malta. The Mediterranean island had selected **Joe Grech** to sing their debut entry 'Marija L-Maltija' ('Maltese Maria'). Joe was from the 'medallion man' school of dressing and appeared on stage in a white suit with the tightest white flared trousers probably ever seen in the contest and a large polka-dot bow tie with

Left: Her second appearance at the contest, Katja Ebstein looked very striking in her silver catsuit, and gave a strong performance, but again had to be content with third place.

Last year's winner Dana congratulates this year's victor Séverine.

matching hanky. Malta finished last.

After what the judges deemed to be the worst song of the night, came the one they considered the best, the entry from Monaco. **Séverine** was the French woman selected to sing for the principality this year. As a child, she had been inspired by former Eurovision winner Jacqueline Boyer, and admitted that she regularly mimicked her idol at home by performing in front of a mirror. She has frequently claimed that she had never set foot in Monaco prior to her win and was somewhat put out that no invitation to do so was forthcoming after her victory. 'Un Banc, Un Arbre, Une Rue' ('A Bench, A Tree, A Road') was well orchestrated, and Séverine belted the song out, giving a very dramatic interpretation that was accompanied by four male backing singers. In addition to the strong musical track, the backing singers cleverly sang the chorus melody while Séverine sang the verse. Although the song ended with a burst of the obligatory 'la la las', it was still a song way above the standard of the others on show, and the judges agreed.

Following her third placing in the 1970 contest, Germany's highest known placing in the contest to date, **Katja Ebstein** was asked back to sing in Dublin, and hopefully finish a couple of places higher. Her song 'Diese Welt' ('This World') was very strong, and Katja raised fashion standards in the contest, wearing an all-in-one silver cat suit. She sang powerfully and was received warmly by the audience. However, she was unable to improve her placing from the previous year. To do that she had to wait until 1980 when she made her third and final Eurovision appearance.

Spain had been enjoying considerable success in the recent contests, and this was extended in Dublin. **Karina** was the artist chosen to sing their 1971 effort, 'En Un Mundo Nuevo' ('A Whole New World'). The song started with a gentle woodwind introduction while Karina sang the

Séverine enjoyed much success around the continent with '**Un Banc, Un Arbre, Une Rue**'. She hit the UK Top 10 with the French version, even though she also recorded it in English. She made No. 1 in Sweden, the Top 20 in the Netherlands and many other countries as well. She also released German and Italian versions, and reportedly made a Spanish version.

ballad for the opening verse. The tempo of the song then stepped up another notch into a rousing, rather typical Euro thigh-slapper, highly reminiscent of Spain's two victorious entries from the late 1960s. It was good enough to earn Spain a second place.

Two French language songs followed next. **Serge Lama** sang 'Un Jardin Sur La Terre' ('A Garden On The Earth') for France, while **Monique Melsen** sang 'Pomme, Pomme, Pomme,' ('Apple, Apple, Apple') for Luxembourg. They could not have been more opposing styles of songs even if they had tried harder. Serge's ballad was very much in the French mould, with heavy emotion and strong orchestration, whereas Monique presented an infuriatingly catchy, bouncy piece of bubble-gum pop from the 'Boom Bang-A-Bang' school of Eurovision composition. Monique's bright blue hot pants and her red boots were possibly the only things to catch the judges' attention.

The BBC were reported to be anxious as to what kind of reception the UK artist would get in Dublin, with the hostilities in Northern Ireland raging at the time. In a stroke of PR genius, they invited Northern Ireland's **Clodagh Rodgers** to perform 'Jack In The Box' in Dublin, thus ensuring that her reception would be nothing but warm both in Britain and in Ireland. This gesture was not appreciated by all, however, and the singer received death threats from paramilitary organisations for her perceived switch of national allegiance.

During rehearsals, Clodagh wore a muslin smock to disguise her dazzling costume, fearing that one of the other entrants may copy it. When she did reveal it at the final

Right: Monique Melsen's bright-blue hotpants and bouncy bubble-gum pop left Luxembourg way down the field in 13th place.

Far right: Séverine sings for Monaco.

dress rehearsal, watched by the judges, she received an awesome reception from the audience. Her silver-trimmed pink blouse and sparkling silver hot pants were certainly the most eye-catching garments of the night. At the other end of the fashion spectrum, Portugal's **Tonicha** wore an outfit that resembled a lumpy patchwork quilt, while Norway's **Hanne Krogh** wore a Victorian costume complete with parasol. The judges were less impressed with the United Kingdom's song than with Rodgers' attire and she faded to fourth.

Belgian TV had suffered many headaches in getting their song into the contest. 'Goeie Morgen, Morgen' ('Good Morning, Morning') was to be sung by Nicole and Hugo, but just days before the event, Nicole came down with an attack of jaundice and was unable to perform. In a last minute scramble, Belgian broadcaster BRTN invited **Lily Castel and Jacques Raymond** to fill in for the ill-fated duo. It is rumoured that Ms Castel had barely enough time to buy a dress for the event, but they did present a very accomplished performance, with some very slick choreography. Nevertheless, the ill-fated Belgians ended up sharing a lowly fourteenth rung with Yugoslavia.

The most significant change in 1971 was in the voting procedure. The number of judges was slashed to two for each country. One judge had to be aged between 16 and 25, the other between 26 and 55. There also had to be at least ten years' difference between their ages. They had to be present in Dublin for the voting and would be seen by viewers casting their votes on screen. Every judge had to award every song a mark of between one and five, excluding the song from his or her own country, of course. At least this meant that no song could score less than 34 points, but it made for a rather tedious procedure.

After the incredibly lengthy scoring was complete, Séverine appeared back on the stage, just as the complex scoreboard was being hoisted back into the rafters. Dana presented the trophy to the winning team and flowers not only to Séverine, but also to the runners-up, Karina and Katja Ebstein, the last time that this happened in the contest. Bernadette Ni Gallchoir made a quick dash from her position in the box overlooking the stage to congratulate the winner in person, before the reprise of the winning song ended the show to mass cheers from the small audience in the theatre.

1971 was a good year for the Eurovision Song Contest. The viewing figures reached 250 million for the first time and, after the shaky start to the decade, the competition was now on a roll. It was fast becoming the premiere TV event of the year in nearly all the participating countries and looked very steady for the future.

country	song	performer	place	score	draw
Monaco	Un Banc, Un Arbre, Une Rue	**Séverine**	1	129	3
Spain	En Un Mundo Nuevo	**Karina**	2	116	6
Germany	Diese Welt	**Katja Ebstein**	3	100	5
United Kingdom	Jack In The Box	**Clodagh Rodgers**	4	98	9
Italy	L'Amore E Un Attimo	**Massimo Ranieri**	5	91	11
Sweden	Vita Vidder	**The Family four**	6=	85	12
Netherlands	De Tijd	**Saskia & Serge**	6=	85	14
Finland	Tie Uuteen Päivään	**Markku Aro & Koivisto Sisters**	8	84	17
Portugal	Menina	**Tonicha**	9	83	15
France	Un Jardin Sur La Terre	**Serge Lama**	10	82	7
Ireland	One Day Love	**Angela Farrell**	11	79	13
Switzerland	Les Illusion De Nos Vingt Ans	**Peter, Sue & Marc**	12	78	4
Luxembourg	Pomme, Pomme, Pomme	**Monique Melsen**	13	70	8
Belgium	Goeie Morgen, Morgen	**Lily Castel & Jacques Raymond**	14=	68	10
Yugoslavia	Tvoj Dječak Je Tužan	**Krunoslav Slabinac**	14=	68	16
Austria	Musik	**Marianne Mendt**	16	56	1
Norway	Lykken Er...	**Hanne Krogh**	17	53	18
Malta	Marija L-Maltija	**Joe Grech**	18	52	2

Winner

Luxembourg

Performer

Vicky Leandros

1972

Title

'Après Toi'

Composers

Klaus Munro/
Yves Dessca/
Mario Panas

Presenter

Moira Shearer

Host & Venue

BBC
Usher Hall

Edinburgh
United Kingdom

After the mammoth success of the Dublin contest, there was just one major headache facing the EBU – the cartel of public service broadcasters who run Eurovision. Who was going to host the seventeenth competition? Radio-Tele Monte Carlo, the rightful hosts, was one of the smallest broadcasters in the organisation and possessed neither the resources nor the technical capability to stage the competition. After failed attempts to find a venue and a rebuff from French TV for help, Monaco turned to the Director General of the BBC, Sir Charles Curran, and invited the British broadcaster to take up the challenge. The BBC agreed, taking the contest out of London to the Scottish capital of Edinburgh. This was presumably in deference to the Scots, who had provided Lulu, the singer of the UK's most recent winner. The chosen venue was the very traditional Usher Hall.

The previous year's winner, Séverine, was in attendance in 1972, seated among the Scottish and international dignitaries, but she looked thoroughly bored throughout the evening. Indeed, during Monaco's entry, which was cheerily sung by **Anne-Marie Godart** and **Peter McLane**, Séverine appeared particularly unimpressed and was observed by television viewers looking at her watch as the duo took their bows.

There were no changes at all to the line-up for the broadcast on the 25th March, and there was also no change in the voting procedure. Like the defending Monegasque pair, a third of all the entrants chose male-female duos, the same number that opted for the more traditional winner, a female vocalist. Those six countries who had opted for happy couples were clearly way off target, as they occupied five of the seven bottom positions in the final shake-up, including the last three positions of all. Two of the three groups ended in the top five, paving the way for more ensembles to enter Eurovision in subsequent years. The

Austrians achieved their best result since 1966, fifth place, with the appropriately named combo **The Milestones**. No Austrian entry has achieved a higher final position at the contest since.

The presenter for the evening was one of the more internationally famous individuals to have handled the job. **Moira Shearer** was a former classical ballet dancer who had found international fame as a movie actress in *The Red Shoes* and the psychological thriller *Peeping Tom*. She later admitted that her daughters had persuaded her to accept the invitation to host the competition – to have something to tease her about in years to come. Not known as a TV presenter at all, she certainly seemed somewhat out of place in the contest.

Among the early performances, Germany's **Mary Roos** stood out, performing in front of a wild, hallucinogenic backdrop. France entered **Betty Mars** singing an unusual song, even by French standards. Mars was dressed in a voluminous white gown as she warbled Piaf-style through the dreary 'Come, Comédie'. Ireland also tried something different in 1972; **Sandie Jones** became the first and, to date, the only performer ever to sing in the Irish language. Dressed in a shimmering, emerald-green beaded gown, she was distressed to see many members of the audience leaving their seats as she came on stage to perform. Someone had thrown muddy water over a row of the audience and BBC staff were

'Après Toi' proved to be one of the most popular winners ever. In addition to French, Vicky Leandros recorded it in English, German, Spanish, Greek, Italian and Japanese. She went to No. 1 in Germany, the Netherlands and Norway, No. 2 in the UK and Sweden, and charted in almost every country on the continent.

Far left: Norwegian viewers had chosen Grethe Kausland and Benny Borg to sing 'Småting' in Edinburgh. The two men with them clasping bouquets are the song's arranger Karå Grøttom (left) and composer Ivar Børsum.

Left: Maltese duo Helen and Joseph. Malta's second attempt at the contest was even less successful than their debut in 1971. They came bottom again, and scored even fewer points.

evacuating the affected group just as the orchestra had begun the introduction to Jones's song. She didn't miss a beat and performed well, but not well enough to sell the song to the assembled jurors.

One of the biggest cheers of the night went out for **The New Seekers**, who were singing for the United Kingdom. The five-member ensemble was the first group ever to sing for the UK, but by no means the last. They were themselves a fairly international collection of artists: Australian **Peter Doyle**, **Marty Kristian,** born in Germany but brought up in Australia, the Scottish **Eve Graham** and English members **Lyn Paul** and **Paul Layton**. They had enjoyed enormous global success in 1971 with 'I'd Like To Teach The World To Sing (In Perfect Harmony)' a huge hit that had started life as a TV advert for Coca-Cola. Their Eurovision song 'Beg, Steal Or Borrow' was already at number two in the UK when the group took to the stage in Edinburgh, the men dressed in multi-coloured velvet suits, ruffled shirts and bow ties and long pink or blue gowns for the two ladies. They sang well,

and received thunderous applause from the audience, but singing fifth, they certainly did not appear to have a favourable draw. Teddy Scholten had won from that position in 1959, but then there had only been 11 entries. It wasn't to be until 1995 that a song performed fifth would win again.

The final two entries of the night proved to be two of the most popular. Greek-born **Vicky Leandros** had represented Luxembourg back in 1967, when she had finished fourth with one of the most commercially successful songs ever to appear in the contest, 'Love Is Blue'. She returned this year with 'Après Toi' ('After You') and gave a faultless performance of what was a stirring ballad. One of her nearest challengers followed, when **Sandra and Andres** sang 'Als Het Om De Liefde Gaat' ('If It's All About Love') for the Netherlands. This was the first of three entries from Sandra Reemer. It was an incredibly lively song, which the duo performed in strikingly garish-green outfits, Sandra even sporting matching green nail varnish. Although there were many choruses of 'na na na' they had the audience clapping

country	song	performer	place	score	draw
Luxembourg	Après Toi	**Vicky Leandros**	1	128	17
United Kingdom	Beg, Steal Or Borrow	**The New Seekers**	2	114	5
Germany	Nur Die Liebe Lässt Uns Leben	**Mary Roos**	3	107	1
Netherlands	Als Het Om De Liefde Gaat	**Sandra & Andres**	4	106	18
Austria	Falter Im Wind	**The Milestones**	5	100	11
Italy	I Giorni Dell'Arcobaleno	**Nicola di Bari**	6	92	12
Portugal	A Festa Da Vida	**Carlos Mendes**	7	90	7
Switzerland	C'est La Chanson De Mon Amour	**Véronique Müller**	8	88	8
Yugoslavia	Musika I Ti	**Tereza**	9	87	13
Spain	Amanece	**Jaime Morey**	10	83	4
France	Come-Comédie	**Betty Mars**	11	81	2
Finland	Muistathan	**Päivi Paunu & Kim Floor**	12	78	10
Sweden	Härliga Sommardag	**The Family Four**	13	75	14
Norway	Småting	**Grethe Kausland & Benny Borg**	14	73	6
Ireland	Ceol An Ghrà	**Sandie Jones**	15	72	3
Monaco	Comme On S'Aime	**Anne-Marie Godart & Peter MacLane**	16	65	16
Belgium	A La Folie Ou Pas Du Tout	**Serge & Christine Ghisoland**	17	55	15
Malta	L'Imhabba	**Helen & Joseph**	18	48	9

The New Seekers performing 'Beg, Steal Or Borrow' – a clear winner from the six short-listed songs performed on *The Cliff Richard Show* on BBC1, which many viewers missed owing to a power cut.

along for what was by far the liveliest song of the night.

After an interval rendition of 'Inverness Gathering' by massed bands of eight Scottish Regiments including the Royal Scots Dragoon Guards – curiously, this marching band surpassed any of the Eurovision entries and topped the UK charts a month after the contest with a version of 'Amazing Grace' – it was time for the voting. Moira Shearer was now seated in front of the black-and-white scoreboard, facing a screen built into the set upon which viewers could see the various juries, who were locked away in the keep of Edinburgh Castle. Achieving the same winning score as the previous year, the result was predictable, with Luxembourg cruising to victory. Their entry was co-written by Yves Dessca who had also penned the lyrics to the 1971 winner, and thus followed Willy van Hemert to become only the second person ever to write two Eurovision winners – an elite club that still only has five members today. For the eighth time, the UK finished second and for the third year in a row, Germany crept into third place, with the highest score yet recorded for

a German song, edging out the Netherlands by one point in the final round. This was due in part to a mark of six from the Dutch themselves, the same mark they had received from the Germans.

At the bottom of the pile Ireland suffered their worst result until 1989, coming fifteenth. The Irish have never sent an entry to Eurovision sung in anything but English since. But this was nothing compared to the indignity suffered by Maltese duo **Helen and Joseph** who were hoping to improve upon on their country's last-place debut in 1971. They actually did worse; not only did they come bottom with 'L'Imhabba' ('Love'), but they also managed to score four points less than their predecessor Joe Grech had earned in Dublin. Portugal had also finished last with their debut entry, as did Austria, Monaco and Lithuania, but no other country managed to do it with their first two songs. Possibly as a result of this dire showing, Malta did not return to the contest until 1975, and all their subsequent entries have been sung in English.

The ratings for the 1972 contest continued to grow, with 22 million viewers watching in the UK alone. The contest was riding high, and was about to take on an even bigger lease of life with dramatic rule changes and the addition of new countries in the coming years.

Winner

Luxembourg

Performer

Anne-Marie David

1973

Title

'Tu Te Reconnaîtras'

Composers

Vline Buggy/ Claude Morgan

Presenter

Helga Guitton

Host & Venue

CLT Nouveau Théâtre

With both Austria and Malta taking a break, only 17 nations lined up for the eighteenth contest in Luxembourg's Nouveau Théâtre. There was a controversial addition to the line-up to replace the absentees, with the debut of Israel. Many viewers were puzzled to see the Middle-Eastern nation competing in Eurovision, but as members of the European Broadcasting Union they were eligible. Following atrocities against Israeli athletes at the Munich Olympic Games the previous autumn, security was heightened to allow Israel to participate comfortably, and

luxembourg

it hasalways been rumoured that their singer wore a bullet-proof vest during her performance. In addition, the audience were warned not to stand during the show at the risk of being shot by security!

Israel was not the only contentious entry of the eighteenth contest, which was broadcast on 7th April. The Swedish entry came to the contest amid a storm of controversy. The focus of complaint was the lyrics of the song, 'You're Summer'. And the offending line was 'Your Breasts Are Like Swallows Nesting' – a very poor metaphor,

not deemed worthy of the lyricist, who was a member of the Swedish Academy which gives away the Nobel Prize for Literature. The two singers performing the song wore brightly coloured suede shirts of yellow and blue. The duo was known in Sweden as Malta, but they wisely renamed themselves **The Nova** for the contest. They'd caused much consternation when they triumphed in the Swedish heats, largely due to the song they beat into third place – 'Ring Ring' by a then-unknown group that were to become Abba.

One major difference between the 1973 contest and previous contests was that the EBU had given permission for participating nations to submit songs in any language. Finland and Sweden opted for English, whereas Norway chose to sing in various tongues, but no one else availed themselves of this relaxation of the rules. In the next few years though, it became a much more popular option.

Finland had drawn the first spot, exactly the same draw **Marion Rung** had had when she had last sung for her country back in 1962. This time around she was much more confident, singing 'Tom, Tom, Tom' with great enthusiasm clearly enjoying the experience enormously. The contest was less fun for the hapless **Nicole and Hugo** who sang second for Belgium. Much has been made of the 'curse' of singing

Anne-Marie David retained the Eurovision title for Luxembourg, with her powerful voice and confident performance of 'Tu Te Reconnaîtras' ('You Will Recognise Yourself').

country	song	performer	place	score	draw
Luxembourg	Tu Te Reconnaîtras	**Anne-Marie David**	1	129	11
Spain	Eres Tu	**Mocedades**	2	125	7
United Kingdom	Power To All Our Friends	**Cliff Richard**	3	123	15
Israel	Ey-Sham	**Ilanit**	4	97	17
Sweden	You're Summer	**The Nova & The Dolls**	5	94	12
Finland	Tom Tom Tom	**Marion Rung**	6	93	1
Norway	It's Just A Game	**The Bendik Singers**	7	89	6
Germany	Junger Tag	**Gitte**	8=	85	4
Monaco	Un Train Qui Part	**Marie**	8=	85	5
Portugal	Tourada	**Fernando Tordo**	10=	80	3
Ireland	Do I Dream?	**Maxi**	10=	80	14
Switzerland	Je Vais Me Marier, Marie	**Patrick Juvet**	12	79	8
Italy	Chi Sarà Con Te	**Massimo Ranieri**	13	74	10
Netherlands	De Oude Muzikant	**Ben Cramer**	14	69	13
Yugoslavia	Gori Vatra	**Zdravko Čolić**	15=	65	9
France	Sans Toi	**Martine Clémenceau**	15=	65	16
Belgium	Baby Baby	**Nicole & Hugo**	17	58	2

second over the years, but the Belgian duo were already cursed in the contest. Having had to drop out at the last minute in 1971, they finished last in 1973. They did manage to provide one of the most dramatic appearances this year – matching purple cat suits and daring choreography. Competing in the fashion stakes was **Patrick Juvet**, who was described as Switzerland's answer to David Cassidy sporting more purple eye-shadow than any of the female singers in the show! His song was little more than a list of girls' and boys' names, interspersed with cries of 'Alley-Oopee'. Another visual highlight came from the Dutch, who dimmed the lights to almost pitch black for their entry as **Ben Cramer** performed wearing a luminous white suit. The song was written by Pierre   Kartner, an artist who later achieved world-wide fame and success under the name of Father Abraham, singing along with animated creations, the Smurfs.

Spain seemed to base their song on Elvis Presley's standard 'Can't Help Falling In Love With You'. **Mocedades** were a six-piece group – two girls plus four guys strumming guitars – from Bilbao chosen to sing 'Eres Tu' ('You Are'). It was a very strong entry that British entrant **Cliff Richard** had tipped as his most dangerous competitor. Although they never held the lead, the Spanish were a threat throughout the voting and in the end ran the winner a very close second.

Spain had been the only country ever to retain the Eurovision title so far, doing so on home ground in 1969 when they shared first place. Luxembourg went one better this year, when **Anne-Marie David** took 'Tu Te Reconnaîtras' ('You Will Recognise Yourself') to the top of the judges' table exclusively. It was not an easy victory though, and Luxembourg trailed narrowly for large parts of the voting. Anne-Marie, dressed in scarlet, had one of the most powerful voices on show in 1973 and gave a very confident and expressive performance of this home-crowd pleaser. Although the UK was the bookies' favourite, Anne-Marie clearly had the backing of the somewhat partisan audience and exited the stage to rapturous, yet seated applause.

Like Sweden, Ireland was having its own share of problems in the Grand Duchy. The singer **Maxi's manager** refused to make changes to her song 'Do I Dream' despite requests from Irish TV. The showdown went as far as RTE Ireland flying in another singer, Tina Reynolds, as a late replacement. With no accreditation or security clearance she was not permitted to enter the heavily guarded Nouveau Théâtre. The farcical situation continued until the morning of the competition when it was agreed Maxi could sing the song as she desired. The

Right: Postcard votes pour in for the UK's six short-listed songs, performed by Cliff Richard on the highly rated *Cilla* show, hosted by his close friend Cilla Black. Viewers overwhelmingly selected 'Power To All Our Friends', with 125,505 postcard votes.

Far right: After her successful outing, Anne-Marie tried her luck at the contest again in 1979, when she sang for her native France. On that occasion she finished in third place and promptly disappeared. In 1981, when the BBC publication *Radio Times* tried to track her down, she proved impossible to trace.

alternative would have been for Ireland to withdraw from the contest. Tina Reynolds ended up in her hotel room, watching Maxi give a poor and nervous performance.

British viewers selected the punchy song 'Power To All Our Friends' for him, but Cliff was much more nervous than he had been in 1968. It is alleged that in order to calm his nerves, his manager had given him Valium a few hours before the show. This had left him drowsy and his entourage had great difficulty waking him for his performance. He woke up to give a vocally confident performance, but sadly, his bizarre choreography was not quite so impressive. Waving his arm, and demonstrating some remarkable leg movements, he came across looking somewhat ridiculous. Towards the end of the song, he almost fell over after attempting to spin on the spot and his performance is now often seen on TV as an example of the silly antics the contest is sadly known for. Regardless, 'Power To All Our Friends' was one of the strongest songs in the contest and one of the better UK entries. After his performance, Cliff opted not to sit in the 'artists' enclosure' as he called it, and hid in the bathroom, as he had done on his previous trip to Eurovision. As he said, he didn't want to be seen by viewers trying to look pleased that he was losing! In the voting, his song led

from the start, but towards the end it suffered fatigue, and finished in a closely run third place.

Luxembourg ended on 129 points, the highest score ever attained under the voting system that allowed two jury members for each nation. It was the most comprehensive win ever achieved in the contest. Spain was four points behind in second place, and the UK two points behind the Spanish song. Despite the furore, the Eurovision judges liked the Swedish entry and The Nova finished in fifth place, Sweden's best showing since 1966. With bullet-proof vest or not Israel's Ilanit finished in fourth place, the best showing of any new nation since Denmark had finished third in 1957.

The tension and excitement of the scoring was enlivened by the contribution of the senior Swiss juror who flamboyantly displayed his votes with a theatricality and costume worthy of Liberace. Whether it was his antics or the closeness of the result, this voting system was retired and jurors remained unseen in future years.

Once again, the contest could not be considered anything but a huge success. In the UK alone, 24 million viewers – almost half the population – had tuned in, and more and more nations were taking the broadcast and were anxious to compete. The show was riding high, and was about to reach its zenith.

'Tu Te Reconnaîtras' was a popular winner in the hall and with the general public, too. Anne-Marie recorded six versions, including two different recordings in Italian. The English version climbed to No. 13 in the UK, with the original French version reaching the Top 10 in the Netherlands, Sweden, and many other countries.

Winner

Sweden

Performer

Abba

1974

Title

'Waterloo'

Composers

Stig Anderson/
Benny Andersson/
Björn Ulvaeus

Presenter

Katie Boyle

Host & Venue

BBC
The Dome

Brighton
United Kingdom

Eighteen countries had registered for the nineteenth contest, but in the end only seventeen songs competed in Brighton in the UK. The French President Georges Pompidou died just days before the competition and his funeral was scheduled for the broadcast date of April 6th. In deference, French TV withdrew and their singer, Dani, had to be content with a seat in the audience.

Mistress of ceremonies **Katie Boyle** presented the contest for a fourth time. This year, she was exercising her linguistic talents far more, but had a much bigger worry on her mind throughout the live broadcast. Katie carried her prompt cards in a strangely 'low' manner, well below her waist, and the reason emerged afterwards. Upon arrival in Brighton for the final stages of dress rehearsals, she discovered that the dress being made for her appearance, in salmon-pink satin, had not been made to the right size. It was far too small and wouldn't even meet around her bust. Although the BBC costume designer worked through the night to alter the dress, it was still very tight, and under the stage lights, Ms Boyle's undergarments were clearly visible to the cameras. With seconds to go before she made her entrance, stagehands had to cut her out of her underwear, leaving her feeling very vulnerable as she stepped out onto the Dome stage.

Finland opened the contest, and the second spot had been drawn by the host nation. **Olivia Newton-John** representing the UK, felt she needed some luck for the show. She had let it be known that she would prefer to sing a ballad in Brighton, and made no secret of her disappointment when 'Long Live Love' was chosen by the British public as their song for Europe. It has been said that, when a fan wished her luck, she retorted that she would need more than luck with such a lousy song. But once in Brighton, Olivia seemed more relaxed, gave many interviews and turned in some great rehearsals. For the big night she wore a vast blue chiffon affair and turned in a very enthusiastic performance.

Spain was looking to improve on their second place from 1973, but ended up way off the mark. Solo male artist **Peret** brought along a Spanish guitar, which he used as much as a prop as an instrument, twirling it around throughout the performance. The song was very much in the mode of traditional Spanish rumba music, with the five backing singers providing much hand clapping and false tabs. It was a brave attempt to do something outside of the normal pop mould, but it did not impress the judges.

Anne-Karine Strøm, who had appeared for Norway the previous year as a member of the Bendik Singers, returned this year with the Bendik Singers backing her. Norway had not finished last in the contest since 1969. But they were back to their usual form in Brighton, ending equal bottom.

Marinella sang the very first Greek entry to the contest. She dressed in a very simple outfit, black trousers and a striped shirt, but was joined on stage by five singers in traditional Greek costumes. The song had very heavy Greek undertones, with a bouzouki, and a sing-a-long chorus of 'la, la, las' – an ever popular Eurovision refrain.

Far left: Katie Boyle's underwear had to be removed minutes before the broadcast began as it could be seen on camera through her dress. A vulnerable Katie then attempted to protect her modesty with her prompt cards throughout the show.

Left: Taking their collective name from the initials of their four members, Agnetha Faltskog, Björn Ulvaeus, Benny Andersson and Anni-Frid (Frida) Lyngstad, Abba were two happy couples who had enjoyed considerable success apart before pooling their resources in 1972. They had performed 'Waterloo' in Swedish in the heats, and risen to No. 1 in the charts, but had translated the song into English for their appearance in Brighton.

'Waterloo' shot to the top of the charts in the UK, Germany, Ireland, Australia, Belgium, Norway, Finland, Denmark and many other countries. Abba released Swedish, English, French and German versions, and even made the Top 10 in the US *Billboard* chart – the first Eurovision winner to do so.

Israel and Yugoslavia were both represented by an all-male band: **Poogy** for Israel and Belgrade band **Korni** for Yugoslavia. Poogy, a motley crew of six guys in striped knitwear, had a folksy sound and Korni's offering was more in a rock vein. The Yugoslav song had sound effects of bombs dropping, and the band members all wore brightly coloured lamé jackets to confuse the theme even further.

The Swedish quartet that followed were about to give the contest its biggest jolt since its cosy inception back in 1956. **Abba** came to Brighton clear winners of the Swedish heat, having missed out on victory the year before when 'Ring Ring' reached third place.

This year, they had performed 'Waterloo' in Swedish in the heats, but had translated the song into English for their appearance in Brighton. When they arrived in England they found themselves the bookies' favourites to win, but by the day of the broadcast, had slipped to 20-1, well behind the British and Dutch songs.

But when they took to the stage in the Dome with their shimmering, and somewhat daring costumes, for an electric performance, there could be no doubt that the prize would be theirs. To add to the overall effect, their conductor, Sven-Olof Waldoff, dressed in Napoleonic garb to the delight of the audience and the commentators.

After this drama, Luxembourg, Monaco and Belgium followed with the tried and trusted format of ballads sung in French. British singer **Ireen Sheer** singing for Luxembourg, sang in French, but with a pronounced English accent. **Romuald**, representing the Principality in a sparkling jacket, sang a well-orchestrated, dramatic ballad, which could have done very well in any other year. And, as part of a cost-saving exercise for Belgium, Gérard Départdieu look-a-like **Jacques Hustin** appeared with the same four backing singers as Romuald had. He walked round the stage in a dark suit with an open-neck shirt, grasping the air with his hands. TV critic Clive James commented in the UK's *Observer* newspaper that he appeared to be trying to grab an invisible apple.

The Netherlands came into the contest as joint favourites with the UK. **Mouth and MacNeal** certainly gave an interesting performance, dressed as hippies, with an assortment of backing musicians and singers in tow. The hairy and bearded Mouth had a gruff voice, which belied a happy-looking fellow clearly enjoying the whole experience. Blonde Maggie MacNeal also exuded a sense of fun. Joining

Poogy were Israel's most popular band, but their folksy sound and sartorial statement of knitted tank tops failed to set the contest alight.

Mouth (in black trousers) and MacNeal (to his right), and puppets made in their image (on the barrel organ), gave a lively performance for the Netherlands.

them on stage was, among others, a man playing a barrel organ, with puppets of the two main singers set on top. It was a very strong song, but perhaps let down by the antics of the performers.

Tina Reynolds, singing for Ireland, had great difficulty remembering the lyrics of her song as a result of a knock in a recent car accident. She had scribbled the words onto her hand, but they became smudged and illegible. In the end, she delivered a faultless performance of the up-tempo song, which contained more 'la, la, las', than any song since 'La, La, La' itself had won for Spain back in 1968.

The most intriguing story of the night came with the Portuguese entry. **Paulo de Cavalho** sang the gentle 'E Depois Do Adeus' ('And After Goodbye') alone on stage. He shared last place, but the song was assured a place in history at home. It was to be used as a trigger for an uprising in Portugal that would overthrow the government. The troops' signal to mobilise was the debut broadcast of the song on national radio. This remains the only Eurovision entry to have actually started a revolution.

Finishing the presentation of the songs was the Italian entry. **Gigliola Cinquetti** had won the contest as a sixteen-year-old prodigy in Copenhagen in 1964 and had become something of an icon in Italy as a result. She returned with another impressive performance, but her fans back home were not permitted to see it for several days. Italy was engaged in a referendum about divorce at the time and RAI did not want to appear to be attempting to influence the result by transmitting the contest with the song 'Si' ('Yes').

After Gigliola left the stage, Katie Boyle returned to present the interval act. The Wombles must have seemed very odd to non-British viewers. They were a group of over-sized furry puppets, performing their first two singles, both of which made the British Top five.

At the end of the voting, tense as ever, the glorious Abba were declared the winners and made their way to the stage to collect their medals, only to be stopped, in Benny and Björn's case, by an over-zealous security guard who did not recognise them.

For Abba, Eurovision was the launch pad to even greater stardom. Although their immediate follow-up singles didn't do as well as 'Waterloo', by the end of 1975 they were well on their way to becoming the biggest group on the planet since The Beatles.

Uncle Bulgaria with Agnetha Faltskog. Interval act The Wombles were characters from a children's TV series, but the animals must have baffled the rest of Europe.

country	song	performer	place	score	draw
Sweden	Waterloo	**Abba**	1	24	8
Italy	Si	**Gigliola Cinquetti**	2	18	17
Netherlands	I See A Star	**Mouth & MacNeal**	3	15	12
United Kingdom	Long Live Love	**Olivia Newton-John**	4=	14	2
Luxembourg	Bye Bye, I Love You	**Ireen Sheer**	4=	14	9
Monaco	Celui Qui Reste Et Celui Qui S'en Va	**Romuald**	4=	14	10
Israel	Natati La Khaiai	**Poogy**	7=	11	6
Ireland	Cross Your Heart	**Tina Reynolds**	7=	11	13
Spain	Canta Y Se Feliz	**Peret**	9=	10	3
Belgium	Fleur De Liberté	**Jacques Hustin**	9=	10	11
Greece	Krassi Thalassa Ke T'Agori Mou	**Marinella**	11	7	5
Yugoslavia	Generacija '42	**Korni**	12	6	7
Finland	Keep Me Warm	**Carita**	13	4	1
Norway	The First Day Of Love	**Anne Karine Strøm**	14=	3	4
Germany	Die Sommermelodie	**Cindy & Bert**	14=	3	14
Switzerland	Mein Ruf Nach Dir	**Piera Martell**	14=	3	15
Portugal	E Depois Do Adeus	**Paulo de Calvalho**	14=	3	16
France	La Vie A Vingt-Cinq Ans	**Dani**	WD		

WD = Withdrawn

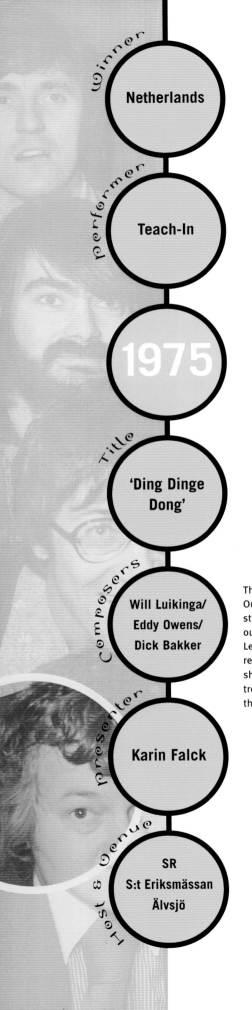

Netherlands

Teach-In

1975

'Ding Dinge Dong'

Will Luikinga/ Eddy Owens/ Dick Bakker

Karin Falck

SR S:t Eriksmässan Älvsjö

Stockholm
Sweden

Immediately following Abba's ground-breaking win in Brighton, things got back to normal in the Eurovision Song Contest, when a song generally regarded as one of the weakest winners ever took the honours. The Swedish TV service chose the St Eriksmässan Älvsjö, a collection of now silvery, then orange-coloured, buildings on the outskirts of Stockholm, as the venue for the broadcast on 22nd March 1975. A record-breaking 19 nations had entered songs for this, the twentieth contest. Greece had opted not to take part after only one year in the line-up, but France and Malta were active again and Turkey were making their debut.

The organisers had a large headache to deal with before the contest got underway. There had been demonstrations in the Swedish capital by left-wing activists, who were opposed to commercial music and who had chosen to vent their anger at the Eurovision Song Contest as an exponent of it.

Swedish TV personality **Karin Falck** was the host of the twentieth contest. She wore a frock designed to blend in with the blue set, giving the show a uniform look not yet seen before. Falk skipped onto the stage to a fanfare from the orchestra and greeted viewers in Swedish, English

The Netherlands' Teach-in. Outlandish, science-fiction-style costumes were brought out for the final performance. Lead-singer Getty Kaspers recently mused that at the time she thought they looked very trendy, but now she sees that they looked totally ridiculous.

and French. As she explained to the English-speaking viewers, she was very excited. In fact she admitted to being somewhat surprised that she hadn't fainted with the excitement of it all! Just to make sure she didn't get even more excited, she then recounted a few lines from a Danish poem: 'To think that fun is simple fun while earnest things are earnest, shows all too plain that neither one though truthfully is honest.' It wasn't entirely clear why this particular text had been chosen, but Karin explained that everyone could learn something from the words.

Short films introduced each performer, showcasing their artistic talents, as they were then shown painting a portrait of themselves and the flag of their nation onto a large blank canvas. It was a neat idea, but soon became tedious. For many of the performers, it was obvious why they were singers and not artists.

To open the show, the Netherlands once again drew the first spot. This was the fifth time the Dutch had had to sing first. For the first time ever, though, the first song would turn out to be the winning entry, and so the Netherlands both opened and closed the 1975 contest, with an English song entitled 'Ding Dinge Dong'. The six-piece band **Teach-in**, led by Getty Kaspers, at least had the good sense not to try to copy the Abba formula too closely, except perhaps in their choice of costumes. Getty herself wore a white blouse with a floral print over voluminous white satin trousers. Her five male companions were dressed in extremely odd garb, looking more like extras from a low budget sci-fi series than a pop group. The lyrics of the song were also fairly ridiculous, consisting of a chorus encouraging the listener to 'ding-a-dong every hour, when you're picking flowers, even when your lover is gone, gone, gone'. It was hardly Eurovision's finest moment, but the melody was exceptionally catchy. The song ended with a single beat on a triangle, which was the signal for the xylophonist to hit a silver glass bauble that shattered onto the stage. It was a very small gimmick, but may have been enough to lodge the performance in the judges' minds. Still, with 18 songs to go, most were probably expecting that something better would turn up!

Another English-language song followed as Ireland took to the stage to sing in the accursed second slot. **Jimmy and Tommy Swarbrigg** were the two brothers singing their own composition, 'That's What Friends Are For'. Jimmy was stricken with flu during the rehearsals and found it hard to sing along with his brother on the night, but a trio of Irish lasses provided vocal support and aided them in their task. The two brothers were also sporting very high platform shoes, which they later conceded made them feel very

country	song	performer	place	score	draw
Netherlands	Ding Dinge Dong	**Teach-In**	1	152	1
United Kingdom	Let Me Be The One	**The Shadows**	2	138	9
Italy	Era	**Wess & Dori Ghezzi**	3	115	19
France	Et Bonjour A Toi L'Artiste	**Nicole Rieu**	4	91	3
Luxembourg	Toi	**Geraldine**	5	84	5
Switzerland	Mikado	**Simone Drexel**	6	77	7
Finland	Old Man Fiddle	**Pihasoittajat**	7	74	15
Sweden	Jennie Jennie	**Lars Berghagen & The Dolls**	8	72	18
Ireland	That's What Friends Are For	**The Swarbriggs**	9	68	2
Spain	Tu Volveras	**Sergio Y Estibaliz**	10	53	17
Israel	At Ve' Ani	**Shlomo Artzi**	11	40	12
Malta	Singing This Song	**Renato**	12	32	10
Yugoslavia	Dan Ljubezni	**Blood & Ashes**	13=	22	8
Monaco	Une Chanson C'Est Une Lettre	**Sophie**	13=	22	14
Belgium	Gelukkig Zijn	**Ann Christy**	15	17	11
Portugal	Madrugada	**Duarte Mendes**	16	16	16
Germany	Ein Lied Kann Eine Brücke Sein	**Joy Fleming**	17	15	4
Norway	Touch My Life With Summer	**Ellen Nikolaysen**	18	11	6
Turkey	Seninle Bir Dakika	**Semiha Yanki**	19	3	13

Right: Italy's Wess and Dori Ghezzi. Wess had a strong deep voice, contrasting well with Dori's mezzo-soprano tone. Finland made it their top pick and six juries placed it second, but others were less impressed, and Italy fell back to third from their second plcce in 1974.

Far right: The Shadows had been, and indeed still are, the most successful instrumental band in the history of British pop music, but were not a widely popular choice, with many critics feeling the band too old and outdated.

precarious. It was not one of Ireland's better efforts, and, like Sweden, the Irish were still competing under the shadow of high expectations following a hugely successful earlier win.

Cliff Richard's association with the contest extended yet another year in 1975, albeit somewhat tenuously as his former backing group, **The Shadows,** took up the challenge for the UK. Although known for their twanging guitar instrumentals, they had enjoyed a few hits with Bruce Welch on vocals. Critics thought 'Let Me Be The One' was somewhat outdated and the group weren't helped in Stockholm when Welch forgot the second line of the song. He recovered well and they gave a good performance, with the audience giving the song by far the best cheer of the night.

Although a small part of the Turkish nation does fall into European soil, they are more generally regarded as an

The reception of **'Ding Dinge Dong'** from the record-buying public was lukewarm. It didn't even manage to top the Dutch charts, stalling at No. 3. This was still ten places higher than they reached in the UK charts. Teach-in's biggest commercial success with their winner was in Sweden where they hit No 2.

Asian country. Unlike Israel, which tends to have songs in a more recognisable pop mould, Turkey has typically stuck to a more Middle-Eastern flavour with its entries. The Turkish debut was no exception. 'Seninle Bir Dakika' ('A Minute With You'), which was sung by **Semiha Yanki,** was a beautiful and haunting ballad but not one likely to impress the judges.

Sweden opted once again to present a song in English. This was hardly surprising considering the success of their last entry. **Lars Berghagen,** who sang his own song 'Jennie, Jennie', was accompanied on stage by The Dolls – the backing group provided by the producers for any of the artists not bringing their own to the Swedish capital. The Dolls had sung with The Nova in 1973, so were used to the experience. The three ladies in the backing group had also dressed in similar frocks and scarves to that of presenter Ms. Falk. The song followed a formula that was very popular in 1975 and had a slow verse, building to a sing-a-long chorus. It was well thought of, but never likely to win and in the end only managed eighth place.

A new scoring system was introduced for 1975 and has remained in place ever since. Each jury was made up of 11 members, six between the ages of 16 and 25, and five more between 26 and 55. They secretly awarded marks for all songs except their own immediately after each entry was performed. The votes were then added up and the most popular song was awarded the top mark of 12 points. The second song received ten, the third song eight, and then the songs placed fourth to tenth received seven points to one point each. It seemed very complicated, but the only part of

the process seen by the viewers was the announcement of the ten songs to which each country had elected its top picks. It was a much longer process than normal, but much fairer and much more exciting than the experiments used in the early 1970s.

Teach-in won with a margin of 14 points over The Shadows who were in turn 23 ahead of Italy's **Wess and Dori Ghezzi**. France was back in the fray this year after their last-minute exit from Brighton, with **Nicole Rieu** performing the sophisticated yet gentle 'Et Bonjour A Toi L'Artiste' ('Good Morning To You, The Artist'), which finished fourth.

The biggest national improvement of the night came from a country-and-western band called **Pihasoittajat** (courtyard musicians) who represented Finland. The Finns had never yet managed to place a song in the top five at Eurovision. This year, their fourteenth attempt, was no exception, but their song did much better than most of their entries, finishing in seventh place. Among the lower placings, **Renato** finished twelfth and was given a hero's welcome back in Malta, such was their relief at not finishing last again. Despite this relative success, Malta would not be seen in the contest again until 1991. Turkey joined Malta and Portugal as one of the nations who came last at their first attempt, amassing a paltry three points in total.

The contest was still very popular with television viewers, and the weak nature of the year's winner can now be viewed as a blip on the chart, as it was inevitable that following the success of Abba and 'Waterloo' was an impossible task for any act.

Winner
United Kingdom

Performer
Brotherhood of Man

1976

Title
'Save Your Kisses For Me'

Composers
Tony Hiller/ Lee Sheridan/ Martin Lee

Presenter
Corry Brokken

Host & Venue
NOS
Nederlands Congresgebouw

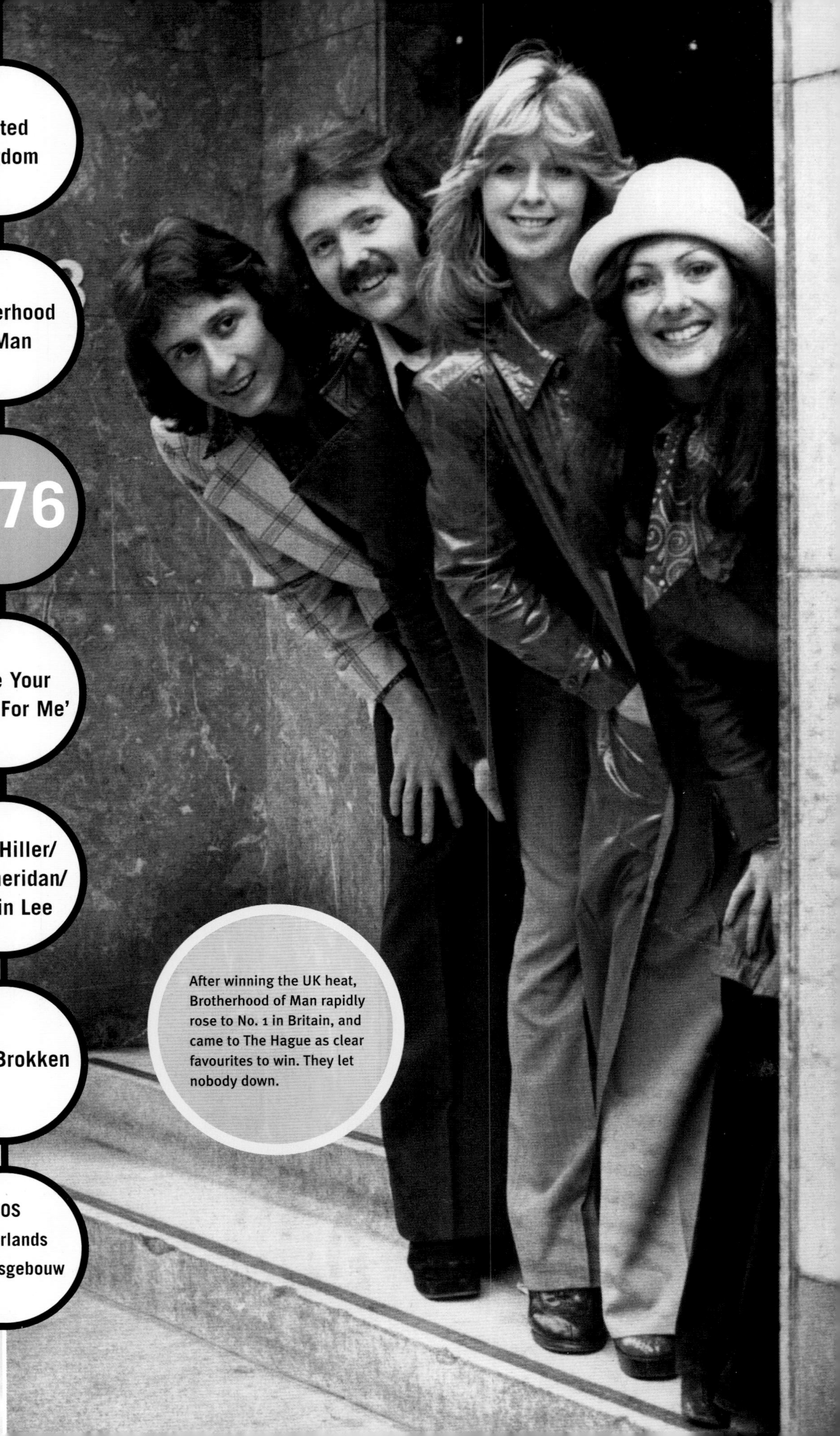

After winning the UK heat, Brotherhood of Man rapidly rose to No. 1 in Britain, and came to The Hague as clear favourites to win. They let nobody down.

For the third time, the Eurovision Song Contest came to the Netherlands in 1976, to another Dutch city. The Hague is the seat of the Dutch government and the site of the huge modern complex: the Nederlands Congresgebouw. The twenty-first contest, broadcast on 6th April, did not have as many entrants as the twentieth, with a number of countries playing musical chairs and opting in and out of the line-up. Sweden, Malta and Turkey all declined to enter, but Austria was taking part for the first time since 1972 and Greece was back in for their second entry. Sweden's absence was highly

the Hague
The Netherlands

controversial, particularly as they had been the host nation only one year earlier. It was, in fact, partly fear of winning and bearing the costs for hosting the contest again that kept them away, but pressure from the anti-Eurovision Song Contest lobby played a part in the decision too.

Corry Brokken came out of retirement at the request of the show's producer, Fred Oster, to act as the mistress of ceremonies. Corry had been studying law since retiring from show business in 1971, fourteen years after becoming the very first Dutch singer to win the Eurovision Song Contest in 1957. She certainly had adopted the appearance of a lawyer, wearing a long black skirt with a white blouse under a black jacket for the show. Her oversized glasses completed the studious look. Corry showed off her fluent grasp of languages throughout the show and performed an extremely competent job, even if it was an unglamorous one.

There were a number of innovations on show this year including an illuminated scoreboard, i-dents to bookend

'Save Your Kisses For Me' remained at No. 1 for six weeks in the UK. They were soon top of every singles chart in Europe, although in Sweden, who had not taken part in 1976, they only made No. 6. As an added bonus, they also made the US top thirty, the most successful UK entry there until 1996.

the video postcards and an ingenious stage set made up of moving pieces that could transform itself into any number of shapes and change colour at the lighting director's whim.

The draw had placed the United Kingdom in pole position for the third time and the British came to the contest with their highest hope for many years. **Brotherhood of Man** consisted of two young men, Martin Lee and Lee Sheridan, who took lead vocals for their performance assisted by blonde Sandra Stevens and the brunette Nicky Stevens. They were extremely well prepared for their big night, the boys dressed in black and white suits and the girls in white and red jumpsuits, topped off with matching berets. Their choreography was exceptionally slick and is still fondly remembered. Their song, 'Save Your Kisses For Me', was a twee tale of a father going to work, leaving his three-year-old behind, but it was heart-warming and hit the right spot with the audience and judges. At the end of the performance they were presented with bouquets of flowers, as all the singers were throughout the evening. It was a very good start to the contest and set a pace that no one else could match.

Peter, Sue and Marc were back for their second attempt at the Euro crown for Switzerland, this time singing in English, albeit a song with a German title: 'Djambo, Djambo' ('Jumbo, Jumbo'). A drummer, bass player and a clown, who played both guitar and the barrel organ, presumably impersonating Djambo (Jumbo) himself, joined the trio. Peter Reber tried to accommodate a plethora of instruments, playing mouth organ, piano and guitar, and rushing to and fro on the stage in an effort to manage all three. Sue and Marc took the main vocals, dressed in denim outfits.

Germany was having a number of problems in 1976. **Tony Marshall** had won the German selection process with the song "Der Star," ('The Star'). Almost immediately afterwards his victory was declared null and void and ARD allowed the second-placed entry to go to The Hague instead. 'Sing, Sang, Song' was the highly unoriginal title of the replacement, performed in a mixture of German and English by the **Les Humphries Singers**. This particular ensemble was a well-known singing group, made up of 13 artists from various countries and ethnic backgrounds. The rules of the contest, of course, only allowed six of them to appear on stage and so only two girls and four boys were chosen for the final line-up. They had worked well on their harmonies, but the paucity of the song could not be hidden. Ralph Siegel's composition could only manage to place fifteenth.

Israel managed to capture a little more attention than their last couple of entries had received, aided in part by their choice of artists. The three 'Chocolate Girls,' or **Chocolate Menta Mastik** as they were known, sang 'Emor Shalom' ('Say Hello'), dressed in matching white suits with the voluminous flared trousers so popular at the time. They certainly had a very catchy song, which was performed with a very slick routine. Although not quite as successful as their debut entry, the judges approved and the girls achieved sixth place. All three ladies had met while performing their National Service in the Israeli army and had continued to sing together after they were de-mobbed. One of their members, Yardena Arazi, went on to become a huge star in her country as a soloist and three years later became the second former contestant to act as mistress of ceremonies when the show was staged in Jerusalem.

More often than not, the home team tends to do well in the contest and obviously with this in mind, **Sandra Reemer** returned to the fray four years after her last excursion to sing for the Netherlands again. By now she had abandoned her partner Andres, cut her hair and added her surname to her moniker, yet her dress sense was no less outlandish than before. To sing 'The Party's Over Now' she was wearing a pale blue frock with a chiffon cape that enveloped her arms, topped off with a ruffled collar. Her song was smart and catchy and got a very enthusiastic reception from the audience, but fared less well in the voting where she was placed ninth, exactly halfway down the score sheet.

Greece opted for a very unusual song and performer for their second appearance in the contest. From Greece, the rotund **Mariza Koch** had spent many years living in London. A bouzouki player strummed along as Mariza sang the rather harsh-sounding lyrics in a somewhat screeching tone. 'Panaghia Mou, Panaghia Mou,' (My Homeland, My Homeland) was a protest song at the Turkish invasion of Cyprus, and certainly attracted controversy. It was too much for the juries, although scored better than many predicted, to place thirteenth.

Finland failed to build on their relative success of 1975 but **Fredi**'s entry 'Pump, Pump' was great fun. Joined by a motley crew known as the Friends, Fredi towered over the two girls singing lead with him as he invited viewers to let their 'hips go hippety pump, pump'.

The UK finished with 164 marks, a score that would not be bettered until 1986, and in terms of marks received from the total scores available, it remains the second highest ever recorded, and, at a whopping 80 per cent, the best score under this system of voting. It was indeed a crushing win.

Brotherhood of Man winning the UK heat at London's Royal Albert Hall.

There was a problem with the final score, however, although it affected the other end of the roster. Yugoslavia ended the night in last place with a total score of six points, which they had amassed from only three nations. It later transpired that scrutineer Clifford Brown had not noticed that France had not awarded four points to any country. When the show was over, it was revealed that the French nation's four points should have gone to Yugoslavia, lifting them to ten, three points ahead of Norway. For the second time, **Anne-Karine Strøm** finished last after all.

At the start of the evening the Norwegian singer was hotly tipped to fare much better with her song 'Mata Hari', with its rousing, catchy chorus. Alas, Strøm had taken some bad advice on how to present the song and for no apparent reason she and her three backing singers had decided to wear sunglasses for their performance, which were put on and taken off at regular intervals. Anne-Karine herself was dressed in a one-piece catsuit made from gold brocade, worn with a matching headband. Not for the first time, a promising effort came unstuck with a poorly thought-out performance. Like another Norwegian, Kirsti Sparboe before her, Anne-Karine made her third and final Eurovision effort her least successful, placing last with seven points.

The four members of Brotherhood of Man were seen leaping about back stage in great excitement, before making their way to the stage to receive their awards and more flowers from Getty Kaspers of Teach-In. The band got a hero's welcome back in Britain, where they remained at number one for six weeks, outselling every other single in the UK charts that year, which included Abba's 'Dancing Queen' and Elton John and Kiki Dee's 'Don't Go Breaking My Heart'. They were soon at the top of every singles chart in Europe, although in Sweden, which had not taken part this year, they only made number six.

Belgium's low-key ballad by **Pierre Rapsat** also did well in his homeland and hit the Dutch charts too, while Fredi and Friends just missed the top of the Finnish charts. Later in the year, the Friends ditched Fredi and recorded a Finnish version of 'Save Your Kisses For Me'.

The winning entry recorded the highest ever sales for a winning song on single, although when album sales are added in, 'Waterloo' still outranks all other Eurovision entries. With such a successful winner, continued success in the ratings and with more and more countries watching, the contest was still riding high – nobody could have foreseen the disasters that would beset the show in 1977, which would stop the contest dead in its tracks.

country	song	performer	place	score	draw
United Kingdom	Save Your Kisses For Me	**Brotherhood of Man**	1	164	1
France	Un, Deux, Trois	**Catherine Ferry**	2	147	17
Monaco	Toi, La Musique Et Moi	**Mary Cristy**	3	93	16
Switzerland	Djambo Djambo	**Peter, Sue & Marc**	4	91	2
Austria	My Little World	**Waterloo & Robinson**	5	80	14
Israel	Emor Shalom	**Chocolate Menta Mastik**	6	77	4
Italy	Noi Lo Rivivremo Di Nuovo	**Al Bano & Romina Power**	7	69	13
Belgium	Judy Et Cie	**Pierre Rapsat**	8	68	6
Netherlands	The Party's Over Now	**Sandra Reemer**	9	56	8
Ireland	When	**Red Hurley**	10	54	7
Finland	Pump Pump	**Fredi and The Friends**	11	44	11
Portugal	Uma Flor De Verde Pinho	**Carlos de Carmo**	12	24	15
Greece	Panaghia Mou, Panaghia Mou	**Mariza Koch & Dimitris Zouboulis**	13	20	10
Luxembourg	Chansons Pour Ceux Qui S'Aiment	**Jürgen Marcus**	14	17	5
Germany	Sing Sang Song	**Les Humphries Singers**	15	12	3
Spain	Sobran Las Palabras	**Braulio**	16	11	12
Yugoslavia	Ne Mogu Skriti Svoju Bol	**Ambassadori**	17	10	18
Norway	Mata Hari	**Anne-Karine Strøm**	18	7	9

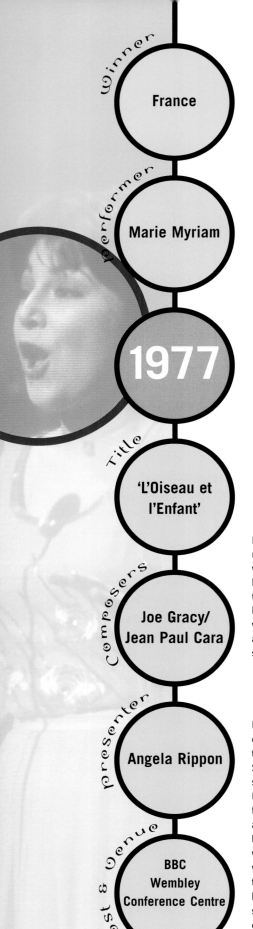

France

Performer

Marie Myriam

1977

Title

'L'Oiseau et l'Enfant'

Composers

Joe Gracy/
Jean Paul Cara

Presenter

Angela Rippon

Host & Venue

BBC
Wembley
Conference Centre

The Eurovision Song Contest returned to London in 1977, although only just. Industrial action by BBC cameramen had led to the United Kingdom's heat not being shown on TV and threatened the Eurovision final itself. The Netherlands stepped in with an offer to play host for the second year running, but once the Dutch TV unions heard of this proposal they stated their support for their British counterparts, as did unions across Europe. Reluctantly, the 2nd April broadcast date was abandoned, and the contest shelved.

london
United Kingdom

Once the industrial strife was resolved, the BBC swiftly announced a revised broadcast date of May 7th, from the newly opened Wembley Conference Centre. It was only the second time – the last had been the inaugural competition in 1956 – that the contest had been held as late as May.

There were further difficulties when Tunisia, who were making their debut, pulled out of the line-up, having been drawn fourth in a one-off attempt to take part in Eurovision. Then Norway and Sweden objected to the video postcards

Right: France's Marie Myriam recently admitted that she was very nervous and that her hands shook throughout. But the only hitch was outside her control: the caption telling viewers the song's title wobbled around the bottom of the screen providing comic relief.

Far right: The judges were disdainful of a heavy dig at the contest from Austria's Schmetterlinge. Added to the silliness of the lyrics of 'Boom Boom Boomerang' was a fairly ridiculous dance routine and the male performers' bizarre costumes. The boys wore spandex suits, but when they turned their backs to the camera, they were in black-and-white tuxedos, with smiling masks on the back of their heads.

that were to be shown before each performance – they'd been filmed at a nightclub a few days before the contest and the Norwegians felt it showed their young singer behaving badly. Shots of the audience replaced the rejected intermissions.

One major change to the rulebook was that the songs again had to be performed in one of the official languages of the country being represented. Germany and Belgium were given dispensation, as their selection processes were well underway. In the end both nations fielded songs sung in English. The rule stayed in place until 1999, when after continued pressure from competitors because of repeated wins for English-language songs, Eurovision's organisers relaxed the rule once more.

The set for the evening was simple and well designed. The BBC concert orchestra was in a circular pit under three large arches, which could be revolved. In front of them were three circular stages of different sizes, stacked in a step formation. Coloured lighting changed for each performance. To the viewers' right was a separate platform, from whence the evening's mistress of ceremonies, the TV newsreader **Angela Rippon**, welcomed the viewers in English and French.

As Rippon finished her opening remarks, she introduced the first nation, Ireland. **Noel Kelehan** immediately took to the conductor's podium and the song began. This abrupt start was really only a return to the format used in the contest until 1969. Jimmy and Tommy Swarbrigg were making their second appearance in the contest, joined on this occasion by two ladies, Alma Carroll and Nicola Kerr. As **The Swarbriggs Plus Two**, they were singing a strong opener that took their nation closer to the title than any other Irish song since Dana's victory seven years earlier.

Monaco also did well, although they slipped one place from their 1976 result to fourth. **Michèle Torr** had sung for Luxembourg in 1966 and had now switched her allegiance to the small principality. The song itself had a bouncy chorus, breaking out of a much slower verse. Throughout the verses she was seen on TV in 'soft focus', an optical effect that was not explained.

Heddy Lester performed a strong ballad, but did less well than the three previous Dutch entries. It did not go unnoticed that they had all been sung in English. The Austrian song this year has become almost synonymous with all

things regarded as awful in Eurovision. **Schmetterlinge** were four boys and one girl whose song was having a very heavy dig at the contest and, even more, the recording industry. Although officially in German, 'Boom Boom Boomerang' had many lyrics in English and a chorus in the language of nonsense. Still, it's the only Eurovision entry to mention kangaroos, didgery-doos and *Kojak*! Added to the silliness of the lyrics were a fairly ridiculous dance routine and the bizarre costumes of the male performers. They wore white spandex suits, but when they turned their backs to the camera, they were in black-and-white tuxedos, with smiling masks on the back of their heads. Comedy has never been particularly well received at Eurovision and the judges were particularly disdainful of this particular effort. A total score of 11 points from four juries meant they weren't last – that fate fell to Swedish all-male band, **Forbes**, and their dreadful homage to the Beatles – but the Austrians were only one place higher.

Germany fielded the biggest stars of the night, the disco divas **Silver Convention**. Singing in English, they came to London as one of the hot favourites to take the top prize, but like so many other notable stars to have tried their luck in the contest, they became completely unstuck with the jurors and finished in a disappointing eighth place. They continued to release singles, but slumped into ever-deepening obscurity shortly thereafter.

Punk rock was the dominant youth cult in the United Kingdom in 1977, but the music of **Lynsey de Paul and Mike Moran**, performing 'Rock Bottom', was a million miles away from the sound of The Sex Pistols. The duo adopted a highly original concept for their presentation of the song, seated back-to-back, each playing a black grand piano. They dressed in formal business suits, in the style of city stockbrokers, as did **Ronnie Hazlehurst**, who conducted the orchestra using a furled umbrella. Lynsey began the song behind a newspaper, which carried the headline: 'Where are we? Rock Bottom'. Although they weren't, they didn't win either. For a staggering tenth time, the UK had to be content with second place, even though they received more top marks than any other nation.

Greece was seen as a real challenger for the prize for the first time this year. They had a sing-a-long pop song, well presented by a group of four singers, **Pascalis, Marianna, Robert & Bessy**, that ran through the musical alphabet, 'Do-Re-Mi-Fa-So-La-Te-Do'. The foursome included some mock conducting of its own, dressed in purple and white. They were certainly hopeful of doing well and, although they only finished in fifth place, this remained the highest placing for a

Spain's Micky was joined by three singers, a banjo player and a man playing a jug. Micky himself wore an old woollen sweater.

Marie made French, German, English, Spanish, Portuguese and Italian versions of 'L'Oiseau Et l'Enfant'. She made No. 5 in Sweden, No. 17 in the Netherlands but only No. 42 in the UK. The song charted in many other countries, but only achieved lasting success in her homeland.

Greek entry until 2001, and remains the best for a song sung entirely in the Greek language.

Belgium had gone for a more modern sound, and one that was tipped to do very well. 'A Million In One, Two, Three' was sung in English and had a very good beat and hook. But the director had problems filming the Belgian group, as the BBC had objected to their revealing blouses. In the end, careful camera angles were used so that their cheeky attire would not offend anyone at home. As with the Germans, though, the judges were not looking for contemporary in 1977, and Belgium failed again to secure their first win, finishing in a disappointing seventh place.

French ballads had dominated the contest from its inception through to 1973, when ten of the winners had followed that model. With the arrival of Abba in 1974, the old format had been swept away and groups had dominated for the last three years, with most performers using the English language. But in 1977, France proved that the judges could be persuaded otherwise when they achieved a record-breaking fifth Eurovision victory. **Marie Myriam** had been a hit-maker from a very early age, making her first records back in 1968. Of Portuguese descent, she had been born in the Congo in Africa, and came to London with the whole of France behind her to sing 'L'Oiseau Et l'Enfant' ('The Bird

And The Child') – an exceptionally simple song that built with each verse and carried a very memorable melody. Compared to the choreographic excesses of many of the favourites, the song's simplicity certainly helped to make it stand out from the crowd.

As befitted a contest that had been cursed with problems, the voting process had numerous mistakes that plagued the process – Israel initially failed to award four points to anyone, possibly to compensate for the Greeks having done so twice! France also got their scoring wrong, giving seven marks to Portugal and six to Italy, when it should have been the other way around.

Backstage, Marie Myriam waited for Angela Rippon to confirm her victory and broke down in tears with all the other artists embracing her with congratulations. She was so busy receiving their praise that she was delayed getting back onto the stage. The cameraman who was filming the backstage scenes fell backwards as he recorded her progress, blocking her exit and giving himself a black eye. Marie recalls that she immediately stopped crying and tried to help the poor chap.

Despite all the disasters the 1977 contest had faced, it proved to be a successful broadcast. In 1978, the contest continued to grow, with many old friends returning to the fold.

country	song	performer	place	score	draw
France	L'Oiseau Et 'Enfant	**Marie Myriam**	1	136	18
United Kingdom	Rock Bottom	**Lynsey de Paul & Mike Moran**	2	121	9
Ireland	It's Nice To Be In Love Again	**The Swarbriggs Plus Two**	3	119	1
Monaco	Une Petite Française	**Michèle Torr**	4	96	2
Greece	Mathema Solfege	**Pascalis, Marianna, Robert & Bessy**	5	92	10
Switzerland	Swiss Lady	**Pepe Lienhard band**	6	71	12
Belgium	A Million In One, Two, Three	**Dream Express**	7	69	17
Germany	Telegram	**Silver Convention**	8	55	6
Spain	Enséñame A Cantar	**Micky**	9	52	14
Finland	Lapponia	**Monica Aspelund**	10	50	16
Israel	Ha'ava Hi ShirLishnayim	**Ilanit**	11	49	11
Netherlands	De Mallemolen	**Heddy Lester**	12	35	3
Italy	Libera	**Mia Martini**	13	32	15
Portugal	Portugal No Coração	**Os Amigos**	14	19	8
Norway	Casanova	**Anita Skorgan**	15	18	5
Luxembourg	Frère Jacques	**Anne-Marie B**	16	17	7
Austria	Boom Boom Boomerang	**Schmetterlinge**	17	11	4
Sweden	Beatles	**Forbes**	18	2	13

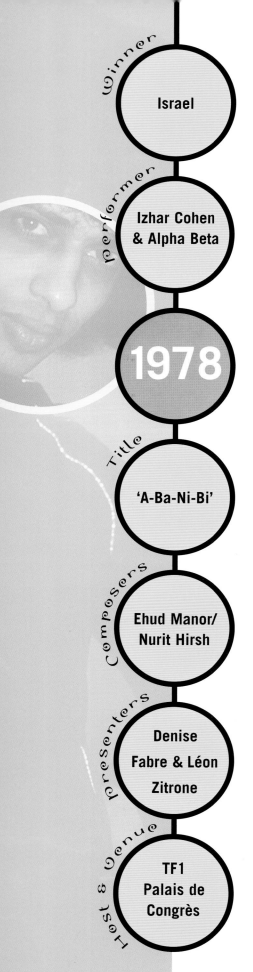

Winner

Israel

Performer

Izhar Cohen & Alpha Beta

1978

Title

'A-Ba-Ni-Bi'

Composers

Ehud Manor/ Nurit Hirsh

Presenters

Denise Fabre & Léon Zitrone

Host & Genue

TF1 Palais de Congrès

paris
france

The twenty-third Eurovision Song Contest came to Paris in 1978, for the first and only time so far. The broadcast date was 22nd April, which aside from the first contest and the delayed 1977 event, was the latest date yet scheduled for the show. Strangely, the production was a very laid-back affair, with a distinct air of *laissez-faire* surrounding the whole broadcast, which was dogged by technical hiccups and an unimaginative black and white set.

Denmark and Turkey were the two additions to the line-up from London. The Danes were making their first appearance since 1966, the second longest absence ever recorded from the contest, while Turkey had returned after missing the past two years' competitions.

Denise Fabre and **Léon Zitrone** were the two presenters recruited to act as hosts for the show, the first time there was more than one person assigned to the task. Zitrone was also the first male presenter of the contest since Lohengrin Filipello hosted the inaugural event in 1956.

For the second year in a row, Ireland performed first.

Right: Israel's Izhar Cohen had been very confident of victory, even though no one had rated the song prior to the big night. Izhar was pretty much a soloist, joined by five backing artists but, unlike so many other entrants, this fivesome were given full credit for their efforts.

Far right: Harmony was the trio engaged to sing the Dutch entry, one girl backed by two male singers.

Having tried the popular two-girl-two-boy scenario in 1977, they now went for a male soloist, the least popular type of winning artist. Their chosen singer, **Colm T. Wilkinson**, gave an incredibly energetic vocal performance that must have blasted the ears of those present in the Palais de Congrès. Such was the power of his voice that he had to adopt a somewhat bizarre semi-crouch to belt out the words of 'Born To Sing'. He may have been, but not this type of song. As the critic Clive James said in the British newspaper *The Observer* the following morning – 'Born to sing? How wrong can you be?'

As a French ballad had claimed the prize in 1977, many countries thought that perhaps this was still the way to the juries' hearts. A quarter of all the entrants presented songs in French. They were almost right. Three of the top four places went to French ballads, although not the place that mattered – first. For the host nation, **Joël Prévost** presented the very typically French chanson 'Il Y Aura Toujours Des Violons' ('There Will Always Be Violins'). It was very well thought of by the judges, and France became the first and only country ever to receive marks from every jury for three

successive years, even if by finishing third this was their poorest showing since 1975.

Instead of the ill-fated video postcards, the French director had decided to use footage of the acts backstage as a way of introducing each entry. Cheryl Baker, a singer with the British six-piece **Co-Co**, made good use of the idea by calling out 'Hello, Mum'. Unfortunately, once on stage the band gave a very weak and off-key vocal performance.

Trying to build on their relative success from the previous year, Greece tried another entry in the sing-a-long Euro-pop mould, but with less success. **Tania Tsanaklidou** appeared on stage to sing 'Charlie Chaplin', replete with full Chaplin-esque attire, including bowler hat and walking stick. It was an odd, distracting effort that finished in eighth place, Greece's second best result to date.

As with the Germans the year before, Luxembourg had turned to the biggest female group currently doing the pan-European circuit to sing for them in Paris. **Baccara** was a Spanish twosome. The duo, which primarily worked for an American record label based in Germany, were singing in French and chosen to represent Luxembourg! They were the

undoubted favourites going into the final and, despite what the judges thought, they probably still were afterwards. The two ladies, Maria Mendiola and Mayte Mateos, had shot to the top of the charts with the seductive disco hit, 'Yes Sir, I Can Boogie' followed by another smash, 'Sorry, I'm A Lady'. Those two songs were unbelievably similar to their Euro-effort, 'Parlez-vous Français?' (Do You Speak French?'). Maybe this is why the judges gave it a disappointing seventh place. Certainly, they gave the most polished and professional performance of any artist in Paris. The two girls gave a tremendous visual show, but it was not to be. For 1978, the judges wanted something just a little bit more unusual.

They got it with the Israeli entry that came from a six-piece group sent to Paris by way of a coin toss at the Israeli heat. There has always been much conjecture as to exactly what **Izhar Cohen and Alpha Beta**'s song 'A-Ba-Ni-Bi' really means. The young children of Israel had developed their own language so as to disguise what they were saying to adults, by inserting a B after every word. 'A-Ba-Ni-Bi' means 'I love you' in this 'B' language. The song had a power that was perhaps lacking in the other 19 entries and was certainly

presented with enormous enthusiasm, slick choreography and an air of great excitement. Izhar himself had a strong voice, which was well suited to the ever-changing tempo and mood of the song.

The final entry was by Sweden's **Björn Skifs**, who had made a name for himself in the United States thanks to an enormous hit, 'Hooked On A Feeling', which he'd enjoyed with the band Blue Swede. He accompanied himself on piano for the first half of the song, opening in Swedish-sounding gibberish as he struggled to remember the lyrics, before rising to complete the song standing. It was a very low-key effort and had an exceptionally soft ending, which may have caught the judges by surprise. It ended in fourteenth position, despite a promising start in the voting.

Israel's win proved something of a headache for a number of the non-competing Arabic nations that were showing the contest – the show was now reaching 450 million viewers in Europe, Africa and the Middle East. During the Israeli performance, most of the Arab broadcasters had switched to a commercial break, not allowing their viewers even to see the Israeli song. When Israel took the lead and looked like the

Right: The costumes worn by the UK's Co-Co came in for some serious criticism. They went for a circus theme, including some clown make-up for good measure, and glittered in golds and other metallic hues.

Although Izhar Cohen did record the original Hebrew version of 'A-Ba-Ni-Bi' for inclusion on Israeli compilation albums, it was only the English version that was available on single. In the UK, it just made the Top 20, was No. 12 in the Dutch chart and No. 9 in Sweden.

clear winner, many decided to kill the transmission entirely. Jordan finished the remainder of the show with an image of a bunch of daffodils on screen. Doubtless, they are still waiting to hear which country won Eurovision in 1978.

Not for the first time, Norway was to be found at the bottom of the pack. This time, however, it was even more humiliating than usual, as the Norwegian song failed to gain a single point. It was the first time since 1970, and the first time ever under this scoring method, that a song had failed to garner any support at all, a scathing comment from the assembled jurors. **Jahn Teigen** may have been disappointed when his song did so badly, but he used the infamy to great advantage and is better remembered and more famous than many artists who have won the contest. Dressed in red trousers and tie, a white shirt and gold braces and sunglasses, he had some highly comical moves, including a split jump in the air at the end of the song. His vocal ability was somewhat questionable, too, and hitting the higher notes proved a problem. His own nation loved it – after Eurovision the song went to Number One and spent 20 weeks in the Norwegian charts.

One other interesting note is that Luxembourg's jury picked the Israeli song as their favourite entry. It was the first time since 1969 that the judges from the Grand Duchy had correctly identified the winning song, and it was to be the last. They never again gave top marks to the winning entry, and in the thirty-seven contests Luxembourg competed, their jury only identified the winning song on six occasions. There are countries that have never yet picked the winner at all, but no other nation than Luxembourg has got it wrong so many times. With Cyprus and Greece invariably awarding each other 'douze points' it inevitably means that they rarely choose the winning song either.

Many critics argued that Israel should not even be competing in the 'Eurovision' contest, but this did not sour the victory for the Israelis. The band was given a huge welcome back in Tel Aviv, with Izhar being carried off the plane high above the heads of the welcoming crowd.

As for Eurovision itself? Ratings began to slip around the continent and the comparable lack of success of the winning song, for the second year in a row, meant that the contest was in need of a new injection of life.

country	song	performer	place	score	draw
Israel	A-Ba-Ni-Bi	Izhar Cohen & Alpha Beta	1	157	18
Belgium	L'Amour Ça Fait Chanter La Vie	Jean Vallée	2	125	10
France	Il Y Aura Toujours Des Violons	Joël Prévost	3	119	6
Monaco	Les Jardins De Monaco	Caline & Oliver Toussaint	4	107	14
Ireland	Born To Sing	Colm T. Wilkinson	5	86	1
Germany	Feuer	Ireen Sheer	6	84	13
Luxembourg	Parlez-vous Français?	Baccara	7	73	17
Greece	Charlie Chaplin	Tania Tsanaklidou	8	66	15
Spain	Bailemos Un Vals	José Velez	9=	65	7
Switzerland	Vivre	Carole Vinci	9=	65	9
United Kingdom	The Bad Old Days	Co-Co	11	61	8
Italy	Questo Amore	Ricchi E Poveri	12	53	3
Netherlands	'T Is OK	Harmony	13	37	11
Sweden	Det Blir Alltid Värre Framåt Natten	Björn Skifs	14	26	20
Austria	Mrs Caroline Robinson	Springtime	15	14	19
Denmark	Boom Boom	Mabel	16	13	16
Portugal	Dai-Li-Dou	Gemini	17	5	5
Finland	Anna Rakkaudelle Tilaisuus	Seija Simola	18=	2	4
Turkey	Sevince	Nazar	18=	2	12
Norway	Mil Etter Mil	Jahn Teigen	20	0	2

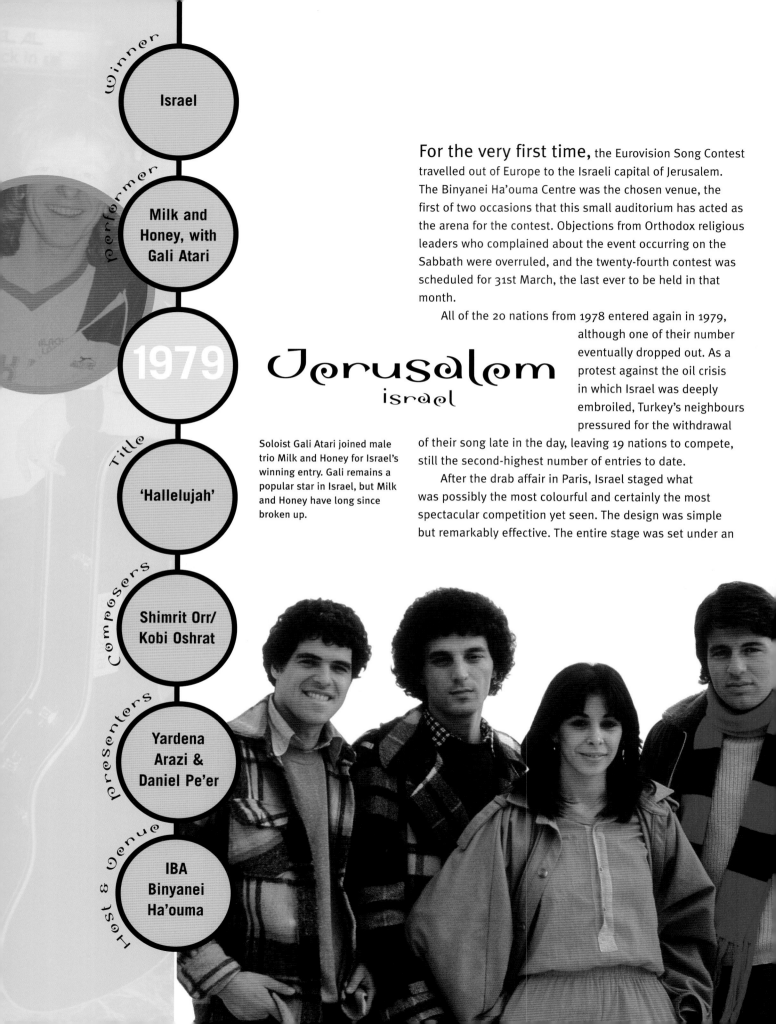

Winner

Israel

Performer

Milk and Honey, with Gali Atari

1979

Title

'Hallelujah'

Composers

Shimrit Orr/ Kobi Oshrat

Presenters

Yardena Arazi & Daniel Pe'er

Host & Venue

IBA Binyanei Ha'ouma

Jerusalem
israel

For the very first time, the Eurovision Song Contest travelled out of Europe to the Israeli capital of Jerusalem. The Binyanei Ha'ouma Centre was the chosen venue, the first of two occasions that this small auditorium has acted as the arena for the contest. Objections from Orthodox religious leaders who complained about the event occurring on the Sabbath were overruled, and the twenty-fourth contest was scheduled for 31st March, the last ever to be held in that month.

All of the 20 nations from 1978 entered again in 1979, although one of their number eventually dropped out. As a protest against the oil crisis in which Israel was deeply embroiled, Turkey's neighbours pressured for the withdrawal of their song late in the day, leaving 19 nations to compete, still the second-highest number of entries to date.

After the drab affair in Paris, Israel staged what was possibly the most colourful and certainly the most spectacular competition yet seen. The design was simple but remarkably effective. The entire stage was set under an

Soloist Gali Atari joined male trio Milk and Honey for Israel's winning entry. Gali remains a popular star in Israel, but Milk and Honey have long since broken up.

illuminated proscenium arch. Everything was bare, except for a centrepiece of three concentric rings, propped upright, which could turn independently to form any number of patterns. Throughout the night, the set was illuminated in a series of striking colours that matched the costumes of the performers and the mood of the songs. It worked well, and was a very spectacular backdrop.

Two presenters were again deemed necessary, and **Yardena Arazi** and **Daniel Pe'er** were invited to act as the contest's hosts. Yardena had taken part in the 1976 contest as part of the group Chocolate Menta Mastik and became the second former contestant to present the competition. She concentrated on the French portion of the script, while the slightly older and somewhat stiffer Daniel Pe'er took care of the English presentation. They shared the Hebrew announcements, of which there were many. Daniel claims to have become something of a cult figure in the Netherlands as a result of his appearance, although exactly why remains a mystery. Yardena obviously had such a good time that she entered the contest again, as a soloist in 1988, and was seen many other times in the Israeli heats.

Yardena had elected to wear a long chiffon gown in a very pale cream, her long hair parted in the centre and pinned back behind her ears. The bespectacled Daniel was in a less flattering, brown, three-piece lounge suit, which contrasted oddly with the tuxedos of the men in the audience. They offered greetings in English, French and Hebrew, before giving very lengthy introductions and explanations in the same three languages.

In a novel innovation, the 'postcards' that introduced each song were comical short movies, which supposedly summed up the intrinsic nature of each nation. The majority of the films were tongue-in-cheek jibes at the relevant country, but others were just plain baffling. Portugal opened the show for the first time since 1968, and their postcard showed fisherman hauling a huge bottle of port out of the sea. It didn't seem to distract **Manuela Bravo** who was singing 'Sobe, Sobe, Balão Sobe,' ('Rise, Rise, Balloon, Rise'), in a tiered yellow dress, on the by now yellow-lit set. Four backing singers joined her, in equally bright hues of yellow, red, purple and blue. Her preview video had been somewhat bizarre, showing Manuela running in and out of the ocean, where her four-poster bed had been placed for no apparent reason. Her on-stage performance was far more routine – a very bright opener, but not a winner, finishing ninth.

The famous 'curse of number two' struck once again in 1979. It is hard to imagine why the Italian song was the pre-contest favourite based on the performance given by **Matia Bazar**. Performing without the orchestra, using only a backing track, they gave by far the worst vocal performance of the night, possibly of anyone ever in the contest. The two lead singers hit a bad note from the beginning and never managed to find the correct key again. The female singer, Antonella Ruggiero, was particularly flat and when the two leads sang together, it was a painful aural experience.

Denmark was able to improve the standard again, with a very strong offering from **Tommy Seebach**, making the first of his three appearances in the Eurovision contest. Seated at the piano in a golden-brown suit, he was joined by three singers in purple to perform 'Disco Tango', a song that became the only Eurovision entry ever to have mentioned John Travolta! As expected, the song followed the tango rhythm and was a very catchy number, which did well for the Danes, reaching sixth place. Another crowd-pleaser was the entry from Greece, which was an ode to the famous philosopher Socrates, proclaiming him to be the first Greek superstar. It was a very energetic song, with a tremendously rousing climax.

The audience also loved Germany's entry – it had been thought that a German song glorifying Ghengis Khan, who waged war on Israel, was highly inappropriate. Nevertheless, the song did get the blessing of German broadcaster ARD to compete and, despite all the worries of offending the host's sensibilities, the performance brought the house down. The five singers in the group were dressed in outrageous costumes and were joined by a male dancer, presumably

'Hallelujah' leapt to No. 5 in the UK chart and was enormously successful elsewhere. It went to No. 1 in Sweden and made No. 8 in the Netherlands. The group recorded German and French versions as well, with the Hebrew version on the B-side.

country	song	performer	place	score	draw
Israel	Hallelujah	Milk & Honey With Gali Atari	1	125	10
Spain	Su Canción	Betty Missiego	2	116	19
France	Je Suis L'Enfant Soleil	Anne-Marie David	3	106	11
Germany	Dschingis Khan	Dschingis Khan	4	86	9
Ireland	Happy Man	Cathal Dunne	5	80	4
Denmark	Disco Tango	Tommy Seebach	6	76	3
United Kingdom	Mary Ann	Black Lace	7	73	17
Greece	Socrates	Elpida	8	69	7
Portugal	Sobe, Sobe, Balão, Sobe	Manuela Bravo	9	64	1
Switzerland	Trödler Und Co.	Peter, Sue & Marc and Pfuri, Gorps & Kniri	10	60	8
Norway	Oliver	Anita Skorgan	11	57	16
Netherlands	Colorado	Xandra	12	51	14
Luxembourg	J'ai Déjà Vu Ça Dans Tes Yeux	Jeane Manson	13	44	13
Finland	Katson Sineen Taivaan	Katri Helena	14	38	5
Italy	Raggio Di Luna	Matia Bazar	15	27	2
Monaco	Notre Vie C'est La Musique	Laurent Vaguener	16	12	6
Sweden	Satellit	Ted Gärdestad	17	8	15
Belgium	Hey Nana	Micha Marah	18=	5	12
Austria	Heute In Jerusalem	Christina Simon	18=	5	18

representing Ghengis himself. The dramatic presentation would not have looked out of place in a Broadway musical and won **Dschingis Khan** a standing ovation.

Ossi Runne, to date the contest's most frequent conductor, took to the podium for the Finnish entry. Ossi had conducted every Finnish entry since 1966, the year he had written their song himself. He was back again this year to direct the music for **Katri Helena**. Her song had an excellent orchestration and a catchy chorus, yet still achieved Finland's second worst result since 1968.

Switzerland had turned once again to **Peter, Sue and Marc** who had teamed up with another trio, three men called **Pfuri, Gnorps and Kniri**, proponents of what was known as 'trash music'. The latter three had brought along possibly the most bizarre complement of instruments, if that's what they were, ever seen on the Eurovision stage. Garden hoses, watering cans, rakes, shutters, plastic bags, saucepans and metal cans were just some of the 'junk' that had been assembled to provide the song's backing. Singing in German, they seemed to be enjoying themselves, even if this was not the reaction of the judges.

Flemish singer **Micha Marah** represented Belgium, singing 'Hey Nana.' She was possibly the tallest lady in the contest, her height boosted further by her very high heels. She wore her blonde hair tightly swept up in a bun and a long blue glittering gown. Such was the awfulness of her entry that she could not be persuaded to commit it to disc herself – instead the composer Charles Dumolin recorded the only known version. Micha may have been right, since despite a very jolly performance, Belgium could only scrape together five points from three nations to finish equal last.

When it was time for Israel's entry, the audience's anticipation had reached fever pitch. **Gali Atari** was the female soloist who had been invited to join the male trio Milk and Honey to sing 'Hallelujah'. The song opened with a simple piano accompaniment as Gali sang the first verse alone on the stage in a pink frock. She was joined for the second verse by the first member of Milk and Honey, dressed in white with sparkling braces and matching bow tie. The orchestra then kicked in, as the two remaining members of the ensemble joined them on stage. With each verse, the song grew in pace and more and more parts of the orchestra joined in with the music. It was a very effective presentation of the catchiest song of the night and once again the crowd was on their feet cheering before the song had even finished. Certainly there was no doubt in their minds that

themselves around her feet. The song was highly reminiscent of the successful Spanish entries of a decade earlier and built after a slow start to a bouncy chorus, injected with 'la la las' from the four children. They eventually rose to their feet for one final burst of 'la la la' before the song ended with them unfurling banners saying 'thank you' in English, Spanish, French and, most importantly, Hebrew. It was without doubt the most manipulative performance of the night and, together with Israel, Spain dominated the voting, although it was to be their own jury that eventually decided the winners.

As the voting reached its climax, Spain was one point in the lead with 116, to Israel's 115. It was up to the Spanish jury to decide the fate of its own entry. One point to Israel would force a draw and a play off, two points or more would rob it of victory. Twelve went to the Germans, their fourth of the night, before the Madrid spokeswoman announced in French 'Israel, dix points!' The audience erupted in cheers, and backstage Milk and Honey and Gali Atari hugged each other with joy. Even Spain's Betty Missiego looked happy for them. It was the first time ever that the song in second place had come from behind to win on the final vote and the first time that the leading country had caused their own defeat.

The winning song was enormously successful across Europe and Gali Atari remains a popular star in Israel, but Milk and Honey have long since disbanded. The lads tried to represent their nation again, but failed to qualify. Two of their number then appeared in Dublin in 1988, backing the 1979 hostess Yardena Arazi with her eighth-placed entry.

The biggest act to emerge from the 1979 contest was the British quartet **Black Lace** who had finished seventh with a song that was accused of plagarising the hit group Smokie. They slimmed down to a duo and had enormous European success in the early eighties with a series of party sing-a-longs including smash hit 'Agadoo', which has become a by-word for terrible music and regularly features on albums celebrating the worst records ever made, but it made the group a household name in a way that Eurovision never did.

The production and the winning entry of the 1979 contest were both triumphs. Nevertheless, ratings suggest that viewers were becoming disenchanted with the contest across the continent. As video recorders, cable TV and alternative entertainment began to erode the domination of domestic TV, the audiences were beginning to slip. It was with this in mind that the twenty-fifth anniversary of the contest loomed the following year.

A strike by unions responsible for lighting and sound over a dispute about who should operate the scoreboard pulled the plug on the live UK heat final. Regional juries were asked to cast their votes on audio-tapes of the 12 finalists and Black Lace were the surprise winners.

Israel was going to do it again, but the judges were not so clearly persuaded. The voting was the most exciting since 1969.

France had turned to Luxembourg's last winner, **Anne-Marie David**. Dressed in a cream gown with heavy gold embroidery, she certainly turned in a passionate performance, aided by three ladies in purple and two men in white. It was something of a dreary melody, but the dramatic nature of Anne-Marie's interpretation lifted it out of the realms of the ordinary. However, the dramatic French ballad had clearly had its day and although she led at one stage in the voting, she eventually finished in third place.

Austria had entered a song entitled 'Heute In Jerusalem' ('Tonight In Jerusalem'), the first time any entry had mentioned the host city, but Spain went one better to spread goodwill. Their song had enough heart-wrenching sentiment to almost sweep the board. After the first verse, **Betty Missiego** was joined by four young children, one of whom had the task of interrupting her in a jocular manner, before seating

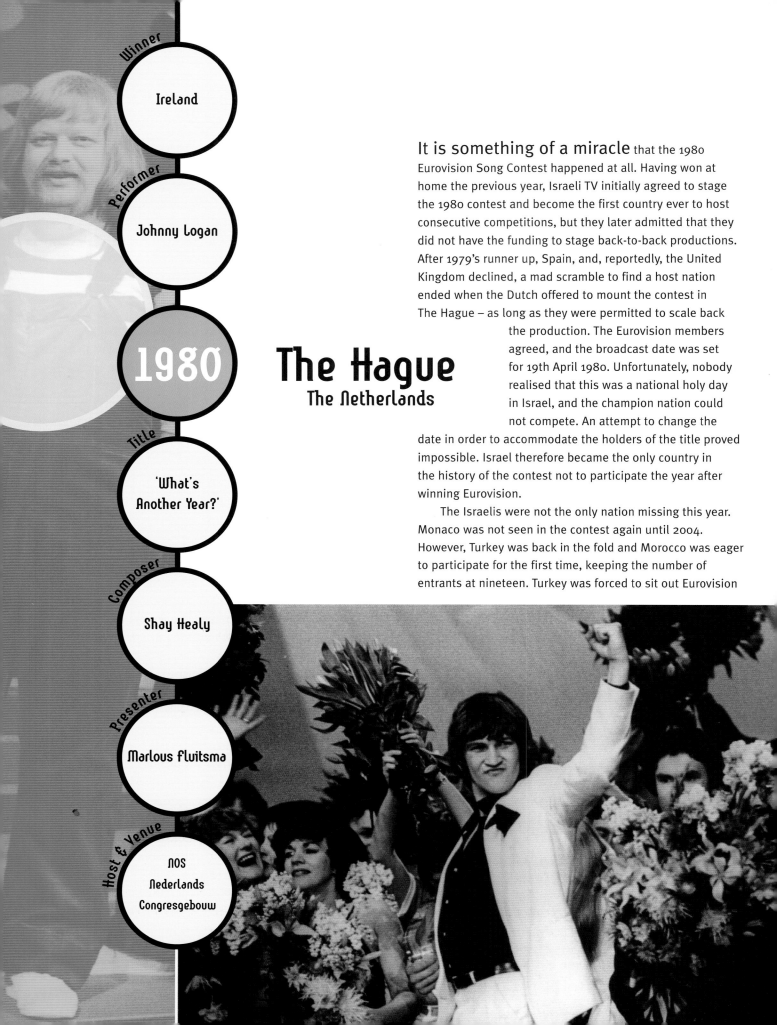

1980

The Hague
The Netherlands

Title

'What's Another Year?'

Composer

Shay Healy

Presenter

Marlous Fluitsma

Host & Venue

NOS
Nederlands
Congresgebouw

It is something of a miracle that the 1980 Eurovision Song Contest happened at all. Having won at home the previous year, Israeli TV initially agreed to stage the 1980 contest and become the first country ever to host consecutive competitions, but they later admitted that they did not have the funding to stage back-to-back productions. After 1979's runner up, Spain, and, reportedly, the United Kingdom declined, a mad scramble to find a host nation ended when the Dutch offered to mount the contest in The Hague – as long as they were permitted to scale back the production. The Eurovision members agreed, and the broadcast date was set for 19th April 1980. Unfortunately, nobody realised that this was a national holy day in Israel, and the champion nation could not compete. An attempt to change the date in order to accommodate the holders of the title proved impossible. Israel therefore became the only country in the history of the contest not to participate the year after winning Eurovision.

The Israelis were not the only nation missing this year. Monaco was not seen in the contest again until 2004. However, Turkey was back in the fold and Morocco was eager to participate for the first time, keeping the number of entrants at nineteen. Turkey was forced to sit out Eurovision in 1979, after extreme pressure was put on their government by Arab nations, in protest at the contest taking place in Jerusalem. Threats had been made to cut off Turkey's petrol supplies if they competed. In their own protest, the Turks' 1980 song paid homage to the precious liquid itself. 'Petr'oil' was an unusual entry. It was performed by **Ajda Pekkan**, a huge star in her native land, who was surrounded on stage by singers and musicians dressed in traditional Turkish costumes. Finger cymbals, bongos and other unusual instruments combined to give the most dramatically different entry of the evening. The judges were not overly impressed, however, although the Turks did at least achieve a considerably better tally than their previous two other entries combined!

The Turks were not alone in entering a protest song. Norway's entry was a demonstration against the building of a hydroelectric power plant. In sharp contrast to Turkey's Mediterranean neighbours, Greece chose an upbeat song about hitchhiking, 'Autostop', which featured motor horn sound effects.

Luxembourg's 1980 song became one of the most mocked entries in Eurovision history. **Sophie and Magaly** were twin sisters with long blond hair and matching pink-and-blue costumes. Three ladies in white with sparkling black tailcoats accompanied them, along with a very large gentleman dressed to resemble a giant penguin who provided the comic relief. Overall, 'Le Papa Pingouin' ('The Father Penguin') was not such a bad song, but seeing a grown man jumping and waddling around the stage in full penguin regalia was just too much to take, even for the long-suffering Eurovision audience.

Oddly, the writers of Luxembourg's ode to father penguins, Bernd Meinunger and Ralph Siegel, had also penned the German entry 'Theater' – they were only the second writers to have two songs entered into the same contest, following in the footsteps of Didier Barbelivien in 1978. Their chosen singer, **Katja Ebstein**, was herself setting a new record. This was her third appearance for her nation, having finished in third place in both 1970 and 1971. The song was highly reminiscent of something from *Cabaret* and was performed extremely well indeed, despite the addition of four backing singers dressed as clowns. Ebstein ended in second place, which put her into the history books as the only singer to have finished in the top three on three occasions, without ever actually winning the contest.

Morocco fared very badly with its debut entry, which managed to combine Arabic sounds with that old Eurovision standby of endless 'la la las'. Only Italy awarded the Moroccans any marks at all, although they did manage to avoid finishing bottom of the heap. That fate fell, not for the first time, to Finland, whose song about a flute player only

Left: 'I love you, Ireland!' An exuberant Johnny Logan celebrates his win.

Right: Denmark fielded the rather odd-looking quartet Bamses Venner (Bamses's Friends), each member dressed in denim dungarees and striped shirt, and fronted by the large and bearded Bamses himself.

impressed the Norwegian and French juries.

Since the Congresgebouw had been the scene of the Brotherhood of Man's victory in 1976, the United Kingdom saw the chosen venue as a good omen. **Prima Donna**, a six-member boy-girl group, was formed especially to sing at Eurovision. They were in very much the same vein as Brotherhood of Man, yet proved alarmingly unpopular with the British public. Indeed, 'Love Enough For Two' was the first British entry since 1964 that did not register on the UK charts before the contest, although it did sneak up to 48 in the weeks after the group sang in The Hague. Despite the lack of enthusiasm for the group at home, the Eurovision judges were somewhat more impressed with Prima Donna, and the UK surprised many when it took third place in the competition.

The home team followed next with 'Amsterdam', a song in praise of the Dutch city, so it was a pity the contest was being held at the Hague. **Maggie MacNeal** gave a very enthusiastic performance of the bookies' pre-contest favourite. The song was very much in the traditional Eurovision mould and, with its strong orchestration, it appeared to be an impressive contender, but it was perhaps a bit too old-fashioned for the juries. Unlike the Dutch, France has very rarely taken the route of choosing up-tempo

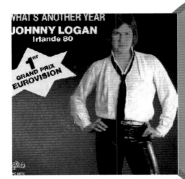

'What's Another Year?' was an instant success throughout the continent, climbing quickly to No. 1 in the UK and in many other countries. But Johnny Logan's follow-up singles were largely ignored and, although regular TV appearances kept him visible, he was unable to shake off lawsuits or the stigma attached to being a Eurovision winner.

sing-a-long songs for Eurovision and their rare exception in 1980 possibly shows why. 'Hé, Hé, M'sieurs, Dames' ('Hey, Hey, Ladies And Gentlemen') was a very trite effort indeed.

Singing for Ireland was **Johnny Logan**, an Australian-born Irishman who performed a song composed by Shay Healy, an employee of the Irish TV channel RTE. Logan looked confident and relaxed on the stage in The Hague. Dressed in a white suit with a black shirt, he followed Dana's example of perching on a stool to perform his song 'What's Another Year?' A well-structured and gentle ballad, punctuated by a saxophone solo, Johnny always looked like the winner, although he was run close in the voting by the equally strong, but very different German song.

Belgium was the final competitor and, as befitted the

country	song	performer	place	score	draw
Ireland	What's Another Year?	**Johnny Logan**	1	143	17
Germany	Theater	**Katja Ebstein**	2	128	12
United Kingdom	Love Enough For Two	**Prima Donna**	3	106	13
Switzerland	Cinéma	**Paola del Medico**	4	104	9
Netherlands	Amsterdam	**Maggie MacNeal**	5	93	15
Italy	Non So Che Darei	**Alan Sorrenti**	6	87	6
Portugal	Um Grande Grande Amor	**José Cid**	7	71	14
Austria	Du Bist Musik	**Blue Danube**	8	64	1
Luxembourg	Le Papa Pingouin	**Sophie & Magaly**	9	56	4
Sweden	Just Nu	**Tomas Ledin**	10	47	8
France	Hé Hé M'sieurs, Dames	**Profil**	11	45	16
Spain	Quedate Esta Noche	**Trigo Limpio**	12	38	18
Greece	Autostop	**Anna Vissi & The Epikouri**	13	30	3
Denmark	Tænker Altid På Dig	**Bamses Venner**	14	25	7
Turkey	Pet'r Oil	**Ajda Pekkan**	15	23	2
Norway	Samiid Ædnan	**Sverre Kjelsberg & Mattis Hætta**	16	15	11
Belgium	Eurovision	**Telex**	17	14	19
Morocco	Bitakat Hob	**Samira Bensaid**	18	7	5
Finland	Huilumies	**Vesa-Matti Loiri**	19	6	10

first contest of the new decade, it attempted something very different and contemporary. The trouble was, the song really wasn't very good. An electronic backing track thumped incessantly as the group, **Telex**, performing a song that was appropriately called 'Eurovision', tried to recreate the success that they had had in the European charts the previous year. It was a brave but unsuccessful effort, and its casual presentation was not what the judges were looking for. However, it remains the only entry ever to mention the contest by name and to feature the Eurovision theme tune, 'Te Deum', as part of its melody.

For a change, the voting did not appear to be conducted along national preferences, unlike so many other years. The Germanic triumvirate of Austria, Switzerland and Germany were somewhat generous to each other, which rather went against their normal behaviour. The UK was very fond of the Irish song, awarding it top marks, but more typically the Irish gave exactly half that amount in return.

After the final scores were tallied, Johnny Logan rushed back on to the stage, raising his arms in triumph and blowing kisses to the cameras and the audience. After Shay Healy, dressed somewhat oddly in a striped jacket and straw boater, had accepted the writer's prize from Marcel Besançon, the 'Father' of the contest, Johnny prepared to sing the winning song again. As the reprise reached its climax, Johnny announced, 'I love you, Ireland'. It was an emotional climax for the silver anniversary of the contest, and after the reprise, the rest of the year's contestants joined Logan on stage to celebrate as the final credits of the show rolled.

The victorious Irish song was an instant success throughout Europe. Johnny seemed destined for a successful career, certainly matching that of Dana. However, he faltered after this initial breakthrough and went through many personal difficulties, continually changed his musical (and hair) style, and even re-branded himself 'Logan'. None of it worked and a few years after triumphing at Eurovision and topping the charts, he had all but

disappeared. However, it was not the end of his story by any means and in 1987 he managed to complete a remarkable Eurovision double.

The 1980 contest was lucky to have made it on to the screen at all, yet thankfully, with such a strong and popular winner, things looked secure for the new decade.

Germany's Katja Ebstein was accompanied by four backing singers dressed as clowns, together with a pianist. It was a very polished entry, and one destined to do well.

Winner

United Kingdom

Performer

Bucks Fizz

1981

Title

'Making Your Mind Up'

Composer

Andy Hill/ John Danter

Presenter

Doireann Ni Bhriain

Host & Venue

RTE RDS Simmonscourt Pavilion

Dublin
Ireland

Twenty countries lined up on the starting grid for the twenty-sixth Eurovision Song Contest, which took place at the Royal Dublin Society's Simmonscourt Pavilion on 4th April 1981. Italy had withdrawn, amid speculation that they believed their entries had been unjustly placed in low positions in recent years. Morocco also declined to enter, having fared badly with their debut entry in 1980; they also objected to the return of Israel. Like the Israelis, Yugoslavia had returned to the competition, in this case for the first time since 1976. Cyprus was the only completely new nation on show and they were to make one of the contest's most successful debuts.

Despite having acoustics that had all the subtlety of an aircraft hanger, the production team took full advantage of the vast arena, constructing three separate stage areas inside the auditorium. In the centre stood a multi-tiered performing area for the artists, with the orchestra seated to the right and a separate stage for the scoreboard and presenter to the left. The entire set design was based on the clasp of the Celtic kilt, with four large, circular pieces overhanging the performance area. The stage itself was made up of circular platforms, which were designed to appear as steps. The set remained unchanged for each country but coloured lighting made the stage appear entirely

unique for each performance.

Each song was preceded by an animated sequence pinpointing the appropriate country on the European map. A film of the artists, composers and authors enjoying a slice of Irish life followed this. These included a trip to the zoo, government buildings and a heavy plug for Guinness.

It was the third time in the contest that the opening slot had gone to the same country for two successive years, with Austria opening the show. **Marty Brem** had been one of the singers of Austria's 1980 song, but this year he took solo credit for the song 'Wenn Du Da Bist' ('When You Are Here'). The slow ballad built well, but was severely hampered by the bizarre on-stage performance that accompanied it. Each of the five female backing singers wore a totally different and highly inappropriate outfit – one of them was even dressed in a body stocking and an American football helmet. The second slot was also taken by the same country as the year before – Turkey, who dropped political protest this time and entered a folky sing-along song called 'Dönme Dolap' ('Carousel').

For the third year in a row, a composition by Ralph Siegel and Bernd Meinunger had won the German heat. Following the success of last year's song by the duo, **Lena Valaitis** had high hopes of going one better and securing the

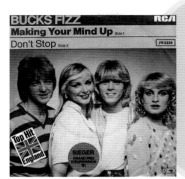

'**Making Your Mind Up**' shot to the top of the UK charts, where it stayed for three weeks. They also went to No. 1 in the Netherlands, Belgium, Spain, Israel, Norway, Denmark, Ireland, Germany, Austria and No. 2 in Sweden. It was a mammoth success and their follow-up singles did well too.

title for Germany. Dressed in a black dress emblazoned with brightly coloured embroidery, she looked very relaxed as she sang the gentle ballad. Accompanied by a group of four singers dressed all in black and a male mouth organist wearing blue, Lena sang the song of blind Johnny Blue and his love of music. A very catchy song, it gained even more raucous approval once the final strains ended.

Jean-Claude Pascal had won Eurovision for Luxembourg in Cannes back in 1961, and now, 20 years later, he was trying his luck again. This was the longest span for any winner to make a second attempt at the Eurovision prize. Sadly, despite crooning a strong French-language ballad, the debonair, tuxedo-wearing singer seemed somewhat dated. Other returning entrants included the serial Eurovision performers **Peter, Sue and Marc**, marking their fourth appearance singing a melodious, pan-pipe-accompanied ballad in a fourth language, Italian. Also back were Denmark's **Tommy Seebach and Debbie Cameron** who had previously appeared in the 1979 contest in Jerusalem, where Debbie had provided backing vocals for Tommy's 'Disco Tango'. 'Krøller Eller Ej' ('Frizzles Or Not') was another up-tempo disco number that sang of racial unity, highly appropriate for the black (Debbie) and white (Tommy) singers. It was a simple plea to love children, no matter what their racial background or hairstyle. Message songs tend to do well in Eurovision, but this effort was hampered by some very strange and over-the-top choreography that was provided by Debbie in her white-fringed dress and pillbox hat and two anonymous female dancers. Tommy was seated at the keyboard, thus avoiding the frenzy.

Yugoslavia had not been seen in the contest since 1976, and the nation's welcome return this year triggered a much more successful period in the contest than they had previously achieved. This year it was Sarajevo who had won the right to submit the Yugoslav song. Called 'Leila' it was performed by the bearded, husky-voiced **Seid Memić-Vajta**.

Left: Victorious Bucks Fizz came to Dublin as hot favourites, and were riding high in the UK chart. They were certainly regarded as the one to beat, although the media had questioned their vocal ability all week.

Above: Turkey entered a jolly number presented in a stylish manner by the Modern Folk Trio and Aysegül. The trio was considerably older than Aysegül, and there was very little that was 'modern' about them.

Finland went for a very new and radical direction for their entry: reggae! **Riki Sorsa** was the blond Rod Stewart lookalike chosen to sing 'Reggae, OK!'. Dressed in pink and yellow harlequin checks, Riki was as far from a reggae act as it is possible to get. Also trying something new were Belgium, with a disco song performed by a singer wearing a revealing toga, and France who chose the Tahitian heartthrob **Jean Gabilou** to sing a powerful anthem rather than a typical French ballad. Ireland, meanwhile, looked to an all-girl group for the first time. A trio called **Sheeba** shimmied through an upbeat pop number in extremely skimpy, sparkling emerald-green gowns, but they had to settle for fifth place in the voting.

After the shock of the new, Norway could be relied on for consistency and scored 'nul points' with a gentle song strummed on a guitar by a man wearing a blue football shirt.

The United Kingdom was fielding a group formed from extensive auditions. The singers who made the final line-up included former contestant Cheryl Baker, who had done so badly in the contest as a member of Co-Co in 1978. **Bucks Fizz** was formed of four blondes – two boys and two girls – who had been selected more for their appearance than their singing ability, which, as they proved in Dublin, was pretty poor. Their song 'Making Your Mind Up' was a very strong, up-tempo dance number, but what really made it stand out was the choreography. Moves included a hand jive, a real jive in the instrumental break and, the most eye-catching trick of all, the boys ripping the girls' skirts off for the final chorus. This idea had come from their manager, Nichola Martin, who had previously been part of a fairly unsuccessful group called Rags. They had entered the UK's 1977 heat and tried the same trick in their routine. A BBC strike blacked out TV coverage of that contest, so Martin waited until she had the chance to reinstate it as part of Bucks Fizz's routine.

On the night, the group sang way off-key, but had such enthusiasm that the judges overlooked this in favour of the song, which provided the UK with their fourth win in the contest.

Following such an impressive entry is always difficult, but the Portuguese entry wasn't helped by the dress sense

Right: Lena Valaitis wins the German heat. She was one of the pre-contest favourites and had high hopes of securing the title, but was pipped by Bucks Fizz.

Far right: The debonair Jean Gabilou's performance on the night took the French back into the running this year to finish a close-run third.

of **Carlos Paião** who wore a 'fake' tuxedo, painted onto his shirt and a blue plastic jacket, while his four backing singers all wore boiler suits. The band's antics included sticking their microphones in their ears.

Closing the contest was Sweden's **Björn Skifs,** who had also ended the 1978 contest. He hadn't done too well on that occasion, but he gave a strong performance in Dublin and managed to squeak into the top ten with his rock-inspired effort, 'Fångad I En Dröm' ('Caught In A Dream').

After an interval display by the dance troupe Planxty it was time for the voting. The scoring went smoothly until a third of the way through when the hostess **Doireann Ni Bhriain** called Yugoslavia for their scores. There was silence from Belgrade. Doireann repeatedly tried to make contact with the Yugoslav jury but to no avail. Eventually, just as Doireann was about to give up, the Yugoslav announcer, Helga Vlahovic, finally managed to get through to Dublin, but when asked for the scores, snapped: 'I don't have it'. It brought gales of laughter from the audience and later did the rounds of out-takes on many programmes dedicated to

TV blunders. From that point on, the UK held the lead and won, despite only being the top choice of two nations, Israel and the Netherlands.

'Making Your Mind Up' shot to the top of the charts in the UK, where it stayed at number one for three weeks. It was a mammoth success and the group proved it was a force to be reckoned with when its follow-up singles did well, too. By the time of the 1982 contest, they had scored three number ones in the UK alone.

Later that summer, to celebrate 25 years of the contest, the International Red Cross hosted a gala in Norway featuring all but seven of the winners of the contest. Norway hardly seems an appropriate host for such an event, but it was part of an annual open-air gala, which had previously featured such stars as Abba, Vera Lynn, Julie Andrews and Charles Aznavour. It was a very fitting celebration of Eurovision and the Red Cross later released a double album consisting of all the winning songs to commemorate the occasion. The contest appeared to be thriving, but would take an unexpected faltering step in the next edition.

country	song	performer	place	score	draw
United Kingdom	Making Your Mind Up	**Bucks Fizz**	1	136	14
Germany	Johnny Blue	**Lena Valaitis**	2	132	3
France	Humanahum	**Jean Gabilou**	3	125	9
Switzerland	Io Senza Te	**Peter, Sue & Marc**	4	121	19
Ireland	Horoscopes	**Sheeba**	5	105	12
Cyprus	Monica	**Island**	6	69	18
Israel	Ha'laylah	**Habibi**	7	56	5
Greece	Feggari Kalokerino	**Yiannis Dimitrias**	8	55	17
Netherlands	Het Is Een Wonder	**Linda Williams**	9	51	11
Sweden	Fångad I En Dröm	**Björn Skifs**	10	50	20
Luxembourg	C'est Peut-être Pas L'Amérique	**Jean-Claude Pascal**	11=	41	4
Denmark	Krøller Eller Ej	**Tommy Seebach & Debbie Cameron**	11=	41	6
Belgium	Samson	**Emly Starr**	13	40	16
Spain	Y Solo Tu	**Bacchelli**	14	38	10
Yugoslavia	Leila	**Seid Memić-Vajta**	15	35	7
Finland	Reggae OK	**Riki Sorsa**	16	27	8
Austria	Wenn Du Da Bist	**Marty Brem**	17	20	1
Turkey	Donme Dolap	**Modern folk trio & Aysegül**	18=	9	2
Portugal	Playback	**Carlos Paião**	18=	9	15
Norway	Aldri I Livet	**Finn Kalvik**	20	0	13

Winner

Germany

Performer

Nicole

1982

Composers

Bernd Meinunger/
Ralph Siegel

Title

'Ein Bisschen
frieden'

Composers

Bernd Meinunger/
Ralph Siegel

Presenter

Jan Leeming

Host & Venue

BBC
Harrogate Centre

Harrogate
United Kingdom

The BBC announced the venue for the 1982 contest in the summer of 1981, just a few months after Bucks Fizz had secured the UK's fourth victory in Dublin. The chosen venue, the small town of Harrogate in North Yorkshire, was certainly something of a surprise, as it was one of the rare occasions that the contest was held outside of a major city centre.

On a sour note, France announced that it would not be taking part in the twenty-seventh contest, with the main French TV channel, TF1, citing the competition as a 'monument to drivel'. With Italy also staying home for the second year in succession and Greece making a late withdrawal, the future of the contest was in question. Only 18 countries lined up to take part, the lowest number since 1977.

The show opened with an animated sequence answering the question that certainly must have been on the lips of many of the 300 million viewers watching: 'Where is Harrogate?' As the sequence ended, the question was answered and viewers were treated to a lengthy video of traditional Yorkshire sites, including a heavy plug for the local manufacturers of the fabric Crimplene.

The influence of the previous year's winning group, Bucks Fizz, was felt throughout the competition. Clearly, many of the competitors had closely copied the foursome's penchant for slick choreography.

Left to right:
Germany's first winner, Nicole, with writers Bernd Meinunger and Ralph Siegel.

Bill van Dijk's gymnastic choreography garnered only eight points for the Netherlands.

Leather-clad Kojo – keeping the recent run of disasters firmly in the Nordic circle.

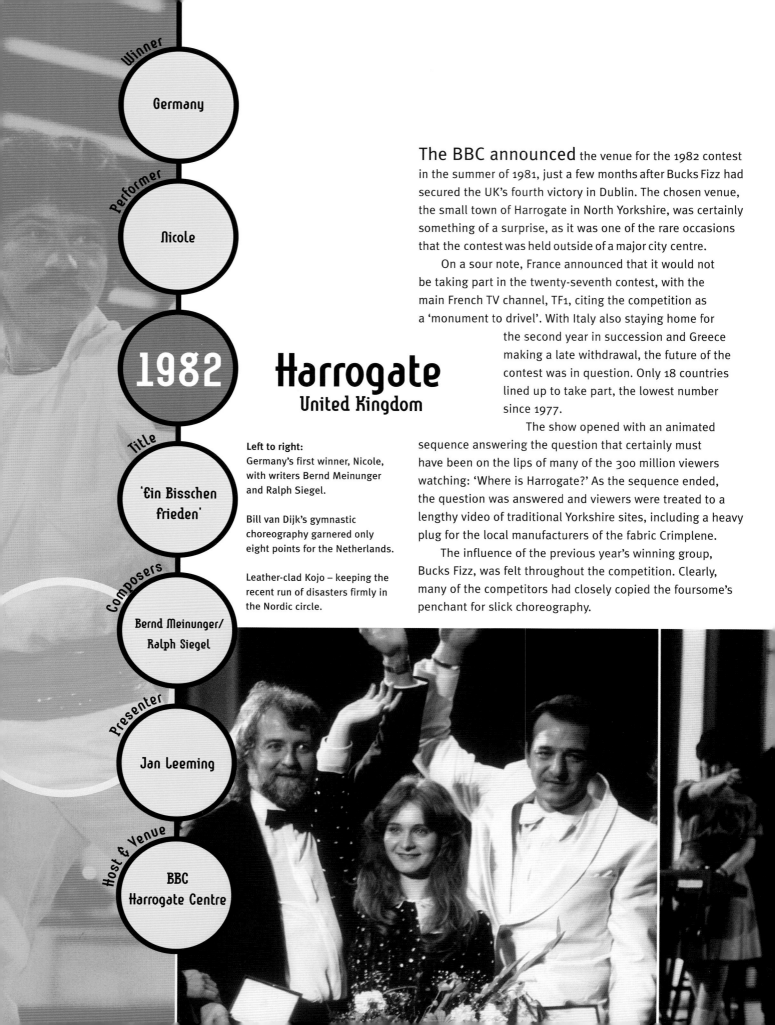

Nicole went on to great chart success throughout Europe and beyond with **'Ein Bisschen Frieden'**. The English version of the song spent two weeks at the top of the UK charts, the third consecutive Eurovision winner to do so, but the first ever that had not been originally performed in English at the contest.

Portugal's **Doce** opened the show. The all-girl group were dressed in sequinned 'cavalier' outfits, highly reminiscent of Adam and the Ants, who were extremely popular at the time. Doce's costumes could have been an attempt to disguise the weakness of their song, which featured numerous repetitions of its title 'Bem Bom', a phrase that was thoughtfully translated into English as 'Bim Bom'. However, worse was to follow.

Following their dismal performance in 1981, Norway been approached by an English academic named René Herail with an offer to help them with their entry. His task was to ascertain the key ingredients of all the previous Eurovision winners and come up with the ultimate formula for Eurovision success. One of his observations was that the harsh Nordic consonants needed to be omitted from the lyrics of the song, and this was achieved with the international sounding title 'Adieu'. It worked – despite

employing two former losers **Jahn Teigen and Anita Skorgan**. As a duet, the luckless Norwegians achieved their best result since 1973!

As in 1977 the United Kingdom chose a duet to follow the winning quartet of the previous year. **Bardo** was made up of children's TV presenter Sally-Ann Triplett, who had sung at Eurovision with Prima Donna in 1980, and singer-actor Stephen Fischer. Like many of the other entrants this year, they were perhaps concentrating too much on their dance routine and not enough on their song. Despite Sally-Ann's prior experience at the competition they turned in a nervy and vocally unsound performance that cost them dearly. For the third time in the show's history, the British ended in seventh place, their worst-ever showing on home ground.

Finland followed a rushed and somewhat breathless Turkish entry. Translated as 'I Slept Too Late' and featuring the cheery line 'Don't drop that neutron bomb on me', the red-leather-clad **Kojo** certainly didn't seem to be taking the job of representing his country too seriously. As he belted out his song, his backing musicians, seemingly dressed as the Blues Brothers, distracted the audience with various items, including a large bass drum that the keyboard-player/drummer continually failed to strike on cue. It was pretty obvious by the time the performance ended that Finland was heading for a very low score, and indeed they were. For the first time since 1963, not one jury could be persuaded that

Finland's song was worthy of a single mark, keeping the recent run of disasters firmly placed in the Nordic area.

Finland had been widely tipped for bottom place, but it was Switzerland that provided probably the biggest surprise of the night when **Arlette Zola** turned in a rousing performance of 'Amour, On T'Aime' ('Love, We Love You'), to finish third. **Anna Vissi**, who had sung for Greece in 1980, returned to the contest, but this time performing for her native Cyprus. Wearing a simple black-and-white dress, Anna performed 'Mono I Agapi' ('Only Love') quite beautifully and certainly appeared to be among the contenders for the title.

Sweden was hotly tipped this year with a duo called **Chips**, whose song was highly reminiscent of Abba's 'Waterloo'. In defence of the Swedes, this was the first time they had even attempted to copy their most successful entry to date and it lifted them up to eighth place, their best showing since their triumph in 1974.

Spain used a dramatic presentation for an otherwise strong entry. As **Lucia** passionately sang the story of 'El' ('Him'), a male dancer repeatedly circled her with passionate and wildly exaggerated dance moves, while another couple tangoed on the other side of the set and made no vocal contribution to the song. Other choreographic nightmares included the Israeli entry. **Avi Toledano** had to perform in the middle of a wildly enthusiastic dance troupe, which was hampered by lack of space on stage and sent their microphones crashing into the audience. Belgium's entrant, a Eurovision veteran named **Stella**, who had sung in both 1970 for the Netherlands and 1977 for Belgium as part of The Hearts of Soul and Dream Express respectively, used a clockwork ballerina as a prop.

Denmark attempted to bring a semblance of 1980s electro-pop to the show, but failed miserably with the judges. Performed by the all-male band called **Brixx**, the lyrics of 'Video Video' told the story of the group's purchase of a video recorder and listed some of the programmes they watched. The list included Björn Borg at Wimbledon, Humphrey Bogart and Prince Charles and Lady Diana's wedding. Naming names is a trick often used in the contest, but it rarely pays off and again this year, the juries were not impressed, giving the song only five points to leave the Danes in seventeenth place. Nor were they particularly pleased with Yugoslavia's effort, which was performed by a female trio called **Aska**. Trying the tried and tested formula of an international greeting, 'Halo, Halo' ('Hello, Hello') was not warmly received, despite the three girls giving it their all and interspersing their lyrics with many 'shoo-be-doo-wahs'.

Far left: Portugal's Doce were certainly a lively opener, but it would not be unfair to suggest that the group had perhaps concentrated a little too much on style and presentation.

Left: As Lucia passionately sang the story of 'El' ('Him'), her male cohort provided the comic highlight of the night. As he tantalised her on stage, she was clearly unaware that he was pulling the most ridiculous faces behind her back.

country	song	performer	place	score	draw
Germany	Ein Bisschen Frieden	**Nicole**	1	161	18
Israel	Hora	**Avi Toledano**	2	100	15
Switzerland	Amour, On T'Aime	**Arlette Zola**	3	97	7
Belgium	Si Tu Aimes Ma Musique	**Stella**	4	96	11
Cyprus	Mono I Agapi	**Anna Vissi**	5	85	8
Luxembourg	Cours Après Le Temps	**Svetlana**	6	78	2
United Kingdom	One Step Further	**Bardo**	7	76	4
Sweden	Dag Efter Dag	**Chips**	8	67	9
Austria	Sonntag	**Mess**	9	57	10
Spain	El	**Lucia**	10	52	12
Ireland	Here Today, Gone Tomorrow	**The Duskeys**	11	49	17
Norway	Adieu	**Jahn Teigen & Anita Skorgan**	12	40	3
Portugal	Bem Bom	**Doce**	13	32	1
Yugoslavia	Halo Halo	**Aska**	14	21	14
Turkey	Hani	**Neco**	15	20	5
Netherlands	Jij En Ik	**Bill van Dijk**	16	8	16
Denmark	Video Video	**Brixx**	17	5	13
Finland	Nuku Pommiin	**Kojo**	18	0	6

By the time Germany's **Nicole** took to the stage for the last song in the contest, it was apparent that the audience and judges alike were still waiting for the one entry that would stand out from all the others. The 18-year-old Nicole did not disappoint them. Her song, 'Ein Bisschen Frieden' ('A Little Peace'), was simple and yet infuriatingly effective. Well-structured and cleverly orchestrated, the young schoolgirl sang perched on her stool with her white guitar to sing the very simple anthem accompanied by a female harpist. It contrasted sharply with some of the choreographic excesses put forward by her challengers. There was never any doubt that Germany had the twenty-seventh contest sewn up. It marked the fourth consecutive year that Bernd Meinunger and Ralph Siegel had composed the German song, and with runners-up credits in the last two contests, they were indeed hungry for victory. Pleas for peace, harmony and brotherly love among different people and nations had long been a popular theme in the contest, but this was the first time that anyone had got the necessary ingredients of a winning entry down so perfectly. The audience showed their appreciation with lengthy applause at the song's conclusion.

At first during the voting, it appeared the juries were swayed by a number of different entries and the first four countries all picked different songs as their favourites. But once Turkey gave the Germans their second 'douze points' of the night, there was no stopping Nicole, who became the nineteenth female soloist to take the Eurovision title and the sixth to be known by only a single name. It was the first victory for Germany in the contest and only the second winner so far to be sung in the German language.

To close the show, Nicole reprised her winning song, singing the victorious number in German, English, French and Dutch – a move that helped register the song in the minds of the record-buying public around the continent. She went on to great chart success throughout Europe and beyond with the winning entry. The English version of the song, 'A Little Peace', spent two weeks at the top of the UK charts. Her popularity continued in Germany for some time to come and she has repeatedly featured as a commentator for German TV at subsequent contests.

Siegel and Meinunger continued to write songs for the competition and have become Eurovision's most prolific songwriting team. Their 1982 winner was itself the target of a plagiarism charge, which ended in the German courts with defeat for the Eurovision winners. But this was only a small blight on Germany's victory, which would bring the next year's contest back to the republic for the first time since 1957.

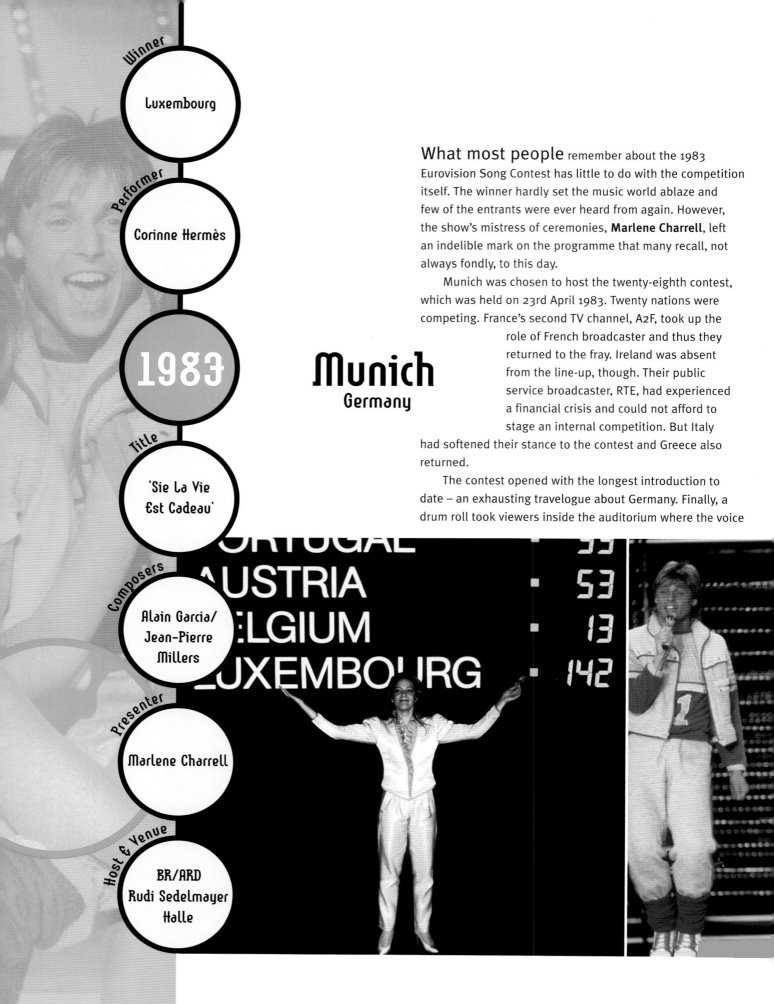

Winner

Luxembourg

Performer

Corinne Hermès

1983

Title

'Sie La Vie Est Cadeau'

Composers

Alain Garcia/
Jean-Pierre
Millers

Presenter

Marlene Charrell

Host & Venue

BR/ARD
Rudi Sedelmayer
Halle

Munich
Germany

What most people remember about the 1983 Eurovision Song Contest has little to do with the competition itself. The winner hardly set the music world ablaze and few of the entrants were ever heard from again. However, the show's mistress of ceremonies, **Marlene Charrell**, left an indelible mark on the programme that many recall, not always fondly, to this day.

Munich was chosen to host the twenty-eighth contest, which was held on 23rd April 1983. Twenty nations were competing. France's second TV channel, A2F, took up the role of French broadcaster and thus they returned to the fray. Ireland was absent from the line-up, though. Their public service broadcaster, RTE, had experienced a financial crisis and could not afford to stage an internal competition. But Italy had softened their stance to the contest and Greece also returned.

The contest opened with the longest introduction to date – an exhausting travelogue about Germany. Finally, a drum roll took viewers inside the auditorium where the voice of the aforementioned Ms Charrell welcomed everyone in German, English and French. Her next duty was to introduce every competing team and one by one the artists taking part ran up the stairs of the huge set. The stage soon became very crowded, but this opening was one of the more spectacular starts to the competition. Charrell was speaking in three languages throughout, but as she made her opening remarks it became clear that, although she was fairly belting out her German and English pronouncements, she was sexily whispering the French version in a deep, husky tone. Sadly, it was a sign of things to come. It isn't entirely unfair to speculate that Charrell may have missed the point of the Eurovision Song Contest, and was somehow under the misapprehension that it was her show and that the songs and voting were an irritating intrusion into her airtime. Atlong last, after the lengthy multi-lingual welcome ended, the competition was ready to begin.

Some 15 minutes into the show France's **Guy Bonnet** performed the first entry. It was Bonnet's third attempt at winning the coveted prize. He had written the French entry in 1968, which finished third, and he performed his own song

in 1970, which ended up a respectable fourth. His song 'Vivre' ('Live') had the same title as the 1978 Swiss entry. This was the very first time that two entries had ever shared exactly the same title and spelling. Norway followed with **Jahn Teigen** also making his third appearance. His song, 'Do-Re-Mi', was a simple ditty based on the musical alphabet. It was well received and nicely performed by Teigen and his four uncredited female backing singers, one of which was his wife, Anita Skorgan. In her introduction, Marlene Charrell was clearly already flagging under the sheer weight of her responsibilities and forgot the name of the song's conductor. After a painful pause, she blurted out 'Johannes Skorgan'. Sigurd Jansen, who was actually waving the baton, grinned widely as he took the podium.

Dressed in grey tracksuits trimmed in primary colours, the United Kingdom's group, **Sweet Dreams**, performed seated on stools. Thankfully, they were using wireless radio microphones so didn't repeat their mishap from the UK heat, when their microphone leads became entangled in their chair legs. Sadly, the performance by the winsome trio could only be described as trite at best.

Corinne Hermès did not achieve great commercial success with '**Si La Vie Est Cadeau**'. She recorded German and English versions and did make the Dutch and Swedish Top 20, but failed to chart at all in the UK. This began an era of lack of widespread success for Eurovision winners.

Far left: Corinne Hermès' victory was expected, but the voting was tense and it was only towards the end that she pulled away from the pack, while the voting itself was not helped by Marlene Charrell announcing each score in three languages.

Left: UK trio Sweet Dreams, featuring Carrie Grant (centre), now famous in the UK as one of the resident vocal coaches on TV talent shows *Pop Idol* and *Fame Academy*.

Sweden fielded the youngest competitor of the evening, 16-year-old **Carola Häggkvist**. Carola had a strong entry that she performed with great gusto. It was warmly received by both the audience and the judges, despite its poor slot in the contest – like position number two, no song performed fourth had yet won the competition.

Turkey performed the most interesting song of the night, even if it was destined to be snubbed by the juries. **Cetin Alp And The Short Waves** were dressed in an assortment of dramatic costumes that were clearly intended to highlight Turkey's song title, 'Opera'. It was a bizarre mix of musical styles, too. Starting as a ballad, it moved on to Dixieland, which was followed by a couple of operatic choruses, before it rose to a dramatic climax. In fairness, it was a brave attempt to circumnavigate the rule of singing in native tongue, something other countries had tried many other times. It was also terrible.

Yugoslavia enjoyed its most successful contest to date. **Daniel**, half Belgian, half Montenegrin and singing for Montenegro, he performed a rousing rock and roll number called 'Džuli' ('Julie') to wild applause from the audience. His performance was helped enormously by two young ladies who danced feverishly throughout the song in tiny miniskirts. Although finishing fourth with 125 points, it was the best yet showing by a Yugoslav entry and the song became the biggest seller of the 1983 entries.

The Germans had taken quite a different direction after their winning entry the year before. Two brothers, Gunther and Michael Hoffmann, known as **Hoffmann and Hoffmann**, and their backing band had entered a catchy and memorable ballad that was much stronger than most of the other entries on show. However, the rather casual presentation by the home team may not have helped their cause and, despite the song's commercial success and early strong showing in the voting, the host nation eventually finished in fifth place.

Israel's **Ofra Haza** went on to become one of the most successful artists to emerge from Eurovision in the 1980s. She enjoyed many international hits and shortly before her death from an AIDS-related illness in February 2000 she recorded the soundtrack for Disney's *Prince Of Egypt*. She was a very strong contender for the 1983 Eurovision title. As with most Israeli songs of the time, the singer was presented in a white outfit while her backing singers and dancers

country	song	performer	place	score	draw
Luxembourg	Si La Vie Est Cadeau	**Corinne Hermès**	1	142	20
Israel	Hi	**Ofra Haza**	2	136	16
Sweden	Främling	**Carola**	3	126	4
Yugoslavia	Džuli	**Daniel**	4	125	12
Germany	Rücksicht	**Hoffmann & Hoffmann**	5	94	14
United Kingdom	I'm Never Giving Up	**Sweet Dreams**	6	79	3
Netherlands	Sing Me A Song	**Bernadette**	7	66	11
France	Vivre	**Guy Bonnet**	8	56	1
Norway	Do Re Mi	**Jahn Teigen**	9=	53	2
Austria	Hurricane	**Westend**	9=	53	18
Italy	Per Lucia	**Riccardo Fogli**	11=	41	5
Finland	Fantasiaa	**Ami Aspelund**	11=	41	9
Portugal	Esta Balada Que Te Dou	**Armando Gama**	13	33	17
Greece	Mou Les	**Christie Stassinopolou**	14	32	10
Switzerland	Io Cosi Non Ci Sto	**Mariella Farré**	15	28	8
Cyprus	I Agapi Akoma Zi	**Stavros Sideras & Constantina**	16	26	13
Denmark	Kloden Drejer	**Gry Johansen**	17	16	15
Belgium	Rendez-vous	**Pas de Deux**	18	13	19
Turkey	Opera	**Cetin Alp & The Shortwaves**	19=	0	6
Spain	Quién Maneja Mi Barca	**Remedios Amaya**	19=	0	7

appeared in bright yellows and reds. Again, the song, 'Hi', was probably strong and catchy enough not to warrant such over-exuberant choreography. And there was much more to it: 'Hi' means 'Alive', and the refrain 'Am Israel hi' translates as 'Israel still exists'. And performed in Munich where Hitler's career started and where the Olympic massacre took place in 1975, Israel's entry was highly symbolic.

After over two hours, longer than the entire 1982 broadcast, the final song rolled around. **Corinne Hermès** had been the bookies' and pundits' favourite before the contest, and she let nobody down on the night. It was a flawless performance of a very strong ballad, very much of the style that had dominated the first 20 years of the competition. Dressed all in pink, with very pale green eyes, Hermès was visually as stunning as her powerful voice. She was indeed the entry to beat and, ultimately, nobody could.

In many ways 'Si La Vie Est Cadeau' ('If Life Is A Gift') was a final hurrah for the French-dominated contests of the 1960s and 1970s. Only two French-language songs have won since; Luxembourg has not been seen in the contest since 1993 and Monaco's long absence began in 1979 and didn't end until 2004. The French themselves are still without a win since 1977.

Marlene Charrell returned to the main stage to describe the voting and introduce the interval act – 'The Song Contest Ballet' – which, she revealed, featured herself in a key role. Based around the orchestral delights of many well-known German songs and international hits, Marlene flung off her long skirt to reveal a shorter version beneath that allowed her the freedom to trip the light fantastic alongside her fellow dancers. It was another lengthy presentation, but viewers at home were probably very thankful that, as it was only music and dance, this one didn't have to be repeated in three languages.

By winning the competition, Luxembourg tied with France for the most number of victories in total, five. Since the French total actually included one shared victory, the Grand Duchy was thus the first country to win five titles outright, a record only bettered by Ireland in 1994. Corinne was the twentieth female soloist to win the contest, although her backing singers of three men and two ladies certainly played a part in the proceedings.

Thankfully, RTL in Luxembourg made much shorter work of the twenty-ninth contest when the show returned to the Grand Duchy for the fourth and last time in 1984.

Israel's Ofra Haza was a very strong contender for the Eurovision title this year, and she went on from the competition to great stardom in Europe and the US.

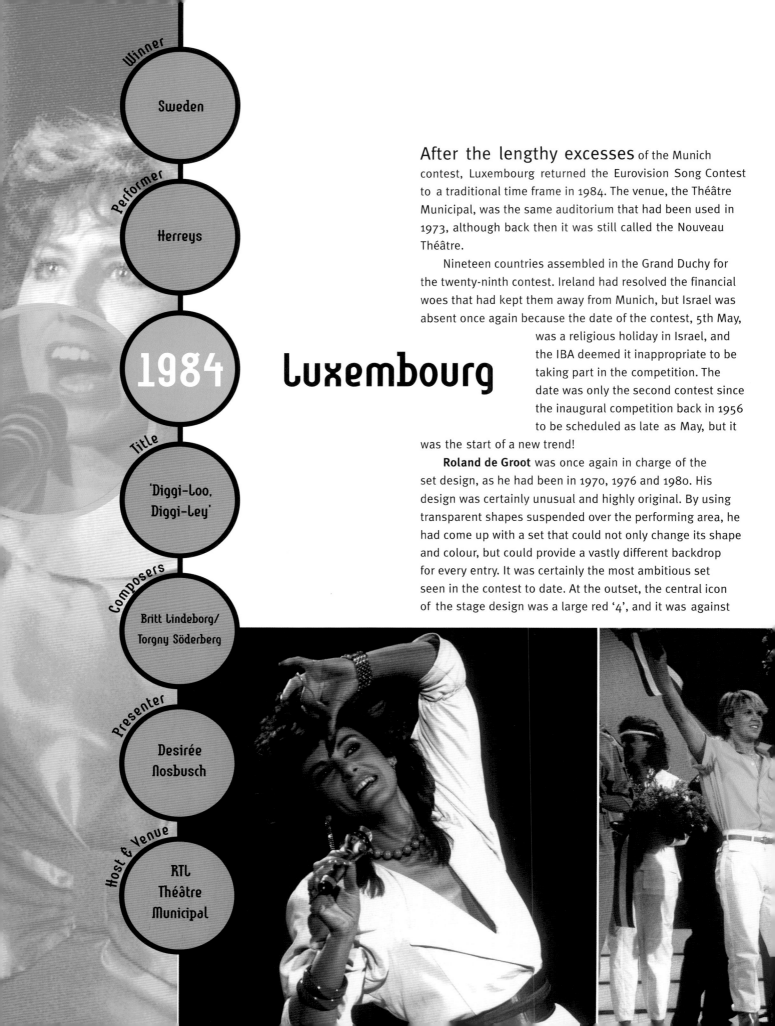

Winner

Sweden

Performer

Herreys

1984

Title

'Diggi-Loo,
Diggi-Ley'

Composers

Britt Lindeborg/
Torgny Söderberg

Presenter

Desirée
Nosbusch

Host & Venue

RTL
Théâtre
Municipal

Luxembourg

After the lengthy excesses of the Munich contest, Luxembourg returned the Eurovision Song Contest to a traditional time frame in 1984. The venue, the Théâtre Municipal, was the same auditorium that had been used in 1973, although back then it was still called the Nouveau Théâtre.

Nineteen countries assembled in the Grand Duchy for the twenty-ninth contest. Ireland had resolved the financial woes that had kept them away from Munich, but Israel was absent once again because the date of the contest, 5th May, was a religious holiday in Israel, and the IBA deemed it inappropriate to be taking part in the competition. The date was only the second contest since the inaugural competition back in 1956 to be scheduled as late as May, but it was the start of a new trend!

Roland de Groot was once again in charge of the set design, as he had been in 1970, 1976 and 1980. His design was certainly unusual and highly original. By using transparent shapes suspended over the performing area, he had come up with a set that could not only change its shape and colour, but could provide a vastly different backdrop for every entry. It was certainly the most ambitious set seen in the contest to date. At the outset, the central icon of the stage design was a large red '4', and it was against this backdrop that hostess **Desirée Nosbusch**, at 19 the youngest ever Eurovision presenter, made her entrance.

For the very first time, Sweden had been drawn in the opening spot. It was represented by a trio of brothers, Richard, Louis and Per Herrey, that called itself **Herreys**. Before they took the stage, the show's producers showed viewers a short video featuring 'The Tourists', a motley crew of actors who were superimposed into video graphic segments showing the tourist high spots of the competing nations. There was a certain amount of tongue-in-cheek humour at the expense of each nation and Sweden's video highlighted the nation's links with the sea, ending with a yellow submarine metamorphosing into a can of smoked fish! It was certainly bizarre, but it proved to be a highly memorable and often extremely amusing approach to the age-old question, 'What do we do in between the songs?'

The Herreys performed their song 'Diggi-Loo Diggi-Ley' with great enthusiasm. A very slick dance routine and bold shirts in primary colours left a memorable image with the judges. Their golden boots are less fondly recalled, but they certainly had worked hard at kicking the show off to a dynamic start. Lyrically, the song was one of the weakest of the night, but the tempo, orchestration and vocals, coupled with the strong presentation, clearly indicated that this was a song that the others had to beat.

Luxembourg, despite being the clear favourite with the

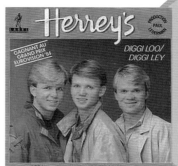

'Diggi-Loo Diggi-Ley' was not a huge commercial success. It charted in the UK, but failed to break into the Top 40. It fared better at home, where it reached No. 2; it also hit the Dutch Top 5.

bookmakers, were not going to provide any competition. Quite simply, young **Sophie Carle** could not sing. Added to the already disadvantageous position of singing second, Carle's performance was one of the worst of the night, although the song still attracted enough support to finish tenth. France followed next, and contrasted starkly with a very strong performer called **Annick Thoumazeau**.

After the improved performances of the Norwegians since their 'nul points' of 1981, **Dollie Deluxe** disappointed with their song 'Lenge Leve Livet' ('Long Live Life'). Dressed in white, red and black, the most popular colour scheme for winning songs, the two writers of the song, Ingrid Bjornov and Benedicte Adrian, who made up **Dollie Deluxe**, provided a modern look to accompany their tune. But it lacked that vital spark and was only deemed worthy of 29 points, leaving Norway in seventeenth place out of the 19 entries.

The most controversial performance of the night, and quite possibly in the history of the contest, came from the United Kingdom. Britain as a nation was not exactly popular in the Grand Duchy, thanks to a particularly shocking piece of soccer hooliganism the previous autumn, when English football fans had run riot in the Luxembourg capital and caused untold damage to the city. Against this backdrop, the three girls who called themselves **Belle And The Devotions** were unlikely to receive the warmest of welcomes to the contest, despite a cheery song that borrowed heavily from the Motown songbook. Dressed in shockingly coloured, dayglo plastic mini-skirts, with each member of the group sporting hair coloured in a different luminous hue, the group were certainly somewhat striking. It wasn't until after the contest that it emerged that they were barely a group at all! Kit Rolfe, aka Belle, was in fact the primary focus of the trio. Her cohorts, Linda Sofield and Laura James, The Devotions, had been recruited more for their dancing ability than anything else. Three other girls, who were never seen by the

Far left: Flame-haired Linda Martin had sparked quite an interest in the Irish media. Indeed, the bible of the Irish music scene, *Hot Press*, had been in hot pursuit of their representative throughout the Eurovision week.

Left: The golden-booted Herreys: Richard, Louis and Per.

viewers, actually performed most of the backing vocals. This caused a few problems for the BBC. Naturally, the backing trio wanted to be seen supporting their nation's entry, but since it would have been obvious that they were doing the majority – if not all – of the actual singing, they were kept off camera. The BBC maintained this was because one of the three was pregnant, but why this would mean they could not be filmed is a mystery.

When the UK's off-key presentation was over, loud boos and jeers were heard coming from the audience. It was the first time a song has ever been heckled from the stage in the history of the Eurovision Song Contest.

Having taken a break from the contest in 1983, and having performed less than satisfactorily in 1982, Ireland had turned to Johnny Logan, the singer of its last winning entry, to write the Emerald Isle's 1984 offering. Performed by **Linda Martin**, 'Terminal Three' was an upbeat number with a strong melody, but it couldn't deflect attention away from Martin's flaming red locks and white leather outfit.

Yugoslavia stirred up controversy when they submitted the video of 'Ciao Amore' for the preview programmes.

Izolda and Vlado were seen skinny-dipping in the video clip and certainly both appeared to be topless. But they failed to live up to expectations and turned in a tame performance.

Two of the three German-language entries followed each other. **Anita**, a secretary who had been catapulted to the top of the Austrian charts, looked very pretty in pink, but despite having one of the more original melodies and tempos of the night, with heavy country influences, she was destined to end up at the bottom of the scoreboard with only five points. Germany also fared badly, but certainly did better than its neighbours. **Mary Roos** was back in the contest, 12 years after finishing third in Edinburgh. Her song was dramatically orchestrated, but somehow, like so many others on the night, it seemed to be lacking the punch it had shown in the heats.

Turkey had put something of an effort into its entry after scoring 'nul points' the previous year and the foursome **Bes Yil Önce On Yil Sonra** performed very well indeed to lift their nation up to twelfth place, its best position to date.

Italy provided the penultimate act of the night. **Alice and Franco Battiato** were possibly the classiest entry of

Right: In her second shot at representing her country, Maribelle sings at the Dutch final in Hilversum, this time going through. Maribelle and her sisters entertained the contest delegates throughout the week's rehearsals with imported smoked eel, a Dutch delicacy. Unfortunately, the judges were not overwhelmed by the stories of the singer's hospitality, and the gentle ballad was not highly regarded.

the evening and recovered from fluffing their opening lines to perform well, accompanied by a trio of operatic singers dressed in the colours of the Italian flag. It was certainly all very impressive, but it was perhaps a little too sophisticated for the Eurovision jurors.

Maria Guinot ended the presentation of the 19 songs with her effort for Portugal. She gave a somewhat stilted performance seated behind a grand piano with a single backing singer joining her on stage. It was one of the weakest endings to the contest seen in recent years and scored only 38 points, placing Guinot in eleventh position.

The voting was very smooth and with only Portugal left to vote, the Herreys brothers led Linda Martin by only six points. Sadly, the Portuguese did not prolong the tension for long, when they awarded Ireland just two points, ending the speculation that they might overturn the leader. The contrary Portuguese then only awarded four points to the Swedes, saving their top marks for neighbours, Spain. For the first time since 1980, all the nations participating managed to achieve a score, with Austria the lowest ranked at only five points.

Desirée Nosbusch wished the viewers good night, adding to the confusion on the stage by stating that she would see viewers again at the same time next week. Presumably nobody had told her that the Eurovision Song Contest is an annual event!

At only two hours and five minutes long, this was the shortest contest since 1974, and one that set new standards in set design and video production. Although some of the videos used to introduce the songs were certainly bizarre, they were all very well made and well thought out.

By contrast, the winning song itself has unfortunately, in some quarters, become something of a byword for bad Eurovision winners, and it is certainly not unheard of for 'Diggi-Loo Diggi-Ley' to be listed as one of the worst winners, if not entries, of all time. Certainly, Herreys were unable to follow Abba into the popular music history books, but it did at last take the Swedes out from under the super group's shadow, and prove that 'Waterloo' was not the only Swedish entry capable of taking the Grand Prix at Eurovision.

country	song	performer	place	score	draw
Sweden	Diggi-Loo Diggi-Ley	**Herreys**	1	145	1
Ireland	Terminal Three	**Linda Martin**	2	137	9
Spain	Lady Lady	**Bravo**	3	106	4
Denmark	Det Lige Det	**Hot Eyes**	4	101	10
Belgium	Avanti La Vie	**Jacques Zégers**	5=	70	8
Italy	I Treni Di Tozeur	**Alice & Franco Battiato**	5=	70	18
United Kingdom	Love Games	**Belle & The Devotions**	7	63	6
France	Autant D'Amoureux Que D'Etoiles	**Annick Thoumazeau**	8	61	3
Finland	Hengaillaan	**Kirka**	9	46	16
Luxembourg	100% D'Amour	**Sophie Carle**	10	39	2
Portugal	Silencio E Tanta Gente	**Maria Guinot**	11	38	19
Turkey	Halay	**Bes Yil Önce On Yil Sonra**	12	37	15
Netherlands	Ik Hou Van Jou	**Maribelle**	13=	34	11
Germany	Aufrecht G'hen	**Mary Roos**	13=	34	14
Cyprus	Anna-Mari Elena	**Andy Paul**	15	31	7
Switzerland	Welche Farbe Hat Der Sonnenschein	**Rainy Day**	16	30	17
Norway	Lenge Leve Livet	**Dollie Deluxe**	17	29	5
Yugoslavia	Ciao Amore	**Izolda & Vlado**	18	26	12
Austria	Einfach Weg	**Anita**	19	5	13

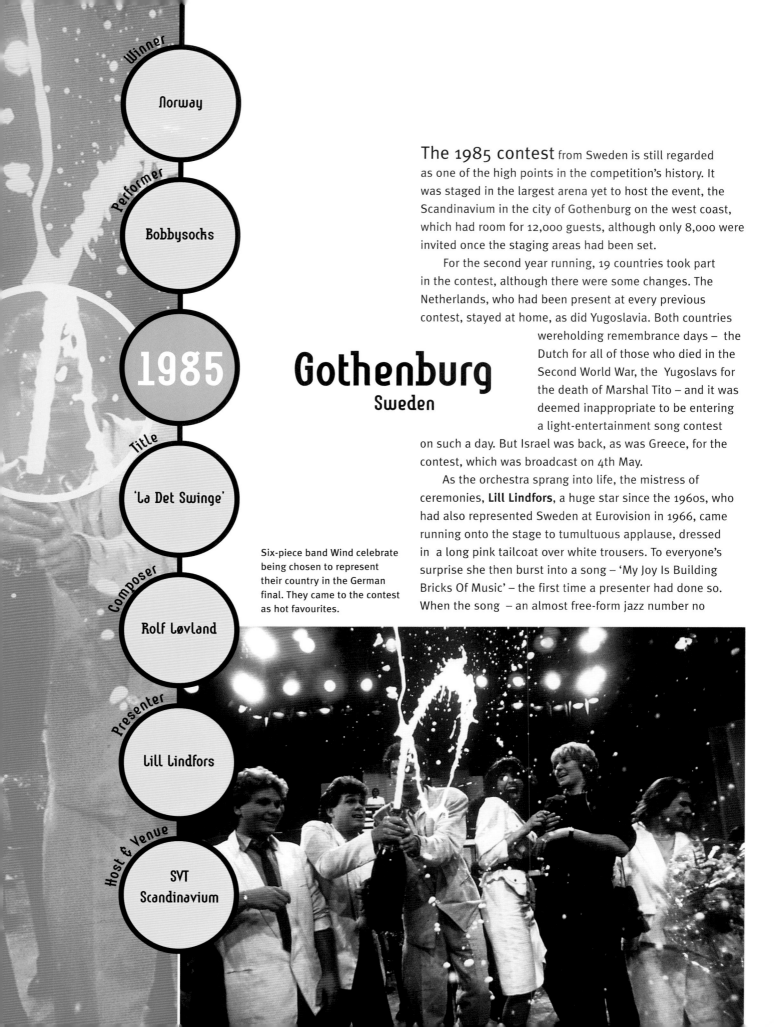

Winner
Norway

Performer
Bobbysocks

1985

Title
'La Det Swinge'

Composer
Rolf Løvland

Presenter
Lill Lindfors

Host & Venue
SVT Scandinavium

Gothenburg
Sweden

The 1985 contest from Sweden is still regarded as one of the high points in the competition's history. It was staged in the largest arena yet to host the event, the Scandinavium in the city of Gothenburg on the west coast, which had room for 12,000 guests, although only 8,000 were invited once the staging areas had been set.

For the second year running, 19 countries took part in the contest, although there were some changes. The Netherlands, who had been present at every previous contest, stayed at home, as did Yugoslavia. Both countries wereholding remembrance days – the Dutch for all of those who died in the Second World War, the Yugoslavs for the death of Marshal Tito – and it was deemed inappropriate to be entering a light-entertainment song contest on such a day. But Israel was back, as was Greece, for the contest, which was broadcast on 4th May.

As the orchestra sprang into life, the mistress of ceremonies, **Lill Lindfors**, a huge star since the 1960s, who had also represented Sweden at Eurovision in 1966, came running onto the stage to tumultuous applause, dressed in a long pink tailcoat over white trousers. To everyone's surprise she then burst into a song – 'My Joy Is Building Bricks Of Music' – the first time a presenter had done so. When the song – an almost free-form jazz number no

Six-piece band Wind celebrate being chosen to represent their country in the German final. They came to the contest as hot favourites.

Am Anfang der Zeit. . . . .
Sehnsucht nach einem Gefühl. . . .
Du bist da . . . .
Also lebe ich . . . .
Für alle. . . . .
Die Glocken von Rom. . . . .
Solang wir träumen, leben wir . . . .
König und Dame. . . . .
Hier, da und überall . . . .
Kinder der Erde . . . .
Grün, Grün . . . .

'La Det Swinge' topped the Norwegian charts and did well in other parts of Scandinavia and the rest of Europe. The English version of the song charted in the UK, but did not break the Top 40. However, this was to be the penultimate Eurovision winner to enter the UK charts until 1992.

This was the first of three wins for the group Wind at the German final. Wind underwent many personnel changes, but they were back to represent their country in the contest in 1987 and again in 1992.

less – ended, Lindfors began the business of welcoming the viewers to Sweden.

In keeping with the arena the set was vast. Pink seemed to be the dominant colour of the stage, and there were all sorts of spheres, palm fronds and trellis flats dotted around the performers' platforms. Lighting enhanced the set to create different effects for each performance and its sheer size allowed the director to place the contenders on different parts of the stage.

As the show was about to begin, Lindfors informed viewers that shots of the writers and composers, filmed in various locations around Gothenburg, would precede each song. It was in such a setting that viewers now saw the composer of Ireland's song, Brendan Graham, jogging around the harbour in his patriotically green tracksuit. The Irish entrant **Maria Christian**, who wore a pale blue strapless gown, had generated much pre-contest publicity after winning her heat, as she suffered from a rare disease that was slowly turning her blind. It was Graham's second attempt to win the contest, his first composition having finished tenth back in 1976. Maria scored better with his 1985 entry, to end the night in sixth place, but she was never really in contention. Graham would have to wait until 1994 to finally win the contest.

The Danes were back with another song from Kirsten and Søren, aka **Hot Eyes**, who had done so well in 1984. It was a rather bizarre presentation, featuring the evening's

youngest performer – Søren's very young daughter whose job was to remove articles of clothing from the backing singers and put them on herself. In a year when Scandinavian countries did particularly well in the voting, the Danes rather let the side down.

Another disappointment was Spain's entry, which was written by Juan Caldos Calderon, who had penned the hugely successful 1973 entry 'Eres Tu'. The singer was **Paloma San Basilio**, who, if not the best performer in the contest, was certainly the most glamorous. Indeed, her silver gown alone was reputed to have cost £1,400. It was a well-structured song of great quality but, despite all the pre-contest chatter, it never attracted much support from the juries and finished in a very disappointing fourteenth place.

France was also left in the cold by the judges with a lushly arranged song that was performed by the darkly handsome **Roger Bens**. Maybe it was the singer's irritating habit of licking his lips after each line that put them off.

Turkey sent along three guys by the names of **Mazhar, Fuat and Özkan**, who together were collectively known as MFO and were obviously attempting to replicate last year's winning trio with their phonetic ditty 'Didai Didai Dai'. Dressed in white suits, with blue shirts and white trilbies, the song was very well presented, even though, like so many other Turkish entries, it was not widely appreciated among the judges.

Lill Lindfors loses her skirt in a pre-arranged accident. Apparently, scrutineer Frank Naef was not too amused, and Mrs Naef was reportedly shocked at the stunt.

One of the most emotionally charged songs of the night was from **Adelaide** of Portugal. At the end of the performance, she sank to her knees and buried her head. She remained in this position, with her shoulders shaking, until the next 'postcard' introduced the German song. It certainly appeared that Adelaide was overcome either with emotion or disappointment with how she had acquitted herself. At any rate, she finished second to last with nine points.

Germany had been the hottest of hot favourites for the title long before the contest began. By the day of the competition, bookmakers were only offering odds against them winning! The six-piece band called **Wind** turned in a great performance and there was no reason to think they would not go all the way. The only glitch seemed to be when the group lined up to take their bows. The enthusiastic percussionist could not find a place in the line-up and, despite his best and rather frantic efforts, he finally had to settle for standing behind the rest of the group.

When Norway's entry took to the stage, the primarily Swedish audience erupted into huge cheers. Hanne Krogh, a veteran of the 1971 contest, and Elisabeth Andreasson, aka **Bobbysocks**, ran onto the stage at full throttle dressed in black with pink sequinned jackets. They turned in a tremendously enthusiastic performance, without ever going over the top. Accompanied by a vocal trio and the composer Rolf Løvland on piano, they gave a flawless performance of a very Abba-esque song 'La Det Swinge' ('Let It Swing') to receive the biggest reception of the night.

The British entrant **Vikki** appeared on stage with a white-painted chair, a prop she had picked up at a second-hand store back in England. Her gentle song was not expected to do well, despite its catchy chorus, but it contrasted well with the exuberance of the Norwegian entry and picked up marks from all but one jury, although it wasn't the top choice of any, to end up in fourth place.

Kikki Danielsson, the host nation's entrant, was joined on stage by two dancers who were dressed to resemble Michael Jackson. The dancers threw themselves into their carefully rehearsed routine, but the song was probably strong enough in itself not to warrant their participation and it's perhaps possible that they had a negative rather

country	song	performer	place	score	draw
Norway	La Det Swinge	**Bobbysocks**	1	123	13
Germany	Fur Alle	**Wind**	2	105	10
Sweden	Bra Vibrationer	**Kikki Danielsson**	3	103	16
United Kingdom	Love Is	**Vikki**	4	100	14
Israel	Olé Olé	**Izhar Cohen**	5	93	11
Ireland	Wait Until The Weekend Comes	**Maria Christian**	6	91	1
Italy	Magic Oh Magic	**Al Bano & Romina Power**	7	78	12
Austria	Kinder Dieser Welt	**Gary Lux**	8	60	17
Finland	Eläköön Elämä	**Sonja Lumme**	9	58	2
France	Femme Dans Ses Rêves Aussi	**Roger Bens**	10	56	5
Denmark	Sku' Du Spør Fra No'en	**Hot Eyes**	11	41	4
Switzerland	Piano Piano	**Mariella Farre & Pino Gasparini**	12	39	15
Luxembourg	Children Kinder Enfants	**Margo, Franck Olivier, Chris Roberts, Malcolm Roberts, Ireen Sheer & Diane Solomon**	13	37	18
Spain	La Fiesta Terminó	**Paloma San Basilio**	14=	36	6
Turkey	Didai Didai Dai	**MFÖ**	14=	36	7
Cyprus	To Katalava Arga	**Lia Vissi Pilouri**	16=	15	3
Greece	Miazoume	**Takis Biniaris**	16=	15	19
Portugal	Penso Em Ti, Eu Sei	**Adelaide**	18	9	9
Belgium	Laat Me Nu Gaan	**Linda Lepomme**	19	7	8

than a positive effect on the judges.

The blond Greek, **Takis Biniaris,** ended the thirtieth anniversary contest. Often the last performed song has done remarkably well in the contest, but Greece could not take advantage of the draw this year. It was a weak ending to the competition and not even the Cypriots could muster maximum support for the song.

With all of the performances completed, Lill Lindfors returned to the stage from a side staircase, sporting a long green dress. As she stepped out onto the platform, she contrived to catch the skirt on some protuberance, and it ripped away from the top, revealing her long lithe legs. The audience was stunned as she did her best to cover her modesty. But she then proceeded to unwrap the top section of the dress to reveal a long white gown that slid to its full floor-length.

It was one of the most amusing moments in the history of the contest and deserved all the applause it received from the now laughing audience. As she took her seat next to the scoreboard, she remarked, 'I just wanted to wake you all up a little!'

Norway's Bobbysocks won the competition, albeit with the lowest score ever recorded for a winning song under the current voting system. The audience's enthusiasm was enormous, and a casual viewer could almost have though it was the home team that had emerged victorious! Wild celebrations followed as last year's winners, the Herreys brothers, danced with their successors. Lindfors congratulated them both, adding that she felt they 'really deserved this, because Norway has been last on so many times!' It was a remarkable win, coming only four years after their last 'nul points'.

The 1985 contest was a huge success for Swedish TV. Lill Lindfors is often cited as the fans' favourite presenter, and Norway was one of the most popular winners in the competition's history, emotionally if not commercially. Having waited so long and suffered so many humiliating, ignominious defeats along the way, Norway now got to host the contest for the first time.

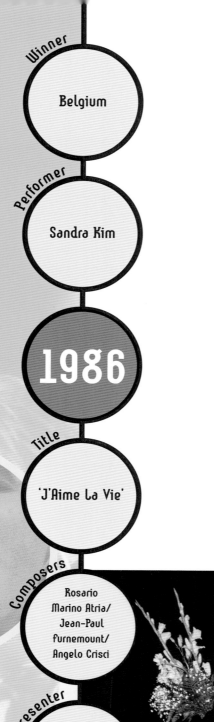

Winner

Belgium

Performer

Sandra Kim

1986

Title

'J'Aime La Vie'

Composers

Rosario Marino Atria/ Jean-Paul Furnemount/ Angelo Crisci

Presenter

Åse Kleveland

Host & Venue

NRK Grieghalle

The line-up of nations was once again different from the year before, with a record-equalling 20 nations opting to take part in the thirty-first Eurovision Song Contest on 3rd May 1986. Greece and Italy had once again taken a year off from the contest, but the Netherlands and Yugoslavia returned to the competition after their one-year break and Iceland was making its debut, the first newcomer to compete since Cyprus in 1981 and the last until 1993.

Bergen
Norway

The venue for the thirty-first contest was the Grieghalle in Norway's second city of Bergen, the birthplace of Norway's most prolific classical composer, Edvard Grieg. Norway had waited a long time to stage the Eurovision Song Contest. Since their first entry in 1960, they had only once been within stalking distance of the prize – a third place in 1966 – before Bobbysocks finally pulled off a notable win in 1985. It was therefore not inappropriate that the performer responsible for that previous worthy achievement was invited to act as compère for the 1986 contest. So Norway's icon from the 1960s, **Åse Kleveland** – who later that year was named as a candidate for the nation's Minister of Culture by the newly elected Prime Minister – followed in the footsteps of her fellow

contestant Lill Lindfors. Like her Swedish counterpart the year before, Kleveland began by singing her introduction to the contest. Using multi-lingual greetings she ended her brief semi-operatic piece with one of the most cringe-worthy efforts in the history of the contest. To the tune of the 'Te Deum', she sang 'Soon we will know who'll be the best, in the Eurovision Song Contest.' Ouch!

The French entry had a good pedigree, as it was written by Eurovision's most prolific performers, Michel and George Costas. The two brothers had sung for more entries and for more countries (six), than any other artists, albeit always as unnamed backing singers. But their song, performed by four ladies called **Cocktail Chic**, was merely an unimaginative list of European cities and people, such as Boy George and Lady Diana. France has rarely entered songs in the typical Eurovision mould and whenever they have it has usually ended in disaster. This year was no different.

The host country had courted controversy with their entry. **Ketil Stokkan** appeared with two dancers dressed in costumes resembling the French fashions of Marie Antoinette, complete with heavy make-up and white powdered wigs. However, one of the 'female' dancers was in fact a man and the act was part of a well-known drag show.

Ketil himself was somewhat soberly dressed by comparison in a bright pink suit. The contest has always attracted a huge gay following and many of the performers have been openly so, but this was the first example of any cross-gender performers, although by no means the last! 'Romeo' was a catchy number but it was not a groundbreaking effort.

Among the many entries by groups this year were Iceland's imaginatively named **Icy**; a spectacularly unpopular rock group from the UK called **Ryder**; a family quartet made up of two sisters and their two cousins, **Frizzle Sizzle**, for the Netherlands and Ireland's female-led **Luv Bug** who finished fourth, the best placing ever for an Irish band. Turkey called on two bands to sing their entry, which was an ode to the coming Halley's Comet. **Klips and Onlar** were two girls and three boys who performed a familiar mix of pop and traditional rhythms that at long last allowed the Turks to break into the top ten, ending the contest in ninth place.

The Israeli pairing was a well-known comedian named **Moti Giladi** with an actress called **Sarai Tzuriel**, who was known to Israeli TV viewers for her work on the children's educational programme 'Sesame Street'. Thankfully, she decided against wearing her costume from that show, the yellow giant 'Big Bird'.

Far left: Belgium's reputedly 15-year-old Sandra Kim celebrates her victory with last year's winners Bobbysocks. She had seemed unstoppable from the first round of voting, and admitted to hostess Åse in a charming manner that she had expected to win 'a little'.

Left: Norway's Ketil Stokkan was accompanied on stage by an intriguing dance act, featuring a man in drag.

'J'Aime La Vie' was a huge hit in Belgium and charted in many other countries with great success, but not in the UK, where it went ignored. When Miss Kim did reveal that she had deceived the audience about her age, Swiss TV petitioned to have the song disqualified, but to no avail.

Among the early performances, Switzerland's young and glamorous **Daniela Simons** seemed to be the act to beat, with a lushly orchestrated offering reminiscent of many previous French winners of the competition. As the song reached its climax, Daniela took a hand mike and moved forward to stand at the front of the stage for a dramatic, powerful ending. However, she was soon to be upstaged...

Sandra Kim had been the focus of the majority of the press coverage in the build-up to this year's competition. Reputedly aged 15, she came to Bergen as the youngest soloist Eurovision competitor since Jean-Jacques had sung for Monaco in 1969, or that was the official story. Born Sandra Calderone, in Belgium of Italian parents, she successfully united the two Belgian communities, the French and the Flemish. Singing an upbeat disco number she was the hot favourite with the bookies to take the crown. Accompanied on stage by backing singers and musicians, including Patricia Maessen from the Hearts of Soul and latterly Dream Express, she appeared on stage looking older than her 15 years in a white jacket with pink trousers and matching bow tie around her neck. Her penchant for large ice creams had been noted by the press in the rehearsals and had been seen in evidence in the preview videos. It was certainly a catchy

number and the appeal of such a young artist singing in a very contemporary mode was bound to catch the judges' eyes, and it did. However, Ms Kim was not the innocent 15-year-old she appeared to be at all. The truth, which emerged later, was that she was in reality only 13! Quite why her man ager had found it necessary to disguise her age, other than to fit the lyrics of the song, is a mystery. Her performance was one of the best that night and was in many ways even more impressive considering the tender age of the young singer.

Germany had to follow this outstanding performance and did so very well. **Ingrid Peters** had a strong entry with an excellent orchestral arrangement. Despite attracting top marks from the UK, the German song was possibly overshadowed by the Belgian entry that preceded it and did not fare as well in the voting as had been anticipated. Neither did Cyprus. **Elpida** was making her second appearance in the contest and joined a very select band of performers who have appeared for more than one nation. Her previous entry was for Greece in 1979, when she had finished a very credible eighth. This year, there were rumours she was not too happy with the song and had reportedly threatened not to take the stage at all, only relenting at the very last moment. In order to raise her flagging morale, the song's conductor Martyn Ford

Sandra Kim was only 13, but looked older.

joined the performers on stage to encourage the audience to clap along. It was a brave attempt, but Cyprus finished last in the contest, a fate that would possibly have been avoided had Greece been in the competition.

Austria did little better this year with **Timna Brauer**. She was an Austrian Jew and arrived at the contest under pressure to withdraw from Israeli critics, angered by the politics and Nazi past of Austria's newly elected president, Kurt Waldheim. The damaging publicity and the general attitude to Austrian politics across Europe at the time was not likely to win Brauer many votes, despite the unusual nature of the song. It was a very dramatic piece, with a slow gentle verse erupting into a brash chorus. It was quite experimental in many ways, but obviously not the type of experiment appreciated by the juries. Still, despite the furore, and somewhat ironically, Ms Brauer won more votes to finish ahead of Israel, but only just.

The most bizarre performance of the night came from Sweden's **Lasse Holm and Monica Törnell**. Although the two singers were soberly dressed in black, they were joined onstage by a trio of backing singers in very weird outfits: a French maid, a circus 'muscle man' (who was anything but) and a gentleman in a lilac suit and bowler hat! When not singing the trio got up to all sorts of antics, including somersaults and acrobatics. During the instrumental break, TV producer Sten Carlberg, who was naked from the waist up, joined the throng to play electric guitar. Such was his effect on the French maid that she feigned a fainting fit on stage!

For the interval this year singer **Sissel Kyrkjebø** and musician **Steinar Ofsdal** performed various Norwegian songs around the city of Bergen, and Sissel appeared live on stage to perform the final song of their repertoire. It had a big impact on the audience at home, and Sissel went on to become the biggest star to emerge from the 1986 contest.

Sandra Kim cruised to victory. Belgium had waited longer than any nation in the contest's history, a full 30 years, to achieve their first victory, having been present at every contest since the first in 1956. Sadly for the Belgians, like the Germans, who waited 26 years to win, it has remained their sole victory to date. When Kim later revealed that she had deceived the audience about her age, Swiss TV petitioned to have the song disqualified, but to no avail. Sandra Kim had made history as the youngest-ever winner of the contest, a feat that under current rules at least can never be beaten. However, in 1987, another artist was to write themselves into the Eurovision history books.

country	song	performer	place	score	draw
Belgium	J'Aime La Vie	**Sandra Kim**	1	176	13
Switzerland	Pas Pour Moi	**Daniella Simons**	2	140	10
Luxembourg	L'Amour De Ma Vie	**Sherisse Laurence**	3	117	1
Ireland	You Can Count On Me	**Luv Bug**	4	96	12
Sweden	E' De' Det Här Du Kallar Kärlek	**Lasse Holm & Monica Törnell**	5	78	17
Denmark	Du Er Fuld Af Løgn	**Lise Haavik & Trax**	6	77	18
United Kingdom	Runner In The Night	**Ryder**	7	72	5
Germany	Uber Die Brücke Geh'n	**Ingrid Peters**	8	62	14
Turkey	Halley	**Klips and Onlar**	9	53	8
Spain	Valentino	**Cadillac**	10	51	9
Yugoslavia	Zeljo Moja	**Doris Dragović**	11	49	2
Norway	Romeo	**Ketil Stokkan**	12	44	4
Netherlands	Alles Heeft Ritme	**Frizzle Sizzle**	13	40	7
Portugal	Não Sejas Mau Para Mim	**Dora**	14	28	20
Finland	Paiva Kahden Ihmisen	**Kari**	15	22	19
Iceland	Gledibankinn	**Icy**	16	19	6
France	Europiennes	**Cocktail Chic**	17	13	3
Austria	Die Zeit Ist Einsam	**Timna Brauer**	18	12	16
Israel	Yavoh Yom	**Moti Giladi & Sarai Tzuriel**	19	7	11
Cyprus	Tora Zo	**Elpida**	20	4	15

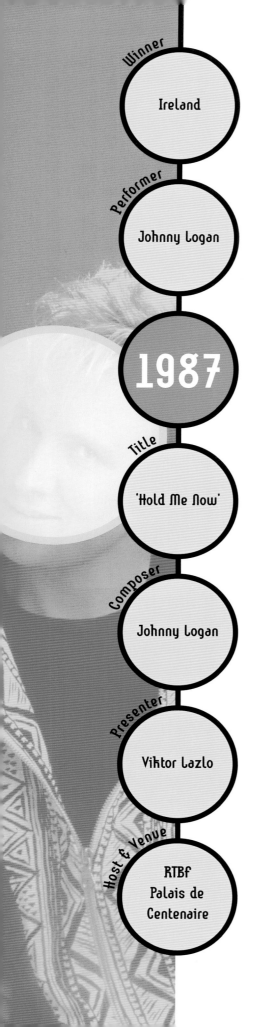

Winner

Ireland

Performer

Johnny Logan

1987

Title

'Hold Me Now'

Composer

Johnny Logan

Presenter

Viktor Lazlo

Host & Venue

RTBF
Palais de
Centenaire

Brussels
Belgium

Having found the youngest winner ever in 1986, another record was to be set in 1987 and, similarly, it was one that many had chased over the years!

Singer **Viktor Lazlo** was the appointed mistress of ceremonies for the contest on 9th May 1987, which was Europe Day. Despite having taken her name from a male character in the movie *Casablanca*, Viktor continued the Eurovision tradition of being a female presenter. Rather unusually, she not only got to present the contest, but plug her new single heavily into the bargain. After the fairly traditional filmed introduction, giving viewers a taste of Belgium's highlights, Viktor burst into a performance of the song 'Breathless'. As Ms Lazlo sang, viewers were able to take in the truly magnificent set, the main focus of which was a laser show, which shone out from beneath a huge globe that seemed to float at the back of the stage. To the viewers' right was a large entryway leading to the performing area and a giant inverted cone that formed the side backdrop. This use of geometric shapes was extremely effective. To the left was the orchestra, dressed all in grey and blending in perfectly with the high-tech look of the production. Above the stage was a bright pink 'scaffold' from which the lighting rigs were suspended, and encircling the entire area was a curved arrow pointing to the stage. It was extremely spectacular and certainly gave the impression that the contest was trying to catch up with the modern world.

Viktor emerged from the laser display wearing a bright pink strapless gown, with a long trailing skirt and matching evening gloves. Her dark hair was piled on top of her head, and suspended from her ears were possibly the largest pink earrings ever seen in European television history! There were a record 22 nations taking part in Brussels.

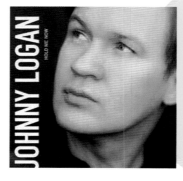

'Hold Me Now' went to the top of the charts all over the continent and to No. 2 in the UK, thus lifting the dreaded 'one-hit wonder' tag from Logan's shoulders.

Italy and Greece had both returned to Eurovision and all
20 of the previous year's competitors had entered again.
The contest was beginning to take longer and longer to
complete so the EBU set 22 as the maximum number of
competitors. This provided problems over the next few
years as new and returning nations indicated an interest in
taking part, but could not be accommodated.

Kate Gulbrandsen of Norway was the first act of the
night. Wearing a light blue jacket over black, thigh-high
boots, her long hair had been styled to stick straight up
into the air. Her song was a strong opener and had a good
pedigree. It was written by 1985's winning composer Rolf
Løvland, with lyrics by one of the ladies who sang that
particular number, the ex-Bobbysoxer Hanne Krogh. It was
not to be a second win for Norway, however, despite a
strong performance from Kate.

Israel had possibly the most controversial song with
their entry 'Shir Habatlanim' ('Lazy Bums'). Very unlike
anything the Israelis had ever submitted for Eurovision

Performing the reprise, Johnny Logan was so overcome with emotion
that he was unable to complete the final note of the song and, as he
had in 1980, added to the lyric that he 'still loves you, Ireland'.

before or since, it was a knockabout comedy song
presented by two actor-comedians, **Datner & Kushnir,**
dressed similarly to the Blues Brothers in dark suits,
white shirts, dark ties, black trilbies and sunglasses.
Comedic efforts have never really appealed to the
Eurovision judges. Of those that had been tried before, only
Sweden's 1986 entry had approached anything like
a good placing (fifth). The Israelis themselves were also
less than keen on this particular effort, with the culture
minister threatening to resign if 'Lazy Bums' went to
Brussels. It did, but he didn't!

Iceland's **Halla Margret Árnadóttir** was making her
debut on the world's stage with a beautifully sleepy song.
Sadly, its lyrics were hard to interpret, let alone understand.

The previous year, Sandra Kim had been the youngest person to win Eurovision and indeed the youngest ever to represent Belgium. **Lilianne St Pierre** could well have been the oldest. Dressed in a dramatic black suit, with a tailcoat swirling behind her, she attacked her song with great vivacity and energy. It was a strong effort, although it was not wholly appreciated by those judging the competition.

Italy returned to Eurovision with a vengeance this year. **Umberto Tozzi** was already a successful performer and songwriter – his song 'Gloria' had topped the charts worldwide in 1983 for Laura Brannigan. Singing with Raf, another artist who had achieved success at home, they had co-composed their ballad 'Gente Di Mare', ('People Of The Sea'). It was a strong entry from the Italians, who had now waited twenty-three years since Gigliola Cinquetti had scored their one and only win in 1964. The two singers seemed to have a fairly relaxed approach to the contest, and their choice of costumes gave them a certain unkempt air, but regardless, it was clearly going to be a tough song to beat.

After many absences from the Eurovision stage during the 1980s, Greece returned with perhaps their best attack on the prize since they had finished at a high of fifth place in 1977. **Bang** were two handsome lads selected to sing a rockabilly-inspired number called 'Stop!'. Their similarity to Wham!, in terms of appearance, if not in music, was noted by many, but this duo were not nearly as successful.

Luxembourg was only four years on from their last win and their recent fortunes had been good. This may have helped inspire Euro punk rocker **Plastic Bertrand** to try his luck with the Grand Duchy, rather than his native Belgium. He had soared to the top of the charts all over Europe in the late 1970s with 'Ça Plane Pour Moi' and Eurovision marked his comeback. It was an up-tempo number, and Plastic moved around the stage with great energy, but nothing could be done to hide the weakness of the song and his very low score bore this out.

The United Kingdom's **Rikki**, or Richard Peebles as he was known back home, was once a singer for 1960s' hit-makers Marmalade, although more recently he had been driving a mini cab around Glasgow. On stage he appeared all in black, with a white jacket, and for the contest he added a tartan cloak to his jacket shoulder. Alas, the total lack of

Right: Johnny received a standing ovation from his fellow competitors as he made his way to the stage to receive the writer's award – a glass pyramid etched with this year's contest logo – from Sandra Kim. He sent his bouquet of flowers cascading into the orchestra, for no apparent reason.

Far right: Opening the contest for Norway, Kate Gulbrandsen had styled her long hair so that it stuck straight up in the air.

interest in the song from the UK public was almost mirrored by the contest's juries. Israel certainly liked the song, but hardly any other support could be rallied from the other 20 nations and the UK slumped to their worst-ever placing in Eurovision history up to this time, a dismal thirteenth.

France also fared badly, as did Turkey whose singer **Seyyal Tanner** had boasted to a radio DJ that she was going to win, but ended last with nul points. Denmark impressed with a cleverly orchestrated song by Anne Cathrine Herdorf that was somewhat reminiscent of Nicole's 1982 winner. But in the end the evening belonged to one man.

When **Johnny Logan** won the 1980 Eurovision Song Contest he had tried to launch an enduring career. However, he failed to ignite the charts and remained a 'one-hit wonder' across the Continent. Plagued by legal and contract battles, he admitted that he had lost all the money earned from his 1980 victory. This year, he was back in the game and after a place in the contest's history as the only singer to win twice. No singer had yet won the competition on two occasions, although two singers, Lys Assia and Gigliola Cinquetti, had come close. Logan was not daunted by this poor track record and submitted his own composition 'Hold Me Now'. Wearing all white and backed by a trio of singers in navy and white, he sang very well, and received an enthusiastic roar of approval from the audience for his gentle ballad. Similarly structured to his earlier winner, this song was clearly the favourite in the hall.

At the end of the proceedings, Johnny Logan had a 31-point lead over Germany, with Italy just breaking over the century thanks to top marks from Ireland and Yugoslavia and a good score from the Swiss. It was a resounding victory, much easier than in 1980 when again Germany had come second to Logan's first. His place in the Eurovision history books was assured. Germany's **Wind**, who had performed a catchy, almost reggae-style song, were also worthy of a footnote, as they became the only act to finish second on two occasions, without ever winning the competition.

Rather than launch a bigger career, Logan's win seemed to cement his reputation as a Eurovision artist, and he never did shake off the tag and enjoy any lasting success. Indeed, his brother quipped that he was asked on a number of occasions 'Doesn't your brother get any other gigs?'

country	song	performer	place	score	draw
Ireland	Hold Me Now	**Johnny Logan**	1	172	20
Germany	Lass Die Sonne In Dein Herz	**Wind**	2	141	16
Italy	Gente Di Mare	**Umberto Tozzi & Raf**	3	103	7
Yugoslavia	Ja Sam Za Ples	**Novi Fosili**	4	92	21
Netherlands	Rechtop In De Wind	**Marcha**	5=	83	12
Denmark	En Lille Melodi	**Anne Cathrine Herdorf & Bandjo**	5=	83	19
Cyprus	Aspro Mavro	**Alexia Vassiliou**	7	80	17
Israel	Shir Ha'batlanim	**Datner & Kushnir**	8	73	2
Norway	Mitt Liv	**Kate Gulbrandsen**	9	65	1
Greece	Stop!	**Bang**	10	64	11
Belgium	Soldiers Of Love	**Lilianne St Pierre**	11	56	5
Sweden	Boogaloo	**Lotta Engberg**	12	50	6
United Kingdom	Only The Light	**Rikki**	13	47	14
France	Les Mots D'Amour N'Ont Pas De Dimanche	**Christine Minier**	14	44	15
Finland	Sata Salamaa	**Vicky Rosti**	15	32	18
Iceland	Haegt Og Hljótt	**Halla Margret Árnadóttir**	16	28	4
Switzerland	Moitié Moitié	**Carol Rich**	17	26	22
Portugal	Neste Barco A Vela	**Nevada**	18	15	8
Spain	No Estas Solo	**Patricia Kraus**	19	10	9
Austria	Nur Noch Gefühl	**Gary Lux**	20	8	3
Luxembourg	Amour Amour	**Plastic Bertrand**	21	4	13
Turkey	Sarkim Sevgi Ustünne	**Locomotif & Seyyal Tanner**	22	0	10

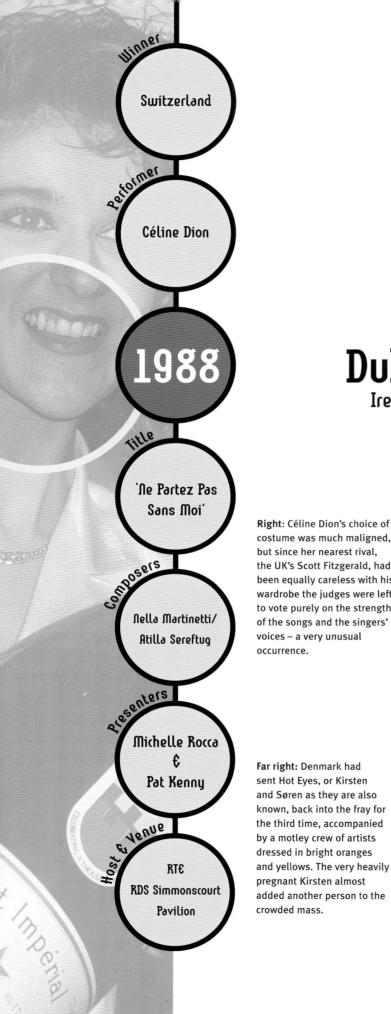

Winner
Switzerland

Performer
Céline Dion

1988

Title
'Ne Partez Pas Sans Moi'

Composers
Nella Martinetti/ Atilla Sereftug

Presenters
Michelle Rocca & Pat Kenny

Host & Venue
RTE RDS Simmonscourt Pavilion

Dublin played host to the Eurovision Song Contest for the third time, choosing the Royal Dublin Society's Simmonscourt Pavilion, which had also staged the 1981 event, as the venue for the thirty-third competition. The maximum of 22 countries entered. However, only 21 made it to Dublin. Cyprus had picked a song that was in fact an updated version of an entry from their 1984 national song contest and was disqualified.

Many innovations were made at this year's competition and certainly the 1988 contest is widely regarded as having given the show a much-needed shot in the arm. The whole concept of the production was designed to attract a younger audience and apparently it achieved its goal. The programme took a huge leap forward in style, even if it remained hampered by the content. The stage design, graphics and overall production continued the high-tech look started in Brussels the previous year and by adding some highly original touches – not least huge video walls – to the finished product, the Irish were able to

Dublin
Ireland

Right: Céline Dion's choice of costume was much maligned, but since her nearest rival, the UK's Scott Fitzgerald, had been equally careless with his wardrobe the judges were left to vote purely on the strength of the songs and the singers' voices – a very unusual occurrence.

Far right: Denmark had sent Hot Eyes, or Kirsten and Søren as they are also known, back into the fray for the third time, accompanied by a motley crew of artists dressed in bright oranges and yellows. The very heavily pregnant Kirsten almost added another person to the crowded mass.

give a whole new feel to the proceedings. In a first for the contest, the previous year's winner Johnny Logan reprised a truncated version of his 1987 winner before the opening Icelandic entry performed.

As had now become customary, each song was preceded by a video 'postcard' showing a slice of Irish culture and life. Thus the two Icelandic hopefuls, Stefan Hilmarsson and Sverrir Stormsker, who together made up the duo **Beathoven**, were seen enjoying a hurling match. Their song was less memorable and featured the traditional Eurovision standby of a chorus of 'la la las' alongside lyrics that name-checked Michael Caine, Sigmund Freud and the less famous John Paul Sigmarson, the world's strongest man, who hailed from Iceland and was brought along to Eurovision as part of the nation's delegation.

With Cyprus's withdrawal, Sweden took the dreaded second slot; the curse affected the much-fancied **Tommy Körberg** when he was stricken with throat problems upon his arrival in the Irish capital. He missed several rehearsals, but recovered sufficiently to perform what had been one of

Celine Dion

'Ne Partez Pas Sans Moi' did not fair too well in the charts around the continent, despite Céline recording both French and German versions. Indeed, the record label, Carrere, took the unprecedented step of deciding not to release the song in the UK or Ireland.

the pre-show favourites. Accompanied on stage by a trumpet solo the Swede sang well, although he did not impress the judges much. For their postcard, the Finnish group, **Boulevard**, was seen cycling the Irish countryside with Tour de France winner Steven Roache. He was not able to bring them much luck, and as Ossi Runne took his twenty-first bow for Finland at the end of the song, it was pretty clear that he had conducted his twenty-first losing entry.

A worker at Glasgow's meat market, the United Kingdom's **Scott Fitzgerald** performed in a powder-blue suit that seemed to be several sizes too small for him. In his introduction to the UK act, the contest's co-presenter Pat Kenny reminded viewers that UK entrants tended to remove articles of clothing for their performances, citing Sandie Shaw's bare feet and Bucks Fizz's skirt-ripping routine as examples. Thankfully, Scott kept all his clothes on to sing his ballad, the first slow-tempo song to represent the UK since 1966.

Turkish superstars **MFÖ** returned, after their failure in the 1985 contest, to sing another of their compositions. The strong orchestration and catchy melody could not help the fact that their song was constructed around the repetitive lyric 'Sufi, Sufi, Sufi, hey-a hey'. It was certainly not a groundbreaking effort.

Singing for Israel, **Yardena Arazi** was accompanied by two members of 1979's winning group Milk and Honey. Arazi is deeply superstitious and only agreed to represent her nation when a tarot reader told her the ninth song would win this year's competition. At that time, with Cyprus still in the draw, Israel was indeed the ninth entry, but by the time the contest rolled round and Cyprus had withdrawn, the ninth spot had gone to Switzerland.

Céline Dion, a native French-Canadian who had been singing professionally since she was 12 years old, had upset some quarters of the Swiss media when she entered the Swiss heats – especially as her song was co-written by a

non-Swiss national, Turk Atilla Sereftug. But all doubts were dismissed when she appeared on stage at the Swiss final, sweeping away the opposition with the sheer power of her voice and stage presence. At only 19, she had the dynamic vocal range to carry any song and the bookies installed her as the pre-contest favourite.

On stage in Dublin, Dion certainly gave the song everything, although her choice of costume was much maligned, consisting of a long white jacket, trimmed in gold, worn over a white puffball skirt. She had not chosen a look to flatter. Although the song could not be described as the most original ever heard in the contest, it was performed with such vocal style and force that it was clear that the bookies were right: this was the one to beat.

Not really surprisingly, the biggest cheer of the evening was saved for **Jump The Gun,** the five-piece all-male band selected to sing the Irish entry. They were more in a rock vein than the middle-of-the-road music offered by most of the other contestants and certainly looked set to do well for the home nation.

Germany had pulled out all the stops for their entry this year, with veterans Ralph Siegel and Bernd Meinunger once again at the songwriting helm. Looking to improve on their second place from the year before and recapture the crown, they turned to the mother and daughter team of **Maxi and Chris Garden**. It was the first-ever example of a mother-and-daughter singing in the contest and it was a gimmick that some had doubts about, especially as the cameras focused almost entirely on the youngster, Maxi, who performed from behind an unusually designed white piano with a permanently fixed grin on her face. Mother Chris also sat at the keyboards of her regular-sized grand.

In contrast to the youngest singer of the night, Austria's entrant was the ageing rocker **Wilfried Scheutz**, who sang 'Lisa, Mona Lisa'. He brought along a young lady dressed in an oversized pink jacket to help him out. But it wasn't going to be enough to avoid a humiliation for the Austrians, who were now without a win since 1966.

Greece enhanced **Afrodite Fryda**'s performance with a clown. The song included false laughter among the repetitive lyrics of the chorus. With Cyprus absent, points were going to be hard to come by for the Greeks,

country	song	performer	place	score	draw
Switzerland	Ne Partez Pas Sans Moi	Céline Dion	1	137	9
United Kingdom	Go	Scott Fitzgerald	2	136	4
Denmark	Ka' Du Se Hva' Jeg Sa'	Hot Eyes	3	92	13
Luxembourg	Croire	Lara Fabian	4	90	17
Norway	For Vår Jord	Karoline Krüger	5	88	15
Yugoslavia	Mangup	Srebrna Krila	6	87	21
Israel	Ben Adam	Yardena Arazi	7	85	8
Ireland	Take Him Home	Jump The gun	8	79	10
Netherlands	Shangri-la	Gerard Joling	9	70	7
France	Chanteur De Charme	Gérard Lenorman	10	64	19
Spain	La Chica Que Yo Quiero	La Decada	11	58	6
Sweden	Stad I Ljus	Tommy Körberg	12=	52	2
Italy	Ti Scrivo	Luca Barbarossa	12=	52	18
Germany	Lied Für Einen Freund	Maxi & Chris Garden	14	48	11
Turkey	Sufi	MFÖ	15	37	5
Iceland	Sokrates	Beathoven	16	20	1
Greece	Clown	Afrodite Fryda & Choir	17	10	14
Belgium	Laisser Briller Le Soleil	Reynaert	18=	5	16
Portugal	Voltarei	Dora	18=	5	20
Finland	Nauravat Silmät Muistetaan	Boulevard	20	3	3
Austria	Lisa, Mona Lisa	Wilfried Schuetz	21	0	12

and indeed they were. Especially as Norway, who could formerly have been relied upon to finish last, had entered a beautiful ballad performed by the charming **Karoline Krüger** that was a popular vote- winner.

At one stage of the voting the UK looked to be cruising to victory, but after the penultimate jury they led Switzerland by just five points. When the jury in Ljubljana awarded only six to the Swiss, it all appeared to be over and backstage Céline Dion looked crestfallen. However, the tension continued as one by one, the Yugoslav spokeswoman eliminated the remaining scores. Now one point behind, the UK had to receive one of the remaining four scores in order to win. As each score was announced in turn, seven to the Netherlands, eight to Germany, ten to Norway, the tension became almost unbearable. Everyone held their breath as the voice from Ljubljana announced, 'And finally... France, 12 points!' – a quote that became the title of a behind-the-scenes documentary about this year's contest.

It was the closest-ever competition and, for only the third time in the history of the contest, the winning song came from behind and overtook the leader on the final vote.

Céline Dion broke down in tears of joy, hugging her assembled delegation. **Scott Fitzgerald** was left disconsolate. Perhaps understandably, a certain amount of bitterness seems to have accompanied his defeat. He vented his frustration to both the British and Dutch press, with particular anger reserved for the failure of the Dutch jury to award him any marks at all.

The winning entry did not fare very well in the charts around the continent, despite the fact that Dion recorded both French and German versions of the song. However, in the next decade Céline Dion emerged as the biggest female artist in the world, her albums selling hundreds of millions of copies around the globe.

For RTE, the plaudits for their accomplished production were many indeed. The show was given a much-needed fillip and became the model on which most contests were based for many years to come, as indeed was the winning song! And In addition to the tension and excitement of the battle at the top of the scoreboard, some other notable things happened in the voting. Probably most significantly, for the very first time in the contest's history, Turkey voted for Greece!

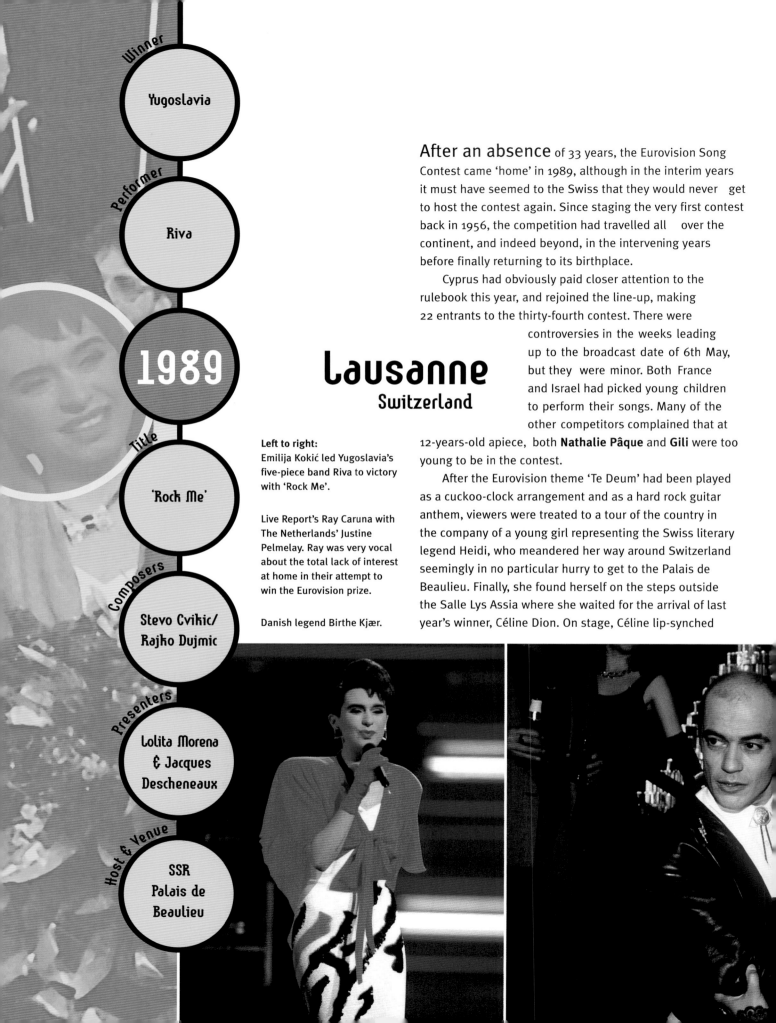

Winner
Yugoslavia

Performer
Riva

1989

Title
'Rock Me'

Composers
Stevo Cvikic/ Rajko Dujmic

Presenters
Lolita Morena & Jacques Descheneaux

Host & Venue
SSR Palais de Beaulieu

Lausanne
Switzerland

Left to right:
Emilija Kokić led Yugoslavia's five-piece band Riva to victory with 'Rock Me'.

Live Report's Ray Caruna with The Netherlands' Justine Pelmelay. Ray was very vocal about the total lack of interest at home in their attempt to win the Eurovision prize.

Danish legend Birthe Kjær.

After an absence of 33 years, the Eurovision Song Contest came 'home' in 1989, although in the interim years it must have seemed to the Swiss that they would never get to host the contest again. Since staging the very first contest back in 1956, the competition had travelled all over the continent, and indeed beyond, in the intervening years before finally returning to its birthplace.

Cyprus had obviously paid closer attention to the rulebook this year, and rejoined the line-up, making 22 entrants to the thirty-fourth contest. There were controversies in the weeks leading up to the broadcast date of 6th May, but they were minor. Both France and Israel had picked young children to perform their songs. Many of the other competitors complained that at 12-years-old apiece, both **Nathalie Pâque** and **Gili** were too young to be in the contest.

After the Eurovision theme 'Te Deum' had been played as a cuckoo-clock arrangement and as a hard rock guitar anthem, viewers were treated to a tour of the country in the company of a young girl representing the Swiss literary legend Heidi, who meandered her way around Switzerland seemingly in no particular hurry to get to the Palais de Beaulieu. Finally, she found herself on the steps outside the Salle Lys Assia where she waited for the arrival of last year's winner, Céline Dion. On stage, Céline lip-synched through a truncated version of her victorious number, before presenting her first English language recording.

After Italy's opener, Israel had drawn the graveyard second spot for the second time in three contests. Despite this bad omen, the Israelis were among the hot favourites to take the title, even having attracted a fair amount of controversy with one of the performers of their song. Twelve-year-old Gili was accompanied by the slightly older **Galit Burg**. It certainly was a strong offering and the two performers complemented each other well with a variety of harmonies, backed up by another female duo. The trouble was Gili himself. Although there would be a large number of judges who would sigh and consider him adorably cute for his age, there were possibly an equal number who wouldn't have minded giving him a clip around the ear!

Ireland, with a particularly weak song by Kiev Connolly, suffered their worst placing in the contest to date, eighteenth, and this surprised no one in particular. Turkey also came to the contest with low expectations and was destined for just five points. But, despite a truly dreadful song, the performance and vocal dexterity of the girl-boy group, **Pan**, was spectacular and deserved higher marks. Iceland suffered the ignominy of their first ever 'nul points' with only their fourth Eurovision entry. **Daniel Ågust Haraldsson** sang in a very lacklustre style. The reason for his disdain could possibly be put down to the fact that his prize for winning the right to sing for his country had been a cactus! His costume, very

baggy trousers, an oversized white shirt and huge medallion, was perhaps the most interesting of the night.

The UK's **Live Report** was a six-piece band led by Maltese-born Ray Caruana. The only female member of the band, Maggie Jay, had disguised herself in the run-up to the competition, fuelling speculation that it was Annie Lennox of the Eurythmics. It wasn't. Despite looking rather drab, Caruana gave a vocal performance worthy of any singer who has ever sung for their country. However, despite receiving more 12-point scores than any other song on the night, it was to be a record-breaking twelfth time that a British song took second place.

Sweden's **Tommy Nilsson** presented a rousing rock-inspired anthem that sounded exactly like the sort of thing that Eurovision needed if it wanted to survive and indeed thrive, a view shared by three nations who gave it maximum points in the voting. Denmark's entry provided a touch of class with **Birthe Kjær**, probably the oldest performer in the 1989 contest. A Danish legend, she certainly brought an air of professionalism and vitality to the show with her vivacious presence. It was a finger snapping, sing-a-long number that was perhaps too outdated to win.

Austria had sent wannabe heartthrob **Thomas Forstner** to sing one of two songs in the contest written by Joachim Horn-Bernges and Dieter Bohlen. It was the first time since 1980 that writers had provided songs for two different countries in the same contest, as this pair of composers was

Despite recording English and Serbo-Croat versions, '**Rock Me**' failed miserably almost universally and, like 1988's winner, was not even released in the UK. Riva themselves could not build on their victory and were not even present at the 1990 contest in Zagreb.

also responsible for the German entry. Forstner sang without the orchestra and wore a lavender-coloured suit with his long hair flowing down his back. This may not have been the best appearance he could have chosen, but the ballad was perhaps strong enough to overcome the visual handicaps. Certainly, Austria equalled their best result since winning the contest 23 years earlier. As for Germany, they were very confident of their chances of a second win. Represented by **Nino de Angelo**, himself a hit-maker across the continent, the song had a much more contemporary feel than a lot of the other entries. Angelo sang with passion, but the lack of live music seemed to hamper the overall presentation and the Germans finished very poorly in the voting.

Finland did much better than usual with its flamenco-fringed offering, although it fell one place short of equalling its best result yet. Ossi Runne had been conducting Finland's songs since 1966, when he had also written the Finnish entry himself. Since then, 1981 was the only year he had not waved the baton for the hapless nation and he made this, one of his most successful appearances, his last. Only

two other men, Franck Pourcel and Noel Kelehan, have conducted more entries over the years.

France's young **Nathalie Pâque**, who just beat Israel's Gili for youngest performer, gave a rather sugary, but nonetheless strong presentation of the pre-contest favourite, but again it's possible that her youth alienated as many voters as it impressed. Switzerland entered a song sung in the fourth and least widespread of their native languages, Romansch. Composer **Marie-Louise Werth** sat at the piano and took the vocal lead, while her three male escorts provided a rather pseudo-operatic accompaniment. It was certainly a little different and seemed to be popular with the juries at first. However, halfway through the voting the Swiss faded from contention.

Greece did a lot better than in recent years when **Marianna** took to the stage to sing 'To Diko Sou Asteri' ('Your Own Star'). The song was much appreciated by the other juries and Greece was placed in the top ten for the first time since 1981.

The last song has often done well in Eurovision and in

country	song	performer	place	score	draw
Yugoslavia	Rock Me	**Riva**	1	137	22
United Kingdom	Why Do I Aways Get It Wrong?	**Live Report**	2	130	7
Denmark	Vi Maler Byen Rød	**Birthe Kjær**	3	111	12
Sweden	En Dag	**Tommy Nilsson**	4	110	10
Austria	Nur Ein Lied	**Thomas Forstner**	5	97	13
Spain	Nacida Para Amar	**Nina**	6	88	16
Finland	La Dolce Vita	**Anneli Saaristo**	7	76	14
France	J'ai Volé La Vie	**Nathalie Pâque**	8	60	15
Italy	Avrei Voluto	**Anna Oxa & Fausto Leali**	9=	56	1
Greece	To Diko Sou Asteri	**Marianna Efstratiou**	9=	56	19
Cyprus	Apopse As Vrethoume	**Fanny Polymeri & Yiannis Savidakis**	11	51	17
Israel	Derech Ha'melech	**Gili & Galit**	12	50	2
Switzerland	Viver Senza Tei	**Furbaz**	13	47	18
Germany	Flieger	**Nino de Angelo**	14	46	21
Netherlands	Blijf Zoals Je Bent	**Justine Palmelay**	15	45	4
Norway	Venners Nærhet	**Britt Synnøve Johansen**	16	30	8
Portugal	Conquistador	**Da Vinci**	17	39	9
Ireland	The Real Me	**Kiev Connolly & the Missing Passengers**	18	21	3
Belgium	Door De Wind	**Ingeborg**	19	13	6
Luxembourg	Monsieur	**Park Café**	20	8	11
Turkey	Bana Bana	**Pan**	21	5	5
Iceland	Pad Sem Enginn Sér	**Daniel Águst Haraldsson**	22	0	20

1989 it proved a lucky draw once again. Yugoslavia had drawn the spot for the second year in succession, and for the third year running had turned to Rajko Dujmic and Stevo Cvikic to compose their entry. 'Rock Me' could be understood in any language, and certainly the music lived up to the song's title. **Riva** were the five-piece band chosen to perform the song, led by the group's only female, Emilija Kokić. Dressed in white and black, with flashes of red, they danced enthusiastically to the most up-tempo song of the night, clearly enjoying the rock 'n' roll rhythm. The song was barely noticed by pundits in the run-up to the competition, but it proved to be one of the darkest horses to ever have run in Eurovision. Yugoslavia was only to appear in the contest on three more occasions after this year, although in subsequent years the member states of the former Yugoslav nation did take part in the contest. Croatia had in fact been responsible for this year's entry and in subsequent years has re-written Eurovision history in order to take credit for this victory.

After the exuberant Yugoslavs had taken their leave, hosts **Lolita Morena and Jacques Descheneaux** introduced one of the most bizarre Eurovision interval acts ever – an attempt to put a modern spin on the story of William Tell with the use of high-powered crossbows. Alas, the spectacle failed when the final arrow aimed at an apple atop Guy Tells's head missed. After this debacle, the scoring ran smoothly.

Yugoslavia was the seventeenth nation to claim the Eurovision title and remained the last new country to win the top prize for the next 12 years. However, some things about the 1989 result stayed the same – the UK finished second, with Denmark third, both for the second year in a row.

Such was the surprise of the victory that many observers were very caustic in their comments after the show ended. The BBC TV's commentator Terry Wogan called it 'the death knell' for the contest and indeed the record-buying public seemed to agree. The unpopularity of the winner led to a certain amount of criticism and disappointment in many quarters and the future of the contest was being called into doubt once again. As the 1980s made way for the 1990s, the future of the Eurovision Song Contest was not looking too secure.

Riva's 'Rock Me' was not a popular winner. Runner-up Ray Caruana of Live Report complained bitterly about being beaten by such a weak song.

Winner

Italy

Performer

Toto Cutugno

1990

Title

'Insieme: 1992'

Composer

Toto Cutugno

Presenters

Helga
Vlahović &
Oliver Mlakar

Host & Venue

JRT/RTZ
Koncertna Dvorana
Vatroslav Lisinski

Zagreb
Yugoslavia

The same 22 countries that had competed in 1989 lined up in Zagreb for the first contest of the 1990s, with 5th May chosen as the broadcast date. The only significant change to the rules, which came following complaints lodged in the previous year, was that singers had to have turned 16 in the year of the contest in order to compete. This was relevant to the UK as it had chosen a 15-year-old artist to sing its entry, but no rules were broken as her birthday was later that year .

The presenters for the big night had no problems fulfilling the age requirement. Helga Vlahović and Oliver Mlakar were certainly over sixteen and were quite possibly the oldest people yet to act as the contest presenters. Helga had been associated with the contest since 1974, when she had announced the Yugoslavian votes in a very haughty tone. In 1981, she became something of a contest legend, when she provided the comic highlight of that year's event by being totally unprepared when called upon by Doireann Ni Bhriain to give her results. Fifty-five-year-old Oliver Mlakar was very well known as a talk show host and anchorman and also fronted a popular game show 'Kviskoteka'.

Eurovision proved to be a big headache for the Yugoslav organisers, with numerous problems besetting the pre-production and a near disaster on the actual night. A severe shortage of cash was the main worry prior to the contest. The local media were particularly incensed that a reputed four million pounds was being spent on the production, when the average Croatian wage at that time was only one thousand pounds a year. Tickets were also highly priced and changed hands on the black market at exorbitant amounts. Nevertheless, the production came to pass, although it did not run particularly smoothly and there were numerous technical difficulties.

The contest got off to a terrible start when the backing tape being used by Spain's Azucar Moreno failed to start. The tape then began midway through the second bar, and the conductor could not cue the orchestra. The two sisters

Ketil Stokkan had sung for his nation on home ground in 1986. This time he had dropped his supporting drag act, and in an enormous pair of black trousers was the first singer to take the common theme of the night, the political changes in Europe.

Many observers were surprised by the final result and once again the record-buying public made their feelings known. Toto Cutugno only made No. 10 in Italy with 'Insieme: 1992' and No. 20 in the Netherlands, but didn't make the Top 20 in any other chart.

made their entrance, and started their routine centre-stage before they realised that the music was out of synch. They walked back off-stage, as the tape continued to play. The sound director stopped the music, and confused applause filled the auditorium. It was possibly the worst nightmare for any performers in the contest's history. The sound problem was eventually resolved and second time around everything went very smoothly. The two sisters must have had their nerve shaken, but they did not let it show. Their highly catchy and dramatic number, with a lengthy flamenco-disco introduction, was a very strong opener and despite all the problems, or possibly because of them, Spain had its best result since 1979, finishing in fifth place.

In an attempt to curry favour with the local audience, Belgium's **Philippe Lafontaine** sang an ode to a Macedonian lady, in this case his wife. The song had other references to the disputed Yugoslav republic, including lines about the Adriatic Sea, but it did little to impress. Although he managed twelfth place, a big improvement on the last two Belgian efforts, Lafontaine did not persuade either of the two nations spanning Macedonia, the Yugoslavian and Greek juries, to give his song any marks.

Luxembourg employed a French teenager to perform their song 'Quand Je Te Rêve' ('When I Dream Of You'). It was a dramatic ballad, much in the French-language tradition, and **Céline Carzo** appeared all in black, with similarly coloured lipstick. She was certainly a tempestuous-looking lovely, but opted for a rather odd and certainly unique presentation style. Standing rigid at centre-stage, the microphone in her right hand, her left hand flat against her thigh, she made no movement whatsoever throughout her performance, staring straight into the camera and not changing her facial expression once. It was odd, to say the least, but certainly memorable.

The United Kingdom came to Zagreb with very high hopes for young **Emma Booth**, who was singing a song with an environmental message. She wore Welsh red for her performance, during which two male and three female backing singers joined her. Miriam Stockley provided the majority of the vocal support, but it was billed as a solo effort. Despite all the promise, Emma gave a disappointing performance, possibly indicating her lack of experience, and could not manage better than sixth place. It was a wise move to choose a topical theme in 1990; in this instance, it just turned out to be the wrong one.

The UK came to Zagreb with very high hopes indeed. Fifteen-year-old Emma Booth had won the 'Song for Europe' contest easily, polling 97,625 votes, far more than double the score of her nearest rival.

The contest came to Yugoslavia for the first time in 1990 and it arrived at a time when the old Communist regimes had all but disintegrated. Thus, many of the nations competing took the momentous events reshaping the political and social landscape of the continent as their theme for the night and for one, at least, it paid off.

Finland and Norway had the right idea, but ended up at the bottom of the heap with their songs recalling the momentous events of autumn 1989, when Berlin had torn down its wall and reunited East and West Germany. Austria fared slightly better with their anthem to peace and harmony, which called for 'no walls anywhere'. Their singer, **Simone,** had caused something of a stir before the contest when she had appeared topless in some newspapers. It's unknown whether this won or lost her votes, but tenth place was a respectable position, anyway.

Not really surprisingly, considering the tumultuous events of the past year, the Germans had embraced the evening's favourite theme and sang a song about freedom. With the juries keen to hear compositions about European unity, this could have been their year. As an added bonus, a 34-year-old Yugoslav, **Daniel Kovac**, was brought in to sing the song, alongside 25-year-old Chris Kempers, a Marie Osmond lookalike. It may have been an attempt to win local support at least, but the song did not fare as well as expected, although it did at least make the first ten, finishing ninth, the best showing of the three German-language songs in the competition.

Israel was off-message this year, with their sultry singer **Rita** giving a steamy performance dressed in a revealing slit skirt. Like so many experienced stars before her, she came a cropper at Eurovision and ended an embarrassing seventeenth. Seventeen was the age of the Danish singer, **Lonnie Devantier**, who performed a song called 'Hallo, Hallo', which probably needed no translation, although it was of course sung in Danish.

The most exciting entry of the night was from **Joelle Ursull**, a dancer, choreographer, fashion model, actress and singer from the Antilles who had been selected to sing 'White And Black Blues' for France. It was sung in French, despite the English title, and penned by Serge Gainsbourg, the legendary Svengali of the French music scene and writer of 1965's winning song. Ursull was hoping to become the first black singer to win the contest since its inception and sang a song about racial harmony. She did not win, but came very close, ending in equal second place. She almost got the biggest hand of the night, but that was saved for the home team, who sang next. **Tajci**, a Croatian representing Yugoslavia, was only 19, but had been performing since she was six years old. She poured everything into her performance and her body into a very tight pink mini-dress, giving the liveliest performance of any of the singers, but it was not to be her night.

The Portuguese effort was 'Ha Sempre Alguem' ('There's Always Someone'), sung by the sultry **Nucha**. It was not a groundbreaking effort and Nucha had made a poor choice of costume. Wearing what looked like black cycling shorts under a short, black, velvet dress, she walked back and forth on the stage, giving the impression that something was preventing her from standing still. **Liam Reilly** was very still, however, seated at the piano to perform the Irish entry, 'Somewhere In Europe'. There have been lots of examples over the years of songs simply regurgitating lists of well-known names and landmarks, but none perhaps as blatant, and certainly not as successful, as this year's Irish effort. Liam himself had been lost 'Somewhere in Europe' earlier in the week, when his flight from Dublin was delayed, and he missed his first rehearsal. This didn't prevent him doing very well on the night, though, tying for second place with the French song.

Italy had been in and out of the contest in the past decade, citing the show on a couple of occasions as 'rubbish' and taking umbrage at the poor placing some of its songs had achieved. Lack of interest in the contest among Italians was now widespread and in 1990 the nation did not even carry the broadcast live. The Italian entrant, **Toto Cutugno**, was a major star in his home country and across Europe. He wrote his own song, 'Insieme: 1992' ('All Together: 1992'), a song dedicated to the forming of closer European ties with the coming of the single market in 1992. It did not impress much in the previews, but had been completely rearranged for Zagreb. It was an anthemic piece, much more rock orientated than many of the other songs, and it certainly had

a memorable hook. Despite this, and Cutugno's international fame, it was not a well-regarded song and caught most commentators by surprise when it romped to victory.

Later, after the voting, as Toto Cutugno was celebrating backstage, the head of the French delegation made a formal protest to scrutineer Frank Naef and the EBU about the Italian voting. Italy had certainly awarded some odd marks, having first identified themselves as the Spanish jury! They gave nothing at all to either of their nearest rivals on the scoreboard, France and Ireland, who were only 11 and six points behind them when they came to vote. Whatever investigation was made into the conduct of the Italian jury, it was largely irrelevant. Ultimately, Italy's votes did not count, as its entry was sufficiently ahead on points to have won, even if its jury had given top marks to one of the runners-up, but it was still a controversial and unexpected win.

Many observers were surprised by the final result, and once again the record-buying public made their feelings known. Toto Cutugno was rewarded by being invited to compère the event the following year. This was quite possibly the worst decision ever taken in Eurovision history.

country	song	performer	place	score	draw
Italy	Insieme: 1992	**Toto Cutugno**	1	149	19
France	White And Black Blues	**Joëlle Ursul**	2=	132	14
Ireland	Somewhere In Europe	**Liam Reilly**	2=	132	17
Iceland	Eitt Lag Enn	**Stjórnin**	4	124	8
Spain	Bandido	**Azucar Moreno**	5	96	1
United Kingdom	Give A Little Love Back To The World	**Emma**	6	87	7
Yugoslavia	Hajde Da Ludujemo	**Tajći**	7	81	15
Denmark	Hallo Hallo	**Lonnie Devantier**	8	64	11
Germany	Frei Zu Leben	**Chris Kempers & Daniel Kovac**	9	60	13
Austria	Keine Mauern Mehr	**Simone**	10	58	20
Switzerland	Musik Klingt In Die Welt Hinaus	**Egon Egemann**	11	51	12
Belgium	Macédomienne	**Philippe Lafontaine**	12	46	3
Luxembourg	Quand Je Te Rêve	**Céline Carzo**	13	38	6
Cyprus	Milas Poli	**Anastazio**	14	36	21
Netherlands	Ik Wil Alles Met Je Delen	**Maywood**	15	25	5
Sweden	Som En Vind	**Edin-Ådahl**	16	24	18
Israel	Shara Barechovot	**Rita**	17	16	10
Turkey	Gözlerinin Hapsindeyim	**Kayahan**	18	21	4
Greece	Horis Skopo	**Christos Callow**	19	11	2
Portugal	Ha Sempre Alguem	**Nucha**	20	9	16
Norway	Brandenburger Tor	**Ketil Stokkan**	21=	8	9
Finland	Fri?	**Beat**	21=	8	22

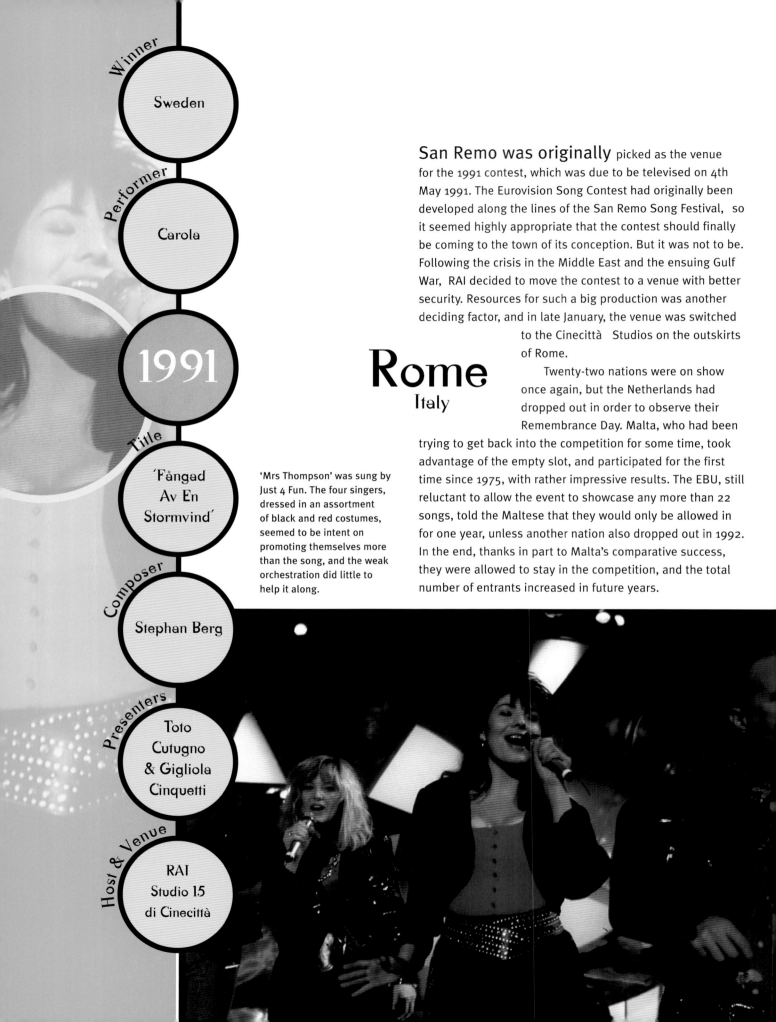

Winner
Sweden

Performer
Carola

1991

Title
'Fångad Av En Stormvind'

Composer
Stephan Berg

Presenters
Toto Cutugno & Gigliola Cinquetti

Host & Venue
RAI Studio 15 di Cinecittà

San Remo was originally picked as the venue for the 1991 contest, which was due to be televised on 4th May 1991. The Eurovision Song Contest had originally been developed along the lines of the San Remo Song Festival, so it seemed highly appropriate that the contest should finally be coming to the town of its conception. But it was not to be. Following the crisis in the Middle East and the ensuing Gulf War, RAI decided to move the contest to a venue with better security. Resources for such a big production was another deciding factor, and in late January, the venue was switched to the Cinecittà Studios on the outskirts of Rome.

Rome
Italy

Twenty-two nations were on show once again, but the Netherlands had dropped out in order to observe their Remembrance Day. Malta, who had been trying to get back into the competition for some time, took advantage of the empty slot, and participated for the first time since 1975, with rather impressive results. The EBU, still reluctant to allow the event to showcase any more than 22 songs, told the Maltese that they would only be allowed in for one year, unless another nation also dropped out in 1992. In the end, thanks in part to Malta's comparative success, they were allowed to stay in the competition, and the total number of entrants increased in future years.

'Mrs Thompson' was sung by Just 4 Fun. The four singers, dressed in an assortment of black and red costumes, seemed to be intent on promoting themselves more than the song, and the weak orchestration did little to help it along.

What most people remember about the 1991 contest is chaos – and lots of it! The whole production seemed to have been thrown together at the last minute, with precious little thought or planning involved and apparently hardly any rehearsal. The show's compère, **Toto Cutugno**, created much of this impression. He was joined for the night by Italy's only other Eurovision winner, **Gigliola Cinquetti**, who was not exactly best equipped for the task in hand either. One of the problems was that Toto seemed unable to speak any language other than Italian. Another was that neither Toto nor Gigliola appeared to have any concept of the contest's rules or format, despite their first-hand experiences.

What rehearsals there were had been a shambles, not helped by the incessant rain that had deluged the Italian city. On most days, the orchestra failed to arrive until several hours after the appointed time and many of the singers vented their frustrations at the lack of preparation.

After a few minor glitches to the opening travelogue, Toto and Gigliola made their entrance and explained why they were there. Toto was in a black tuxedo, while Gigliola looked casual at his side, in a blue knee-length dress, decorated with white stars. She looked as if she had come straight from the office. The show finally got underway with the two presenters singing – or in Cutugno's case miming – their winning Eurovision songs. Then the first act of the night took to a stage that appeared to have been cobbled together out of some rusty iron girders and leftover sets.

For the inter-song postcards, each competing artist had been invited to perform a well-known Italian song, in karaoke style, in the format of the San Remo Song Festival. It was a well-executed idea, and the singers certainly did a very good job of each of their chosen efforts. As they gave a short burst of the song, they were seen superimposed into famous Roman landmarks, supposedly chosen to best represent their personalities. When this interlude ended, the presenters introduced the song's conductor, and the competition was finally underway.

Yugoslavia had drawn the opening slot and theirs was certainly a humorous beginning for the contest and provided one of the weirdest acts of the night. **Baby Doll** was the name of the highly camp and outrageous lady singing 'Brazil', an ode to the South American nation. She was a very tall woman who wore a blonde wig, which combined both long hair and a tall beehive that was decorated with a wide band of small, circular mirrors. Her make-up was startling too, as

Carola was already a well-known singer in Sweden, but struggled to have any impact outside of Scandinavia. She took 'Fångad Av En Stormvind' to No. 3 in Sweden, and charted in Belgium, but had little success elsewhere, despite releasing an English version of the song.

was her bouffant mini-dress, which was fashioned from pale-blue chiffon and covered with pastel-coloured flowers. For the final touch her legs were entirely encased in pale-blue tights, ending in silver heels. Her backing singers were both dressed in sombre black and provided quite a contrast with three dancers cavorting their way around the stage. Sadly, the judges were almost universally unimpressed. The Maltese jury, always contrary, gave Baby Doll one point, but no other nation could be persuaded to award Yugoslavia a single mark. It is possible that the other judges were just too stunned to remember to write down a score.

Following that highly original effort would be tough for anyone and Iceland drew the short straw. As Toto came on stage to introduce the Icelandic postcard, a telephone starting ringing somewhere off stage, which he chose to ignore, and he introduced **Stefan and Eyfi**. Stefan Hilmarsson had been in the 1988 contest with the group Beathoven and he now teemed up with Eyfi for this slower ballad. Eyfi wore an aqua coloured jacket, with a purple bandanna covering his receding hairline, while Stefan sported the same jacket in mauve. They didn't do too well, ending in fifteenth place.

Poor Greece had some major problems with the performance of its entry. All went well into the first chorus of the powerful ballad, but the song was then massacred by the orchestra's elderly saxophonist. Whether it was intentional is debatable, but he completely failed to hit any of the right notes and contributed a tuneless, painful, but nonetheless comic, musical interlude. Luxembourg's effort was also orchestrally interrupted by a breaking guitar string.

Two of the favourites for the contest appeared back-to-back. Sweden and France were both widely tipped to take top prize, but nobody could actually have predicted the outcome. **Carola** was back for her second attempt at the prize for Sweden, hoping to improve on her third place from 1983. It was certainly the liveliest up-tempo song on offer and she attacked it with enormous vivacity. She had two male dancers in business suits leaping around behind her and three backing singers tucked away behind. A wind machine helped blow Carola's long hair around her shoulders, adding to the overall effect. Unfortunately, midway through the performance, the sound failed inside the hall. Nothing seemed untoward to the viewers or the judges, who heard and saw everything perfectly, but in the auditorium, no amplified sound could be heard at all. This must have been unnerving to say the least, but the Swedish singer didn't miss a beat, and gave the song everything she possibly could. When it was over, the audience leapt to their feet.

France could not have found a song that contrasted more strongly with the Swedish effort. The French entry was sung by the Algerian actress **Amina Annabi**, who in writing the song with Wassis Diop, had certainly brought more of an Arabic feel to the melody and lyrics than a French one. Amina was somewhat underdressed in a black pin-stripe suit, which was decorated with an orange scarf that she used to great effect in her performance. It was a highly original piece and she gave an impressive, sultry performance. Many observers and critics thought it too quirky to impress the judges; others commented that it was simply too good for the contest. Both opinions were proved wrong.

There were other highlights and lowlights – Portugal's **Dulce** raised fashion eyebrows by stitching two dresses together, Israel had a strong entry with an all-dancing extravaganza, Spain's **Sergio Dalma** set hearts a-flutter with a rich ballad and the UK's **Samantha Janus** made more of an impression with her pink lace-up bodice than her badly sung entry. But the main memory of the evening was the voting. Not that it excited Toto and Gigliola much. Both the presenters seemed more interested in chatting with the jury spokespersons in pidgin English and French than giving the scores, which they did with a marked lack of enthusiasm.

The voting was eccentric, to say the least, with many different nations picking up the big scores. Sweden got 12 points from Iceland, but nothing from the next two nations. Cyprus got 12 points from both Malta and, somewhat less surprisingly, Greece; Cyprus gave ten to Greece in return. In the end the whole result hinged on the Italian jury's final pronouncement, with both the leading competitors, the

Sweden's Carola wore a brown double-breasted sleeveless jacket over a sparkling white shirt and mauve leggings. She certainly had a powerful voice and, as she has said since, the dancers, in business suits behind her, highlighted the energy of the song.

Israeli and Swedish contestants, on the edges of their seats. When Rome awarded 12 to the French, with nothing at all to the two countries that were at that stage leading, the scores were levelled with both Sweden and France on 146. It was a tied result – the first since 1969.

From 1970 until 1988, the rules stated that should there be a draw, the tied songs would be performed again and voted upon by the other countries one more time. In 1989, the rule had been changed and the song that had received the most 12-point scores would win. If there was still a tie, then the number of ten-point scores awarded would be taken into account. If they were still tied after that, then the songs would be awarded the Grand Prix jointly. This year, both Sweden and France had received 12 points four times. When it came to the tens, Sweden had five, compared with France's two. Many were unhappy with this result, feeling it unjust to examine only the top scores. Certainly, a closer look at all the voting would have swung the result to the French. But rules are rules and the result stood. For the second year running, France had to be content with second place, despite their protests.

Malta did much better than on previous occasions with its first effort in 16 years, the longest absence yet of any nation from the line-up. Having been away since 1975, Malta's fourth Eurovision entry gained the tiny island its highest placing to date, sixth place. Norway returned to form, limping in at seventeenth, with a last-minute substitute entry featuring former winner **Hanne Krogh**. The dishonour of last place fell to Austria and poor **Thomas Forstner**, with his shoulder-length blond hair and jazzy purple suit sadly receiving the dreaded 'nul points'.

Many who were present do not remember the 1991 contest fondly and the antics of the two hosts overshadowed much of the competition. The excitement of the result certainly made up for a lot, but it was not a vintage year. SVT in Sweden had a lot of credibility to restore the following year, a task they accepted with alacrity. Meanwhile, Europe as an entity was continuing to move on. Old nations were changing and new countries were emerging and they wanted to take part in Eurovision. The 1992 competition turned out to be the last one ever held that permitted entrants to participate without pre-qualification.

country	song	performer	place	score	draw
Sweden	Fångad Av En Stormvind	**Carola**	1	146	8
France	C'est Le Dernier Qui A Parlé Qui A Raison	**Amina**	2	146	9
Israel	Kaan	**Duo Datz**	3	139	15
Spain	Bailar Pegados	**Sergio Dalma**	4	119	19
Switzerland	Canzone Per Te	**Sandra Simo**	5	118	5
Malta	Could It Be?	**Paul Giordimaina & Georgina**	6	106	3
Italy	Comme E Doce O Mare?	**Peppino di Capri**	7	89	22
Portugal	Lusitana Paixão	**Dulce**	8	62	12
Cyprus	S.O.S.	**Elena Patroclou**	9	60	21
Ireland	Could It Be That I'm In Love?	**Kim Jackson**	10=	47	11
United Kingdom	A Message To Your Heart	**Samantha Janus**	10=	47	20
Turkey	Iki Dakika	**Can, Izel & Reyhan**	12	44	10
Greece	Anixi	**Sophia Vossou**	13	36	4
Luxembourg	Un Baiser Volé	**Sarah Bray**	14	29	7
Iceland	Nina	**Stefan & Eyfi**	15	26	2
Belgium	Geef Het Op	**Clouseau**	16	23	18
Norway	Mrs Thompson	**Just 4 Fun**	17	14	14
Germany	Dieser Traum Darf Niemals Sterben	**Atlantis 2000**	18	10	17
Denmark	Lige Der Hvor Hjertet Slår	**Anders Frandsen**	19	8	13
Finland	Hullu Yö	**Kaija**	20	6	16
Yugoslavia	Brazil	**Baby Doll**	21	1	1
Austria	Venedig Im Regen	**Thomas Forstner**	22	0	6

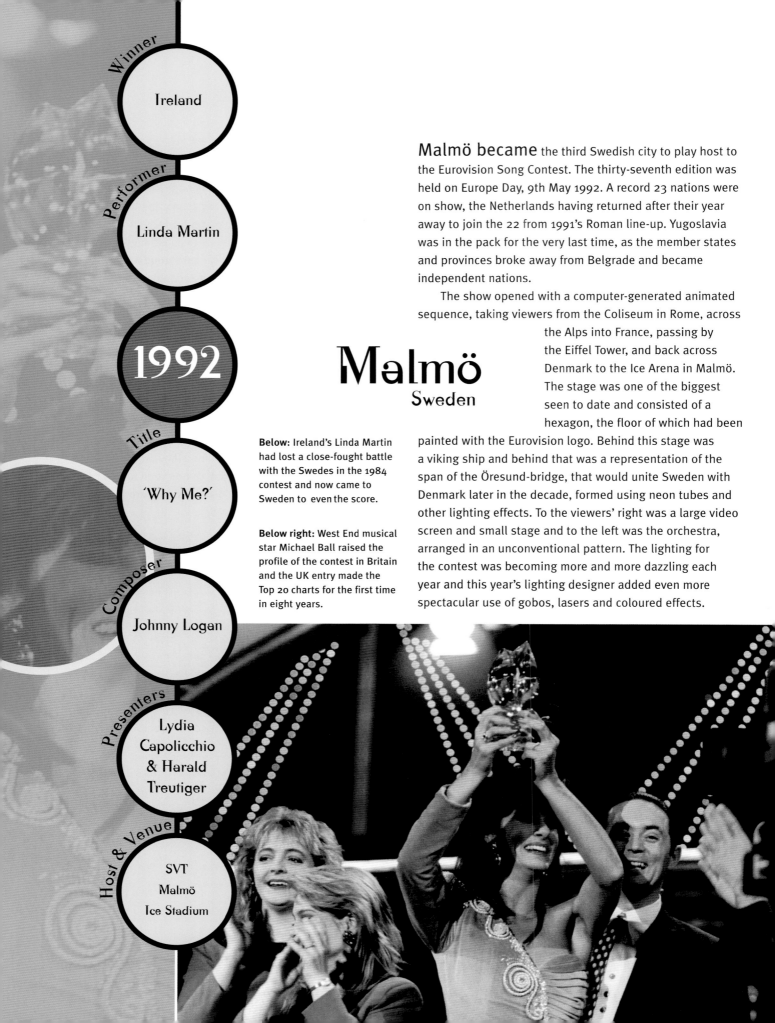

Winner

Ireland

Performer

Linda Martin

1992

Title

'Why Me?'

Composer

Johnny Logan

Presenters

Lydia Capolicchio & Harald Treutiger

Host & Venue

SVT Malmö Ice Stadium

Malmö became the third Swedish city to play host to the Eurovision Song Contest. The thirty-seventh edition was held on Europe Day, 9th May 1992. A record 23 nations were on show, the Netherlands having returned after their year away to join the 22 from 1991's Roman line-up. Yugoslavia was in the pack for the very last time, as the member states and provinces broke away from Belgrade and became independent nations.

The show opened with a computer-generated animated sequence, taking viewers from the Coliseum in Rome, across the Alps into France, passing by the Eiffel Tower, and back across Denmark to the Ice Arena in Malmö. The stage was one of the biggest seen to date and consisted of a hexagon, the floor of which had been

Malmö
Sweden

Below: Ireland's Linda Martin had lost a close-fought battle with the Swedes in the 1984 contest and now came to Sweden to even the score.

Below right: West End musical star Michael Ball raised the profile of the contest in Britain and the UK entry made the Top 20 charts for the first time in eight years.

painted with the Eurovision logo. Behind this stage was a viking ship and behind that was a representation of the span of the Öresund-bridge, that would unite Sweden with Denmark later in the decade, formed using neon tubes and other lighting effects. To the viewers' right was a large video screen and small stage and to the left was the orchestra, arranged in an unconventional pattern. The lighting for the contest was becoming more and more dazzling each year and this year's lighting designer added even more spectacular use of gobos, lasers and coloured effects.

The hosts, **Lydia Capolicchio** and **Harald Treutiger**, welcomed everyone in English to what they called 'the biggest game show in the world' and introduced viewers to an animated creature, 'Eurobird'. This character was to introduce each country by turning the pages of a book to reveal their national flag.

Spain's entrant, **Serafin**, was the first blind singer to appear in the contest and remains one of only a few such handicapped performers to reach the final. There had been much speculation that his blindness would win sympathy votes from the judges, but since he finished fourteenth, Spain's worst placing since 1987, this prediction was not borne out.

Kali was the Rastafarian singer from the Caribbean island of Martinique who was chosen to sing the French entry. His song was sung in French Creole, the only use of that language in the history of the contest. Dreadlocked Kali played a small banjo and was accompanied by a band wearing lively tropical outfits. It was certainly a very unusual entry, perhaps too different to win universal support. France finished outside the top four for the first time in four years, ending in eighth place, despite huge support from the audience in Malmö.

Not surprisingly, even bigger support went to the Swedish song, although it was enthusiasm that was not matched by the judges' marks. **Christer Björkman**'s lushly

Linda shot to the top of the Irish charts with **'Why Me?'** and did the same in Austria, but was not so well thought of elsewhere. In the UK, she became the first Irish winner not to get to the top, spending just two weeks in the list, peaking at No. 59. In the Dutch chart she did better, climbing to No. 23 but didn't register in Sweden at all.

orchestrated ballad had a memorable melody, and served as a stark contrast to Carola's winner the year before, but any hopes of a second consecutive win were dashed when Sweden had to wait until the sixth round of voting for a single point and ended up in twenty-second place, the worst placing by the home nation for 34 years. At least they had their Nordic neighbours for company – Finland only scored three with 'Yamma Yamma', a song about the noise that comes from a radio when browsing the frequencies, the lyrical depth of which was equal to the Eurovision classic 'Boom Boom', while Norway returned to type with a rousing song that was nonetheless highly unpopular.

Mary Spiteri was the diva of the night and gave a very powerful performance to finish third, Malta's best entry to date. For the first time since 1960, Luxembourg chose a song in Luxembourgian for their entry. On that occasion, Luxembourg had ended in last place, which may have been the reason why all its subsequent entries, including its five winners, were sung in French. **Marion Welter**, dressed in a highly colourful jacket and a yellow skirt, was joined by remnants of the 1989 group Park Café, only they were now known as **Kontinent**. Few commentators were unable to resist a joke about Marion being 'in-kontinent'. The judges were able to resist the song almost completely, with Malta being the only country to award it any votes at all, a remarkably high ten, which left Marion in twenty-first place, still ahead of her hosts.

The Danish entry had the cleverest lyrics of the evening – a conversation set to music. One half of the duo, **Kenny Lübcke**, was a successful rock singer in Denmark, but the other, **Lotte Nilsson**, was taking time away from her usual job as a schoolteacher. **Mia Martini** had appeared in the 1977 contest in London, without much success, but was better appreciated this time around. She had been consistently rated as one of Italy's most popular and successful singers over the last decade and a half, hitting the charts many times and building a huge reputation. Her sister, Loredana Bertè, was also a popular singer and the two vied for the public's attention throughout their highly successful careers. Martini's entry was a dramatic piece that started slowly and built to a climax. Her voice had some of the earthy sound of Edith Piaf. She was not even put off when a fan called out 'good luck' to her just as the music started. In the end, the Italian song proved to be either enormously popular or not rated at all among the judges, but Martini still managed fourth place. It was almost the last highlight of her career, as she died in mysterious circumstances in 1995.

Germany's **Wind**, the only act ever to have secured two second places in the contest, were back for their third try at the Eurovision crown. With only two of the orginal members left, they were almost unrecognisable from their first appearance in Gothenburg in 1985 and their anthemic entry ended in sixteenth place.

Dismayed by the results of its recent efforts, the United Kingdom persuaded the highly regarded singer **Michael Ball** to enter Eurovision. He came to Malmö as the hot favourite to win, even if his song was a little dated. Many voiced concerns that his deep tones were more suited to slow ballads, but he reiterated that he was glad to be able to present a more up-tempo number in contrast to his usual singing style. He gave the song a tremendous performance, certainly the best given by any UK singer since the mid-1970s. His confidence and professionalism were evident, but it was not enough to take the song to first place. Despite leading, and running neck-and-neck with the winner for much of the voting, Ball eventually had to settle for the UK's thirteenth second place.

It was quite a year for well-known artists to be in the field. All of the top four artists were well-established performers with many successes under their belts. In 1990s Eurovision, this was quite an unusual occurrence. **Linda Martin**, singing for Ireland, had been one of the Emerald Isle's best-known artists since she came to the fore with the

Linda Martin and Johnny Logan collect the Grand Prix. It was the fourth time Ireland had taken the title since their debut in 1965. A delighted Linda thanked the audience and everyone in Ireland. Johnny sent messages to his parents in Australia and also sent a heartfelt greeting to Shay Healy, the writer of his first winning song 'What's Another Year?'

band Chips in the mid-1970s. As a soloist, she had finished second with the Johnny Logan penned 'Terminal Three' at the 1984 Eurovision. She was hoping to go one better this year with another Logan effort, 'Why Me?'.

Johnny Logan admits that it appealed to him to have won the contest in 1980 singing someone else's song; to have won again in 1987 singing his own song; and to have another singer win with one of his songs in 1992. It was certainly something no other singer or writer had yet achieved, or indeed attempted, in the contest.

Martin was not daunted by having to follow the far more luminous Michael Ball on to the stage and she gave a very confident and controlled performance, wearing a pale green off the shoulder number, decorated in silver. Although it did not have the impact of either the Maltese, British or Italian entries, it was the one the judges favoured among the top-ranked songs and took the honours for the Irish, their fourth win to date. It was the start of a remarkable run of success for the small island nation.

Linda Martin became only the third person ever to finish both first and second in the contest, although unlike Lys Assia and Gigliola Cinquetti, she achieved her first win at her second attempt, having finished second with her first. It was also the fourth time Ireland had taken the title since their debut in 1965.

Michael Ball continued his highly successful career, even surpassing the successes he had experienced prior to his Eurovision appearance. UK Channel ITV gave him his own TV series and he had a string of hit albums, including a chart-topping CD containing five of the songs from the UK heat. In an interview with the BBC shortly after he sang in Malmö, he was asked if we would take part again. He replied that he'd '... rather stick needles in my eyes.'

After the debacle of the Roman production, the Swedes certainly deserved praise for their excellent show in 1992. The contest seemed to be back on track, and ratings were creeping up again after their nadir in the late 1980s. The scene was set for an equally memorable broadcast in 1993.

country	song	performer	place	score	draw
Ireland	Why Me?	**Linda Martin**	1	155	17
United Kingdom	One Step Out Of Time	**Michael Ball**	2	139	16
Malta	Little Child	**Mary Spiteri**	3	123	10
Italy	Rapsodia	**Mia Martini**	4	111	19
Greece	Olou Tou Kosmou I Elpida	**Cleopatra**	5	94	5
Israel	Ze Rak Sport	**Dafna**	6	85	3
Iceland	Nei Eda Ja	**Heart 2 Heart**	7	80	11
France	Monté La Riviè	**Kali**	8	73	6
Netherlands	Wijs Me De Weg	**Humphrey Campbell**	9	67	23
Austria	Zusammen Geh'n	**Tony Wegas**	10	63	15
Cyprus	Teriazoume	**Evridiki**	11	57	9
Denmark	Alt Det Som Ingen Ser	**Lotte Nilsson & Kenny Lübcke**	12	47	18
Yugoslavia	Ljubim Te Pesmama	**Extra Nena**	13	44	20
Spain	Todo Estas Es La Musica	**Serafin**	14	37	1
Switzerland	Mr Music Man	**Daisy Auvray**	15	32	13
Germany	Träume Sind Für Alle Da	**Wind**	16	27	22
Portugal	Amor D'Agua Fresca	**Dina**	17	26	8
Norway	Visjoner	**Merethe Trøan**	18	23	21
Turkey	Yaz Bitti	**Aylin Vatankos**	19	17	4
Belgium	Nous On Veut Des Violons	**Morgane**	20	11	2
Luxembourg	Sou Fräi	**Marion Welter & Kontinent**	21	10	14
Sweden	I Morgon Är En Annan Dag	**Christer Björkman**	22	9	7
Finland	Yamma Yamma	**Pave Maijanen**	23	4	12

Winner

Ireland

Performer

Niamh Kavanagh

1993

Title

'In Your Eyes'

Composer

Jimmy Walsh

Presenter

Fionnuala Sweeney

Host & Venue

RTE Green Glens Arena

Millstreet
Ireland

As Linda Martin was singing her reprise on stage in Malmö, out in the west of Ireland, an entrepreneur by the name of Noel C. Duggan was composing a letter to Irish broadcaster RTE before Linda Martin had even finished performing her song. Mr Duggan was the owner and driving force behind the Green Glens Arena, a large indoor stadium, used primarily for show jumping and horse trials. It was not dissimilar to the RDS complex in Dublin, which had hosted the event in 1981 and 1988, but it was located outside of the nation's capital. Way outside. The venue was situated in the tiny village of Millstreet, a dot on the map in County Cork, far to the west of Dublin. It boasted no infrastructure save for a small railway station and had a population of only 1,500. It wasn't that the contest had not been to small towns before – Lugano and Harrogate were hardly bustling metropolises – but never before had such a tiny village been considered. But Mr Duggan impressed RTE, who agreed with his vision to bring an Irish-based contest outside of Dublin for the first, and to date, only time.

There were many obstacles to be overcome for the broadcast on 15th May, even after the contracts were signed. The floor of the arena needed to be dug out to expand the ceiling height and changes to the infrastructure of the town, including expanding the railway line and station, all took considerable effort. But by the time the contest rolled

Below: Ireland's Niamh Kavanagh wore a burgundy jacket over a long black skirt. This may have been in deference to her mother, who had reputedly criticised her for wearing trousers in the Irish heat.

Below right: Munchener Freiheit were one of Germany's most popular bands, but success eluded them at Eurovision.

around, all the necessary changes were completed. The performers and delegates were housed in Cork City and Killarney, 30 miles away, and shuttle buses had to bring everyone to the arena for the rehearsals.

The EBU had altered the rules to permit a record 25 nations to enter the 1993 contest, making it the biggest field to date. However, only 22 made it there automatically. The remaining three places would go to the top three songs from a preliminary heat to be staged in Ljubljana, Slovenia. Speculation circulated that anything upwards of 20 nations would compete in the qualifier alone, but in the end only seven countries actually took part, with the three former constituencies of Yugoslavia – Bosnia-Herzegovina, Croatia and Slovenia – making it through to the Millstreet final. There they joined the 22 nations from 1992 who had all been given automatic entry. The only missing country was what remained of Yugoslavia, who had been expelled as broadcaster JRT had ceased to exit. It was also determined that the bottom placed nations would be relegated from the next contest.

This was a Eurovision Song Contest with a far bigger media profile than in previous years. Much of the pre-publicity for the show centred on the highly unusual location of the contest, and it wasn't always positive – a BBC newsreader commented that the contest was being staged in a cowshed. The inclusion of the three ex-Yugoslavian republics also attracted much media interest, not least because the entries from Bosnia-Herzegovina and Croatia were political songs about the war dividing them. The Bosnian band had fled Sarajevo under gunfire to reach Millstreet, leaving their conductor trapped on the tarmac.

The set design for the contest was quite dazzling. For the first time, a completely translucent set had been built, which was lit from beneath by neon tubes and from above with I-beams and other lighting effects. It was a very successful effect, allowing the motionless set to appear different for every act. Suspended above the performing area was a mirror image of the floor and the slanted backdrop gave the whole concept a slightly distorted perspective. In the centre of the stage was a hidden doorway that was used for the entrance of hostess **Fionnuala Sweeney** and for the winner's triumphant return at the close of the show.

The postcards shown between each song varied little from the concept already used for both the Dublin contests of 1981 and 1988, except that the use of corporate sponsorship was certainly now more prominent. Thus it was that viewers were able to see the Slovenians disembarking from their Aer Lingus jet; the Danes enjoying some Jameson's Whiskey; the Icelandic singer doing a bit of shopping in Dublin and the Italians at Waterford Castle.

Enrico Ruggeri's style of singing was not dissimilar to the gravelly sounds of Rod Stewart. This was somewhat out of kilter with the mood of the song, which was essentially a ballad. It built well and had a memorable hook, but as an opener for the contest, it was somewhat low-key.

IN YOUR EYES
Eurovision Song Contest Winner, 1993

Niamh achieved great success with 'In Your Eyes', registering the biggest-selling single of the year in Ireland, and making it to No. 24 in the UK charts. She did not return to her job at the bank but, surprisingly, did not return to the charts either.

This was to be Italy's last regular contribution to the contest. They placed twelfth and have only competed once since. Germany was fielding one of the night's most familiar names in this year's line-up: **Münchener Freiheit**. They had hit the charts all over Europe in the late 1980s but like so many successful acts before them, the white-clad, male sextet discovered that name recognition means precious little to the Eurovision juries.

The Swiss had the only emotive French ballad of the 1993 edition, with the Canadian **Annie Cotton** pouring great passion into it. She was well appreciated by the judges, achieving third place.

Tommy Seebach has never had much appreciation in Eurovision. He had twice before represented Denmark in the contest, finishing sixth and eleventh. For his third and final effort in 1993, he was part of the Tommy Seebach Band, a folksy group that performed standing in a circle in the centre of the stage, while the cameras moved around them. Including a whistling interlude, a rarity amongst Eurovision songs, it was not enough to stop the Danes from being relegated. They scored just nine points and finished in twenty-second place – falling foul of the rapidly expanding contest's new rules alongside Luxembourg, Israel, Turkey, Belgium and the debutant Slovenia.

Tony Wegas had a disappointing result in Malmö and came straight back to Millstreet to try again for Austria to fare even worse. His song was a much cheerier number than his earlier effort and was the first really up-tempo song of the night. Yet again, it was not the Austrians' year, and they

Above left: Spain's entry was sung by Eva Santamaria, with two backing singers and three highly excited dancers.

Above: The UK's Sonia rehearses her number, 'Better The Devil You Know'.

slipped down to fourteenth place. Tony Wegas also slipped personally when he was jailed just a few years later for stealing from two elderly women in Vienna to buy drugs. It was a fairly ignominious end for the Romany singer.

Having experimented with different musical styles over the last few years, France entered what could really be described as a very typical piece of Eurovision music for 1993. 'Mama Corsica' ('Mother Corsica') was sung by the young heartthrob **Patrick Fiori**, and was an infectiously catchy song that ended in a strong fourth place.

The Irish bookies had great faith that Ireland would take the Eurovision prize for the second year running, but few really believed the judges would choose the same nation again, especially as the song was not so inherently different from the 1993 winner, 'Why me?'. Singer **Niamh Kavanagh** had to take time off from her job as a clerk with the Allied Irish Bank in order to compete in Millstreet. Her employers took a full-page advertisement in the national Irish press on the day of the contest, telling her to take the following Monday off if she won! She was not without some high-profile experience, however, having contributed tracks to the soundtrack of Alan Parker's hit movie *The Commitments*. Not surprisingly, she received an overwhelming ovation from the audience after a confident performance of Jimmy Walsh's 'In Your Eyes'.

country	song	performer	place	score	draw
Ireland	In Your Eyes	**Niamh Kavanagh**	1	187	14
United Kingdom	Better The Devil You Know	**Sonia**	2	164	19
Switzerland	Moi Tout Simplement	**Annie Cotton**	3	148	4
France	Mama Corsica	**Patrick Fiori**	4	121	12
Norway	Alle Mine Tankar	**Silje Vige**	5	120	25
Netherlands	Vrede	**Ruth Jacott**	6	92	20
Sweden	Eloise	**Arvingarna**	7	89	13
Malta	This Time	**William Mangion**	8	69	7
Greece	Ellada, Hora Tou Fotos	**Kati Garbi**	9	64	6
Portugal	A Cidade Até Ser Dia	**Anabela**	10	60	11
Spain	Hombres	**Eva Santamaria**	11	58	22
Italy	Sole d'Europa	**Enrico Ruggeri**	12	45	1
Iceland	Pá Veistu Svarid	**Inga**	13	42	9
Austria	Maria Magdalena	**Tony Wegas**	14	32	10
Croatia	Don't Ever Cry	**Put**	15	31	21
Bosnia-Herzegovina	Sva Bol Svijeta	**Fazla**	16	27	18
Finland	Tule Luo	**Katri Helena**	17	20	17
Germany	Viel Zu Weit	**Münchener Freiheit**	18	18	3
Cyprus	Mi Stamatas	**Zymboulakis & Van Beke**	19	17	23
Luxembourg	Donnez Moi Une Chance De Te Dire	**Modern Times**	20	11	15
Turkey	Esmer Yarim	**Burak Aydos**	21	10	2
Denmark	Under Stjernerne På Himlen	**Tommy Seebach Band**	22=	9	5
Slovenia	Tih Deževan Dan	**1 x band**	22=	9	16
Israel	Shiru	**Lamakat Shiru w/ Saraleh Sharon**	24	4	24
Belgium	Iemand Als Jij	**Barbara**	25	3	8

Ireland's main rival was the United Kingdom's **Sonia** – a hugely successful pop star who'd been nominated to enter by the British arm of the Eurovision fan club. She became only the sixth act ever to sing for the UK who had a number one single under their belt before entering the contest.

On the night, Sonia – wearing a purple catsuit – turned in possibly the best performance on the Millstreet stage. Her presence was very strong, and she played to the camera perfectly. It was greeted with strong, but not over-enthusiastic applause from the partisan Irish audience, but certainly looked like a winning entry, even if it was rather a weak composition, and provided one of the most exciting voting sequences yet seen. The tension during the voting was heightened by the failure to reach the Maltese jury. In the end Malta voted last and their decisions were crucial. The Irish only needed one point to win, but the UK could still clinch the title if they received 12 and the Irish received nothing at all. Malta certainly kept the atmosphere alive.

After awarding Luxembourg ten points the tension in the hall and backstage reached fever pitch. If the UK got the 12, they had won. If not, even if the points did not go to Ireland, the Irish had it. The Maltese spokesman certainly played out the drama, when, after a pause, he announced 'Ireland, 12 points'. The audience went wild, while backstage cameras showed Sonia looking crushed, but still making an effort to congratulate the jubilant winner.

Niamh Kavanagh achieved great success with her winning song, registering the biggest selling single of the year in Ireland and making it to number 24 in the UK charts. She did not return to her job at the bank, but surprisingly did not return to the charts either.

The 1993 contest was a triumph for Irish broadcaster RTE, but gave them a big headache as to whether they could stage the contest again the following year, according to the rules. They did not fail in their duty, becoming the first country ever to stage the show two years in succession.

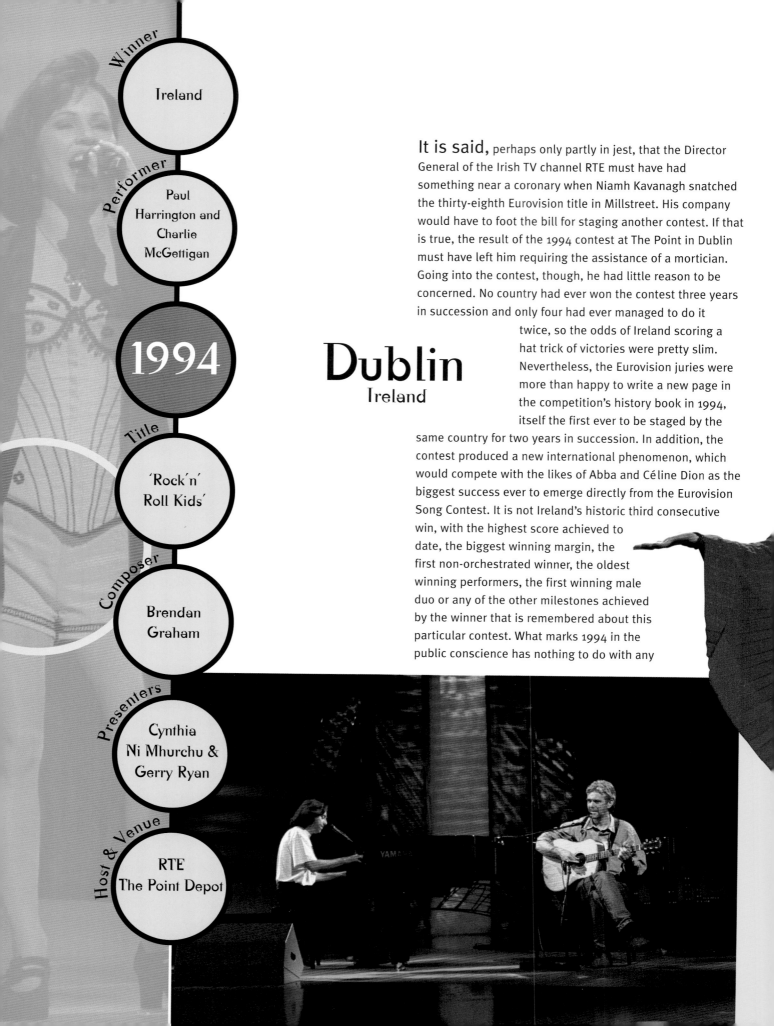

Winner

Ireland

Performer

Paul
Harrington and
Charlie
McGettigan

1994

Title

'Rock'n'
Roll Kids'

Composer

Brendan
Graham

Presenters

Cynthia
Ni Mhurchu &
Gerry Ryan

Host & Venue

RTE
The Point Depot

Dublin
Ireland

It is said, perhaps only partly in jest, that the Director General of the Irish TV channel RTE must have had something near a coronary when Niamh Kavanagh snatched the thirty-eighth Eurovision title in Millstreet. His company would have to foot the bill for staging another contest. If that is true, the result of the 1994 contest at The Point in Dublin must have left him requiring the assistance of a mortician. Going into the contest, though, he had little reason to be concerned. No country had ever won the contest three years in succession and only four had ever managed to do it twice, so the odds of Ireland scoring a hat trick of victories were pretty slim. Nevertheless, the Eurovision juries were more than happy to write a new page in the competition's history book in 1994, itself the first ever to be staged by the same country for two years in succession. In addition, the contest produced a new international phenomenon, which would compete with the likes of Abba and Céline Dion as the biggest success ever to emerge directly from the Eurovision Song Contest. It is not Ireland's historic third consecutive win, with the highest score achieved to date, the biggest winning margin, the first non-orchestrated winner, the oldest winning performers, the first winning male duo or any of the other milestones achieved by the winner that is remembered about this particular contest. What marks 1994 in the public conscience has nothing to do with any of the songs or singers in this year's competition at all – it is what happened during the seven minutes that the juries were adding up their scores.

The producers had commissioned Bill Whelan to compose some traditional Celtic music for the interval to which the world champion Irish dancers Jean Butler and Michael Flatley added dramatic interpretations alongside a plethora of other dancers. The piece was named '**Riverdance**' and inadvertently started a phenomenon that swept the world and made Flatley a multi-millionaire,

The stage set for the thirty-ninth contest was designed to resemble Dublin. All around the backdrop were neon-lit representations of tall buildings and skyscrapers, which incorporated video screens and lighting effects into their structures. Beneath the stage was a snaking path of under-floor lights representing the Liffey River, and on either side of the vast set was a column-lined podium for the presenters **Cynthia Ni Mhurchu** and **Gerry Ryan**.

After the formalities – and informalities, among which was a parade of giant papier-mâché heads featuring Irish stars such as Bono and Sinead O'Connor – the show began with the Swedish entry.

Marie Bergman had come to Dublin some 23 years earlier to sing with the Family Four, now she returned in tandem with **Roger Pontare**. They were both somewhat oddly dressed. Pontare inexplicably as an American Indian and Bergman in a sleeveless gown and a bowler hat. Sweden's eastern neighbours came next, with **Cat Cat** singing for Finland. The two sisters, a blonde and a brunette, came to Dublin with what was possibly Finland's most hotly-tipped entry to date, but unwisely opted to wear what one pundit described as their mother's underwear. Despite having arrived in the city as one of the favourites, the Finns once again found themselves languishing at the bottom end of the results table.

Unimpressive was the word that most critics used to describe the host nation's effort. Indeed there was a strong media rumour circulating that Ireland had deliberately chosen a song deemed certain to lose. Not since Séverine had won for Monaco had the contest been won by the third song and that was 23 years ago when Dublin had played host for the very first time. This in itself should have provided a clue as to the potential of the Irish entry and there were many similar portents to examine. Not only were the Irish going for their third consecutive win and singing in third place, but it was the third time the Irish entry had been penned by **Brendan Graham** and the third time a male duo had represented the country. Jimmy and Tommy Swarbrigg had sung twice for Ireland in the 1970s and now **Paul Harrington** and **Charlie McGettigan** were hoping to go where they had failed, and both of Graham's earlier efforts had stopped short.

Left: Russian contestant Youddiph's dramatic and versatile outfit was likened to a sun-dried tomato by the UK's commentator, Terry Wogan.

Far left: Paul Harrington and Charlie McGettigan's low-key ballad was a highly unusual entry. Many were sceptical about the selection process, and a whispering campaign circulated that RTE had deliberately chosen a song deemed unlikely to win.

Commercially, 'Rock'n'Roll Kids' fared badly. In Ireland it only got to No. 2, kept off the top by the single release of the 'Riverdance' music. In the Dutch chart, the Irish duo climbed to No. 23, but barely registered anywhere else. It remains the only Irish winner of the contest not to chart in the UK at all.

The two male singers accompanied themselves on piano and guitar, with no other musical or vocal backing. The title of the song, 'Rock'n'Roll Kids' suggested perhaps an upbeat number with a finger-snapping beat, but the song was actually a very low-key ballad, with little variation in tempo or mood. It told the story of two older men reminiscing about their younger days back in 1962, when Elvis was the top of the pops. It was a very simple piece that was in strong contrast to almost everything else on offer this year, yet it was not widely expected to do well. As they finished, it was clear the audience was behind them and they received a massive cheer.

It wasn't the biggest of the night, though, which was saved for the second entry from Bosnia-Herzegovina. **Alma and Dejan** were so taken aback by the tumultuous reception given to their arrival on stage that conductor Sinan Alimanović had to wait for the cheering and applause to die down before he could cue the song. The audience seemed oblivious to the need to hear the Bosnian entry and continued their deafening support even after the music started. Dejan, the male half of the duo, could not hear anything at all and missed all of his first lines, mumbling in an almost inaudible attempt to catch up. Many commentators felt that this show of support for the troubled nation might well influence the judge's decision, but in fact it did not. Bosnia did improve on their debut showing, but only by one place to end in fifteenth position.

Six nations had been relegated from the line-up from the previous year, with Italy choosing to stay away by choice. Estonia, Hungary, Lithuania, Poland, Romania, Russia and Slovakia took the vacant slots in the largest-ever influx of new countries in a single contest. But there were disappointing entries from the new nations. Romania, Lithuania and Estonia made terrible debuts, whereas Poland and Hungary excelled. Poland climbed to second place, the best yet showing for a debutant country. But the Polish entry was not without criticism, particularly when, at the dress rehearsal viewed by the judges, **Edyta Gorniak** partially sang in English, against all the contest rules.

Bernd Meinunger and Ralph Siegel were back for another go this year and had turned to three youngsters, **Mekado**, to sing 'Wir Geben 'Ne Party' ('We're Giving A Party'). It was the tenth entry the German duo had penned for the contest and it was certainly the most hotly tipped to provide a German win since Nicole had sung one of their earlier efforts in Harrogate. The three girls, Melanie, Kati and Dorkas, were newly formed as an act, yet they came to the contest very well prepared. The song was, of course, performed in German, but Siegel had cleverly selected phrasing that at the very least sounded the same in any language. The title alone sounds uncannily like the English translation.

Among the new nations, Slovakia had picked their most popular band, **Tublatanka,** to sing their very first song in the final. The long-haired, six-piece group looked more like a band from the early 1970s than a thrusting 1990s outfit and ended equal nineteenth, which meant that Slovakia would not return to Eurovision until 1996. Lithuania would not be back until 1999, as they followed in Portugal's footsteps by failing to score a single point with their debut effort.

The appearance of the Russians in the contest was the main focal point of much of the media interest and coverage of the competition. Young **Youddiph**, or Judith or even Piligrim, her pen name as lyricist, depending apparently

Above: Choreography played a big part in the German presentation from Mekado. The routine devised by the girls was very slick, though it caused them some problems in the final dress rehearsals and some extra last-minute practice was required to get things right.

Left: The two sisters of Finland's Cat Cat wore corsets, one in pink and one in green, with long black coats over the top. Two male dancers accompanied their singing with some eccentric, but nonetheless accomplished dancing, but the whole effect was very unimpressive.

on the time of day or the young lady's whim, gave many interviews expressing her joy at being in the contest. It was a strong effort, enhanced perhaps by the most unusual outfit of the night. Apparently dressed in a cowl, the youngster was able to wrap the fabric of the unusually designed dress into various different styles, adding visual appeal to her strong vocal performance. Unkind commentators noted that one of the styles she adopted during the song made her resemble a sun-dried tomato.

After the tremendous reception for 'Riverdance,' it was apparent that the Irish would storm to victory at least half-way through the voting and the audience became wildly excited at the thought. Every time the entry received top marks, they started to chant 'olé, olé, olé', the Irish mantra that was usually reserved for international soccer and rugby events. Gerry Ryan had to repeatedly ask the audience to quieten down, but they were too excited at the prospect of another win.

The two singers of the winning song seemed as shocked by the result as everyone else was and sat backstage looking somewhat stunned. When they made their way onto the stage, they were elated, and hugged everyone in sight. As fireworks erupted around the stage and over the Dublin docks outside, Paul Harrington and Charlie McGettigan began their reprise of the most unlikely winner to take the title to date.

It had been a very exciting and accomplished production, with RTE proving that their consummate production skills were equal to creating two successive contests that were unique in style and presentation. They had a very large problem ahead of them to consider, though, and retreated to discuss quite how to approach this unexpected victory. In the outside world, the Irish win was not warmly welcomed at all, particularly in the ever-growing fan base where disbelief, disdain and protestations at the winning song were rife.

country	song	performer	place	score	draw
Ireland	Rock'n'Roll Kids	**Paul Harrington & Charlie McGettigan**	1	226	3
Poland	To Nie Ja	**Edyta Gorniak**	2	166	24
Germany	Wir Geben 'Ne Party	**Mekado**	3	128	14
Hungary	Kinek Mondjam El Vétkeimet	**Friderika Bayer**	4	122	22
Malta	More Than Love	**Moira & Chris**	5	97	12
Norway	Duett	**Elisabeth Andreasson & Jan Werner Danielsen**	6	76	17
France	Je Suis Un Vrai Garçon	**Nina Morato**	7	74	25
Portugal	Chamar A Musica	**Sara Tavares**	8	73	8
Russia	Vechni Stranik	**Youddiph**	9	70	23
United Kingdom	We Will Be Free (Lonely Symphony)	**Frances Ruffelle**	10	63	6
Cyprus	Ime Anthropos Ki'ego	**Evridiki**	11	51	4
Iceland	Nætur	**Sigga**	12	49	5
Sweden	Stjärnorna	**Marie Bergman & Roger Pontare**	13	48	1
Greece	Diri Diri	**Kostas Bigalis & The Sea Lovers**	14	44	19
Bosnia-Herzegovina	Ostani Kraj Mene	**Alma & Dejan**	15	39	18
Croatia	Nek Ti Bude Ljubav Sva	**Toni Cetinski**	16	27	7
Austria	Für Den Frieden Der Welt	**Petra Frey**	17	19	20
Spain	Ella No Es Ella	**Alejandro Abad**	18	17	21
Switzerland	Sto Pregando	**Duilio**	19=	15	9
Slovakia	Nekonecna Piesen	**Martin Ďurinda & Tublatanka**	19=	15	15
Romania	Dincolo Di Nori	**Dan Bittman**	21	14	11
Finland	Bye Bye Baby	**Cat Cat**	22	11	2
Netherlands	Waar Is De Zon?	**Willeke Alberti**	23	4	13
Estonia	Nagu Merelaine	**Silvi Vrait**	24	2	10
Lithuania	Lopšiné Mylimai	**Ovidijus Vyšniauskas**	25	0	16

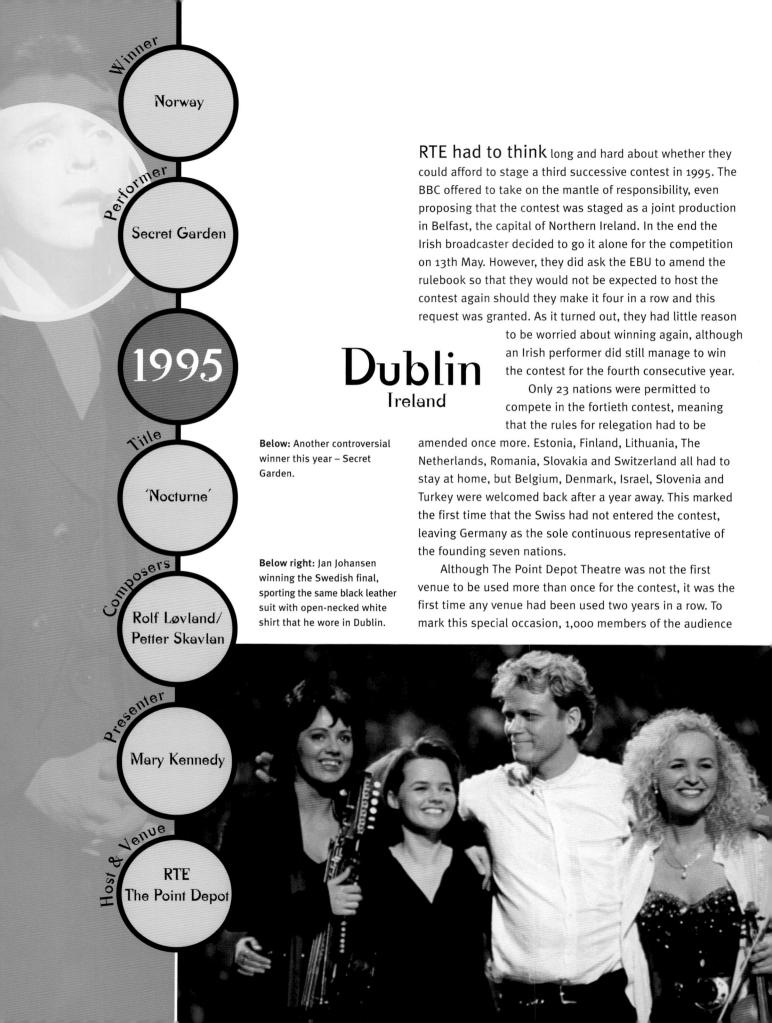

Winner

Norway

Performer

Secret Garden

1995

Title

'Nocturne'

Composers

**Rolf Løvland/
Petter Skavlan**

Presenter

Mary Kennedy

Host & Venue

**RTE
The Point Depot**

Dublin
Ireland

Below: Another controversial winner this year – Secret Garden.

Below right: Jan Johansen winning the Swedish final, sporting the same black leather suit with open-necked white shirt that he wore in Dublin.

RTE had to think long and hard about whether they could afford to stage a third successive contest in 1995. The BBC offered to take on the mantle of responsibility, even proposing that the contest was staged as a joint production in Belfast, the capital of Northern Ireland. In the end the Irish broadcaster decided to go it alone for the competition on 13th May. However, they did ask the EBU to amend the rulebook so that they would not be expected to host the contest again should they make it four in a row and this request was granted. As it turned out, they had little reason to be worried about winning again, although an Irish performer did still manage to win the contest for the fourth consecutive year.

Only 23 nations were permitted to compete in the fortieth contest, meaning that the rules for relegation had to be amended once more. Estonia, Finland, Lithuania, The Netherlands, Romania, Slovakia and Switzerland all had to stay at home, but Belgium, Denmark, Israel, Slovenia and Turkey were welcomed back after a year away. This marked the first time that the Swiss had not entered the contest, leaving Germany as the sole continuous representative of the founding seven nations.

Although The Point Depot Theatre was not the first venue to be used more than once for the contest, it was the first time any venue had been used two years in a row. To mark this special occasion, 1,000 members of the audience won their seats in the auditorium by drawing winning scratch cards on the Irish National Lottery.

To commemorate the fortieth Eurovision Song Contest, a montage of previous entries was displayed across the stage. The screens were pulled back to reveal the set and presenter **Mary Kennedy** appeared at the top of a very high staircase, which was hoisted up into the rafters, not to be seen again, once she reached the bottom. The set resembled a giant arrow, sweeping down from the back of the stage area, with the pointed head forming the platform for the performers. Two 'wings' jutted out of the side of the stage for the use of backing singers and musicians.

Poland began the evening with an unusual and haunting piece performed by the singer **Justyna**. It was a brave attempt to broaden the musical horizons of Eurovision, and the song showed off her impressive vocal range. But the departure from convention was not hugely appreciated by the judges, and she ended up in 18th place.

Ireland's Eurovision record from 1992 to 1997 is as follows: first, first, first, fourteenth, first and second. It would not take a genius to work out from these results which year the Irish song was sung in the dreaded second slot! **Eddie Friel** was not daunted by this seemingly luckless draw, but had other concerns. Continual criticism and harassment dogged him about his song, which many believed plagarised an old hit by singer Julie Felix. Narrowly avoiding disqualification, Friel performed, seated on a stool

and accompanied by an accordion player. It is hard to see why this particular Irish song was so unappreciated by the judges, as it was not wholly dissimilar to any of the songs that had won for them, and indeed, in many camps, it was regarded as a superior effort to the 1994 winner. Regardless, it was not to be Ireland's year.

The most unusual and controversial entry was from Norway's **Secret Garden**. The exact configuration of the group's membership was unclear, but the main focus was on the Norwegian composer Rolf Løvland and Irish violinist Fionnuala Sherry, who had met at the previous year's contest when Sherry was performing for the house orchestra. For the performance three other artists were brought in to add to the group playing a keyfiddle and whistle. A singer named Gunnhild Tvinnereim performed the lyrics – those that there were – for 'Nocturne' consisted of only 24 words spread over seven lines. There are many examples of Eurovision songs having few lyrics, but these songs tended to simply repeat them over and over. The words of 'Nocturne' were sung only twice, once at the beginning and once at the end of the song. The rest of the 'song' was purely music, performed largely by violinist Sherry.

Many predicted good things for this highly distinctive effort, but others felt it was too obscure to win, particularly as it barely constituted a song at all, being predominantly an instrumental number. When it romped home to the top spot, the song's critics made their voices even louder, forcing

Secret Garden found lasting success around the world, but limited success with the single of **'Nocturne'**, making the Top 10 in Ireland and Belgium and falling just short in the Netherlands. However, the single had a fairly limited release, not appearing in UK stores until November and not issued at all in Norway.

changes to the rules regarding the structure of future entries. It was too late for this year, and Norway took the prize after leading from the front. It was a particularly good year for the Scandinavian nations, all of whom ended the contest in the top five.

Austria had chosen a jazz song by well-known black singer **Stella Jones** as their entry. No black performer had yet won the contest. It was a lively effort, but Jones's odd choice of costume, a maroon-and-white trouser ensemble, possibly did her no favours, nor did the antics of the female saxophonist who made it blatantly clear that she was miming, which, although perfectly permissible, seemed out of place. Another fashion faux pas came from the flamboyant Russian, **Philipp Kirkorov**, who wore a billowing white shirt, skin-tight black trousers, calf-length black boots and a chest full of heavy gold medallions. Sadly, this outfit didn't detract from a poorly received entry.

Belgium was back from their year away, but only scored five more points than the song that had led to their relegation in 1993. 'La Voix Est Libre' ('The Voice Is Free'), was sung by **Frédéric Etherlinck**, a handsome young man from French-speaking Wallonia. It was an anthemic piece, but performed in a careless manner that cannot have helped its cause.

The United Kingdom, as ever, arrived at Eurovision to much fanfare. In an attempt to modernise the contest, a multicultural rap group called **Love City Groove** had been chosen for the contest, but despite their attempts to add a streetwise flavour to the contest, they ultimately floundered only just inside the top ten due to an inability to sing live.

Sweden had been one of the two most favoured entrants among the bookies and certainly appeared to be the favourite with the audience. **Jan Johansen** sang the moody 'Se På Mej' ('Look At Me') in a black leather suit with an open-necked white shirt. It was a very strong ballad that he performed in a smouldering, smoky tone. The arrangement for the live presentation of the song included a lush string accompaniment, but unfortunately, due to a technical error with the sound, the strings went unheard by the juries and

Right: Eddie Friel accumulated 44 points and ended fourteenth, which to date was the third worst showing ever for an Irish entry.

Far right: Germany was to fare even worse than the Irish, scoring only one single point. Husband-and-wife team Stone and Stone were singing their own composition, a moody piece with changing rhythms and a pitch that seemed hard for Cheyenne, dressed in a shapeless white frock, to master. It was a very contemporary sound, but not what the judges wanted.

audience alike. The voters liked it, though, but not enough in the final count and yet again the favourites were beaten, ending the night in third place. The Swedes' neighbours, Denmark, made an impressive return to the contest, with a song by **Aud Wilken** that had a syncopated rhythm and a banjo accompaniment. It completed the trio of Scandinavian songs in the top five – the third best showing for a Danish song since their return to the contest in 1978.

Unlike the previous year there was no 'Riverdance' to set the world alight, but there was again a resounding victory from one entry. The Norwegians had set the pace of the voting from the start, picking up six 12-point scores in total. By the time Israel had voted, Norway had secured its victory, its second in the contest. It was a sweeping win, if an unexpected one, and Rolf Løvland joined the very exclusive club of men who have written two winning songs.

Despite losing, there was cause for celebration for Spain too. **Anabel Condé** gave a very strong performance, which carried her to second place, albeit a distant one. Cyprus, in finishing ninth, without the usual 12 points from Greece, had their best showing since 1987.

Lower down the pecking order, Poland scored only 15 points and ended in eighteenth place, the lowest placing to date for the opening number. Germany – who had been represented by husband and wife duo **Stone and Stone** – fared even worse than the Irish, scoring only one single point, their lowest score since gaining zero in 1965 and their worst placing yet. The Russians ended in seventeenth place with marks from only three nations, but viewers in Russia got a very different perspective. They did not receive the transmission live and, although it was not stated, it was heavily hinted that **Phillipp Kirkorov** was the winner. His song was presented last, with none of the voting shown at all.

Although Ireland had not won the 1995 contest, they did stage an impressive production and provided Norway with the key performer for their victory – there was a distinctive Celtic feeling to the Norwegian winner. Only one year later, the Irish were back to form.

country	song	performer	place	score	draw
Norway	Nocturne	**Secret Garden**	1	148	5
Spain	Vuelve Conmigo	**Anabel Condé**	2	119	9
Sweden	Se På Mej	**Jan Johansen**	3	100	18
France	Il Me Donne Rendez-vous	**Nathalie Santamaria**	4	94	12
Denmark	Fra Mols Til Skagen	**Aud Wilken**	5	92	19
Croatia	Nostalgija	**Magazin & Lidija**	6	91	11
Slovenia	Prisluhni Mi	**Darja Švajger**	7	84	20
Israel	Amen	**Liora**	8	81	21
Cyprus	Sti Fotia	**Alexandros Panayi**	9	79	17
United Kingdom	Love City Groove	**Love City Groove**	10=	76	15
Malta	Keep Me In Mind	**Mike Spiteri**	10=	76	22
Greece	Pia Prosefhi	**Elina Konstantopoulou**	12	68	23
Austria	Die Welt Dreht Sich Verkerht	**Stella Jones**	13	67	8
Ireland	Dreamin'	**Eddie Friel**	14	44	2
Iceland	Núna	**Bo Halldórsson**	15	31	7
Turkey	Sev	**Arzu Ece**	16	21	10
Russia	Kolybelnaya Dlya Vulkana	**Philipp Kirkorov**	17	17	6
Poland	Sama	**Justyna**	18	15	1
Bosnia-Herzegovina	Dvadeset I Prvi Vijek	**Davor Popović**	19	14	4
Belgium	La Voix Est Libre	**Frédéric Etherlinck**	20	8	14
Portugal	Baunilha E Chocolate	**To Cruz**	21	5	16
Hungary	Új Név A Régi Ház Falán	**Csaba Szigeti**	22	3	13
Germany	Verliebt In Dich	**Stone and Stone**	23	1	3

Winner

Ireland

Performer

Eimear Quinn

1996

Title

'The Voice'

Composer

Brendan Graham

Presenters

Ingvild Bryn & Morten Harket

Host & Venue

NRK Oslo Spektrum

Eimear Quinn raises her glass to another Irish victory.

The biggest Eurovision hit for 20 years came out of the 41st contest in Oslo, although (not for the first time) it was not the winning song that captured the public interest. Norway had their hands full with the organisation of the 1996 event, hampered in part by new EBU rules that meant they did not know which 22 nations would join the hosts until two months before the broadcast on 18th May.

Twenty-nine nations wanted to join the Norwegians in Oslo, but the EBU decreed that only 22 could be allowed entry. Primarily to appease Germany, who had been relegated from the contest after their poor showing in 1995, all interested parties were invited to select a song that would take part in a preliminary audio-only competition to be voted on by the other 28 nations. The results were intended to remain a closely guarded secret, but over time many of the results have slipped into the public domain. It appears from the results that Sweden were the 'winners', with Ireland in second place. The biggest surprise was the countries that were eliminated, which included three former winning nations – Germany, Denmark and Israel – as well as Russia, Hungary, Romania and the Former Yugoslav Republic of Macedonia, who had

Oslo
Norway

been attempting to make their first-ever appearance in the contest.

The Germans took the defeat badly, particularly as they had selected a very contemporary piece of high-energy music as their entry. Eurovision also stood to lose one of the largest audiences in the continent. Not really surprisingly, the concept of having an audio pre-qualifier did not catch on and this was the only time such a method was used to determine the entries.

Two presenters from opposing backgrounds hosted the event at the 6,000-seater Oslo Spektrum: the New York-based news correspondent **Ingvild Bryn** and the lead singer of Norwegian super-group A-ha, **Morten Harket**. The singer was reluctant to accept the invitation to act as compère, but agreed once he learned that he would have the chance to sing his new solo single at the start of the show. After this, a spectacular film based around Norway's history and the customary multi-lingual welcoming remarks, there was time for some comedy banter between the presenters. Possibly the best joke of the show came when Ingvild Bryn pointed out that their victory in 1995 was not the first time that Norway had won Eurovision. 'No,' replied Morten Harket, 'It's the last!' This remained correct until 2009!

The President of Turkey had survived an assassination attempt earlier in the day, which could have resulted in Turkey's withdrawal, or at the very least a quick last-minute edit of his good luck message in the video postcard preceding **Şebnem Paker**'s song. Many other performers surrounded the young Turk, including a scantily-clad violinist and accordion player, who performed the lengthy introduction of this folksy number.

The UK had possibly the hottest pre-contest favourite in over a decade. **Gina G** was an Australian who had settled in London. She arrived in Oslo to learn that her song 'Ooh Aah... Just A Little Bit' had knocked George Michael off the top of the UK charts. It was a very up-tempo piece of Euro-Pop with a driving hi-energy beat and was possibly the most contemporary song performed in the contest for many years. Sadly, on the night Gina simply did not have the ability to carry off the live performance, hitting a bum note at the start and never recovering.

Like Gina G, Belgium's **Lisa del Bo** was riding high in the charts at home with her song as she arrived in Oslo, an unusual feat for a Belgian Eurovision effort in itself. Dressed in a very odd and somewhat unflattering white 'tutu', Lisa

Eimear Quinn was not even able to take **'The Voice'** to the top of the Irish charts. Eimear appears to have returned to her studies and is yet to make any kind of an impact anywhere, including her home nation.

did not really help her cause with her appearance. The lyrics of the upbeat number were also somewhat trite. 'Life is a card game made of jokers and pokers' was not the stuff that winners are made of.

Cyprus had the handsome **Constantinos**, taking time out from his military service, to sing their entry. He was well liked among the female contingent in the audience, particularly the hostess, Ingvild Bryn, who throughout the show had a running joke with her co-presenter about her fondness for the young Cypriot. Constantinos gave a wink to the camera as he ended the dramatic ballad, perhaps intended for Ms Bryn.

For Austria, the blind blues singer **George Nussbaumer** sat at the piano to sing 'Weil's Dr Gut Got' ('When You're Doing Well') with a troupe of backing singers that quite literally threw themselves into the performance of the gospel number. It was the first time ever that a pure gospel song had been heard in the contest, but it was not widely appreciated, ending in a shared tenth place with Malta.

For Norway, **Elisabeth Andreassen** was making her fourth appearance in the contest, but her first as a soloist. Wearing a black gown designed by Jean-Paul Gaultier, and accompanied by haunting panpipes, she sang her anthemic song well to a rousing reception. As the only song on show that had not had to go through the pre-qualifier, it was therefore the only untested song among the jury system, but the Norwegians had nothing to fear. By finishing in their first-ever second place, Norway achieved their third-best result in the history of the contest, and Elisabeth joined the elite club of four performers to finish both first and second in the contest.

France commenced the second stage of the contest with the Breton song 'Diwanit Bugale' ('May The Children Be Born'). **Dan Ar Braz Et L'Héritage Des Celtes** was the name of the band that Dan himself had assembled for this highly original piece of music, the likes of which had not really appeared in the contest before. The Scott Karen Matheson of the group Capercaillie was one member of the group, alongside the Welsh singer Elaine Morgan. It was a startling departure for the French and was the only entry ever to be sung in Breton, but it was still unable to impress the juries, ending in nineteenth place, the worst placing to date for any French entry.

Having taken a year off from winning in 1995, Ireland cruised to their fourth victory in five years, breaking their own record to score a seventh win. **Eimear Quinn** was a student at the Cork School of Music when she was approached to perform a song that was clearly inspired by the huge success of 'Riverdance' and had much more to do with traditional Irish music and rhythms than the current pop scene. She had a very high-pitched, crystal-clear voice, which suited the haunting style of the music and she was joined onstage by five musicians playing traditional Irish instruments. It may have appeared to be too unusual or

too outdated to be a winner, particularly when compared to the hugely popular entry from the UK, but, not for the first time, the judges were out of step with the public mood and commercial tastes.

With Ireland resuming their role as perennial favourites, Finland came back to the contest to fulfil their tradition of finishing last! And one of Sweden's trio, **One More Time**, was no less than Peter Grönvall, son of Abba's Benny Andersson. Peter got his first song into the national finals at the age of 22 in 1986, and had numerous in the following years. He wrote the song with his wife, and the haunting ballad did well in the contest, despite its unusual style and tempo.

For the scoring segment of the show, Ingvild Bryn made her way to an as yet unseen part of the set, the 'blue' room. For the first time, virtual reality was used in the contest, superimposing the scoreboard graphics onto the screen. Ingvild was in fact standing in an empty space, completely decorated in blue, but to the viewers she appeared to be

Right: The UK's contestant Gina G wore a mini-dress of chain-linked gold discs, which had been created by American designer Paco Rabanne for Cher. Cher had rejected it and Gina acquired it and cut the full-length gown down to size.

Far right: Malta's Miriam Christine was the youngest performer in the contest. Miriam wore a very short mini-skirt and jacket in pale pink, while her backing trio were dressed in green, white and red to represent the Italian flag, in deference to the Italian designer who had provided the costumes.

surrounded by a three dimensional scoreboard.

Sadly, the advance in technology couldn't help prevent glitches, the most notable of which was only spotted months later by the EBU. Spain had awarded six points to the Netherlands, but the mark had incorrectly been given to Poland. The later correction pushed the Dutch above the UK, but had no affect on the winner, which romped to victory.

The result was not appreciated much in the hall, with many leaving their seats before Eimear Quinn had even begun her reprise. As fireworks exploded around the arena and on the stage, the credits rolled as Eimear sang the winner again. The EBU were obviously taking notes. By electing Ireland the winners again, the juries may well have confirmed their own demise. As the contest closed, there were very few left in the audience to encourage Eimear and composer Brendan Graham as they took their bows.

Hits from this year's Eurovision were few and far between, but Gina G went on to huge success. She may not have won the contest and in fact had fallen way below expectations with both her final position and her performance, but it did not stop her commercial progress. Not only did she top the UK chart, but she also made it to number six in Sweden, the top ten in Ireland and Belgium and number 12 in the USA, where the song was nominated for a Grammy award. Although the hits continued into 1997 – she even launched her own line of underwear – a minor scandal broke when she collapsed on a plane flying to Glasgow. She claimed to be exhausted, but rumours of drug abuse circulated in the media. She has not troubled the charts since.

Lucia Moniz, who achieved Portugal's best ever result went on to a starring role opposite Colin Firth, in the hit movie *Love Actually*.

Eimear Quinn appears to have returned to her studies, and is yet to make any kind of an impact anywhere.

With the public's dissatisfaction at yet another Irish win growing, especially among the hardcore fans of the contest, the EBU were prepared to make changes, and indeed sweeping alterations were made to the rulebook for 1997.

country	song	performer	place	score	draw
Ireland	The Voice	**Eimear Quinn**	1	162	17
Norway	I Evighet	**Elisabeth Andreassen**	2	114	12
Sweden	Den Vilda	**One More Time**	3	100	23
Croatia	Sveta Ljubav	**Maja Blagdan**	4	98	7
Estonia	Kaelakee Hääl	**Ivo Linna & Maarja-Liis Ilus**	5	94	11
Portugal	O Meu Coração Não Tem Cor	**Lucia Moniz**	6	92	4
Netherlands	De Eerste Keer	**Maxine & Franklin Brown**	7	78	15
United Kingdom	Ooh Aah... Just A Little Bit	**Gina G**	8	77	2
Cyprus	Mono Gia Mas	**Constantinos**	9	72	5
Malta	In A Woman's Heart	**Miriam Christine**	10=	68	6
Austria	Weil's Dr Guat Got	**George Nussbaumer**	10=	68	8
Turkey	Besinci Mevsim	**Şebnem Paker**	12	57	1
Iceland	Sjúbidú	**Anna Mjöll Olafsdottir**	13	51	19
Greece	Emis Forame To Himona Anixiatika	**Marianna Efstratiou**	14	36	10
Poland	Chcę Znać Swój Grzech	**Kasia Kowalska**	15	31	20
Switzerland	Mon Cœur l'Aime	**Kathy Leander**	16=	22	9
Belgium	Liefde Is Een Kaartspel	**Lisa del Bo**	16=	22	16
Slovakia	Kým Nás Má	**Marcel Polander**	18	19	22
France	Diwanit Bugale	**Dan Ar Braz Et L'Héritage Des Celtes**	19	18	13
Spain	Ay Que Deseo!	**Antonio Carbonell**	20	17	3
Slovenia	Dan Najlepših Sanj	**Regina**	21	16	14
Bosnia-Herzegovina	Za Našu Ljubav	**Amila Glamočak**	22	13	21
Finland	Niin Kaunis On Taivas	**Jasmine**	23	9	18

Winner

United Kingdom

Performer

Katrina and The Waves

1997

Title

'Love Shine A Light'

Composer

Kimberley Rew

...ers

Carrie Crowley & Ronan Keating

RTE The Point Depot

Dublin
Ireland

Having gained their fourth Eurovision victory in five attempts, the Irish broadcaster RTE brought the contest back to The Point in Dublin for the third time in four years in 1997. It was the very first time that any venue was used to stage the contest three times, surpassing the achievements of the RDS Simmonscourt Pavilion across the City. Not only was the venue familiar, but the victor was one of the most successful countries in the Eurovision family, albeit one that had been waiting 16 years for their elusive fifth triumph. What cannot be denied is that when the United Kingdom wins the contest, they usually win it big! Many records were set as the British nation stormed to first place with the first American artist to conquer the European audience.

The hostility shown towards the 1996 result in which such an old fashioned piece of music had won over the far more popular hi-energy sounds on offer, meant that the EBU had relented to growing pressure from within their ranks to revamp the system used to determine the winner. They announced that tele-voting, or voting by phone, would be trialed in this year's event. It proved to be the biggest single alteration to the rule-book since the competition's inception back in 1956. The UK, Germany, Austria, Switzerland and Sweden all gave viewers in their respective nations the chance to determine the

Left: After much deliberation during rehearsal week, Katrina opted for a black velvet coat worn over black leather trousers, with a green shirt she had reputedly picked up in a flea market for less than £1!

Right: Sweden's blond trio, Thomas, Patrik and Gabriel, collectively known as Blond, proved to be way off the mark, and ended in a dismal fourteenth place.

songs they approved of the most; the remaining 20 countries stuck with the traditional jury system.

The process determining which 25 nations would compete in Dublin was once again revised and was now to be based on the best average scores over the past four contests. The broadcast date, 3rd May, coincided with a religious holiday and prevented the Israelis from competing but Italy made a brief return to the bosom of the Eurovision family for the first time since 1993. They have not competed since.

Another major change to the rulebook this year was that permission was granted for songs to be performed without any live music if desired. Backing tracks had been in wide use in the contest since 1973, but the only instruments permitted to be pre-recorded were those seen on stage. This led to the inclusion of performers as part of the competing acts using guitars and keyboards that they clearly had no idea how to play! For 1997, the EBU relented, under pressure, to permit any or all music to be pre-recorded, allowing countries to dispense with the annoyance of having to put artists on stage simply to mime. For many, it was the thin end of the wedge and, sure enough, within two more years, the orchestra was gone altogether.

Two young celebrities were drafted in to give the contest a younger appeal – **Carrie Crowley** was selected to act as the forty-third female presenter, with **Ronan Keating** joining her in the task. Keating also provided the cabaret for the interval act, along with his four colleagues from the hugely popular Irish boyband, Boyzone.

For the first time, Cyprus had the honour of opening the contest, and they did so with the highly catchy 'Mana Mou' ('Mother Land'), which was sung by the brother and sister team of **Hara and Andreas Constantinou**. The song was a very successful combination of traditional Greek instruments and a driving disco beat. Although there was a refrain of 'Dum-dubba-dum', which did little to enhance the song, it was a very effective opening bid for the title and ultimately achieved the highest score yet for a Cypriot song.

Before the Turkish entry, 1988 winner Céline Dion was seen by viewers wishing the participants good luck and recalling her appearance in the contest back in Dublin nine years earlier. Video messages from previous entrants were dotted throughout the show – including stars such as Cliff Richard, Julio Iglesias and Benny and Björn from Abba who joked that Eurovision has never helped anyone's career and that it was a complete waste of time.

Turkey's song was performed for the second year running by **Şebnem Paker**, this time accompanied by the Group Etnic. Şebnem was dressed in a very slinky, black mini-skirt and figure-hugging top and smouldered around the microphone tempestuously while the band and orchestra played the introduction. As was nearly always the case, the Turkish entry was a very ethnic piece of music with little resemblance to the pop music scene of any other culture. But by the time the

Love Shine A Light
Katrina + the Waves

'Love Shine A Light' reached No. 3 in the UK but, with no airplay at all from the nation's largest station, Radio 1, it rose no higher. In other countries, it hit the Top 5 at best. The band spent 18 weeks in the Swedish charts, peaking at No. 5, and made No. 4 in the Netherlands.

Above: Italy made a brief return to the competition with husband-and-wife team Jalisse. The ball gown she is wearing in this rehearsal photo was ditched at the last minute in favour of a black suit.

Left: Switzerland's Barbara Berta wore a velour suit in a snakeskin pattern, accompanied by a trumpet soloist and backing singers. Her forgettable ballad garnered five points.

song reached its chorus, it became obvious that it had a very, very catchy hook and it finally broke the mould of previous Turkish efforts, landing them in the top three for the first time.

If Turkey and Cyprus were transforming their Eurovision form, Norway was back in its more usual position – last with 'nul points!' The Norwegian song, 'San Francisco', was infectiously happy, but references to the Californian city and 1960s culture probably did not help it. Other low points of 1997 were the Greek entry, which included a musician seemingly playing a bunch of grapes; a rap song from Denmark's Kølig Kaj that featured dancers in leopard-skin trousers and a telephonist on stage (the song was about a man who falls in love with someone from directory enquiries); and a techno-inspired effort from Iceland that incorporated dancers in fetish gear cavorting round a white settee.

The Irish entry, sung by **Marc Roberts**, was a gentle ballad that was very much in the nation's usual mould and was the joint favourite with the bookmakers to triumph again. Singing without the orchestra, relying entirely on the assistance of a backing tape, Marc gave a very confident and emotional performance and it brought the house down. Even the Irish President, Mary Robinson, attending her third contest, rose to her feet to support the home entry. In the end, it was no shame for the Irish to end in second place, albeit a distant one.

Stephan Berg, the composer of the Swedish winner from 1991, was back for another stab at the title this year, with a song that bore a striking resemblance to the previous Swedish winner from Herreys, 'Diggi-Loo Diggi-Ley', although lyrically it was perhaps superior. The choreography of the three singers was certainly very slick, if a little over the top. Nevertheless, it was one of the very few songs in the traditional Eurovision style on show in Dublin, which was clearly the wrong note to strike with the judges and it ended in a dismal fourteenth place.

The biggest star of the night, in more ways than one, was the Russian superstar **Alla Pugachova**. Not only was she one of Russia's leading recording artists, but also a huge movie star, stage actress, and designer of her own line of shoes. Staggering out onto the stage in the tallest pair of shoes ever seen in the contest, she hardly looked the part of a superstar. Her blonde hair unkempt and wearing a black sweater over a short black skirt, she may have surprised those who were unprepared for her appearance. Not withstanding, she gave an impassioned interpretation of her own composition and, as she reached the song's rousing climax, the audience, who had cheered every entry with great enthusiasm, almost brought the house down.

Thirty years after Sandie Shaw had first lifted the Grand Prix for the United Kingdom, and 16 years after their last triumph, the Brits stormed back to form in the forty-second

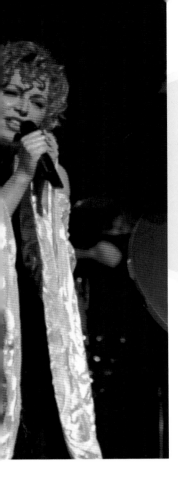

country	song	performer	place	score	draw
United Kingdom	Love Shine A Light	Katrina &The Waves	1	227	24
Ireland	Mysterious Woman	Marc Roberts	2	157	5
Turkey	Dinle	Şebnem Paker & Group Etnic	3	121	2
Italy	Fiumi Di Parole	Jalisse	4	114	9
Cyprus	Mana Mou	Hara & Andraes Constantinou	5	98	1
Spain	Sin Rencor	Marcos Llunas	6	96	10
France	Sentiments Songes	Fanny	7	95	22
Estonia	Keelatud Maa	Maarja-Liis Ilus	8	82	13
Malta	Let Me Fly	Debbie Sceri	9	66	18
Slovenia	Zbudi Se	Tanja Ribič	10	60	6
Poland	Ale Jestem	Anna-Maria Jopek	11	54	12
Greece	Horepse	Marianna Zorba	12=	39	17
Hungary	Miert Kell Hogy Elmenj?	VIP	12=	39	19
Sweden	Bara Hon Älskar Mig	Blond	14	36	16
Russia	Primadonna	Alla Pugachova	15	33	20
Denmark	Stemmen I Mit Liv	Kølig Kaj	16	25	21
Croatia	Probudi Me	ENI	17	24	23
Germany	Zeit	Bianca Shomburg	18=	22	11
Bosnia-Herzegovina	Goodbye	Alma Čardžić	18=	22	14
Iceland	Minn Hinsti Dans	Paul Oscar	20	18	25
Austria	One Step	Bettina Soriat	21	12	4
Switzerland	Dentro Di Me	Barbara Berta	22=	5	7
Netherlands	Niemand Heeft Nog Tijd	Mrs Einstein	22=	5	8
Norway	San Francisco	Tor Endresen	24=	0	3
Portugal	Antes Do Adeus	Celia Lawson	24=	0	15

Poland's entry, performed by Anna-Maria Jopek, was described as 'folk rock' and the musical accompaniment had a very unusual tempo and use of ethnic sounds.

contest. 'Love Shine A Light', which was performed by the American-led **Katrina and the Waves**, was the overwhelming winner and cruised to victory, breaking a host of records in its wake, with the highest yet score and the most number of top marks ever awarded to one song.

The main question that seemed to be directed at the group was whether or not they were concerned about their credibility as a result of appearing in the Eurovision. As Katrina was happy to respond, 'What credibility?' Since scoring an international hit with 'Walking On Sunshine' in 1985, the band had been reduced to touring British and German air-force bases. Their Eurovision song had been written as a theme tune for the Samaritans organisation, before being picked as the UK's unlikely entry. Despite being ignored by the UK media, the band arrived in Dublin as favourites and didn't disappoint, turning in a confident performance in their multi-coloured zoot suits. Unfortunately for the band, the Eurovision win proved something of a

false dawn for them. The decision by their record company to withhold the release of the single robbed them of much-needed pre-contest publicity and airplay. But the song still outclassed almost every other winner since Johnny Logan's 1987 victory and the band found themselves much in demand on the European TV and concert circuit. Tensions within the group began to surface, however, and by the time a follow-up single and a long-awaited album were released in the summer, their own website was announcing they had split up.

For RTE, the 1997 competition was yet another accomplished triumph for their production team, yet it was to be their last contest for a while to come. It was time for Ireland to take a well-earned rest from the winner's podium.

Tele-voting was judged a success, and Eurovision was heading towards the new millennium on the crest of a wave of great enthusiasm.

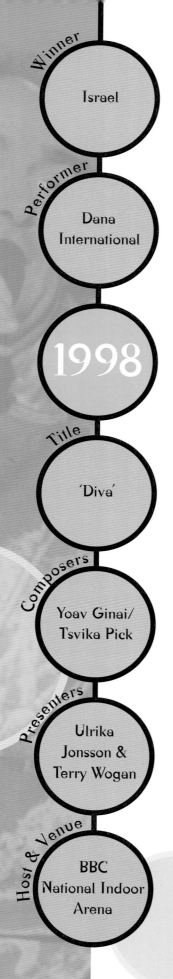

Winner
Israel

Performer
Dana International

1998

Title
'Diva'

Composers
Yoav Ginai/ Tsvika Pick

Presenters
Ulrika Jonsson & Terry Wogan

Host & Venue
BBC National Indoor Arena

Birmingham
United Kingdom

In 1998, the United Kingdom played host to the Eurovision Song Contest for a record eighth time. In the years since they had staged their seventh contest in 1982, Ireland had equalled the BBC's number of productions, but in 1998 the British edged ahead once again. The broadcast date was 9th May, Europe Day, with the 4,000-seat National Indoor Arena in England's second city, Birmingham, chosen as the host venue.

The Former Yugoslav Republic of Macedonia was the only newcomer, with Slovakia, Israel, Romania, Belgium and Finland returning after their absences. The remaining 19 places were given to the countries with the best average score over the contests between 1993 and 1997. This meant that Austria, Bosnia-Herzegovina, Denmark, Iceland and Russia all missed the cut, whereas Italy was absent by choice.

The UK turned to two non-British nationals to present the show. After offering barbed remarks for the BBC as a Eurovision commentator for many years, Irish-born **Terry Wogan** was chosen as the master of ceremonies, joined by the multi-lingual TV presenter **Ulrika Jonsson**, a British TV star who originally hailed from Sweden.

Six months before the final, controversy was already building in a number of the participating countries. In Israel extreme religious and political groups were protesting at their nation's representative, a transsexual singer known as **Dana International**, named after the demure Irish winner from 1970. Germany also had their share of negative publicity surrounding the winner of their domestic heat, 'schlager' singer **Guildo Horn**. The media attention surrounding both of these artists was staggering and did much to attract new viewers to the show.

In Birmingham, the Greeks attracted some negative publicity of their own. Dionysia Karoki and the group **Thalassa** had threatened to quit the contest on the final day of rehearsals, as they were upset at the way the performance was being filmed and demanded changes. Dozens of aggressive tantrums by the composer of their song, Yiannis Valvis, were caught by a documentary crew and, as a result, he was barred from the contest. On the afternoon of the event, the Greeks pulled out of the show, only to return minutes later. Ultimately, they probably shouldn't have bothered. Only one nation awarded their rock anthem any marks at all, which, inevitably, was a 12 from Cyprus. France was having a bad year too. **Marie-Line**'s soul-influenced entry was never going to take her to the top. With only three points and twenty-fourth place, France suffered their worst-ever result in the competition.

The international media that had gathered in Birmingham had set their sights on the Israeli artist from the moment it was announced she would be singing in the contest. Dana International was a superstar in her homeland, with a string of hits to her credit. Only her outrageous and flamboyant personality, as well as the deep emotions she stirred in the more orthodox parts of the Israeli community, matched her popularity. Dana had been born as a man, but had undergone surgery to transform herself into the diva of Israeli pop. No entry had ever attracted so much pre-publicity – or controversy – albeit generated by one of the slickest publicity machines ever hired for the purpose.

Wherever Ms International went, controversy seemed to follow. On her arrival in the country, she was sequestered in the only hotel in Birmingham with bulletproof windows and had armed guards surrounding her at all times. This was not vanity, however; orthodox religious fanatics had threatened her life almost continually since she had emerged into the world of show business. The dress she intended to wear on the night, which had been designed by Jean-Paul Gaultier, was also kept under

armed guard, even though she eventually decided not to wear it for her performance. The anticipation surrounding her entry was huge, although rumours began to circulate in rehearsals of the singer's inability to sing. The rumours proved correct and nobody could argue that Dana International turned in anything approaching a good vocal performance when she took to the Birmingham stage. She didn't care, though! Such was her stage presence and confidence that she turned in an excellent, if vocally flat, show. Wearing a plain silver off-the-shoulder dress, with four female backing singers all in black suits, her low-key appearance probably surprised viewers after all the hype. She had elected not to use the orchestra, performing the hi-energy disco number accompanied by just a backing track. It was enough to take Israel to the top once again, although it was a close call.

If Dana International intrigued the press and public, they were equally enthralled with the German singer Guildo Horn. Accompanied by his backing group, The Orthopaedic Stockings, he had romped home to victory in the German selection, much to the reported shame of the German public. Such was the controversy surrounding his resounding win with 'Guildo Hat Euch Lieb' (Guildo Loves You) that news of his win even made the news broadcasts in many other nations. Dressed in turquoise crushed velvet, with a garish yellow ruffled shirt, he had been entertaining the rehearsal audiences and media all week with his antics.

'Diva' made it to No. 11 in the UK, even though it wasn't until late June that the CD hit the shops, long after the contest was forgotten. It also made No. 11 in the Dutch charts, No. 3 in Sweden, and was a minor hit in many other countries too.

Left: Dana International celebrating her victory, wearing the Jean-Paul Gaultier frock that had been specially designed for the contest, but that she had decided not to wear until this point.

On stage in Birmingham, Guildo discarded his turquoise cape after the gentle opening, as he darted around the stage, leaping off the platform into the audience. He made amorous advances to Katie Boyle – the legendary UK Eurovision hostess, there as the BBC's guest of honour – rang cow bells and ended the song perched high above the set on the platform constructed for the scoreboard. Nothing like this had ever been done in the contest before and it brought the house down.

After all the antics of these two competitors, an un-rated entry of a distinctly different nature became an unexpected challenger for the top prize. **Chiara** was singing an exceptionally simple and gentle ballad for Malta. For her solo performance, all the lights on the stage were dimmed to form a black surround, with candles erected on the stage to cast some dramatic shadows.

Unlike the winning act of 12 months ago, the United Kingdom's **Imaani** was a relative newcomer with no previous success prior to this appearance, although she had performed as a backing vocalist for the former Eurovision winner Lulu. Despite her inexperience, Imaani was clearly boosted by a tremendous show of support and she turned in a faultless vocal performance and also possibly the best performance of any act on the night. In the closest contest seen since 1991, the British were eventually pipped once again, just slipping into second place.

Each year the vast Eurovision scoreboard becomes more advanced. Thus, in 1998, to indicate which country was voting next, the computer guided the viewers around a 3-D map of Europe. It also guided us through a tight contest that was nip and tuck between Israel, Malta and the United Kingdom, right up until the final votes.

Because of the relegation system, the scores were tense across the board. The Netherlands had to finish in the first five to gain enough points to keep their average high enough for automatic entry into the 1999 contest. Their sunny 20-year-old singer **Edsilia Rombley** managed it in charming style, ending the evening in fourth.

When the result was announced viewers saw Dana International and her entourage leaping around the green room backstage and celebrating as they rushed to their dressing rooms. A fanfare from the Royal Lifeguards should

Guildo Horn's performance for Germany brought the house down. The only negative controversy that followed Mr Horn was the promise by legions of his fans to cross the borders into other countries to try to influence the televote from there. They may well have done so, but it wasn't enough to take the title. Many countries did indeed embrace the eccentricity of the entry, but not enough for it to rise above seventh place.

have heralded the triumphant entrance of the winning Israeli team, but they were nowhere to be seen. Dana International was busy changing into the Jean-Paul Gaultier frock that had been specially designed for the contest, clearly not at all perturbed by the need to get back on stage. The striking parrot feathers of the frock was the image beamed across the media around the world in the next few days.

It was the first time a transsexual artist had won the contest, but perhaps more noteworthy for the competition, it was the first time a winning song had not used any live music. The interval act earlier in the evening had actually been the last time any live music was to be heard in the Eurovision Song Contest. Israel had won the contest without having entered the year before, the first nation ever to do so. They were of course already the only nation that had not entered the year after winning, two rather bizarre contest anomalies.

Dana returned to the next contest in Jerusalem and continues to make regular appearances in London and other cities with large gay populations, but she has yet to find any lasting success as a recording artist outside Israel.

As for Chiara, she admits to having spent much of the time after the broadcast in floods of tears, but she recovered her composure to shrug off defeat. When she flew back to Malta the next day, 6,000 people crushed into Valetta airport to give her a hero's welcome back home.

With higher than average viewing figures and widespread media coverage of the winner, the 1998 contest was a huge triumph. In addition, the BBC was able to bring the contest to completion in less than three hours, a triumph in itself! Tele-voting was deemed a success, too. Almost all countries – Hungary and Cyprus being the two known exceptions – had tried the system, and with so many contemporary sounds taking the top slots in the final order, it seemed to be a popular move.

country	song	performer	place	score	draw
Israel	Diva	Dana International	1	172	8
United Kingdom	Where Are You?	Imaani	2	166	16
Malta	The One That I Love	Chiara	3	165	10
Netherlands	Hemel En Aarde	Edsilia Rombley	4	150	18
Croatia	Neka Ni Me Svane	Danijela	5	131	1
Belgium	Dis Oui	Melanie Cohl	6	122	20
Germany	Guildo Hat Euch Lieb	Guildo Horn	7	86	9
Norway	Altid Sommer	Lars A. Fredriksen	8	79	22
Ireland	Is Always Over Now?	Dawn	9	64	13
Sweden	Kärleken Är	Jill Johnsson	10	53	19
Cyprus	Yenesis	Michael Hadjiyianni	11	37	17
Portugal	Se Eu Te Pudesse Abraçar	Alma Lusa	12=	36	14
Estonia	Mere Lapsed	Koit Toome	12=	36	23
Turkey	Unutamazsin	Tuzmen	14	25	24
Finland	Aava	Edea	15	22	21
Spain	Que Voy A Hacer Sin Ti	Mikel Herzog	16	21	4
Poland	To Takie Proste	Sixteen	17	19	7
Slovenia	Naj Bogovi Sliisijo	Vili Resnik	18	17	12
F.Y.R. Macedonia	Ne Zori Zoro	Vlado Janevski	19	16	25
Greece	Mia Krifi Evaesthisia	Dionysia Karoki-Georgopoulou & Thalassa	20	12	2
Slovakia	Modlitba	Katarína Hasprová	21	8	6
Romania	Eu Cred	Malina Olinescu	22	6	15
Hungary	A Holnap Már Nem Lesz Szomorú	Charlie	23	4	11
France	Ou Aller	Marie-Line	24	3	3
Switzerland	Lass 'Ihn	Gunvor	25	0	5

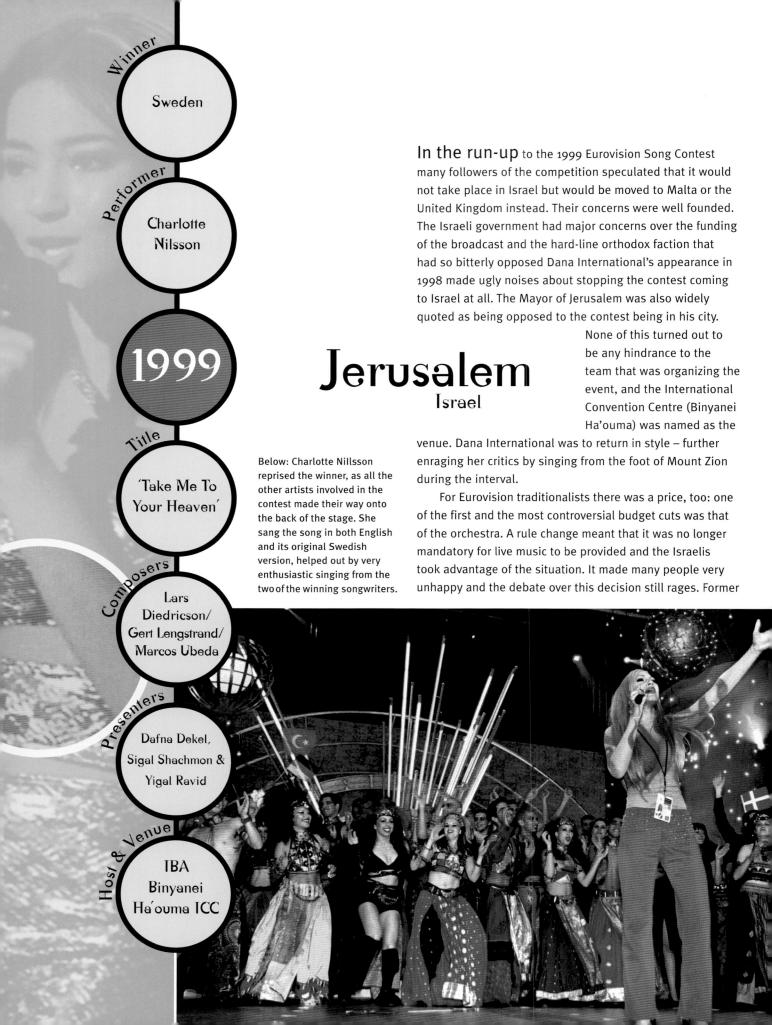

Winner

Sweden

Performer

Charlotte
Nilsson

1999

Title

'Take Me To
Your Heaven'

Composers

Lars
Diedricson/
Gert Lengstrand/
Marcos Ubeda

Presenters

Dafna Dekel,
Sigal Shachmon &
Yigal Ravid

Host & Venue

IBA
Binyanei
Ha'ouma ICC

In the run-up to the 1999 Eurovision Song Contest many followers of the competition speculated that it would not take place in Israel but would be moved to Malta or the United Kingdom instead. Their concerns were well founded. The Israeli government had major concerns over the funding of the broadcast and the hard-line orthodox faction that had so bitterly opposed Dana International's appearance in 1998 made ugly noises about stopping the contest coming to Israel at all. The Mayor of Jerusalem was also widely quoted as being opposed to the contest being in his city.

Jerusalem
Israel

None of this turned out to be any hindrance to the team that was organizing the event, and the International Convention Centre (Binyanei Ha'ouma) was named as the venue. Dana International was to return in style – further enraging her critics by singing from the foot of Mount Zion during the interval.

For Eurovision traditionalists there was a price, too: one of the first and the most controversial budget cuts was that of the orchestra. A rule change meant that it was no longer mandatory for live music to be provided and the Israelis took advantage of the situation. It made many people very unhappy and the debate over this decision still rages. Former

Below: Charlotte Nillsson reprised the winner, as all the other artists involved in the contest made their way onto the back of the stage. She sang the song in both English and its original Swedish version, helped out by very enthusiastic singing from the two of the winning songwriters.

winner Johnny Logan was particularly vehement in his comments, describing the event as 'karaoke'.

An even bigger relaxation in the rules regarded the language each country had to sing in. All countries were now free to sing in whatever language they chose – which usually meant English. Although on the big night itself Slovenia's **Darja Švajger** gave an excellent example of the perils of singing in a language that is not your own when a lyric that should have been 'I tremble in your arms' came out sounding remarkably like 'I trample in your arse'.

It was also announced that for the 2000 event and in subsequent years, the four biggest financial contributors to the EBU – Germany, Spain, the United Kingdom and France – would all be given automatic entry into the contest regardless of their scores. This meant they would never have to miss out, unlike Finland, Greece, Hungary, FYR Macedonia, Portugal, Slovakia and Switzerland, who all failed to qualify for Jerusalem.

After a disagreement over the set design, a new team was brought in late in the day. Inspired by the coming millennium, the centrepiece was a huge sun-like mechanical globe, with constellations of planets and rays of sun rotating around it. It was designed to evoke the passing of time. The stage floor was elevated and a glass catwalk built into it, which was illuminated from beneath.

Spain's Lydia had chosen to wear a full-length gown in vertical stripes in the colours of the rainbow. It's almost impossible to describe how hideous the frock appeared on camera. Even the shape was a very unflattering style for the teenager, let alone the garish colours. With only one point and last place, Lydia doubtless came to reflect upon her choice of outfit in the green room.

Releasing remixed versions of the song, as well as the original Swedish version **'Tusen Och En Natt'** in some countries, Charlotte Nilsson crept into the charts around the continent, reaching No. 2 in Sweden. In the UK she made it to the Top 20. In Belgium the song went to No. 5.

The controversies continued into the evening of the show itself. Bosnia-Herzegovina had to submit a late alternative entry after it was discovered that their original entry had been released in Finland some years previously. Norway objected to Croatia's song using the sound of a male voice choir who weren't on stage with **Doris Dragović**. The Croatians argued that it was a synthesised sample, but a third of their points were docked, nonetheless.

The United Kingdom had been enjoying something of a revival of their Eurovision fortunes over the last couple of years, but the British lost their touch once again in 1999. They entered a very contemporary-sounding all-girl group called **Precious**. However, the sound problems that plagued nearly all the artists in Jerusalem made it almost impossible to hear the music track and the vocals veered off-key. They almost equalled the worst UK result in the history of the contest to date, falling all the way back to share twelfth place.

Like the British, Norway had opted for a very modern look and sound for their entry and the voters had equal disregard for them. **Stig van Eijk** was the black singer recruited to sing 'Living My Life Without You' in English. It was a dance number with a strong beat, performed in a pseudo-rap style, yet with all the lyrics sung rather than spoken. It wasn't a good effort and was rewarded with fourteenth place, no doubt in part due to van Eijk's problems with feedback in his ear-piece, which he complained about bitterly afterwards.

France enjoyed a slightly improved position in this year's contest, but they were still down in nineteenth place, matching their second worst result yet. It was the only French-language song in the competition and proved just how much musical tastes had shifted in the contest over the years. Singer **Nayah** arrived with controversy in tow. After winning the French heat, the first to be staged since 1987, she had been exposed as a member of an unusual religious cult which believed that the world would end in Jerusalem at the dawn of the new millennium and that only members of the cult would be saved in a space ship, which would depart the Earth from within the holy city. Thankfully for Nayah, she did not have to board the vessel prior to ending her performance, but viewers were still not impressed.

In a poll of fans on the internet, Cyprus's entry – an up-tempo dance track by the energetic **Marlain Angelidou** – was widely tipped for victory. But their views were not shared by the public-at-large and with no Greek votes to support the song, only the UK considered it worthy of any points at all.

'Diva' had proved that a hi-energy dance track could indeed take the top prize and the Israeli efforts that immediately follwed it, pursued this format. The four lads who made up **Eden** were a combination of two white Israelis and two African-Americans who were based in Israel. Their performance was augmented by some very dynamic dance moves, which drew comparisons with both the Four Tops and the Temptations from many quarters. They sang the up-tempo number very well, with the occasional burst of English in with the Hebrew. They brought the house down among the partisan crowd, but did not entirely convince the judges, finishing in a very strong fifth place in the final shake-up.

The members of German group **Sürpriz** were possibly very surprised to find themselves in the contest at all. Benefiting from the disqualification of the original German winner, they came to the contest with a very ethnic-sounding song, clearly designed to inspire the Turkish audience and the Eastern Europeans. 'Reise Nach Jerusalem' ('Journey To Jerusalem') was a very original piece, based on the children's game of the same name, also known as musical chairs. The six members of the band, who ranged in age from 16 to 32, were all of Turkish descent and the song owed more to Turkish culture than German pop. It was the tenth collaboration by Ralph Siegel and Bernd Meinunger to represent Germany, making them the contest's most prolific writers. The group performed the song in a mix of Turkish, German, English and Hebrew. It was a very old-fashioned style of entry and was not widely tipped to do well. However, the Germans had their best contest for five years, ending the night in a closely fought third place with 140 points.

Above: Dressed in silver, the apparent colour of choice this year, Malta's Times Three appeared very nervous on stage. They had worked hard at their choreography, but it didn't seem to fit with the song, which would have benefited from a simpler presentation.

Right: As Charlotte took position for her reprise, Dana International pretended the trophy was too heavy to lift. But she slipped and crashed to the floor, bringing the two composers down with her. Security forces threw themselves onto the stage, and when she emerged from the pile of bodies, she scuttled off, hiding her face from the cameras.

Iceland were one of the many countries who had seized the opportunity to present a song in English, having spent 12 years entering songs in their own tongue. Sadly, **Selma** did not appear onstage with the weightlifters, muscle men, fairies and large ladies who decorated her preview video. But it was, nonetheless, a lively performance, featuring two male dancers throwing themselves around the stage in a frenzy of choreography. Selma sang well, despite sound problems, achieving a well-fought and close second place, the best-ever showing for an Icelandic entry.

Much publicity had been gained for the Swedes by referring to Abba's win exactly 25 years earlier. The attention was magnified as **Charlotte Nilsson** wore a striking pink number that was designed to appear as body paint rather than clothing. The swirling mauves and purples on the sheer skin-tight top contrasted with the pink glitter-trimmed trousers. Her backing singers, three men and two women, matched in outfits of grey and white. It was a very catchy number that was likened to Abba's 'Waterloo' in many ways, largely because of its strong brass accompaniment on the soundtrack. Charlotte had a very powerful voice and used it to great effect, presenting the song in a straightforward manner. She ended the song with a toss of her head that sent her long blonde hair whipping across her face. She also wore a broad smile that suggested she knew she had done well, as indeed she had. Despite trailing for the first half of the voting and only edging clear in the last few rounds, she was able to bring Sweden their fourth win in 25 years.

During the voting the audience began to jeer the partisan nature of the scoring, which was the most evident since 1966. The tele-voting, it seems could not prevent the neighbourly exchange of points between friendly allies.

To end the show, the three presenters invited everyone on the stage to join in a rousing rendition of 1979's winning song 'Hallelujah', as a tribute to the victims of the Balkan War who were not able to view the broadcast of the show. The credits rolled over this emotional display of international harmony. After the disharmony, controversy and problems that had plagued the contest it was a fitting end.

country	song	performer	place	score	draw
Sweden	Take Me To Your Heaven	**Charlotte Nilsson**	1	163	15
Iceland	All Out Of Luck	**Selma**	2	146	13
Germany	Reise Nach Jerusalem	**Sürpriz**	3	140	21
Croatia	Marija Magdalena	**Doris Dragović**	4	118	4
Israel	Yom Huledet (Happy Birthday)	**Eden**	5	93	19
Estonia	Diamond Of Night	**Evelin Samuel & Camille**	6	90	23
Bosnia-Herzegovina	Putnici	**Dino & Béatrice**	7	86	22
Denmark	This Time I Mean It	**Trine Jepsen & Michael Teschl**	8=	71	9
Netherlands	One Good Reason	**Marlayne**	8=	71	11
Austria	Reflection	**Bobbie Singer**	10	65	18
Slovenia	For A Thousand Years	**Darja Švajger**	11	50	6
Belgium	Like The Wind	**Vanessa Chinitor**	12=	38	2
United Kingdom	Say It Again	**Precious**	12=	38	5
Norway	Living My Life Without You	**Stig van Eijk**	14	35	8
Malta	Believe in Peace	**Times Three**	15	32	20
Turkey	Dön Artik	**Tugba Onal**	16	21	7
Ireland	When You Need Me	**The Mullans**	17	18	17
Poland	Przytul Mnie Mocno	**Mietek Szcześniak**	18	17	12
France	Je Veux Donner Ma Voix	**Nayah**	19	14	10
Lithuania	Strazdas	**Aiste**	20	13	1
Portugal	Como Tudo Começou	**Rui Bandera**	21	12	16
Cyprus	Tha'ne Erotas	**Marlain Angelidou**	22	2	14
Spain	No Quiero Escuchar	**Lydia**	23	1	3

Winner

Denmark

Performer

The Olsen Brothers

2000

Title

'Fly On The Wings Of Love'

Composer

Jørgen Olsen

Presenters

Kattis Ahlström & Anders Lundin

Host & Venue

SVT Globe Arena

Stockholm
Sweden

The first contest of the new millennium was staged in the biggest venue yet seen in the competition – the Globe Arena, a vast circular structure with seating for over 16,000 – before the biggest live audience to date. A quarter of a century since it was last staged in the Swedish capital, Stockholm once again played host to the 24 nations hoping to be the first winner of the new century.

The logo for the contest, revealed in the early spring of 2000, was a large pair of open lips! The concept behind the design was to present a symbol that represented a new expression and a contemporary design. The lip pattern was described as 'a sensual – yet stylistically pure – mouth representing song, dialogue and speech.' Another advance in the format this year was that a film that was designed to complement each song's theme or its presentation was projected onto five screens, forming a unique backdrop that reflected the subject and mood of each entry, as well as the colour of the artist's costume.

Kattis Ahlström and **Anders Lundin** were the hosts for the evening and made many hilarious remarks. For example, their welcoming address was delivered in a multitude of languages, including English, Swedish, French, German, Hebrew and many others, ending in Swahili – 'just in case,' said Anders.

The show opened for the very first time with the Israeli song. The two male–two female group called **Ping Pong** was in Stockholm to sing the hi-energy dance track 'Sa'me'akh' ('Be Happy'). Perhaps trying to drum up some publicity, the Israeli entrants had caused some controversy with their preview video when the two boys from the group kissed each other, as did the two girls, in between singing into cucumbers and other phallic objects, which were also referred to in the lyrics. The song itself was a cross between the Pet Shop Boys and the Spice Girls and the foursome seemed to have lots of fun on stage, including another male-to-male kiss. However, at the end of the contest, despite the strength of the track, it was not enough to earn many tele-votes and Israel ended with seven marks from only two countries and a dismal twenty-second place.

Nicki French was not only disappointed, she was also humiliated by the tele-voters this year. By far the biggest name to appear in the 2000 contest, she had shot to the top of the charts all over the world in 1995 with a disco version of the Bonnie Tyler hit 'Total Eclipse Of The Heart'. The former stage musical singer did not help matters with a far from strong performance. Her vast experience seemed to desert her on stage, hampered further by her choice of clothing for the show. Consisting of a lilac coat over a purple two-piece bodice and pantaloons, and with her bare midriff exposed, the outfit was entirely unflattering for her figure

and age. Only eight countries awarded the UK any marks at all, earning just 28 points and ended up in sixteenth place. It was the lowest score yet for the UK under the current points system and was the worst ever placing for a British entry up to this point.

The very over-the-top and flamboyant German **Stefan Raab** had clearly enjoyed himself so much at the 1998 contest that he had penned another heavily humorous entry for the Stockholm contest, this time opting to sing the song himself. He performed with a backing band and two girl singers, who were dressed as modern-day cowboys in gold and white reflective suits, with platform shoes that hadn't been seen since the contests of the 1970s. The song, 'Wadde Hadde Dudde Da?' was nonsense of the highest order, with a rap verse performed in German and the chorus in English. It was wacky but well received. By finishing fifth, the Germans had an excellent result, easily putting the woes of the past decade behind them.

The host nation had opted for a bizarre and frankly confusing performance. **Roger Pontare** had sung with Marie Bergman in the 1994 competition in Dublin and returned as a soloist this year dressed once again in the attire of an American Indian. He had brought along a Cree-Indian pow-wow dancer, a Norwegian Sami and a Thule Eskimo for good measure, to illustrate his song about indigenous people fighting for their land. Fire burned around the stage and

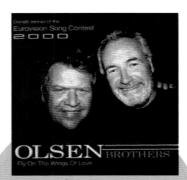

Far left: Denmark's Olsen Brothers, Jørgen, 51 and Niels, 47, were by far the oldest act to compete in this year's event and few pundits gave them any chance of victory, particularly against the tide of youth that was prevalent in this year's competition.

In Denmark, the Olsens' win caught everyone off-guard. The Monday following the contest, 'Fly On The Wings Of Love' sold 100,000 copies in one day alone, a record for the Danish market. It also stormed up the charts elsewhere, hitting the top in Sweden and the Top 10 in Germany.

Left: FYR Macedonia fielded a lively song performed by four teenage girls known as XXL. Dressed in outfits of different colours, they had worked harder on their choreography than on their vocals, which were woefully inadequate.

flames leapt high at explosive intervals, helping to confuse the visual image of the song further. It wasn't to be another win for the Swedes, though, and after a slow start, they finally managed seventh place with 88 points.

One extra country was allowed to compete this year, bringing the number of participants up on the year before to twenty-four. Joining Sweden and the four mandatory entrants, were the absentee nations from 1999 and newcomer Latvia, in addition to the countries with the best average scores from between 1995 and 1999. Latvia proved to be one of the most successful debutante nations in the history of the contest, as a plethora of countries not normally associated with the top places on the scoreboard proved highly successful this year.

The first of those nations to compete was Estonia. Eighteen-year-old **Ines** was widely publicised as being the Estonian answer to the American teenage sensation Britney Spears. Certainly her appearance and singing style were very similar to the more famous youngster. 'Once In A Lifetime' was a lively track with a strong beat and it was a clear challenger for the title.

Like Estonia, neighbouring Russia had turned to a young performer, the youngest in the contest, 16-year-old **Alsou**. For the first time, the Russians were singing in English. Alsou was based in London and there was little connection with Russia at all as the sultry teenager took to the stage in shimmering beige, her skimpy top barely covering her upper body. Although she did not give the best vocal performance, her extremely provocative and sultry dancing and moves more than made up for her lack of singing talent.

Latvia was probably not expecting to do any better with its first-ever entry, but it made a big splash with a song by the all-male band **Brainstorm**, who bore more than a passing resemblance to such international stars as Blur and Oasis. Their lead singer Renars Kaupers had come up with a very catchy song that the group performed with a laid-back charm that grabbed the viewers' attention, as did the aquarium on the screens behind them. Although they benefited from some highly partisan voting, they would have done well in any case.

However, the winner was to come from one of Eurovision's more established but less successful competitors. For Denmark, relegation was a real possibility. Having been made to sit out the 1994, 1996 and 1998 contests, their fortunes had been somewhat revived with a

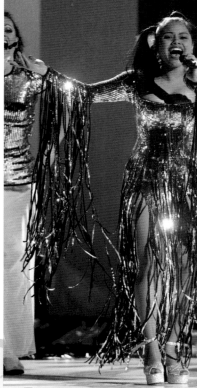

The Netherlands' Linda Wagenmakers started the presentation wearing a vast black and white dress that resembled a circus tent. Hidden beneath the enormous skirt were two male dancers who emerged as the gentle verse gave way to the thumping beat of the chorus, and Linda shed her outer wear to reveal a striking silver gown, shredded from the waist down.

surprise eighth place in Jerusalem. **The Olsen Brothers** came to Stockholm with an unspectacular song that few people were taking particularly seriously – British bookmakers had them listed at 150–1. Jorgen, aged 51, and Niels, aged 47, had been performing together since the 1960s and had often tried to enter Eurovision.

'Fly On The Wings Of Love' was a gentle ballad with a sing-a-long chorus. Special effects were added to the penultimate chorus of the song to give Jorgen's voice an electronic sound, and after the show, the Russians protested at this use of this technology, but to no avail. As they performed the song, which was not entirely dissimilar to

country	song	performer	place	score	draw
Denmark	Fly On The Wings Of Love	**The Olsen Brothers**	1	195	14
Russia	Solo	**Alsou**	2	155	9
Latvia	My Star	**Brainstorm**	3	136	21
Estonia	Once In A Lifetime	**Ines**	4	98	4
Germany	Wadde Hadde Dudde Da	**Stefan Raab**	5	96	15
Ireland	Millennium Of Love	**Eamonn Toal**	6	92	23
Sweden	When Spirits Are Calling My Name	**Roger Pontare**	7	88	18
Malta	Desire	**Claudette Pace**	8	73	7
Croatia	Kada Zaspu Anđeli (Ostani)	**Goran Karan**	9	70	17
Turkey	Yorgunum Anla	**Pinar Ayhan & the SOS**	10	59	22
Norway	My Heart Goes Boom	**Charmed**	11	57	8
Iceland	Tell me!	**August & Telma**	12	45	12
Netherlands	No Goodbyes	**Linda Wagenmakers**	13	40	2
Austria	All To You	**The Rounder Girls**	14	34	24
F.Y.R. Macedonia	100% Te Ljubam	**XXL**	15	29	19
United Kingdom	Don't Play That Song Again	**Nicki French**	16	28	3
Romania	Luna (The Moon)	**Taxi**	17	25	6
Spain	Colgado De Un Sueno	**Serafin**	18=	18	13
Finland	A Little Bit	**Nina Åström**	18=	18	20
Switzerland	La Vita Cos'e	**Jane Bogaert**	20	14	16
Cyprus	Nomiza	**Voice (Christina Argyri & Alexandros Panayi)**	21	8	11
Israel	Sa'me'akh (Be Happy)	**Ping Pong**	22	7	1
France	On Aura Le Ciel	**Sofia Mestari**	23	5	5
Belgium	Envie de Vivre	**Nathalie Sorce**	24	2	10

Ireland's 1994 winner 'Rock'n'Roll Kids', although much more up-tempo, the audience clapped along, waving small lights above their heads during the chorus. They cheered enthusiastically and brought the house down for the finale. What had been the longest shot in the history of the contest romped to victory with a sweeping win and broke some records along the way.

By the final reckoning the Olsen Brothers had 195 points – the third highest total yet scored in the contest – and had received marks from everyone except Croatia and FYR Macedonia, including eight top marks of twelve. Russia was second with 155, including four 12-point scores, with the Latvians joining the Dutch and Turks in failing to award them a mark. Baltic nations took the first, second, third, fourth, fifth and seventh places, with only Ireland spoiling the show in sixth.

It was a clear win for Denmark, ending a thirty-seven year drought for the country, though to be fair, for thirteen of those years, they did not compete at all. They had led from start to finish in the voting, the first winner to do so since 1974. Despite all the partisan voting, there was no doubt they were the overwhelming choice of the televoters and the two oldest singers in the competition took a lengthy walk from the back of the auditorium towards the stage, showered in silver confetti, to receive their prizes. They were the first brothers since Herreys in 1984 to take the title.

The Olsen Brothers' enjoyed huge success at home in Denmark and in Europe with their winning single. In UK, it was a different story. Nicki French's single did finally come out, but spent one solitary week on the charts at number thirty-four. Despite her disastrous result, she bounced back and claimed she would love to do the contest again. She is reported to have put her defeat down to the UK not being part of the European single currency, possibly forgetting that Denmark, Russia, Latvia and Estonia, the top four-placed nations, were not amongst Euro users either.

The biggest contest to date was a triumph for Sweden, but in Denmark they were already planning one even bigger!

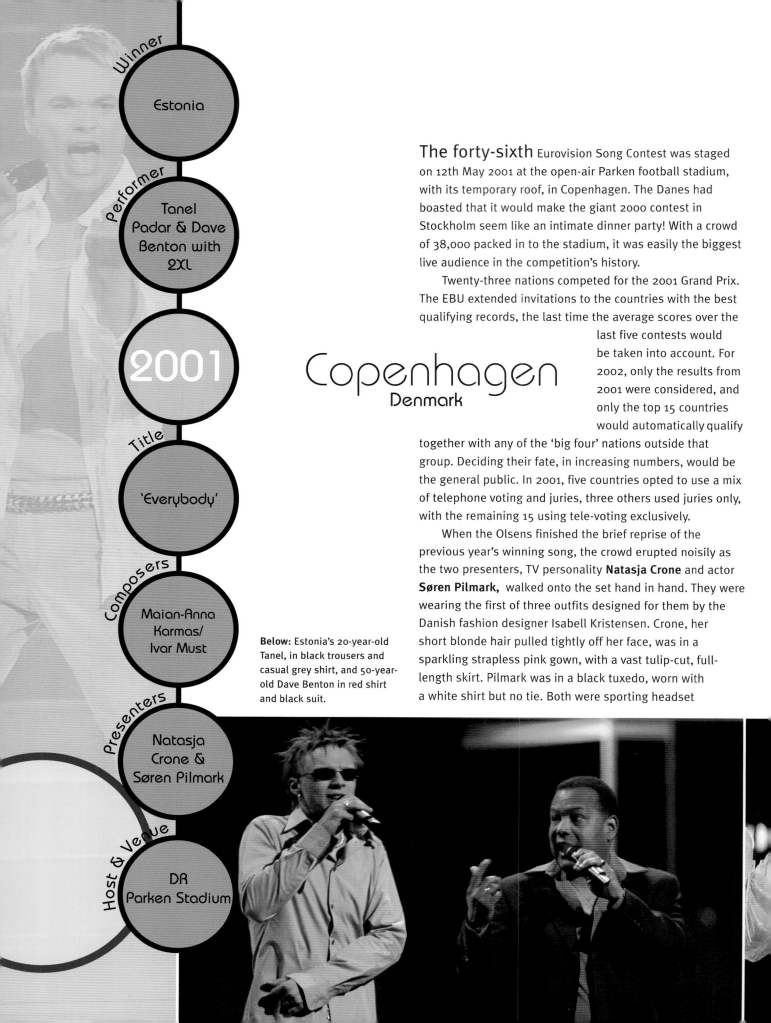

Winner
Estonia

Performer
Tanel Padar & Dave Benton with 2XL

2001

Title
'Everybody'

Composers
Maian-Anna Karmas/ Ivar Must

Presenters
Natasja Crone & Søren Pilmark

Host & Venue
DR Parken Stadium

Copenhagen
Denmark

The forty-sixth Eurovision Song Contest was staged on 12th May 2001 at the open-air Parken football stadium, with its temporary roof, in Copenhagen. The Danes had boasted that it would make the giant 2000 contest in Stockholm seem like an intimate dinner party! With a crowd of 38,000 packed in to the stadium, it was easily the biggest live audience in the competition's history.

Twenty-three nations competed for the 2001 Grand Prix. The EBU extended invitations to the countries with the best qualifying records, the last time the average scores over the last five contests would be taken into account. For 2002, only the results from 2001 were considered, and only the top 15 countries would automatically qualify together with any of the 'big four' nations outside that group. Deciding their fate, in increasing numbers, would be the general public. In 2001, five countries opted to use a mix of telephone voting and juries, three others used juries only, with the remaining 15 using tele-voting exclusively.

When the Olsens finished the brief reprise of the previous year's winning song, the crowd erupted noisily as the two presenters, TV personality **Natasja Crone** and actor **Søren Pilmark,** walked onto the set hand in hand. They were wearing the first of three outfits designed for them by the Danish fashion designer Isabell Kristensen. Crone, her short blonde hair pulled tightly off her face, was in a sparkling strapless pink gown, with a vast tulip-cut, full-length skirt. Pilmark was in a black tuxedo, worn with a white shirt but no tie. Both were sporting headset

Below: Estonia's 20-year-old Tanel, in black trousers and casual grey shirt, and 50-year-old Dave Benton in red shirt and black suit.

'Everybody' got very limited release, primarily in the Nordic countries, where it charted in Sweden only. Once again, the single was not released in the UK or Ireland, despite the song having been the UK televoters' favourite entry.

microphones. As they made their entrance, the perennial BBC TV commentator Terry Wogan referred to them as 'the tooth fairy and Doctor Death'. It was the first of many jokes he made at the pair's expense throughout the evening – later, he called Crone 'the bride of Frankenstein' – and it landed him in trouble with his Danish hosts. His cynicism was not entirely misplaced, however, as they went on to present the entire programme in rhyming couplets!

In pole position came **Michelle**, a 19-year-old singer representing the Netherlands. It was the first time since 1975 that the Dutch had sung first, but the sixth time they had done so in total, itself a record. Her song titled 'Out On My Own' was a simple, rather mournful ballad that was performed by the barefoot singer in a sparkling navy tank top, but its chances of success were hampered by the fact that the Norwegians had entered a song with a very similar title – 'On My Own'. To add to the confusion, the Germans had also entered a young singer called **Michelle**. Eventually, it was doubtful whether the similarities made any impact on the competition – the Netherlands ended in eighteenth place and was out of the next year's contest.

The legendary 'curse of number two' seemed to be at work once again this year, for the first time since 1978 and the eighth time in total, the second performed song came last. Icelandic male duo **Two Tricky** chose to sing in English, as indeed did 15 of the 23 entries this year. Another five were sung at least in part in English, with only three entries including no English at all. Their track was a very up-tempo piece that certainly had a contemporary feel to it, but as history has often proved, contemporary is not usually what the Eurovision voters look for – even tele-voters it would seem – and they had to settle for just three points, two coming from Denmark and one from Norway, who would themselves have to share last place with their Nordic cousins.

For their part, Norway submitted a lush ballad, very much in the mould of former Irish and French winners of the contest, bearing more than just a little similarity to Eric Carmen's 1976 hit single, 'All By Myself'. **Haldor Laegreid** had a very strong and clear voice, but was perhaps let down by his choice of costume – a white lace, frilled shirt, worn open over flared pale-green velvet trousers.

France also received some snide remarks from contest fans about their automatic participation in the contest, but like the Spanish, they had their best result for many years, helping to silence the critics. A hot pre-contest favourite, topping many of the unofficial internet polls, the French seemed to have rediscovered the formula that had allowed them to dominate the first 25 years of the contest, but had brought them scant success in recent years. French-Canadian singer **Natasha St-Pier** was a tall redhead in the Céline Dion mould who had been singing since

Far left: Lithuania's Skamp were reportedly advised to withdraw from the contest after winning the domestic heat, in order to protect their credibility, but they soldiered on. The trio was joined on stage by three lads in crazy-coloured afro-wigs. The singing was rather flat, but it was an enthusiastic effort.

Left: Presenters Natasja Crone and Søren Pilmark.

early childhood. She appeared entirely alone and delivered a faultless performance of her powerful ballad. Perhaps conscious of how disastrously the two French-language songs had fared in 2000, Natasha sang the last verse in English, the first time ever that the French entry had deviated from an indigenous language, but it wasn't quite enough.

Estonia had made a disastrous debut at the 1994 contest in Dublin, when Paul Harrington and Charlie McGettigan had been the first male duo to triumph. Seven years on, 20-year-old **Tanel Padar**, the boyfriend and backing singer of 2000's entrant Ines, had teamed up with 50-year-old Aruban-born singer **Dave Benton** to perform a very bouncy disco number. A lot went against them. Firstly, Benton's ethnicity might have been a handicap, as no black singer had yet taken the Grand Prix. Secondly, male duos were not usually popular – the Olsen Brothers were only the second such pairing to win, and finally, the song just wasn't that good. But, as with the Olsens, the tele-voters did not agree with the pundits or the fans that had placed the song way down the ranking in the unofficial pre-contest internet polls.

They were joined by four young male backing singers and dancers called **2XL**. These lads threw themselves into their routine with enormous energy, break-dancing, somersaulting, spinning and performing other dramatic feats throughout the presentation. The song itself was very nearly a rap, or at least, was highly reminiscent of military marching chants. It had a strong, up-tempo disco beat, and a very catchy chorus that appealed to the audience watching. Notching up 198 points, the third highest score yet achieved, with nine top marks of 12 and racking up three-quarters of the total available vote, they cruised to victory to become the first new nation to triumph in the contest since 1989.

After staying at home for two consecutive years, Greece returned to the contest with a canny ploy up their sleeves to attract the voting viewers. Clearly it had not gone unnoticed by them how well the Scandinavian and Baltic nations were doing in Eurovision, or indeed how chummy the voting had become among these neighbouring nations. Helena and Nikos, known collectively as **Antique**, were Greece's secret weapon – they were Greeks who had been born and raised in

Right: A veteran of many stage musicals, Copenhagen resident Haldor Laegreid brought a great deal of stage presence and professionalism to the Norwegain entry but, for the ninth time in the contest's history, itself a new record, Norway was to finish in last place.

Far right: Sweden's quintet Friends were compared repeatedly to Abba. The two girls who sang lead, Nina Inhammar and Kim Karnfalk, were a blonde and a brunette, just like Agnetha and Frida.

Sweden, where they had built up an enormous following, spreading to other parts of Scandinavia. Their song was the typical mixture of modern and traditional Greek rhythms, but was greatly helped by a driving beat and having the chorus performed in English. Helena appeared dressed in a white, slinky, halter-neck catsuit, which clung to her body, plummeting to the base of her bare spine. Nikos sat on the stool beside her to play his bouzouki. The local bookies had installed the song as the favourite after the rehearsals, and indeed the Greek entry was the only song to receive a mark from every other country, but they had to be content with third place, still two places higher than any previous Greek effort had ever achieved before.

The home entry from Denmark was performed last. **Rollo and King**, a male duo joined by a female vocalist **Signe Svendsen**, had a very unusual up-tempo entry, with country-and-western rhythms, a mouth organ and Jews' harp accompaniment. It set a foot-tapping beat that got the vast audience cheering and clapping along. But it was not enough for Denmark to attain a third Grand Prix win. They came very close, and in doing so, achieved the sixth-highest score yet recorded in the contest, 177 points, the highest score to date for a song that did not win.

Pilmark and Crone returned to the set – this time described as Little Bo-Peep and Dr Phibes by Mr Wogan – to introduce the reprise of each entry, the interval act, Aqua and then the voting.

Despite the crushing nature of Estonia's win, the lower positions provided the most drama. The lowest-ranked countries seemed to be universally loathed across the tele-voting continent, but there were still some shocks. Ireland, the most successful winning nation in the contest's history, was relegated for the first time ever with just six points. With 'big four' status, the UK need not fear relegation, but they had only achieved the cut off point in the rankings required for any other nation, fifteenth.

Estonia had not even existed as an independent nation when Marcel Besançon and his team had created the concept of the Eurovision Song Contest, back in 1956, and yet, almost 50 years on, his idea was still thriving and growing.

country	song	performer	place	score	draw
Estonia	Everybody	**Tanel Padar & Dave Benton with 2XL**	1	198	20
Denmark	Never Ever Let You Go	**Rollo and King**	2	177	23
Greece	Die For You	**Antique**	3	147	22
France	Je N'ai Que Mon Ame	**Natasha St-Pier**	4	142	14
Sweden	ListenTo Your Heartbeat	**Friends**	5	100	7
Spain	Dile Que La Quiero	**David Civera**	6	76	13
Slovenia	Energy	**Nuša Derenda**	7	70	17
Germany	Wer Liebe Lebt	**Michelle**	8	66	19
Malta	Another Summer Night	**Fabrizio Faniello**	9	48	21
Croatia	The Strings Of My Heart	**Vanna**	10	42	10
Turkey	Sevgiliye Son	**Sedat Yuce**	11	41	15
Russia	Lady Alpine Blue	**Mumiy Troll**	12	37	6
Lithuania	You Got Style	**Skamp**	13	35	8
Bosnia-Herzegovina	Hano	**Nino Pršes**	14	29	3
United Kingdom	No Dream Impossible	**Lindsay Dracass**	15	28	16
Israel	Ein Davar	**Tal Sondak**	16	25	5
Portugal	So Sei Ser Feliz Assim	**MTM**	17	18	11
Netherlands	Out On My Own	**Michelle**	18=	16	1
Latvia	Too Much	**Arnis Mednis**	18=	16	9
Poland	2 Long	**Piasek**	20	11	18
Ireland	Without Your Love	**Gary O'Shaughnessy**	21	6	12
Iceland	Angel	**Two Tricky**	22=	3	2
Norway	On My Own	**Haldor Laegreid**	22=	3	4

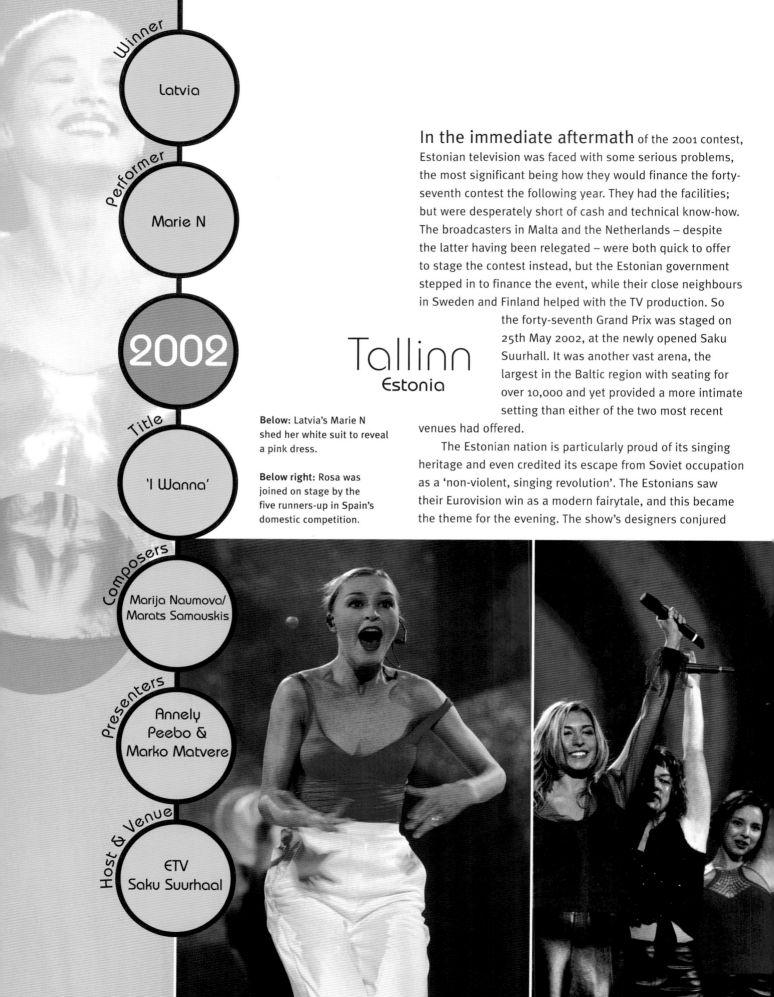

Winner

Latvia

Performer

Marie N

2002

Title

'I Wanna'

Composers

Marija Naumova/ Marats Samauskis

Presenters

Annely Peebo & Marko Matvere

Host & Venue

ETV Saku Suurhaal

Tallinn
Estonia

In the immediate aftermath of the 2001 contest, Estonian television was faced with some serious problems, the most significant being how they would finance the forty-seventh contest the following year. They had the facilities; but were desperately short of cash and technical know-how. The broadcasters in Malta and the Netherlands – despite the latter having been relegated – were both quick to offer to stage the contest instead, but the Estonian government stepped in to finance the event, while their close neighbours in Sweden and Finland helped with the TV production. So the forty-seventh Grand Prix was staged on 25th May 2002, at the newly opened Saku Suurhall. It was another vast arena, the largest in the Baltic region with seating for over 10,000 and yet provided a more intimate setting than either of the two most recent venues had offered.

The Estonian nation is particularly proud of its singing heritage and even credited its escape from Soviet occupation as a 'non-violent, singing revolution'. The Estonians saw their Eurovision win as a modern fairytale, and this became the theme for the evening. The show's designers conjured

Below: Latvia's Marie N shed her white suit to reveal a pink dress.

Below right: Rosa was joined on stage by the five runners-up in Spain's domestic competition.

up a magical and dynamic set that was filled with floating screens and a stage that curved out into the audience.

Their choice of hosts was original, too. **Annely Peebo** was a leading soprano at the Volksoper Opera in Vienna and **Marko Matvere** was a respected classical actor and folk musician with a group called the Association of the Little Concertinas.

The concept for each video postcard followed the set design with modern interpretations of classic fairytales. The postcard introducing the opening Cypriot entry was allegedly based on the story of Aladdin, but it had little to do with the traditional tale of the famous legend. Instead, the video featured an extremely unfortunate-looking bartender in a Tallinn nightclub cleaning a teapot and releasing a series of dancing ghosts. All but one disappeared when the pot was broken, the remaining spectre transforming into a very pretty girl who then accepted a drink from the barman. It couldn't have been more confusing had it tried! The postcards led to a technical hitch during the opening song by Cyprus boyband **One**. Just as their lead singer, Constantinos, began singing a caption bearing the words 'Ugly Duckling' appeared on screen.

As was now becoming the norm, **'I Wanna'** failed to find much international favour after the contest and became the first Eurovision winner not to be released anywhere outside its own territory. If the Latvians were proud of their first win, they didn't show it, buying it in such small quantities it failed to break the Latvian Top 30.

The United Kingdom was one of the several countries tapping into the success of rival TV talent shows to pick its Eurovision entry – its representative **Jessica Garlick** had reached the final stages of 'Pop Idol'. Spain went one better and invented a reality show called 'Operación Triunfo' (Operation Success) to select their Eurovision contestant, launching a TV ratings phenomenon in the process. Combining elements of the cult hit shows 'Big Brother' and 'Pop Idol', Spanish TV had gathered a group of aspiring youngsters together, locked them in a secluded mansion and then filmed their progress, as coaches, choreographers, designers and exercise gurus put the hopeful starlets through gruelling classes in order to turn them into stars. **Rosa**, a shy, somewhat overweight and insecure girl, who had never left her village near Granada before, quickly won the hearts of the viewers as she struggled to attain the standards set by the instructors at the 'school'. Her prize was to sing at Eurovision in Tallinn with the highly catchy 'Europe's Living A Celebration', which was performed in Spanish, despite the English title.

Rosa charged onto the stage wearing a loose-fitting black ensemble and delivered a highly impassioned performance of the up-tempo, sing-a-long anthem. The crowd loved it, but she had to be satisfied with seventh place, one place below Spain's 2001 finish. However, the reward for Spain's TVE was far bigger, as the format for their domestic competition was copied and sold around the world.

Denmark came to Estonia on the crest of its most successful period in the history of the contest. That particular wave came crashing down in Estonia. **Malene Mortensen**, another talent-show winner, sang a passionate ballad that was certainly well received in the hall, but her voice faltered and she looked extremely nervous once she was out on the extended stage area. The previous year's hosts would have to sit out the next contest. This was a great shame – while

Initially appearing in a full-length burgundy ball-gown, Macedonia's Karolina ripped this off mid-way through the song to reveal this skin-tight, contoured, gold bodice resembling body armour, over a flowing, long red skirt.

the populations of other nations, for example the UK, shun Eurovision, in Denmark the viewing figures have peaked, on occasion, at 90 per cent of the population.

Twenty-year-old **Ira Losco** carried the hopes of Malta, Eurovision's most enthusiastic competitors. As her song was criticised for its weak lyrics, Losco concentrated on her performance. Without doubt, her winsome charm won over a good many of the voters, her appeal helped along as she blew glitter towards the camera before upping the tempo of the gentle number for the final verse. It proved to be a successful formula and the Maltese led the voting for almost all of the first half of the scoring, remaining in contention for the Grand Prix right until the very end. Disappointingly, they just missed out on the top prize, having to settle for their best yet result – second with 164 points –and one of the highest scores yet achieved in the contest.

The most controversial entry of the evening came from Slovenia. For the first time ever, a group of performers in drag had made it through to the Eurovision finals, performing under the name of **Sestre**. The stage act of the three chaps – Miss Daphne, Miss Emperatrizz and Miss Marlena – was inspired by airline flight attendants. However, the group was viewed by many Slovenians as a slight on their country. Anti-gay activists and campaigners demanded the trio be barred from representing the nation. Protesters took to the streets of the capital Ljubljana and the controversy even reached

the floor of the Slovenian and European Parliaments. Such violent anti-gay sentiment was perceived by many politicians outside of Slovenia as evidence that the nation was not a suitable candidate for membership of the European Union, which it hoped to join in 2004. Despite the entire furore, few seriously considered the song a likely winner of the contest, although it was an enjoyable and over-the-top performance. No matter how much pre-contest publicity and controversy a group attracts, a novelty act will never overcome the handicap of a weak song, no matter how entertaining.

Portugal was the lowest-placed nation to qualify for the 2002 event, but once RTP had studied their finances, they had opted instead to sit the forty-seventh Eurovision out. Next on the list of eligible nations was Latvia. **Marija Naumova** decided to make the most of her unexpected opportunity. First, she completely overhauled her elected song, turning it from a thumping salsa/disco number into more of a Latin 'cabaret' sound. She then set about devising a stage act to blow the Eurovision audience away. On this point there can be no doubt she achieved her goal.

Perhaps one of the less obvious effects of removing the orchestra and live music in 1999 was that the orchestra had often been a reliable visual aid to illustrate particular entries, which artists now made up for with elaborate stage creations. Appearing on stage in the masculine attire of white suit, black shirt and white trilby, 'Marie N' was backed

country	song	performer	place	score	draw
Latvia	I Wanna	**Marie N**	1	176	23
Malta	7th Wonder	**Ira Losco**	2	164	20
United Kingdom	Come Back	**Jessica Garlick**	3=	111	2
Estonia	Runaway	**Sahlene**	3=	111	8
France	Il Faut Du Temps	**Sandrine François**	5	104	17
Cyprus	Gimme	**One**	6	85	1
Spain	Europe's Living A Celebration	**Rosa**	7	81	5
Sweden	Never Let It Go	**Afro-Dite**	8	72	12
Romania	Tell Me Why	**Monica Anghel & Marcel Pavel**	9	71	21
Russia	Northern Girl	**Prime Minister**	10	55	7
Croatia	Everything I Want	**Vesna Pisarović**	11	44	6
Israel	Light A Candle	**Sarit Hadad**	12	37	10
Bosnia-Herzegovina	Na Jastuku Za Dvoje	**Maja Tatić**	13=	33	15
Belgium	Sister	**Sergio & The Ladies**	13=	33	16
Slovenia	Samo Ljubezen	**Sestre**	13=	33	22
Turkey	Leylaklar Doldu Kalbinde	**Buket Bengisu & Grup Safir**	16	29	19
Greece	S.A.G.A.P.O.	**Michalis Rakintzis**	17	27	4
Austria	Say A Word	**Manuel Ortega**	18	26	3
F.Y.R. Macedonia	Od Nas Zavisi (It Depends On Us)	**Karolina**	19	25	9
Finland	Addicted To You	**Laura Voutilainen**	20	24	13
Germany	I Can't Live Without Music	**Corinna May**	21	17	18
Switzerland	Dans Le Jardin De Mon Ame	**Francine Jordi**	22	15	11
Lithuania	Happy You	**Aivaras**	23	12	24
Denmark	Tell Me Who You Are	**Malene Mortensen**	24	7	14

by two identically dressed males and three ladies in black Spanish-style dresses. The song and choreography owed far more to southern European Latin rhythms than the icy Baltic States and the move to a more universally popular sound certainly paid off. For the first verse and chorus, Marie performed a polished tango with the two male dancers. For the second verse she teamed with one of the female dancers, earning the media description of 'lesbian chic' the next day. As the song progressed, Marie discarded first her hat, then her jacket, shirt and trousers to reveal a short pink mini-dress. On the song's final note, the two male dancers tugged at the hemline, revealing that the dress was in fact a floor-length gown. It was the most carefully choreographed and designed act of the entire show, and the effort paid off. At only their third appearance in the contest, the newest Eurovision nation triumphed in the voting, keeping the contest in the Nordic circle for the fourth consecutive year.

It was a remarkable victory for the youngest Eurovision nation. Having only scraped into the contest when Portugal had withdrawn, Latvia became only the fourth nation to win within their first three attempts and was the first that had not been one of the original seven competing countries. Five countries had placed Latvia first, three had rated them second and four third. Only two countries considered Marie N's entry unworthy of a place in the top seven.

With the awards' presentation over, the credits rolled as Marie performed 'I Wanna' once more, this time with a reverse of her striptease. Initially dressed only in her pink gown, Marie added her white jacket and trilby as she sang the winner, while fireworks exploded around the stage.

Despite all the problems and headaches that had faced EE/ETV and the Estonian capital, the 2002 contest was a production triumph. The success not only of the contest, reaching nearly two hundred million viewers, but also some of the qualifying events gave a renewed impetus to the whole programme. The production values had been extremely high and set a new benchmark for other broadcasters.

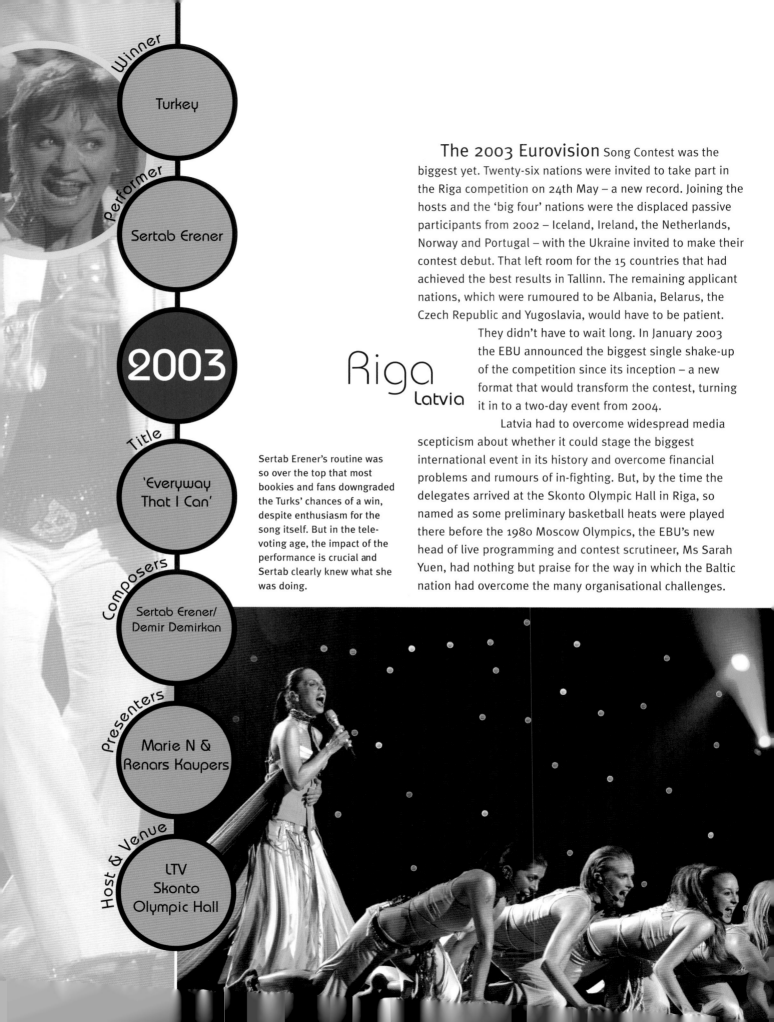

Winner

Turkey

Performer

Sertab Erener

2003

Title

'Everyway That I Can'

Composers

Sertab Erener/ Demir Demirkan

Presenters

Marie N & Renars Kaupers

Host & Venue

LTV Skonto Olympic Hall

Riga
Latvia

The 2003 Eurovision Song Contest was the biggest yet. Twenty-six nations were invited to take part in the Riga competition on 24th May – a new record. Joining the hosts and the 'big four' nations were the displaced passive participants from 2002 – Iceland, Ireland, the Netherlands, Norway and Portugal – with the Ukraine invited to make their contest debut. That left room for the 15 countries that had achieved the best results in Tallinn. The remaining applicant nations, which were rumoured to be Albania, Belarus, the Czech Republic and Yugoslavia, would have to be patient.

They didn't have to wait long. In January 2003 the EBU announced the biggest single shake-up of the competition since its inception – a new format that would transform the contest, turning it in to a two-day event from 2004.

Latvia had to overcome widespread media scepticism about whether it could stage the biggest international event in its history and overcome financial problems and rumours of in-fighting. But, by the time the delegates arrived at the Skonto Olympic Hall in Riga, so named as some preliminary basketball heats were played there before the 1980 Moscow Olympics, the EBU's new head of live programming and contest scrutineer, Ms Sarah Yuen, had nothing but praise for the way in which the Baltic nation had overcome the many organisational challenges.

Sertab Erener's routine was so over the top that most bookies and fans downgraded the Turks' chances of a win, despite enthusiasm for the song itself. But in the tele-voting age, the impact of the performance is crucial and Sertab clearly knew what she was doing.

The previous year's winner, Marie N and Renars Kaupers, who had participated in 2000 as one of Brainstorm, were selected to host the forty-eighth contest. They opened Eurovision in traditional style, making a dramatic entrance in 'crazy costumes' made from multi-coloured fake fur. These were discarded to reveal matching costumes in bright yellow, which were certainly no easier on the eye. They took viewers on a lightning tour of Riga through a collage of photographic images. Greetings were then offered live from the Mir Space Station, where a Latvian cosmonaut was fulfilling a term of duty, before links with Vienna and Nicosia brought good wishes from Elton John (speaking from the venue of the international AIDS charity event The Hair Ball) and the winner of the first Eurovision in 1956, Lys Assia.

The set consisted of swooping arches high above the circular performing area. The floor was actually a giant screen and, throughout the contest, various dynamic images flashed beneath the performers' feet. Lighting effects enhanced the images further as tiny lights glittered on the black backcloth for the set, which hid the artists' green room from the audience of 6,000.

Iceland opened well and was followed by one of the most intriguing and popular artists in the contest, Austria's **Alf Poier**. A former chimneysweep, long-distance runner and night watchman, Alf had built a career as a performance

SERTAB ERENER
Everyway that I can

Sertab enjoyed pan-continental success with the **'Everyway That I Can'**, except in the UK where the single barely scratched the bottom of the charts. Sertab continued to record in English and found success with her follow-up single and album outside the Turkish borders.

artist and had often been named 'comedian of the year' in his homeland. Certainly, his Eurovision entry was full of fun. Dressed in oversized jeans, a red T-shirt and black beret, he was joined on stage by two ladies and four stuffed animals – the song was his comment on animals having to live in the filth created by man. It wasn't expected to do much in the contest, particularly drawn in the ill-fated second place, but such was the quirkiness and bizarre nature of the performance that it earned the Austrians their best result since 1989 and a guaranteed place in 2004's competition.

Many nations had now turned to TV talent shows to select their entries, but Turkey took the approach of commissioning their leading female singer, **Sertab Erener**, to represent her country with a song of her choice. Sung entirely in English, it was by far the most contemporary offering ever entered by the Turks and was backed by a colourful stage presentation. The tiny Erener, dressed in traditional Turkish pink pantaloons with her midriff exposed, was joined by four similarly dressed ladies to present a very over-the-top belly dance. This involved the backing dancers dancing around the stage holding four ribbons that extended from Sertab's bodice, and transformed her into a human maypole. The performance lodged itself in the audience's consciousness and was the clear favourite in the Skonto complex.

There was strife in the Maltese camp and the very unhappy Maltese delegation ended in discord when **Lynn** achieved their worst-ever position with 'To Dream Again'. Ill feeling between the singer and her delegation erupted into a full scale-shouting match on the plane back to Valletta. Female soloists from Bosnia, Portugal and Croatia also failed to impress despite all turning in first-rate performances.

From the moment it was announced that the group **t.A.T.u.** was to represent Russia in Riga, a media feeding frenzy began. The creation of their manager, Ivan Shapovalov, the two teenage girls Lena Katina and Yulia

Volkova had built an image as teenage lesbians, thanks to the very provocative video for their international hit 'All The Things She Said'. A complete media invention, the girls began to crack under the pressure, as neither were lesbians and their manipulation by Shapovalov became as much of a story as their music. Their media campaign to win the contest was carefully scripted, with the press lapping up the hints dropped throughout the run-up that the girls would appear naked on stage, kiss on camera and simulate sexual acts for the audience. Their behaviour beforehand certainly seemed choreographed – the girls arrived late for rehearsals and created tantrums and disorder wherever they went, resulting in a warning from the EBU. However, on the night, their rock effort was weakly performed without any controversy at all, bar a very, very hesitant touch, and the weary audience booed them off the stage to thank them for their week-long antics. Nevertheless, the viewers were captivated and voted for the song in huge numbers.

Chris Crombey and Gemma Abbey were a Liverpudlian duo called **Jemini**, who came to Riga to perform for the UK with very little domestic support and little expectation of success. Yet even the disinterested UK audience was stunned by the final result. No British Eurovision entry had ever been placed lower than sixteenth in the contest and, remarkably, there had only been five previous UK songs placed outside the top ten. In addition, no song sung in English had ever failed to score. However, such was the tuneless and uninspired effort from the hapless duo that all these statistics were swept away by their inept performance. 'Nul points' for the UK was unthinkable, and

with 26 entries this also made Jemini the least-successful entry in the history of the contest so far.

The young Brad Pitt lookalike **Jostein Hasselgard** performed Norway's entry at the piano. Well regarded, the simplicity of the Norwegian ballad took this effort up to fourth place, despite some small pre-contest controversy when the Norwegian commentator **Jostein Pedersen** angered SVT Sweden. Although intended to be a joke, Pedersen had described the Swedish duo, **Fame**, as being 'less charismatic than an IKEA bookcase'! All was forgiven on the night, though, when the Swedes awarded the Norwegians the maximum 12 points.

With four of their own languages to chose from and any of hundreds of others from around the world at their disposal, the Belgian group **Urban Trad** instead opted to make up one of their own. 'Sanomi' was performed entirely in this imaginary tongue, although the rhythm and musical style of the song were very clearly inspired by Celtic and folk traditions. A minor controversy afflicted the band when one of its three female members was thrown out, having been revealed to be a member of a Nazi-inspired cult. The six members who did make it to the contest were hardly tipped for success, but such was the distinct difference and unusual quality of the Belgian entry that the voting viewers were

Hardly in the first flush of youth and highly criticised for her bizarre looks, orange-haired Lou had tried many times to represent Germany and finally made it through this year.

Contrary to rehearsal-week media hype, t.A.T.u. did not appear naked on stage, kiss on camera or simulate sexual acts. Their performance was weak and they were booed off.

clearly impressed. Belgium had not placed in the top five since winning back in 1986, but this year they would be one of the three leading contenders for top place, barely missing out on gold in the final vote.

It was clear from the outset that the voting was a three-horse race this year. Although Norway started incredibly strongly, Turkey, Belgium and Russia dominated the entire voting process, with the lead swapping between each country regularly. By the time Sweden had cast their votes, Belgium led by 162 to Turkey's 157 and Russia's 152. The entire result was in the hands of the Slovenians, who scuppered Belgian chances with a mark of three, but gave victory to Turkey with ten. Slovenia's 12 for Russia was too late for t.A.T.u. Only three points separated the top three songs, the closest contest yet.

Throughout the voting, the curtain separating the green room from the stage was raised, allowing the audience in the hall to see the contestants backstage soaking up the tension of the voting. When the result was announced, Sertab and her dancers made their way from this area back onto the stage, while t.A.T.u's manager, clearly not delighted with the result, was seen yelling at his cohorts. Sarah Yuen and Riga's Mayor Gundars Bojas presented the Grand Prix while 'Everyway That I Can' took the audience by storm in the reprise.

Jemini returned home to the UK as media curios and faced the press and cameras with much humour, but considerable defiance. They put on a brave face and generated more media buzz than any UK effort since Gina G. For t.A.T.u., the bubble had burst and they failed to find much success outside of Russia after the contest.

The Eurovision Song Contest was leaving the Baltics and heading east. The 2004 contest would certainly hold a great deal of Eastern promise.

country	song	performer	place	score	draw
Turkey	Everyway That I Can	Sertab Erener	1	167	4
Belgium	Sanomi	Urban Trad	2	165	22
Russia	Ne Verj, Ne Bojsia, Ne Prosi	t.A.T.u.	3	164	11
Norway	I'm Not Afraid To Move On	Jostein Hasselgad	4	123	18
Sweden	Give Me Your Love	Fame	5	107	25
Austria	Weil Der Mensch Zählt	Alf Poier	6	101	2
Poland	Keine Grenzen – Zadnych Granich	Ich Troje	7	90	20
Iceland	Open Your Heart	Birgitta	8=	81	1
Spain	Dime	Beth	8=	81	12
Romania	Don't Break My Heart	Nicola	10	73	24
Ireland	We've Got The World	Mickey Joe Harte	11=	53	3
Germany	Let's Get Happy	Lou	11=	53	10
Netherlands	One More Night	Esther Hart	13	45	14
Ukraine	Hasta La Vista	Olexsandr	14	30	16
Croatia	Više Nisam Tvoja	Claudia Beni	15	29	8
Bosnia-Herzegovina	Ne Brini	Mija Martina	16	27	6
Greece	Never Let You Go	Mando	17	25	17
France	Monts Et Merveilles	Louisa Baileche	18	19	19
Israel	Words For Love	Lior Narkis	19	17	13
Cyprus	Feeling Alive	Stelios Konstantas	20	15	9
Estonia	Eighties Coming Back	Ruffus	21	14	23
Portugal	Deixa-Me Sonhar (Keep The Dream Alive)	Rita Guerra	22	13	7
Slovenia	Nanana	Karmen Stavec	23	7	26
Latvia	Hello From Mars	F.L.Y.	24	5	21
Malta	To Dream Again	Lynn Chircop	25	4	5
United Kingdom	Cry Baby	Jemini	26	0	15

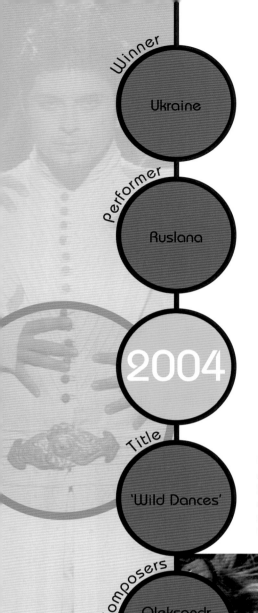

Winner

Ukraine

Performer

Ruslana

2004

Title

'Wild Dances'

Composers

Oleksandr
Ksenofontov/
Ruslana

Presenters

Meltem
Cumbul &
Korhan Abay

Host & Venue

TRT
Abdi Ipekci
Spor Salun

Istanbul
Turkey

The forty-ninth Eurovision Song Contest was easily the largest yet staged and also the first conceived under a radical new format. So that 36 countries could take part, including the returning Monaco (who had not participated since 1979), the EBU had decided, even before the 2003 contest, that the competition would be split into two nights. Although the exact format of the new contest was always under discussion, seemingly up until the very last minute, it was determined before the Riga show that only the top ten scoring countries, together with the 'big four' nations, would make it directly into the following year. The other ten countries to join that elite group would be determined in a semi-final held shortly before the Grand Prix.

Istanbul, the only city in the world that spans two continents, was selected as host for this dramatically different format, in which a semi-final contest of twenty-two nations would take place three days before the event proper on May 15th. Albania, Andorra, Belarus and the former Yugoslav republics of Serbia and Montenegro were the nations competing for the very first time.

Ukranian superstar Ruslana submitted a track from her latest hugely successful album and set about building a stage routine that would blow the international viewers away.

Following logistic complications, the venue was switched late in the day from the Mydonese Showlands to the larger and more secure Abdi Ipekci basketball Stadium. Performing on the same set and introduced by the same postcards as would be used at the final, the semi-finalists' performances were certainly as strong as if they were finalists. Problems with the sound on the broadcast and voting irregularities certainly marred the production and there was huge disappointment in each of the failed nations. All 33 nations televising the contest were permitted to vote, but only the ten qualifiers were announced on screen towards the end of the two-hour show, with Serbia and Montenegro being drawn out first. Immediately after the top ten was announced, the results of the remaining 12 nations were flashed on screen. Israel had just missed the cut-off in eleventh place and, in the ultimate humiliation, Switzerland had failed to score a single point. With potential scores from 33 nations, it was the worst-ever drubbing in the history of the competition, far outstripping the dire performance of the UK the previous year. However, the result was not without controversy. There were so few votes cast in Monaco – less than 100 – that the computer had not been able to recognise the paltry scores and had randomly invented votes instead.

The Saturday final opened with Spain's **Ramon**. The 18-year-old winner of the third 'Operación Triunfo' gave a very spirited rendition of his tempestuous song 'Para Llenarme De Ti' ('To Be Filled With You'). France's **Jonatan Cerrada** sang a dramatic ballad, very much in the traditional Eurovision style. But the French, like so many other nations, clearly felt that song quality would not be enough to win over viewers and thus created a stage act that not only distracted from the song itself but left viewers completely nonplussed. Recreating the story of LE PETIT PRINCE, Jonatan – all in white, this year's colour for performers – was joined on stage by a bald-headed, black woman on six-foot stilts and dressed in white spandex, as were the four backing singers. It was simply so bizarre that no one could possibly have been impressed, and judging by the lack of phone votes, they weren't!

There was speculation that viewers would also be confused by Serbia and Montenegro's debut 'Lane Moje' ('Oh My Fawn'). The video of **Željko Joksimovic** ´ 's entry contained such strange images of swan-plucking that it was hard to concentrate on the haunting music and style of the ballad. Opening with 45 seconds of flute and string

'Wild Dances' was a huge hit at home in the Ukraine, making the top of the charts and going double platinum. It also reached No. 1 in Belgium and Greece, and No. 2 in Turkey.

music from the Ad-Hoc Orkestra, Željko's low-key, very ethnic number had been the pick of almost all the internet fans to deliver the goods on the night and for once they were almost proved right. Such was the unusual quality of the effort, with no distracting choreogr aphy to sway viewers, they were charmed by the haunting melody and orchestration and gave the Serbs their best-ever showing in the contest and equalled the best-ever result for a debut nation, second place.

The Germans had taken their entry to their hearts in a manner unseen since Nicole in 1982, but the low-key jazz number by **Max**, who had won his ticket to Istanbul on the back of an exhaustive TV talent series, failed to interest the viewers.

The Ukraine had made a solid start to its Eurovision campaign in 2003 and had certainly embraced the Eurovision ideal as a result. Determined to do even better this year, the leading Ukrainian superstar, **Ruslana**, was given free rein to choose an entry for Istanbul, following the formula that had proved so successful for the Turks. Clearly taking 'Xena – Warrior Princess' as her inspiration, Ruslana and her five backing singers appeared on stage in leather armour that barely covered any of their bodies. Cracking whips, carrying alpine horns and discarding fur cloaks, such was the energy and dynamism of their stage show that most viewers were left breathless at the spectacle. The pace of the choreography was dazzling and the aggressive stance of the routine was such that at the very first rehearsal, the troupe broke the video screen that served as the stage floor. Their enthusiasm was relentless and won over every delegation at the rehearsals and ultimately the tele-voters on the night. Singing in a mix of English and Ukrainian, Ruslana also proved that viewers were not only attracted by songs in English. She also cemented the concept that to win, the stage show has to be overwhelming, which it certainly was!

Greece came to the contest a hot favourite, helped in part by the confidence of the performer, the Greek superstar **Sakis Rouvas**. Known as much as a product spokesman and model as a singer, Rouvas created a stage show that featured disrobing dancers and a stage frenzy that left the audience excited. It was a stark contrast to all the male balladeers in the contest, particularly overshadowing the Icelandic and Irish entries that followed.

The biggest reception of the night was reserved for Turkish ska band **Athena** who sang 'For Real' immediately after the highly popular Cypriot song. The multi-tattooed duo were unlike any of the other competitors and indeed unlike anything ever contributed to the contest before, least of all from Turkey. Very similar to the sort of hits created by the Specials and Madness in the early 1980s, the song was such a strong contrast to all the other entries that the viewers lapped it up in droves, but it was not quite enough to secure a second Turkish win.

Sanda Ladosi was another barely clothed lady with sensual choreography singing 'I Admit' for Romania, but her performance was almost tame in comparison to **Lena Philipsson** who closed the competition for Sweden. A veteran of the Swedish heats and a huge star at home, Lena turned in a smoulderingly sexual interpretation of 'It Hurts', using her microphone stand as an integral part of her act.

With 36 nations voting, there were distinct fears that the process would simply become too long, but this was resolved by allowing each country a strict time limit of 90 seconds to announce their scores.

Six countries were consistently among the top choices of all nations from the outset, with the lead switching between Ukraine, Turkey, Greece, Serbia and Montenegro continuously and Cyprus and Sweden always just behind. Both the UK and Ireland seemed to be heading for 'nul points' each, but thankfully came to each other's rescue, the British votes being the only marks anyone gave to the

The Macedonians opted for an elaborately staged number, but the antics of the performers, using chairs as their main prop, distracted completely from 'Life', sung by Tose Proeski.

An ecstatic winner, after another highly impassioned performance of 'Wild Dances', Ruslana and her dancers gave a hero's press conference and were fêted by the entire Eurovision community at the post-contest ball.

Irish, and Norway were only saved from a fifth 'nul points' by Sweden. It was the tenth time the Norwegians had placed last and a record eighth time that the third performed song trailed in behind the rest of the field.

Ukraine had won with only their second entry, equalling the achievements of the Dutch and gaining the best-ever result for a new nation other than the original seven competitors. Backstage, Ruslana and her team could not have been more delighted and such was the emotion and celebration from the winners that their arrival back in the auditorium for the reprise was delayed considerably, creating problems for presenters **Meltem Cumbul** and **Korhan Abay**. Ruslana fell to her knees and thanked the audience, her emotion evident to all. As Sertab Erener made her way towards her to present the Grand Prix, she trapped her shoe in a speaker grille and had to be freed by stagehands.

Ruslana returned home to Kiev a national heroine and she was honoured by the President and Prime Minister. Such was Ukraine's pride at winning the contest and taking its place on the international stage that some of the nations who have been competing in Eurovision for longer could do well to examine their approach to the contest if they wish to be successful in the future.

The fiftieth contest was heading to a nation that had not even existed when the competition was created back in 1956. In the months that followed Ruslana's victory, the Ukraine grabbed even bigger headlines around the globe as the people took to the streets in protest to finally break free from Russian ties and, through the Orange Revolution, they forced the government from power, overturning corrupt election results.

Against this background, the state TV station, NTU, left in partial limbo amidst the political turmoil, struggled to organise the contest amidst all the changes taking place, but nonetheless, they succeeded in welcoming the world to the fiftieth contest in style and produced a show certainly worthy of the golden anniversary celebration.

country	song	performer	place	score	draw
Ukraine	Wild Dances	Ruslana	1	280	10
Serbia & Montenegro	Lane Moje	Željko Joksimović	2	263	5
Greece	Shake It	Sakis Rouvas	3	252	16
Turkey	For Real	Athena	4	195	22
Cyprus	Stronger Every Minute	Lisa Andreas	5	170	21
Sweden	It Hurts	Lena Philipsson	6	170	24
Albania	The Image Of You	Anjeza Shahini	7	106	9
Germany	Can't Wait Until Tonight	Max	8	93	8
Bosnia-Herzegovina	In The Disco	Deen	9	91	12
Spain	Para Llenarme De Ti	Ramon	10	87	1
Russia	Believe Me	Julia Savicheva	11	67	14
Malta	On Again... Off Again	Julie & Ludwig	12	50	6
Croatia	You Are The Only One	Ivan Mikulic	13	50	11
F.Y.R. Macedonia	Life	Tose Proeski	14	47	15
France	A Chaque Pas	Jonatan Cerrada	15	40	4
United Kingdom	Hold On To Our Love	James Fox	16	29	20
Poland	Love Song	Blue Café	17	27	19
Romania	I Admit	Sanda	18	18	23
Iceland	Heaven	Jonsi	19	16	17
Netherlands	Without You	Re-Union	20	11	7
Austria	Du Bist	Tie-Break	21	9	2
Belgium	1 Life	Xandee	22	7	13
Ireland	If My World Stopped Turning	Chris Doran	23	7	18
Norway	High	Knut Anders Sorum	24	3	3

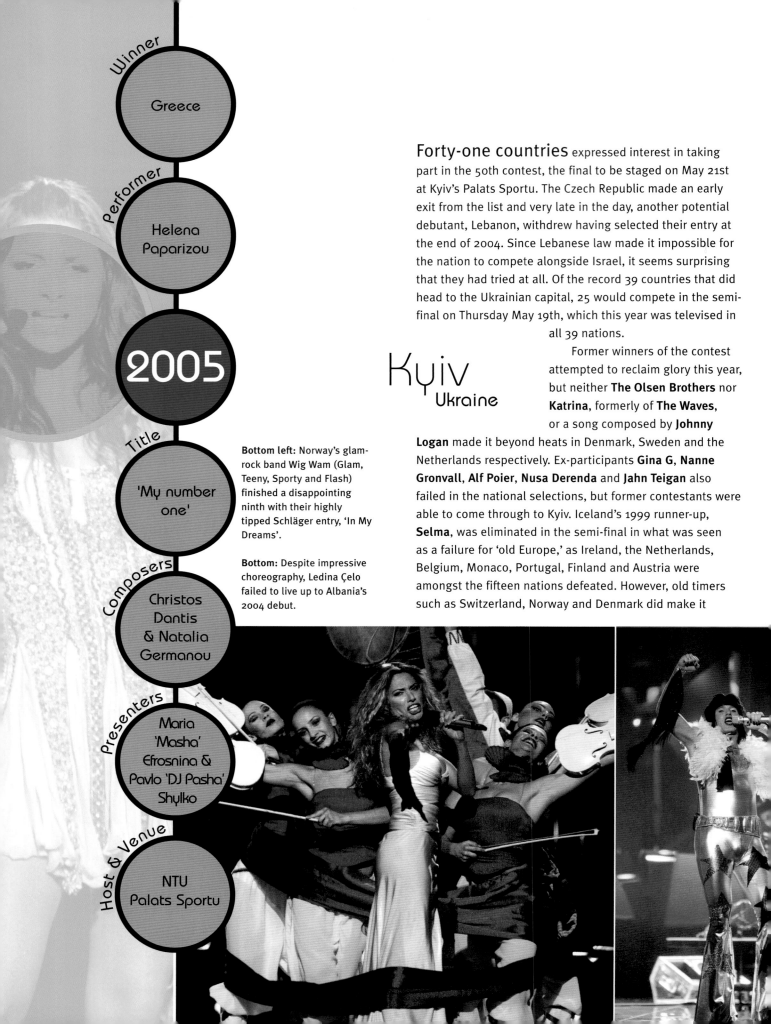

Winner

Greece

Performer

Helena
Paparizou

2005

Title

'My number
one'

Composers

Christos
Dantis
& Natalia
Germanou

Presenters

Maria
'Masha'
Efrosnina &
Pavlo 'DJ Pasha'
Shylko

Host & Venue

NTU
Palats Sportu

Bottom left: Norway's glam-rock band Wig Wam (Glam, Teeny, Sporty and Flash) finished a disappointing ninth with their highly tipped Schläger entry, 'In My Dreams'.

Bottom: Despite impressive choreography, Ledina Çelo failed to live up to Albania's 2004 debut.

Forty-one countries expressed interest in taking part in the 50th contest, the final to be staged on May 21st at Kyiv's Palats Sportu. The Czech Republic made an early exit from the list and very late in the day, another potential debutant, Lebanon, withdrew having selected their entry at the end of 2004. Since Lebanese law made it impossible for the nation to compete alongside Israel, it seems surprising that they had tried at all. Of the record 39 countries that did head to the Ukrainian capital, 25 would compete in the semi-final on Thursday May 19th, which this year was televised in all 39 nations.

Kyiv
Ukraine

Former winners of the contest attempted to reclaim glory this year, but neither **The Olsen Brothers** nor **Katrina**, formerly of **The Waves**, or a song composed by **Johnny Logan** made it beyond heats in Denmark, Sweden and the Netherlands respectively. Ex-participants **Gina G**, **Nanne Gronvall**, **Alf Poier**, **Nusa Derenda** and **Jahn Teigan** also failed in the national selections, but former contestants were able to come through to Kyiv. Iceland's 1999 runner-up, **Selma**, was eliminated in the semi-final in what was seen as a failure for 'old Europe,' as Ireland, the Netherlands, Belgium, Monaco, Portugal, Finland and Austria were amongst the fifteen nations defeated. However, old timers such as Switzerland, Norway and Denmark did make it through, as did the non-European, neighbourless nation of Israel, rather spoiling the accusations that the contest had become a 'vote-for-your-neighbour' contest. Indeed, whereas FYR Macedonia and Croatia came through the semi, Slovenia did not. Hungary, Romania and debutant Moldova made the cut, but Bulgaria and Belarus went home early. Latvia qualified, but Lithuania, Estonia and Poland didn't make it. Despite all complaints to the contrary, it seems that geographic allegiances will never totally outweigh the popularity of the song.

There was very little celebration of the contest's anniversary in Kyiv, as the EBU had commissioned DR to produce a lavish gala to mark the occasion on October 22nd at The Forum, Copenhagen. But some countries did choose to mark the anniversary, notably with three former winners, **Marie N**, **Cheryl Baker** and **Dana** invited to announce the scores from their respective nations.

In the run-up to the contest there had been serious concerns over the organisation of the event, particularly when it was revealed that much-needed renovations to the venue were so far behind that contracts remained unsigned right through to the spring. In the end, the **Klytschko Brothers**, world boxing champions and co-owners of the hall, had to be given parts in the proceedings to gain their cooperation. Ticket sales were a disaster when they finally became available and a very last-minute switch in presenters, when **Ruslana** was dropped in favour of **Masha Efrosnina** to join **DJ Pasha** for the night, did little to inspire confidence that the show would come together. Huge controversy over the selection of the Ukrainian entry was also clouding the run-up to the final. The rock band **Greenjolly** had won the Ukrainian heat with the song that had been the theme of the Orange Revolution, 'Razom Nas Bahato, Nas Nye Podolaty' ('Together We Are Many'), even though it had not been entered in any of the televised qualifying contests that had taken place over several months, but submitted as a last-minute 'wild card,' reportedly to please the incoming government. The favourite for the home nomination, **Ani Lorak**, a vocal supporter of the discredited president, was particularly upset about the organisation of the domestic contest and accusations flew. In the end, the home team fared badly, despite enormous support from the massive partisan audience, and the hosts finished fifth from the bottom. Indeed, it was the bottom-placed nations that attracted the most comment

Helena topped both the Greek and Swedish charts with 'My Number One' and enjoyed top 40 successes in Belgium, Switzerland, Germany and Austria. She toured the US and Australia later in 2005 and continues to be one of Greece's top female artists.

this year as the only nations ranked below the hosts were the other automatic qualifiers, the 'Big Four'. Never before had Germany, France, the UK and Spain found themselves shoulder-to-shoulder at the bottom of the scoreboard, and it once again raised questions about their commitment to the contest and their automatic right of participation, particularly as Belarus, unqualified for the second year running, had spent 5 million Euros on an effort to send their biggest star, **Angelica Agurbash**, to the final. The German entry, which placed last, was in fact marred with problems when it was revealed that its composer, **David Brandes** (who in tandem with contest veteran **Bernd Meinunger**, aka **John O'Flynn**, had written both the German and Swiss songs), had manipulated its chart position in order to make the German final. The track was banned from the German charts and Brandes from attending the contest as a result.

For the returning artists who did make it to Kyiv, it was a particularly successful night. Both **Chiara** and **Helena Paparizou** had placed third on their previous Euro-outings and both singers would improve on those performances this year. Chiara, wearing a sparkling red gown, was the only performer in the final who took to the stage entirely alone to belt out her own composition, 'Angel'. Singing in the third slot, Chiara bucked the trend of this recently fruitless draw to secure Malta's second second place. Romania, who had won the semi-final with 'Let Me Try', performed by **Luminita Anghel and Sistem**, beat all the other semi-finalists again to place third with a rock-inspired anthem that included pyrotechnics on stage that had originally been banned by the producers. Israel and Latvia did much better this year and impressed with traditional Euro-ballads to round out the top five. Moldova, the only debutants in the final, also did well, placing sixth with a highly original rock number aided by the gold toothed 'Grandmamma' on the drum.

The biggest single improvement from the previous year came from the Swiss. Having failed to score a single point in the 2004 semi-final, SF-DRS chose Estonian girl group **Vanilla Ninja** to represent the Swiss, who internally selected the Brandes/Meinunger effort 'Cool Vibes' to be their song. Switzerland was rewarded for their increased effort with eighth place in both contests. **Constantinos**, making his third contest appearance for Cyprus, backed by former Greek contestant **Elena Konstantopolou**, was disappointed with eighteenth place, despite top marks from both Malta and Greece. Sweden's **Martin Stenmarck** had something of a nightmare result, finishing nineteenth, sending the Swedes down into relegation for the first time. There they would be joined by Russia and Turkey whose recent successful runs both ended.

Bosnia-Herzegovina's birthday tribute to Eurovision, 'Call Me' had been much fancied to do better than their eventual fourteenth place, as was the UK's **Javine** who slumped to 22nd after drawing the 'curse of number two', but the clear favourite for the contest from the outset let nobody down. Having split from **Antique**, with whom she had secured third place in 2001, Swedish-born Helena had been invited to represent Greece by ERT and the public had selected 'My Number One', by **Christos Dantis** and **Natalia Germanou** to be her Eurovision entry. Helena admitted it was a gamble to present a song with this title, particularly if she did not indeed achieve number one in the competition. To ensure success, Helena embarked on a European tour, presenting her hugely expensive promo video to audiences across the continent before the big night and developed a dazzling stage show for the live presentation. Backed by former Cypriot contestant **Alex Panayi**, Helena and her four dancers presented a highly polished routine that captured the

country	song	performer	place	score	draw
Greece	My Number One	Helena Paparizou	1	230	19
Malta	Angel	Chiara	2	192	3
Romania	Let Me Try	Luminita Anghel & Sincron	3	158	4
Israel	Hasheket Shenishar (The Silence That Remains)	Shiri Maimon	4	154	11
Latvia	The War Is Not Over	Walters & Kazha	5	153	23
Moldova	Boonika Bate Doba	Zdob Shi Zdub	6	148	7
Serbia & Montenegro	Zauvijek Moja	No Name	7	137	12
Switzerland	Cool Vibes	Vanilla Ninja	8	128	22
Norway	In My Dreams	Wig Wam	9	125	5
Denmark	Talking To You	Jakob Sveistrup	10	125	13
Croatia	Vukovi Umiru Sami	Boris Novković feat. Lado Members	11	115	18
Hungary	Forogj Világ	Nox	12	97	1
Turkey	Rimi Rimi Ley	Gülseren	13	92	6
Bosnia-Herzegovina	Call Me	Feminnem	14	79	21
Russia	Nobody Hurt No One	Natalia Podolskaya	15	57	20
Albania	Tomorrow I go	Ledina Çelo	16	53	8
F.Y.R. Macedonia	Make My Day	Martin Vucic	17	52	15
Cyprus	Ela Ela (Come Baby)	Constantinos feat. Elina Konstantopoulou	18	46	9
Sweden	Las Vegas	Martin Stenmarck	19	30	14
Ukraine	Razom Nas Bahato, Nas Nye Podolaty	Greenjolly	20	30	16
Spain	Brujería	Son de Sol	21	28	10
United Kingdom	Touch My Fire	Javine	22	18	2
France	Chacun Pense à Soi	Ortal	23	11	24
Germany	Run & Hide	Gracia	24	4	17

imaginations of the viewers and vaulted the Greeks to their first ever win in the contest, albeit with a comparatively low percentage of the scores.

The lengthy voting process highlighted the usual regional allegiances, but another anomaly was in evidence. There was a distinction between the songs preferred by the 24 finalists in comparison to those rated by the 15 relegated nations, who announced their scores first. Indeed, the Greeks languished in ninth place after the losing semi-finalists had voted, a long way behind Latvia and Switzerland who led at that stage. But with 12 points from 8 of the 23 other finalists, making 10 in total, Greece pulled ahead of the pack to lead for the final 17 rounds of votes. Helena accepted her award from Ruslana and new **President Viktor Yuschenko**, before reprising her winning song, as 94 per cent of Greeks tuned in to celebrate their first victory, 31 years after making their contest debut, the longest wait for a first win yet.

To celebrate the golden anniversary of the contest, Helena joined many winners and former contestants with hosts **Renars Kaupers** and **Katrina Leskanich** in Copenhagen for a special celebration of the contest's first half century on October 22nd. 14 songs, 10 selected by a vote on the internet, competed for the title of best ever Eurovision song, with 'Waterloo' by Abba emerging as the winner.

As the 51st contest headed to Athens, Marcel Besançon could never have imagined that his creation would not only still be going strong over fifty years after its inauguration, but growing each year and attracting new countries and audiences. To the puzzlement of all those who decry the banality of the songs and the quality of the performers, the Eurovision Song Contest remains the most watched and most popular music event in the world. It began in a tiny theatre in 1956 and grew into a multi-day event featuring upwards of 40 nations, billions of viewers, thousands of dedicated fans and in 2003 spawned a junior event for children aged 8–15. Monsieur Besançon would be very proud indeed.

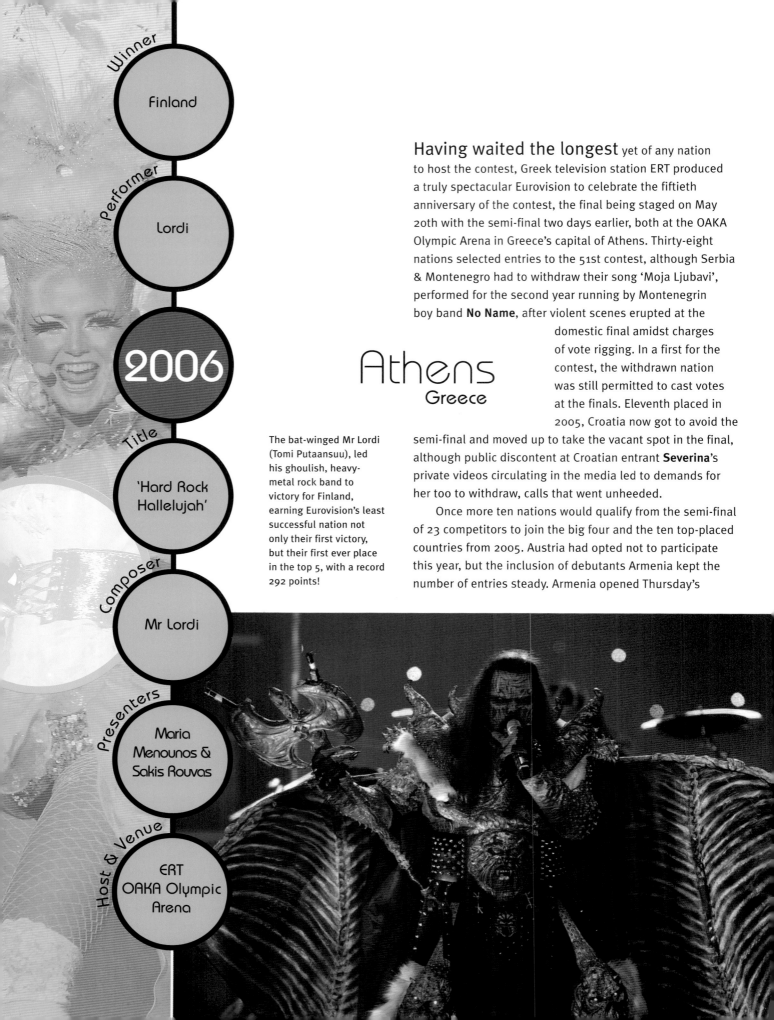

Winner

Finland

Performer

Lordi

2006

Title

'Hard Rock Hallelujah'

Composer

Mr Lordi

Presenters

Maria Menounos & Sakis Rouvas

Host & Venue

ERT OAKA Olympic Arena

Having waited the longest yet of any nation to host the contest, Greek television station ERT produced a truly spectacular Eurovision to celebrate the fiftieth anniversary of the contest, the final being staged on May 20th with the semi-final two days earlier, both at the OAKA Olympic Arena in Greece's capital of Athens. Thirty-eight nations selected entries to the 51st contest, although Serbia & Montenegro had to withdraw their song 'Moja Ljubavi', performed for the second year running by Montenegrin boy band **No Name**, after violent scenes erupted at the domestic final amidst charges of vote rigging. In a first for the contest, the withdrawn nation was still permitted to cast votes at the finals. Eleventh placed in 2005, Croatia now got to avoid the semi-final and moved up to take the vacant spot in the final, although public discontent at Croatian entrant **Severina**'s private videos circulating in the media led to demands for her too to withdraw, calls that went unheeded.

Once more ten nations would qualify from the semi-final of 23 competitors to join the big four and the ten top-placed countries from 2005. Austria had opted not to participate this year, but the inclusion of debutants Armenia kept the number of entries steady. Armenia opened Thursday's

Athens
Greece

The bat-winged Mr Lordi (Tomi Putaansuu), led his ghoulish, heavy-metal rock band to victory for Finland, earning Eurovision's least successful nation not only their first victory, but their first ever place in the top 5, with a record 292 points!

semi-final and having qualified, in a unique twist, closed Saturday's final. The final itself was opened for the very first time by Switzerland, with a six-piece vocal group drawn from Malta, Sweden, Bosnia-Herzegovina, Israel, Portugal and Switzerland – written by the perennial German team of **Bernd Meinunger** and **Ralph Siegel**, and sung in English. Despite the very obvious attempt to curry cross-border favour (the preview video being filmed in Greece itself) the song, 'If We All Give A Little' sunk to 17th place.

Former Greek Eurovision stars were much in evidence during the broadcast, with **Sakis Rouvas** acting as compére for the event alongside Greek-born American **Maria Menounos**, who was brought in from NBC in the USA to co-present the show. Maria's unfamiliarity with Eurovision and her use of the word 'amazing', seemingly in every sentence, plus some technical challenges on the night, did not go unnoticed in the worldwide media. But the two presenters' task was eased somewhat during the voting, when the international spokespersons were only permitted to announce their top three scores of 8, 10 and 12 points, the points from 1 to 7 being added to the scoreboard automatically – a move that shaved almost thirty minutes off the show's running time.

Nana Mouskouri and **Helena Paparizou** also appeared in the final, with the reigning Queen of Eurovision performing both her winning song and her latest single during the show. **Vicky Leandros**, Greece's first Eurovision winner, albeit for Luxembourg, had hoped to be singing the German entry. Alas, she was defeated by an Australian-led country and western band in the German heat. The German song from **Texas Lightning**, 'No, No Never', was by far the most commercially successful entry from this year's contest and it was the pre-contest favourite, but as it turned out the tele-voters were not in sync with the music-buying public or bookies' predictions. Country and western was a highly unusual musical style for Eurovision, and indeed this year's event reflected a far greater musical diversity than usually heard. Denmark entered a twist; the UK had another go at rap; Turkey had their typical Eastern rhythms and Albania sent a haunting ethnic piece, their first entry in their native tongue. High-energy Europop was strongly represented, with Slovenia, Belarus and Malta all attempting the format, albeit with little success. Belgium, Sweden and Estonia went for the more traditional schläger style of pop, whereas Greece, Cyprus and France all tried

Lordi attained solid sales around the continent, most spectacularly at home, where the single was sold out upon their victory. Other major chart success came in Germany, where they reached the top five yet failed to displace the German entry from Texas Lightning off the top of the charts.

emotive ballads by female soloists. There was gospel from Israel, Tahitian rhythms from Monaco, a'capella from Latvia, jungle drums and imaginary lyrics from the Dutch, camp comedy from Iceland and a shouted rant from Lithuania. Ukraine's entry was a combination of folk and high energy, with double-Dutch skipping thrown in. Performed by **Tina Karol**, the lyrics of 'Show Me Your Love' were penned by last year's contest host, **DJ Pasha**. But the real surprise would be a style even more unfamiliar to the Eurovision audience – heavy-metal Goth rock!

The star quotient was also higher than many recent contests. International stars, including Belgium's **Kate Ryan** (who failed to qualify) and Sweden's former contest-winner **Carola** were both highly tipped, as were Ireland's **Brian Kennedy**, Moldova's **Arsenium** and Spain's **Las Ketchup**, all of whom had enjoyed major international successes. The diva of the night was undoubtedly the host nation's own biggest superstar, **Anna Vissi**, making her third contest appearance presenting 'Everything', a dramatic ballad she had co-written. Bringing deafening support from the predominately Greek audience of 18,000 in the hall, Ms Vissi was later castigated by the local media when she slumped to ninth place, only just avoiding relegation for the hosts, yet still one of only two of the pre-qualified nations to place in the top 10.

Russia's top teen heart-throb **Dima Bilan** was also strongly tipped, as was the very ethnic, haunting ballad from **Hari Mata Hari** representing Bosnia-Herzegovina. Hari finally made it to the contest having been disqualified in 1999 and came through the qualifier easily, securing third place in the final with 'Lejla', sung entirely in Serbo-Croat. Although English dominated the line-up, other languages were on show this year, including Norwegian and Turkish, with Romania's **Mihai Trăistariu** even singing a burst of Italian in his popular offering, 'Tornerò', which finished

Far Left: Iceland's Silvía Night caused controversy throughout. She reluctantly omitted the swearing from her song's lyric during the live performance, but her antics failed to qualify her for the final, leading to a foul-mouthed tantrum staged for the world's press.

Left: Greek-born American Maria Menounos and former contestant Sakis Rouvas, made a spectacular, flying entrance to host the 51st contest.

fourth, just ahead of former winner **Carola**'s 'Invincible' for Sweden. Sweden had come through qualifying for the first time and, indeed, many nations not normally associated with the qualifying ranks had to reach the final the same way. Ireland, Russia and Turkey also made it through, together with F.Y.R. Macedonia, Ukraine and Armenia. Two nations who had almost equally woeful Eurovision records qualified for the first time. The all-male sextet **LT United** from Lithuania qualified to the apparent disgust of the audience with their chant 'We Are The Winners' – three minutes of aggressive shouting, demanding votes from the viewers! It clearly worked and the Lithuanians went on to finish sixth in the final, their best showing yet. Iceland's **Silvía Night** tried a similar concept, with her outrageous performance and highly suggestive lyrics to 'Congratulations', yet failed to qualify, despite many attention-seeking tantrums during rehearsals.

For some nations, things remained the same. Portugal, Estonia, Andorra, Bulgaria, Belarus and Slovenia all failed to progress, as was becoming the norm, and unlucky Poland placed 11th, just missing out on the final for the second year running. The ten nations that did make it

through to the final almost repeated their success on the big night, occupying ten of the twelve top places. The top qualifier was the country with the least success of any nation in the history of the competition to date, the always luckless Finns. But this year, Finland was to prove the surprise package of the show.

Having failed continually since 1961 to even gain a place in the first five and with almost permanent residence in the relegation and semi-final zones since their introduction, Finnish TV station YLE approached top death-metal band **Lordi**, the mask-wearing monsters of Finnish rock, to take up the baton in 2006 and finally reverse their fortunes. Easily coming through the Finnish heats with their self-composed 'Hard Rock Hallelujah', the five-piece band caused a storm of controversy in their homeland, with many branding them as 'satanists' and thus inappropriate for the Eurovision audience. Never seen publicly without their grotesque rubber masks and ghoulish costumes, the clamour surrounding the four-male and one-female band was soon being reported across the continent, affording huge amounts of publicity in all the participating countries. Using flaming pyrotechnics to enhance their act, their stunning stage display and the rough, heavy-metal sounds entranced the voters and not only did they secure Finland's first ever win, they did so with the highest score yet recorded in the contest, a total they matched in both the semi-final and final.

Russia's **Dima Bilan**, whose pop ballad 'Never Let You Go' was equally memorably performed, with a ghostly ballerina emerging from a bed of rose petals inside a grand piano, had to settle for second place, much to the Russian superstar's annoyance.

The Finnish rockers were universally lauded after their staggering win, which had achieved vastly increased ratings across the continent on the previous year. Although many continued to question their possible satanic connections and their bizarre appearance, the group was much in demand

around Europe and they hit the charts in many countries. Upon their return to Helsinki, they were fêted as national heroes, having finally broken through the disastrous run for previous Finnish entrants. A crowd of 100,000 fans greeted their first public appearance with the Mayor of Helsinki, where a world record was set for a live karaoke performance of the winning song. A square in their home town of Rovaniemi was renamed in honour of the band. **Lordi** appeared all around the world, conducting friendly and humorous interviews which belied their terrifying appearance, although always maintaining their incognito image.

After shattering Greece's record 32-year wait to win and then stage the Eurovision Song Contest, Finland would now play host for the first time, winning 45 years after their debut and inviting the world to Helsinki for 2007.

country	song	performer	place	score	draw
Finland	Hard Rock Hallelujah	**Lordi**	1	292	17
Russia	Never Let You Go	**Dima Bilan**	2	248	10
Bosnia-Herzegovina	Lejla	**Hari Mata Hari**	3	229	13
Romania	Tornerò	**Mihai Trăistariu**	4	172	12
Sweden	Invincible	**Carola**	5	170	22
Lithuania	We Are The Winners	**LT United**	6	162	14
Ukraine	Show Me Your Love	**Tina Karol**	7	145	18
Armenia	Without Your Love	**André**	8	129	24
Greece	Everything	**Anna Vissi**	9	128	16
Ireland	Every Song Is A Cry For Love	**Brian Kennedy**	10	93	21
Turkey	Süper Star	**Sibel Tüzün**	11	91	23
F.Y.R. Macedonia	Ninanajna	**Elena Risteska**	12	56	11
Croatia	Moja Štickla	**Severina**	13	56	20
Norway	Alvedansen	**Christine Guldbrandsen**	14	36	5
Germany	No No Never	**Texas Lightning**	15	36	8
Latvia	I Hear Your Heart	**Vocal Group Cosmos**	16	30	4
Switzerland	If We All Give A Little	**Six4one**	17	30	1
Denmark	Twist Of Love	**Sidsel Ben Semmane**	18	26	9
United Kingdom	Teenage Life	**Daz Sampson**	19	25	15
Moldova	Loca	**Arsenium ft. Natalia Gordienko & Connect-R**	20	22	2
Spain	Bloody Mary	**Las Ketchup**	21	18	6
France	Il Était Temps	**Virginie Pouchain**	22	5	19
Israel	Together We Are One	**Eddie Butler**	23	4	3
Malta	I Do	**Fabrizio Faniello**	24	1	7
Serbia & Montenegro	*Moja Ljubavi*	*No Name*	*WD*	*WD*	*WD*

WD = Withdrawn

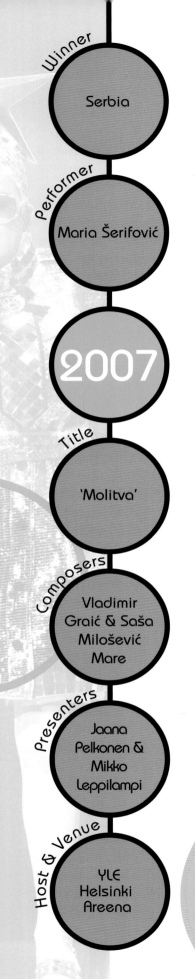

Winner

Serbia

Performer

Maria Šerifović

2007

Title

'Molitva'

Composers

Vladimir Graić & Saša Milošević Mare

Presenters

Jaana Pelkonen & Mikko Leppilampi

Host & Venue

YLE Helsinki Areena

Available prior to the contest in its original, English and remixed versions as a free download, the single of **'Molitva'** was later given a very limited release; largely limited to promotional copies only. In Serbia itself, it failed to register in the official charts, but it did reach the Swedish top 10 and Swiss top 20. The Ukrainian runner up was far more successful, reaching the top 30 in the pan-European chart.

Helsinki
Finland

Having waited even longer than the Greeks to host their first Eurovision, Finnish broadcaster YLE brought the show to their capital Helsinki in 2007, after considering bids from Espoo, Tampere and Turku; coping with the biggest yet field of 42 competing nations and the largest yet semi-final, staged two days ahead of the grand final on May 12th. Twenty-eight countries submitted songs for the semi-final, hoping to be one of the ten that would make it to the Saturday show. Once again, there was controversy and consternation across the Western European media, when the Eastern nations dominated the qualification places. Even before the contest season had officially begun, Monaco had opted not to make another attempt to return to the contest final, announcing their withdrawal, partially it seemed as they doubted their chances of ever qualifying. Other, older Eurovision countries The Netherlands, Denmark, Switzerland, Portugal, Malta, Belgium, Israel, Norway, Cyprus, Iceland and a returning Austria all took part, but were all eliminated, whereas the ten qualifiers were solely representative of nations East of the Danube. Bulgaria, Belarus and debutants Georgia and Serbia all reached the final for the first time ever and Slovenia made it there for the first time since the semi-final process had been inaugurated. Neither of the other contest debutants, Montenegro and the Czech Republic, were able to qualify. The controversy surrounding the apparent advantage the Eastern Diaspora was giving to their home and neighbour entries raged for many days after the contest. Maltese head of delegation **Robert Abela** even indicated that Malta's 12 points for the UK given in the final were more of a protest against their own failure to qualify than the Maltese viewer's true preference. Former German winner **Nicole** went further, telling *Bild* magazine that "It is obvious that Eastern European countries engage in dirty trade with points every year. Germany should withdraw from the competition". In the UK, the scoring was discussed in the British Parliament, with one MP claiming that the voting system was "harmful to the relationship between the peoples of Europe". Indeed, once again it was not a good night for the 'Big Four' countries, with Germany ranking the highest in 19th place. It was also a very bad night for Eurovision's most successful nation, when Ireland finished in last place for the very first time with a folk song performed by the band **Dervish**. Had their one supporter, Albania, not used a jury instead of tele-voting, the Irish may well have ended the night without any points at all. The controversy continued when a similar voting pattern emerged in the final as it had in the semi. The top 17 places all went to nations from the East, with Turkey's fourth and Greece's eighth place being the only top ten achievements for countries established in the contest prior to 1993. Not all the Western media was negative, with the Swedish paper *Expressen* describing a sense of "shame" over the reactions in many Western European nations, going on to say that the Eurovision Song Contest had never been better. Describing the winning entry as a "worthy, historic winner", the paper went on to call the proposals for a separate, Eastern contest "incredibly pathetic". Not withstanding, taking the controversy on board, the EBU began looking at ways to assuage the critics in future contests.

The theme of the contest was "True Fantasy", and it was broadcast in high definition for the first time. The fantasy of the postcards and the kaleidoscope imagery of the graphics continued into the stage design, which was based on the Kantele, a Finnish musical instrument. Presenters **Jaana Pelkonen** & **Mikko Leppilampi** were aided backstage by **Krisse Salminen**, who was given the job of hosting the green room and external show areas during the broadcast, as it was her 'fantasy' to host Eurovision. **Lordi** opened the show with a partially live, partially pre-filmed, explosive rendition of "Hard Rock Hallelujah" bringing fire and excitement

to the stage. The interval act was equally dramatic, with **Apocalyptica** providing dazzling acrobatics during the tallying of the scores. The postcards introducing each song had been filmed in various locations, telling the stories of everyday Finnish life. Finland's own Eurovision fantasy continued to a certain degree, when for the second year running, they were the best placed of all the Nordic countries. Iceland, Norway and Denmark had all fallen at the semi-final stage and Sweden were placed one place lower than the hosts at 18th. Latvia's 16th place was the best result of any of the far Northern nations.

Despite the post-contest complaints, the run-up to the contest was largely dominated by controversies surrounding both the Israeli and Ukrainian entries. Israel's song "Push The Button" by rock group **Teapacks**, seemed to be nuclear themed, however, it wasn't clear if the group weren't in fact making a pointed jibe at American **President George W. Bush**. Eventually, the lyric was approved by the EBU, but the song did not make the final. For the Ukraine, comedic drag act Verka **Serduchka** had caused outrage in his home nation when he won the domestic heat with "Dancing, Lasha Tumbai". His less-than-subtle parody of a nouveau riche Russian housewife did not find favour in many conservative quarters and the Ukrainian culture minister threatened resignation if the song went to Helsinki. Surviving the threat, **Verka** became the most sought-after personality during the contest run-up, arriving in the Finnish capital with his 'mother' in tow and entertaining the media and fans all

Maria Šerifović and the Beauty Queens, dressed in masculine attire, emote the winning song 'Molitva' for Serbia.

week with their antics. Again, the lyric of his song proved controversial when it was pointed out that the gibberish title "Lasha Tumbai" had a similar phonetic sound to "Russia Goodbye", adding to the parody of the entry. As with Israel, the lyric was approved and Verka went on to secure second place in the final, just ahead of the Russian song. Another drag act, Denmark's **DQ** had hoped to be in the final, but was eliminated at the semi-final stages.

Although English was once again the dominant language for the 25 finalists, there was a solid representation of other tongues, with Italian returning to the contest, courtesy of Latvia's operatic opus "Questa Notte" (Tonight). Romania went even further, singing "Liubi, Liubi, I Love You" (Love I Love You) in a mix of Italian, Spanish, English, Romanian, French and Russian. The French opted for a mix of French and English, and Bulgarian was heard in the final for the first time.

To date, Switzerland are the only country to win Eurovision at their first attempt, when by default they won the inaugural contest on home ground in 1956. Since then, both Poland and Serbia & Montenegro had come closest to achieving the same feat, finishing second at their contest debuts. Although Serbia was officially a debutant in 2007, the Serbs had of course been competing under the Yugoslav flag at various times from 1961 until 1992 and had provided the debut entry for Serbia & Montenegro in 2004. For 2007, a newly independent Serbia sent their first entry to the contest (as did their former partner Montenegro) and carried away the title at the Hartwall Areena. In doing so, Serbia's **Maria Šerifović** became the 33rd female soloist to land the Eurovision title; and the first winner since 1998 to perform a winning song with no English lyrics.

Maria Šerifović had come to national prominence in Serbia only a few years earlier, winning the award for best vocal performance at the Serbian Radio

Belarusian Koldun's mother, founder of Princess Diana's fan-club, dreamt of a daughter who would look like Diana. She was thrilled with her son's striking resemblance to the Princess.

Festival, after a few years as a popular artist at local Serbian music festivals. Despite having finished 18th in Serbia & Montenegro's Eurovision heat in 2005, Maria returned to triumph with the song "Molitva" (Prayer) and earn the ticket to Helsinki, where she was immediately installed as one of the pre-contest favourites.

On stage, Maria was joined by an all female vocal troupe of five singers, known later as the **Beauty Queens**, all dressed in masculine black suits, as was Maria herself. The press and fans were quick to point out that there seemed to be Sapphic overtones to the stage performance, but these were dismissed at the press conferences held during the rehearsals. Regardless, the conservative media remained resolute in their perception of the song's presentation, although **Maria Šerifović** didn't seem to allow the controversy to detract from her focus. On the night, the powerful ballad was obviously one of the favourites in the arena and with nine top marks of 12 points and a total of 268 points, the third-highest scoring Eurovision song

to date, it was a clear winner, becoming the first ballad to win the contest in the tele-voting era. Maria received her winner's trophy from Santa Claus, who had also been responsible for launching the voting window, continuing the fantasy theme of the contest.

As a result of the song being promoted for download only by Serbian TV, Maria's commercial success with the winning song was very limited. It was Verka Serduchka who enjoyed the widest commercial success across the continent, reaching the top ten in France, Sweden and Finland and the top 30 in Ireland and the UK. Third placed **Serebro**'s "Song #1" for Russia topped the Russian charts, outselling all other singles for the year in their homeland. **Maria Šerifović** remained one of Serbia's most popular artists after the contest, releasing several albums and becoming one of the European Union's 15 'Intercultural Ambassadors' appointed for the 2008 European Year of Intercultural Dialogue.

YLE's 2007 production was lauded as a success, leaving another daunting challenge for their successor.

country	song	performer	place	score	draw
Serbia	Molitva	**Maria Šerifović**	1	268	17
Ukraine	Dancing Lasha Tumbai	**Verka Serduchka**	2	235	18
Russia	Song #1	**Serebro**	3	207	15
Turkey	Shake It Up Shekerim	**Kenan Doğulu**	4	163	22
Bulgaria	Water	**Elitsa Todorova & Stoyan Yankoulov**	5	157	21
Belarus	Work Your Magic	**Koldun**	6	145	3
Greece	Yassou Maria	**Sarbel**	7	139	10
Armenia	Anytime You Need	**Hayko**	8	138	23
Hungary	Unsubstantial Blues	**Magdi Rúzsa**	9	128	8
Moldova	Fight	**Natalia Barbu**	10	109	24
Bosnia-Herzegovina	Rijeka Bez Imena	**Maria Šestić**	11	106	1
Georgia	Visionary Dream	**Sopho**	12	97	11
Romania	Liubi, Liubi, I Love You	**Todomondo**	13	84	20
F.Y.R. Macedonia	Mojot Svet (My World)	**Karolina**	14	73	6
Slovenia	Cvet Z Juga	**Alenka Gotar**	15	66	7
Latvia	Questa Notte	**Bonaparti.lv**	16	54	14
Finland	Leave Me Alone	**Hanna**	17	53	5
Sweden	The Worrying Kind	**The Ark**	18	51	12
Germany	Frauen Regier'n Die Welt	**Roger Cicero**	19	49	16
Spain	I Love You Mi Vida	**D'Nash**	20	43	2
Lithuania	Love Or Leave	**The 4Fun**	21	28	9
France	L'Amour À La Française	**Les Fatals Picards**	22	19	13
United Kingdom	Flying The Flag (For You)	**Scooch**	23	19	19
Ireland	They Can't Stop The Spring	**Dervish**	24	5	4

Winner

Russia

Performer

Dima Bilan

2008

Title

'Believe'

Composers

Dima Bilan &
Jim Beanz

Presenters

Jovana
Janković &
Željko
Joksimović

Host & Venue

RTS
Beogradska
Arena

By 2007, four performers had achieved the feat of both winning and finishing second at Eurovision. In 2008, Russian superstar **Dima Bilan** was to become the fifth and the first male to achieve the distinction. Yugoslavia had hosted Eurovision in Zagreb, Croatia, in 1990, just two years before the break up of the federation. The former Yugoslav capital Belgrade was now playing host in 2008 for the first independent member of the former federation to stage the competition, although sadly, the run up to the contest final on 24th May was certainly not smooth. Violence erupted in

Belgrade
Serbia

the city in the early spring, with many deaths reported amongst foreign nationals living in the Serb capital after Kosovo's unilateral declaration of independence. Speculation that the show would have to be moved to another nation eventually came to nothing, with the EBU confirming the Serbian hosts just weeks before the transmission. Heightened security measures went some way to reassuring the delegations of their safety. The contest itself was transforming again this year, with two semi-finals taking place on 20th and 22nd May. All countries but the host and the 'Big Four' nations would have to compete for the 20 places – ten from each semi – available in the final, regardless of their placing in the prior year. In an attempt to dispel the controversies created the previous year, the EBU also introduced a system of allocating neighbours and nations that had traditionally supported each other in the voting into separate draws for the semi-final places. In addition, the backup juries that cast votes in case of a breakdown in the tele-voting system would nominate one of the qualifiers in each semi-final, if their top rated song had not qualified through tele-voting alone. In practice, this had no impact on the first semi-final, but in the second, it allowed twelfth-ranked Sweden to reach the final with former winner **Charlotte Nilsson Perrelli**'s 'Hero', letting the 1999 victor avoid the ignominy of being the only prior winner of the contest to lose in the semi-final. Another previous winner, **Dana International**, had composed the Israeli entry, which eased through qualifying in the first semi-final in fifth place. Other nations who had struggled in recent years also reached the final, perhaps in part to the new draw allocation procedures.

Dima Bilan topped the Russian airplay charts with '**Believe**' and enjoyed chart success in Latvia, Sweden and Germany amongst other territories. The commercial success was helped in part thanks to a pre-contest tour of Europe, where the song had been heavily promoted prior to the final.

Portugal, Iceland, Denmark, Israel, Norway and Poland all returned to the final this year. Greece and Ukraine emerged the winners of the respective semis, where favourites Russia were placed third in heat one, behind Armenia. The new structure seemed to have some benefits and certainly the West was better represented in the final this year, although the media was still critical of the system. Another innovation this year was a ceremony staged to officially hand over the 'keys' of the Eurovision hosts from Helsinki to Belgrade, which took place in December 2007.

Perhaps equally controversially, but less worrying, for the first time the host chosen to co-present the contest was also one of the contenders! **Željko Joksimović** had

Like Sandie Shaw 41 years earlier, Dima Bilan went barefoot for his winning Eurovision performance, baring his chest for the viewers too.

represented Serbia & Montenegro in 2004, finishing in second place with his own composition. He then penned the song that represented Bosnia-Herzegovina in 2006. His return this year as the composer of the Serbian entry 'Oro' (Dance), performed by **Jelena Tomašević with Bora Dugic**, placed him in the unique and potentially awkward position of being the only presenter ever to have had an entry in the contest he was hosting. Thankfully, as **Maria Šerifović** had been invited to present the winner's trophies, he would not have faced the tricky task of presenting himself with the award should he win. In the end, Serbia's entry placed sixth, thus avoiding any difficult questions. His partner for the presentation was **Jovana Janković** and they were joined by various celebrity guests, including local basketball hero **Vlade Divac**, tennis superstars **Novak Djokovic** and **Ana Ivanović** and the winner of the very first Eurovision **Lys Assia**, who launched the semi-final voting.

As Belgrade stands on the confluence of the Danube and Sava rivers, the imagery was translated into the theme of this year's contest, "A Confluence of Sound", bringing together the symbolically blue and red rivers to form a treble clef. To underline the theme, the first semi-final was created around a city theme. The contest opened with a panorama of the city of Belgrade forming in the stage's background with two waves sliding down the stage to meet in the centre – at the confluence. The second semi-final was based around a water theme, which was created on stage where water imagery appeared to form the main colours of the set. The final was based on the confluence of both elements. The postcards introducing each nation were highly artistic, with local artisans creating images representing the colours and flags of the competing nations, with an on-screen message welcoming the various countries in their native tongue.

The contest itself had grown bigger once more, with a new record of 43 nations competing for the 53rd grand prix. Austria opted out once again, but both Azerbaijan and San Marino were keen to make their debuts, although for the latter it would end in the disappointment of last place in the first semi-final. It was one of two songs in Italian this year, with the Swiss also opting to perform their entry in the Italian tongue, but like San Marino, they did not make the final. Romania's mix of Italian and Romanian did prove a winner, and **Nico & Vlad** made the final where they would open the show. Azerbaijan's **Elnur & Samir** did well to qualify

and secure eighth place in the final with their song 'Day After Day'. Azerbaijan's entry was performed in a highly surreal style, with black devils and white angels cavorting around the stage. The over-the-top presentation of many of the songs this year drew criticism from many quarters, and indeed some of the bizarre efforts seen in Belgrade did seem to warrant the harsh reaction of many watching. Bosnia-Herzegovina's entry 'Pokušaj' (Try), performed by **Laka** was by most reckoning the most surreal. Although the pregnant brides knitting on stage as his singing partner hung washing around the set in the domestic heat were retained, the black chicken was retired. This was even more bizarre than the puppet **Dustin The Turkey**, who had failed in the semi-final for Ireland. Spain's **Rodolfo Chikilicuarte** was another unusual character, but unlike Bosnia who placed 10th, his effort was not so well thought of and placed 16th, still the best showing of any of the 'Big Four' nations. France's **Sébastian Tellier** had originally intended to sing his song 'Divine' entirely in English, but following an outcry in the French Parliament, French lyrics were added to the performance, which again was highly surreal. It was another bad night for the United Kingdom, who were struck down again by the 'curse of number two', placing last of the 25 finalists, much to the disgust of the BBC's **Sir Terry Wogan**, who shortly after resigned from his role as the UK commentator, having covered the contest since 1971.

Russia's **Dima Bilan** had come to Belgrade the red-hot favourite, and was clearly leaving nothing to chance. Prior to his arrival in the Serbian capital, Bilan had embarked on an extensive European tour, particularly focussing on some of the smaller nations in the contest, where the tele-vote was perhaps better influenced by a local TV appearance. In addition to this careful marketing strategy, his performance on the night was truly spectacular. Having co-written the song with American **Jim Beanz**, with production help from **Timbaland**, he also worked hard on the live presentation, enlisting the help of Russian Olympic gold medalist figure skater and three-time world champion **Evgeni Plushenko**, who performed on a small, artificial ice rink on stage. The Hungarian violinist **Edvin Marton** accompanied the track on his Stradivarius, while two female backing singers provided vocal support. It was a very carefully choreographed routine, and was slickly executed, despite abandoning plans during rehearsals for the singer to climb a ladder on stage. Russia's closest competition came from neighbours Ukraine, who's **Ani Lorak** had put together an equally impressive stage show for her entry 'Shady Lady'. Greece's American singer **Kalomira** also dazzled with an elaborate show for "Secret Combination", as did **Sirusho** performing 'Qele, Qele' in English for Armenia. Despite the Armenian entry attracting the highest number of 12 points in the contest, all the competition fell aside as Russia swept to victory, with a crushing 42-point margin between first and second place.

Unfortunately, despite the efforts of the EBU to address some of the perceived challenges in the voting structure

in the semi-finals, the media rounded on the result of the final, demanding changes in future years. Norway had been the only Western country to finish in the top 10, with **Maria Haukass Storeng** earning fifth place; and Russia's victory earned largely with Eastern support angered many in the West. Talk amongst broadcasters who had been relegated in the semi-finals once more (which included Ireland, The Netherlands, Belgium, Switzerland and other older Eurovision competitors) was of reform. The Big Four, all of whom had fared badly once again, would also lead the way behind the scenes in changing the voting structure for 2009. Despite all the disappointment in the Western media, Serbia had still hosted and executed another exciting contest. **Dima Bilan** continued to build on his already considerable fan base and expanded his superstar status further into Eastern Europe.

country	song	performer	place	score	draw
Russia	Believe	**Dima Bilan**	1	272	24
Ukraine	Shady Lady	**Ani Lorak**	2	230	18
Greece	Secret Combination	**Kalomira**	3	218	21
Armenia	Qele, Qele	**Sirusho**	4	199	5
Norway	Hold On, Be Strong	**Maria Haukass Storeng**	5	182	25
Serbia	Oro	**Jelena Tomašević feat. Bora Dugic**	6	160	23
Turkey	Deli	**Mor Ve Ötesi**	7	134	12
Azerbaijan	Day After Day	**Elnur & Samir**	8	132	20
Israel	The Fire In Your Eyes	**Boaz**	9	124	7
Bosnia-Herzegovina	Pokušaj	**Laka**	10	110	6
Georgia	Peace Will Come	**Diana Gurtskaya**	11	83	17
Latvia	Wolves Of The Sea	**Pirates Of The Sea**	12	83	14
Portugal	Senhora Do Mar (Negras Águas)	**Vânia Fernandes**	13	69	13
Iceland	This Is My Life	**Euroband**	14	64	11
Denmark	All Night Long	**Simon Matthew**	15	60	16
Spain	Baila El Chiki Chiki	**Rodolfo Chikilicuarte**	16	55	22
Albania	Zemrën E Lamë Peng	**Olta Boka**	17	55	3
Sweden	Hero	**Charlotte Nilsson Perrelli**	18	47	15
France	Divine	**Sébastian Tellier**	19	47	19
Romania	Pe-o Margine De Lume	**Nico & Vlad**	20	45	1
Croatia	Romanca	**Kraljevi Ulice & 75 Cents**	21	44	9
Finland	Missä Miehet Ratsastaa	**Teräsbetoni**	22	35	8
Germany	Disappear	**No Angels**	23	14	4
Poland	For Life	**Isis Gee**	24	14	10
United Kingdom	Even If	**Andy Abraham**	25	14	2

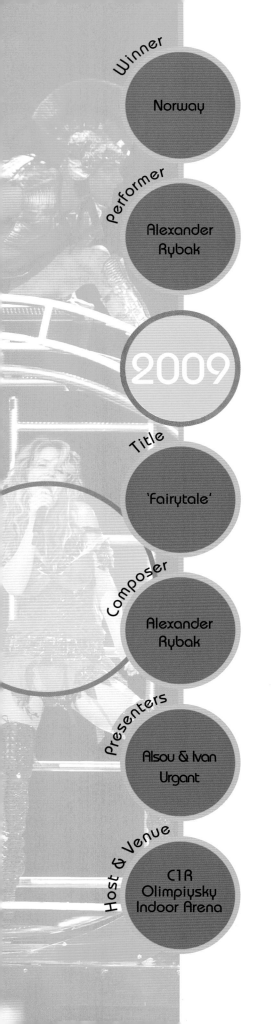

Winner

Norway

Performer

Alexander
Rybak

2009

Title

'Fairytale'

Composer

Alexander
Rybak

Presenters

Alsou & Ivan
Urgant

Host & Venue

C1R
Olimpiysky
Indoor Arena

Although not nearly as large as the vast Parken in Copenhagen, Moscow's Olimpiysky Indoor Arena was still able to handle an audience of nearly 25,000 for the final of the 2009 Eurovision Song Contest on 16th May, following the two semi-finals on 12th and 14th May to decide the 25 finalists. Inside the cavernous arena, Channel One Russia constructed a vast stage, with a 100-metre video wall comprised of the largest number of screens ever assembled. Two-thirds of all the LED screens available in Europe were brought in to create the backdrop.

Moscow
Russia

Following the apparent success of dividing the semi-final competitors into separate draws and allowing the backup jury a say in the final selection, the system was once again used to determine the ten winners from each of the two heats. Perhaps more significantly, the scoring for the final was also to be dramatically overhauled, with the inauguration of

'**Fairytale**' proved to be one of the most successful Eurovision winners for many years. The single topped the Norwegian, Danish, Swedish, Belgian, Belarusian, Greek, Finnish, Russian and Ukrainian charts and was a top ten hit in Ireland, the UK, Germany, Austria and Estonia. It was even a minor hit in Australia.

professional juries. Each nation would provide five members from the music or entertainment industries to cast votes on the songs, providing 50 per cent of the total vote from each country. The remainder would be determined by tele-voting from the viewers. The new measure was welcomed widely and it led to a resurgence of Western success in the contest, although many argued this was more to do with the raising of standards in the Western European efforts, something lauded across the continent's media. Despite these changes, neither Monaco nor Austria was willing to return to the contest and San Marino also opted out after their debut the previous year. Slovakia announced their participation after over a decade away, but no new nations were joining the Eurovision family this year. Both Latvia and Georgia initially declared they would not be taking part in Moscow, but each changed their minds and selected entries. Hostilities between Georgia and Russia were at their peak towards the end of 2008 and it was something of an international coup when the Georgians agreed to participate. However, this

détente turned sour when the Georgian group **Stefane Da 3G** were chosen to represent their nation with a thinly veiled attack on Russian President **Vladimir Putin** with the song 'We Don't Wanna Put In'. Objections from Russian television were raised quickly with the EBU, who agreed that the lyric was deliberately inflammatory, asking that it be re-written. When GTVR refused, the entry was disqualified. Despite this setback, **Stefane Da 3G** became instant celebrities across Europe and beyond and enjoyed much media attention and a major hit as a result. Controversy wasn't limited to Georgia's disqualification; when it emerged after the contest that voters in Azerbaijan had been interviewed by police for supposedly voting for the Armenian entry. This followed criticism of using an image in the Armenian postcard of a monument located in Azerbaijan which had to be edited from the broadcast. Spanish TVE were also in trouble when they were forced to postpone the broadcast of the second semi-final due to an over-run of a live tennis event, possibly leaving them facing financial sanctions. In Moscow itself, a banned gay rights march was scheduled for the same day as the contest, leading to some violent clashes between police and protesters, witnessed by the world's media gathered for the song contest. Despite all these background controversies, the contest itself was almost unanimously praised across the world for its production standards and the quality of the entries.

An even older TV institution joined forces with the contest this year, when the Russian holder of the 58th Miss World title, **Ksenia Sukhinova** was chosen to be the face of the 54th song contest's media advertising and the main feature of the inter-song postcards, which incorporated 3D animation of local landmarks from each nation.

Of the 42 nations that came to Moscow, some were represented by artists that had been there before. Former contest host **Sakis Rouvas** was attempting to better his third place for Greece in 2004 and Malta's **Chiara** was bidding to become the first artist ever to finish first, second and third. Alas, even though they both made the final, both fell way short of their goals. There were other very high

Norway's Belarusian-born Alexander Rybak broke his violin bow during his winning performance, where his dancers and backing singers helped him achieve the highest score yet seen in Eurovision.

profile artists bidding for Eurovision glory this year, with France's **Patricia Kaas** performing her own song, and Lord **Andrew Lloyd-Webber** and **Diane Warren** the prolific team behind the UK effort. Both entries managed to improve the results of these two nations considerably, whereas burlesque star **Dita Von Teese**'s presence did little to help Germany's **Alex Swings Oscar Sings!** Unfortunately, for some of the perennial contenders, success was again elusive. Despite The Netherlands sending their hugely popular male trio **De Toppers**, they were still unable to qualify for the final. A similar fate befell Ireland, Switzerland and Belgium, but otherwise many more of the qualifiers came from the West this year, including a final place for Portugal's **Flor-De-Lis**, after many years of continued failure. Israel also qualified with a joint Israeli-Arab effort performed by **Noa & Mira Awad**, which pled for harmony between Jews and Arabs in the region. The Ukraine also had a message song, with **Svetlana Loboda**'s 'Be My Valentine (Anti Crisis Girl)' marking a campaign against violence towards women. Another Ukrainian singer was in the line up, rather controversially representing the host nation Russia. **Anastasia Prikhodko** had been overlooked for the Ukrainian selection, but Russian TV had invited her to participate in their national final, which she won easily with the song 'Mama', triumphing over bigger local stars, despite her performing the song largely

Below: Armenian sisters Inga & Anush Arshakyan finished 10th. **Below right:** Ukraine's Svetlana Loboda performs in her 'Hell Machine' with a troupe of Roman soldiers.

in Ukrainian. Andorra, Belarus, Slovenia, Slovakia, the Czech Republic and Montenegro all failed again to reach the grand final, which in the case of Andorra, made it their sixth failure in six attempts. Like the Czechs and the Montenegrins, the Andorrans were yet to reach their first final. For the Czechs the result was particularly humiliating as **Gypsy.cz** became only the second act to score 'nul points' in the semi-finals.

Despite the high hopes of many of the international names and the lavish praise awarded to the hosts who had spent a record 40 million Euro on the production, not for the first time it seemed the contest winner had been determined many months before any singers arrived in the Russian capital, when Norway had emerged as favourites at the very start of their own selection process. Belarusian-born Alexander **Rybak** had been installed as the favourite from the first round of the Norwegian heats and he swept the board in Moscow in an unprecedented manner with his own composition, "Fairytale".

In racking up an astonishing 387 points, including 16 top marks of 12 points, Norway triumphed with an absolute margin of 169 over Iceland's second placed **Yohanna**, with her song "Is It True?", a relative margin of nearly 44 per cent. Every one of the other 40 countries awarded Norway a mark, with only the Czech Republic, Bulgaria and Turkey awarding anything less than five points. Such was the runaway nature of his victory that **Alexander** secured his win only half way through the voting sequence. For the viewers, the interest then switched to who would secure the runners-up places, with the outcome only decided on the

final vote – Norway's own – when Iceland's receipt of the final 12 points of the night just edged Azerbaijan's **Aysel & Arash** into third place, ahead of Turkey's **Hadise** and the UK's talent show winner **Jade Ewen**. Had the UK not awarded Turkey 12 points, they would have secured fourth place for themselves!

The success of the Western nations and the fact that the contest was won by the first country West of the Danube since Denmark in 2000, went a long way to vindicating the return of the juries and the splitting of neighbours in the semi-finals. Ironically, Finland had been saved by the backup jury in the first semi-final, having only placed 12th with the tele-voters, but still went on to finish last in the final – a return to form for the Finns after such a relatively successful run. Croatia made the final despite being 13th in their semi, much to the chagrin of neighbours Serbia who had placed 10th but were thus relegated. FYR Macedonia was also knocked out despite finishing 10th in their heat – for the second year running. The media reaction to the contest was

almost uniformly positive, with most commentators hailing the contest as the best ever! The public seemed to agree, with viewing figures increasing universally and the number of hit singles across the continent rising dramatically.

After the contest, the EBU published the full results of both the jury marks and the tele-voting scores which demonstrated some disparities between the two sets of votes. The UK and France in particular had scored better with the juries than they had with the viewers, lifting both into the top ten with their combined scores. Such transparency won the contest new plaudits and the 50/50 split between the professional juries and the viewers was thus to be extended to the semi-finals for 2010. After a few years of criticism from Western nations and a perception among viewers that the contest was being dominated by an Eastern voting bloc, the Moscow contest had proved a huge success and had gone a long way to promoting a more positive image for the venerable competition.

country	song	performer	place	score	draw
Norway	Fairytale	**Alexander Rybak**	1	387	20
Iceland	Is It True?	**Yohanna**	2	218	7
Azerbaijan	Always	**AySel & Arash**	3	207	11
Turkey	Düm Tek Tek	**Hadise**	4	177	18
United Kingdom	It's My Time	**Jade Ewen**	5	173	23
Estonia	Rändajad	**Urban Symphony**	6	129	15
Greece	This Is Our Night	**Sakis Rouvas**	7	120	8
France	Et S'il Fallait Le Faire	**Patricia Kaas**	8	107	3
Bosnia-Herzegovina	Bistra Voda	**Regina**	9	106	12
Armenia	Jan Jan	**Inga & Anush**	10	92	9
Russia	Mamo	**Anastasia Prikhodko**	11	91	10
Ukraine	Be My Valentine (Anti Crisis Girl)	**Svetlana Loboda**	12	76	21
Denmark	Believe Again	**Brinck**	13	74	16
Moldova	Hora Din Moldova	**Nelly Ciobanu**	14	69	13
Portugal	Todas As Ruas Do Amor	**Flor-De-Lis**	15	57	6
Israel	There Must Be Another Way	**Noa & Mira Awad**	16	53	2
Albania	Carry Me In Your Dreams	**Kejsi Tola**	17	48	19
Croatia	Lijepa Tena	**Igor Cukrov feat. Andrea**	18	45	5
Romania	The Balkan Girls	**Elena**	19	40	22
Germany	Miss Kiss Kiss Bang	**Alex Swings Oscar Sings!**	20	35	17
Sweden	La Voix	**Malena Ernman**	21	33	4
Malta	What If We?	**Chiara**	22	31	14
Spain	La Noche Es Para Mí	**Soraya**	23	23	25
Lithuania	Love	**Sasha Son**	24	23	1
Finland	Lose Control	**Waldo's People**	25	22	24

eurostats

WINNERS' TABLE

Country		Years
Ireland	7	70, 80, 87, 92, 93, 94, 96
Luxembourg	5	61, 65, 72, 73, 83
France	5	58, 60, 62, 69*, 77
United Kingdom	5	67, 69*, 76, 81, 97
Sweden	4	74, 84, 91, 99
The Netherlands	4	57, 59, 69*, 75
Israel	3	78, 79, 98
Norway	3	85, 95, 09
Switzerland	2	56, 88
Italy	2	64, 90
Denmark	2	63, 00
Spain	2	68, 69*
Austria	1	66
Monaco	1	71
Germany	1	82
Belgium	1	86
Yugoslavia	1	89
Estonia	1	01
Latvia	1	02
Turkey	1	03
Ukraine	1	04
Greece	1	05
Finland	1	06
Serbia	1	07
Russia	1	08

* Shared victory

LAST PLACE TABLE
Excluding the 1956 contest

Country		Years
Norway	10	**63***, 69, **74***, 76, **78**, **81**, **90***, **97***, 01*, 04
Finland	9	**63***, **65***, 68*, 80, **82**, **90***, 92, 96, 09
Belgium	8	61*, **62***, **65***, 73, **79***, 85, 93, 00
Austria	7	57, 61*, **62***, **79***, 84, **88**, **91**
Germany	5	**64***, **65***, **74***, 95, 05
The Netherlands	4	58*, **62***, **63***, 68*
Spain	4	**62***, **65***, **83***, 99
Switzerland	4	**64***, 67, **74***, **98**
Luxembourg	3	58, 60, **70**
Turkey	3	75, **83***, **87**
Portugal	3	**64***, **74***, **97***
Malta	3	71, 72, 06
Monaco	2	59*, **66***
Sweden	2	**63***, 77
Iceland	2	**89**, 01*
United Kingdom	2	**03**, 08
Cyprus	1	86
Italy	1	**66***
Lithuania	1	**94**
Yugoslavia	1	**64***
Denmark	1	02
Ireland	1	09

Bold: 'nul points'   **Shared place*

MOST ENTRIES IN THE FINAL

Country		Years
Germany	53	56–95, (96), 97–09
France	52	56–73, 75–81, 83–09
United Kingdom	52	57, 59–09
Sweden	49	58–63, 65–69, 71–75, 77–09
Spain	49	61–09
Norway	47	60–69, 71–01, 03–06, (07), 08–09
Belgium	46	56–93, 95–96, 98–00, 02–04, (05–09)
The Netherlands	45	56–84, 86–90, 92–94, 96–01, 03–04, (05–09)
Switzerland	46	56–94, 96–98, 00, 02, (04), 05–06, (07–09)
Austria	41	57–68, 71–72, 76–97, 99–00, 02–04, (05), (07)
Finland	41	61–69, 71–94, 96, 98, 00, 02, (04–05), 06–09
Ireland	40	65–82, 84–01, 03–04, (05), 06–07, (08–09)
Portugal	39	64–69, 71–99, 01, 03, (04–07), 08–09
Luxembourg	37	56–58, 60–93
Italy	36	56–80, 83–85, 87–93, 97
Denmark	36	57–66, 78–93, 95, (96), 97, 99–02, (04), 05–06, (07), 08–09
Turkey	31	75, 78, 80–93, 95–09
Israel	30	73–79, 81–83, 85–93, 95, (96), 98–03, (04), 05–06, (07), 08–09
Greece	30	74, 76–81, 83, 85, 87–98, 01–09
Yugoslavia	27	61–76, 81–84, 86–92
Cyprus	24	81–87, 89–00, 02–05, (06–09)
Monaco	21	59–79, (04–06)
Malta	20	71–72, 75, 91–06, (07–08), 09
Iceland	19	86–97, 99–01, 03–04, (05–07), 08–09
Croatia	16	93–06, (07), 08–09
Bosnia-Herzegovina	15	93–97, 99, 01–09
Russia	13	94–95, (96), 97, 00–09
Romania	11	(93), 94, (96), 98, 00, 02–09
Slovenia	10	93, 95–99, 01–03, (04–06), 07, (08–09)
Estonia	10	(93), 94, 96–03, (04–08), 09
Poland	10	94–99, 01, 03–04, (05–07), 08, (09)
Lithuania	8	94, 99, 01–03, (04–05), 06–07, (08), 09
Latvia	8	00–03, (04), 05–08, (09)
Ukraine	7	03–09
Hungary	6	(93), 94–95, (96), 97–98, 05, 07, (08–09)
FYR Macedonia	6	(96), 98, 00, 02, 04–07, (08–09)
Albania	4	04–05, (06–07), 08–09
Moldova	4	05–08, (08), 09
Armenia	4	06–09
Slovakia	3	(93), 94, 96, 98, (09)
Serbia	2	07–08, (09)
Serbia & Montenegro	2	04–05
Georgia	2	07–08
Morocco	1	80
Belarus	1	(04–06), 07, (08–09)
Bulgaria	1	(05–06), 07, (08–09)
Andorra	0	(04–06)
Czech Republic	0	(07–09)
Montenegro	0	(07–09)
San Marino	0	(08)

(93) (96) (04) (05) (06) (07) (08) (09) Losing semi-finalist – not included in total number of entries

PICKING THE WINNER

Which countries have the best record for awarding their top marks to the winning song?

(x) Excluding any year that a nation won the contest since they can't vote for themselves!

Country			Years
Latvia (1)	5/9	55%	00, 01, _04_, 08, _09_
Hungary	4/8	50%	97, 05, 07, _09_
Lithuania	5/10	50%	01, 02, _04_, _08_, 09
Russia (1)	6/12	50%	94, 95, 97, 00, 04, 09
Estonia (1)	7/15	47%	96, 99, 02, _06_, _08–09_
Israel (3)	13/29	45%	74–76, 81–83, 85, 89, 00, 02, _04_, 08–09
Poland	6/14	43%	95, 96, 01, 04, _06_, _09_
Switzerland* (2)	20/47	43%	57, 61, 62, 67, 69–71, 73, 74, 76–78, 80, 82, 87, 93, 94, 96, 97, 07
Germany* (1)	20/51	39%	61, 62, 65, 68, 69, 71, 72, 74, 77, 78, 80, 84, 85, 88, 91, 94, 00, 02, 05, 09
United Kingdom (5)	18/47	38%	60, 64, 69, 70, 72, 73, 75, 79, 80, 85, 86, 87, 89, 93, 99–01, 05–06
Belgium* (1)	18/49	37%	57, 59, 60, 63, 64, 66, 67, 69–72, 76, 78, 80, 85, 87, 03, _05_
Sweden (4)	16/45	35%	60, 62, 63, 69, 71, 75, 79, 85, 87, 88, 93, 97, 00, 05, 06, 09
Yugoslavia (1)	9/26	35%	61, 62, 64, 66, 71–73, 82, 83
Austria (1)	14/42	33%	57–59, 61, 64, 65, 67, 72, 84, 85, 87, 97, 03, _07_
Belarus	2/6	33%	_08–09_
Ireland (7)	12/36	33%	69, 71, 72, 79, 82, 84, 85, 86, 89, 90, 97, 00
Montenegro	1/3	33%	_07_
Malta	7/22	32%	75, 92, 93, 98, 99, 01, 03
The Netherlands* (4)	15/45	33%	63–65, 69–72, 78, 87, 94, 96, 97, 01, 03, _09_
Norway (3)	14/43	33%	60, 62, 67, 71, 73–76, 79, 80, 93, 94, 99
Turkey (1)	10/30	33%	78, 82, 86, 89, 92, 95, 96, 01, 04–05
Serbia & Montenegro	1/3	33%	05
Slovenia	5/15	33%	93, 95, 01, 07, _09_
Ukraine (1)	2/6	33%	08–09
Iceland	7/22	32%	91, 94, 95, 00, 04, _06_, 09
Denmark (2)	11/37	30%	57, 58, 60, 80, 82, 84, 85, 91, 97, 06, 09
Portugal	13/43	30%	64, 68, 72, 76, 79, 80, 82, 83, 86, 88, 94, 95, 98
Bosnia-Herzegovina	4/15	27%	96, 99, 03, 07
Finland (1)	11/42	26%	61, 63–65, 68, 74, 77, 79, 86, 87, 07
Monaco (1)	6/23	26%	60, 61, 63, 66, 67, 69
Armenia	1/4	25%	08
Greece (1)	7/29	24%	76, 80, 83, 92, 95, 01, 06
Italy* (2)	8/33	24%	58, 59, 61, 68, 72, 83, 87, 93
Bulgaria	1/5	20%	_05_
France* (5)	9/47	19%	59, 67–69, 73, 83, 86, 97, 98
Luxembourg* (5)	6/31	19%	63, 64, 66, 67, 69, 78
Croatia	3/17	18%	94, 97, _07_
Albania	1/6	17%	05
Cyprus	4/27	15%	82, 84, 90, 05
Spain (2)	7/47	15%	75, 76, 80, 82, 90, 02, 09
FYR Macedonia	1/9	11%	07
Romania	0/11	0%	
Slovakia	0/4	0%	
Andorra	0/6	0%	
Morocco	0/1	0%	
Moldova	0/5	0%	
Czech Republic	0/3	0%	
Georgia	0/2	0%	
Serbia (1)	0/2	0%	
San Marino	0/1	0%	

_04_, _05_, _06_, _07_, _08_, _09_ = voted in the final but did not compete

*Excludes the 1956 contest

CONDUCTED MOST WINNERS

Noel Kelehan	5	80, 87, 92, 93, 96 (Ireland 5)
Franck Pourcel	4	58, 60, 62, 69 (France 4)
Dolf van der Linden	3	57, 59, 70 (The Netherlands 2, Ireland 1)

WRITTEN OR COMPOSED MOST WINNERS

Willy van Hemert	2	Netherlands 57, 59
Yves Dessca	2	Monaco 71, Luxembourg 72
Johnny Logan	2	Ireland 87, 92
Rolf Løvland	2	Norway 85, 95
Brendan Graham	2	Ireland 94, 96

WINNING AUTHORS/COMPOSERS CONDUCTING THEIR OWN SONG

Klaus Munro	Après toi	Luxembourg 1972
Nurit Hirsh	A-Ba-Ni-Bi	Israel 1978
Kobi Oshrat	Hallelujah	Israel 1979
Atilla Sereftug	Ne Partez Pas Sans Moi	Switzerland 1988

THE LADY CONDUCTORS

Monica Dominique	1	Sweden 1973
Nurit Hirsh	2	Israel 1973, 1978
Anita Kerr	1	Switzerland 1985

MOST APPEARANCES BY CONDUCTORS (Four or more appearances)

Noel Kelehan	29	Bosnia-Herzegovina 1, Greece 1, Ireland 24, Poland 2, Romania 1
Franck Pourcel	23	Austria 2, France 16, Germany 2, Monaco 1, Sweden 1, Switzerland 1
Ossi Runne	22	Finland 22
Dolf van der Linden	19	Belgium 1, Germany 1, Ireland 1, Luxembourg 1, The Netherlands 13, Sweden 1, Switzerland 1
Harry van Hoof	15	The Netherlands 15
Anders Berglund	14	Sweden 13, Yugoslavia 1
Richard Österreicher	12	Austria 12
Francis Bay	9	Belgium 9
Haris Andreadis	9	Cyprus 2, Greece 7
Kai Mortensen	9	Denmark 8, Portugal 1
Willy Berking	8	Belgium 1, Germany 5, Luxembourg 1, Switzerland 1
Fernando Paggi	8	Germany 2, Switzerland 4, Netherlands 2
Eric Robinson	8	Luxembourg 1, The Netherlands 1, Switzerland 1, UK 5
Øivind Bergh	8	Norway 8
Ronnie Hazlehurst	8	UK 7, Germany 1
Henrik Krogsgaard	7	Denmark 7
Olli Ahvenlahti	7	Finland 7
Eduardo Leiva	7	Spain 7
Curt-Eric Holmquist	7	Sweden 6, Belgium 1
Alain Goraguer	6	France 4, Luxembourg 1, Monaco 1
Sigurd Jansen	6	Norway 6
Thilo Krasmann	6	Portugal 6
Henri Segers	5	Belgium 5
Michalis Rozakis	5	Cyprus 2, Greece 3
Allan Botschinski	5	Denmark 5
Georg de Godzinsky	5	Finland 5
Kobi Oshrat	5	Israel 5
Rogier van Otterloo	5	The Netherlands 5
Carsten Klouman	5	Norway 5
Jože Privšek	5	Slovenia 3, Yugoslavia 2
Rafael Ibarbia	5	Spain 5
Alyn Ainsworth	5	UK 4, Belgium 1
John Coleman	5	UK 5
Nikica Kalogjera	5	Yugoslavia 5
Jean Roderes	4	Belgium 1, Luxembourg 2, Switzerland 1
Sinan Alimanović	4	Bosnia-Herzegovina 4
George Theofanous	4	Cyprus 4
Jean Claudric	4	France 1, Luxembourg 2, Morocco 1
Jean-Claude Petit	4	France 3, Monaco 1
Colman Pearce	4	Ireland 4
Eldad Shrem	4	Israel 4
Raymond Lefevre	4	Monaco 3, Luxembourg 1
Pete Knutsen	4	Norway 4
José Calvário	4	Portugal 4
Mojmir Sepe	4	Slovenia 2, Yugoslavia 2
Juán Carlos Calderón	4	Spain 4
Mario Robbiani	4	Switzerland 4
Miljenko Prohaska	4	Yugoslavia 4

MOST NUMBER OF COUNTRIES CONDUCTED FOR

Dolf van der Linden	7	Belgium, Germany, Ireland, Luxembourg, The Netherlands, Sweden, Switzerland
Franck Pourcel	6	Austria, France, Germany, Monaco, Sweden, Switzerland
Noel Kelehan	5	Bosnia-Herzegovina, Greece, Ireland, Poland, Romania
Willy Berking	4	Belgium, Germany, Luxembourg, Switzerland
Eric Robinson	4	Luxembourg, The Netherlands, Switzerland, UK
Fernando Paggi	3	Germany, Switzerland, The Netherlands
Alan Goraguer	3	France, Luxembourg, Monaco
Jean Roderes	3	Belgium, Luxembourg, Switzerland
Jean Claudric	3	France, Luxembourg, Morocco

WINNING AUTHORS/COMPOSERS PERFORMING THEIR OWN SONG

Udo Jürgens	Merci Cherie	Austria 1966
Lenny Kuhr	De Troubadour	The Netherlands 1969
Benny Andersson (Abba)	Waterloo	Sweden 1974
Björn Ulvaeus (Abba)	Waterloo	Sweden 1974
Martin Lee (Brotherhood of Man)	Save Your Kisses For Me	United Kingdom 1976
Lee Sheridan (Brotherhood of Man)	Save Your Kisses For Me	United Kingdom 1976
Johnny Logan	Hold Me Now	Ireland 1987
Toto Cutugno	Insieme 1992	Italy 1990
Rolf Løvland^ (Secret Garden)	Nocturne	Norway 1995
Kimberly Rew* (Katrina & The Waves)	Love Shine A Light	United Kingdom 1997
Jørgen Olsen (The Olsen Brothers)	Fly On The Wings Of Love	Denmark 2000
Marija Naumova (Marie N)	I Wanna	Latvia 2002
Sertab Erener	Everyway That I Can	Turkey 2003
Ruslana	Wild Dances	Ukraine 2004
Mr. Lordi (Lordi)	Hard Rock Hallelujah	Finland 2006
Dima Bilan	"Believe"	Russia 2008
Alexander Rybak	"Fairytale"	Norway 2009

Although a regular member of Katrina and the Waves, Kimberly Rew did not actually appear on stage with the band in the contest, but his guitar playing was featured on the backing track used in Dublin.

^Rolf Løvland was also on stage for his 1985 winner "La det swinge," but received no credit for this performance accompanying Bobbysocks.*

BEST RECORDS OF PERFORMERS

All performers who have competed on more than one occasion and have placed in the top three at least once.

Johnny Logan	1st 1980	1st 1987	
Elisabeth Andreassen~	1st 1985 (Nor)	2nd 1996 (Nor)	6th 1994 (Nor)	8th 1982 (Swe)
Lys Assia	1st 1956	2nd 1958	8th 1957	Unplaced 1956
Gigliola Cinquetti	1st 1964	2nd 1974	
Linda Martin	1st 1992	2nd 1984	
Dima Bilan	1st 2008	2nd 2006	
Carola	1st 1991	3rd 1983	5th 2006
Isabelle Aubret	1st 1962	3rd 1968	
Anne-Marie David	1st 1973 (Lux)	3rd 1979 (Fra)	
Helena Paparizou++	1st 2005	3rd 2001	
Udo Jürgens	1st 1966	4th 1965	6th 1964
Vicky Leandros	1st 1972	4th 1967	
Izhar Cohen^	1st 1978	5th 1985	
Corry Brokken	1st 1957	=9th 1957	Unplaced 1956
Jean Claude Pascal	1st 1961	11th 1981	
Cheryl Baker*	1st 1981	11th 1978	
Hanne Krogh+	1st 1985	17th 1971	17th 1991
Charlotte Nilsson Perrelli	1st 1999	18th 2008	
Wind	2nd 1985	2nd 1987	15th 1992
Katja Ebstein	2nd 1980	3rd 1970	3rd 1971
Francois Deguelt	2nd 1962	3rd 1960	
Cliff Richard	2nd 1968	3rd 1973	
Chiara	2nd 2005	3rd 1998	22nd 2009
Jean Vallée	2nd 1978	=8th 1970	
Romuald	3rd 1964 (Mon)	=4th 1974 (Mon)	11th 1969 (Lux)
Hot Eyes	3rd 1988	4th 1984	11th 1985
Domenico Mudugno	3rd 1958	6th 1959	=17th 1966
Sally-Ann Triplett †	3rd 1980	7th 1982	
Sakis Rouvas	3rd 2004	7th 2009	
Kikki Danielsson‡	3rd 1985	8th 1982	
The Swarbriggs····›	3rd 1977	9th 1975	
Şebnem Paker‹····	3rd 1997	12th 1996	
Camillo Felgen	3rd 1962	13th 1960	
Mary Roos	3rd 1972	=13th 1984	

Rolf Løvland of Norway's 1995 winning group Secret Garden received no performing credit when accompanying Bobbysocks for their 1985 win for Norway. Both entries won the contest.

Paul Harrington, one half of Ireland's winning duo in 1994, returned as an uncredited backing singer for the 1998 Irish entry, finishing 9th.

Tanel Padar who won the 2001 contest with Dave Benton and 2XL had been an uncredited backing singer for Estonia's 4th placed entry in 2000.

Iceland's Selma was 2nd in the 1999 contest, but failed to qualify for the final in 2005.
The UK's John Farrar of The Shadows placed 2nd in 1975, having been an uncredited backing singer for Cliff Richard in 1973, placing 3rd.

George & Michel Costa are worthy of note even though they have never been credited with performing a Eurovision entry. They provided anonymous vocal backing for three winners for two different nations (1973, 1977 & 1983) and were backing singers for Belgium, Monaco, France, Switzerland & Luxembourg on 13 entries from 1973–1983. They also wrote the French entry in 1986.

~As part of Chips 1982, Bobbysocks 1985, with Jan Werner 1994 and as a soloist in 1996
^As lead singer of Alpha-Beta 1978 and as a soloist in 1985
* As part of Co-Co 1978 and Bucks Fizz in 1981
+ As a soloist 1971, with Bobbysocks 1985 and with Just 4 Fun in 1991
† With Prima Donna in 1980 and as part of Bardo in 1982
‡ As a soloist in 1985 and as part of Chips in 1982
····›As The Swarbriggs in 1975 and as The Swarbriggs Plus Two in 1977
‹···· As a soloist in 1996 and with the Group Etnic in 1997
++ As a soloist in 2005 and with Antique in 2001

WRITTEN OR COMPOSED MOST ENTRIES

(Four or more. Final only, excluding qualifying rounds)

Ralph Siegel~	18	Luxembourg 74, 80, 85
		Germany 76, 79, 80, 81, 82*, 87, 88, 90, 92, 94, 97, 99, 02, 03
		Switzerland 06
Bernd Meinunger~	17	Luxembourg 80, 85
		Germany 79, 80, 81, 82*, 87, 88, 92, 94, 97, 99, 02, 03, 05+
		Switzerland 05+, 06
Pierre Delanoé	8	France 58*, 67, 75
		Monaco 60, 61
		Luxembourg 63, 80
		Switzerland 73
Kjeld Heick	8	Denmark 79, 81, 84, 85, 88, 89, 90, 93
José Calvário	7	Portugal 69, 71, 72, 73, 74, 77, 88
Pierre Cour	6	France 59, 60*, 64
		Luxembourg 67, 71, 75, 77
Ehud Manor	6	Israel 73, 75, 76, 78*, 83, 88
Peter Reber	6	Switzerland 71, 76, 77, 79, 80, 81
Emile Gardaz	5	Switzerland 56*, 57, 61, 62, 63
Géo Voumard	5	Switzerland 56*, 57, 61, 62, 63
Michael Kunze	5	Luxembourg 74
		Germany 77, 84, 85, 90
Karen Kavaleryan	5	Russia 02, 06
		Armenia 07
		Belarus 07
		Georgia 08
		Ukraine 08
Arne Bendikson	4	Norway 66, 69, 71, 73
Brendan Graham	4	Ireland 76, 85, 94*, 96*
Didier Barbelivien	4	France 78, 98
		Monaco 78, 79
Juán Carlos Calderón	4	Spain 73, 75, 85, 89
Søren Bundgaard	4	Denmark 84, 85, 88, 89
Paul Curtis	4	United Kingdom 75, 84, 90, 91
Andre Popp	4	France 60*, 64
		Luxembourg 67
		Monaco 75
Phil van Cauwenburgh	4	Belgium 66, 67, 69, 71
Paul Quintens	4	Belgium 66, 67, 69, 71
Rolf Løvland	4	Norway 85*, 87, 94, 95*
Udo Jurgens	4	Austria 64, 65, 66*, 68
Joachim Horn-Bernges	4	Austria 89, 92
		Germany 89
		Poland 03
Andrej Babić	4	Croatia 03
		Bosnia-Herzegovina 05
		Slovenia 07
		Portugal 08
Tonči Huljić	4	Croatia 95, 99, 01, 09
Vjekoslava Huljić	4	Croatia 95, 99, 01, 09

*Winning song
+Under the pseudonym "John O'Flynn"
~Siegel & Meinunger also co-wrote Montenegro's 2009 entry that failed to qualify.

MULTIPLE ENTRIES IN ONE CONTEST BY AUTHORS/COMPOSERS

Didier Barbelivien	2	France & Monaco 1978
Ralph Siegel	2	Luxembourg & Germany 1980
Bernd Meinunger	2	Luxembourg & Germany 1980
Joachim Horn-Bernges	2	Austria & Germany 1989
Dieter Bohlen	2	Austria & Germany 1989
David Brandes	2	Germany & Switzerland 2005
Bernd Meinunger (aka John O'Flynn)	2	Germany & Switzerland 2005
Karen Kavaleryan	2	Armenia & Belarus 2007
Karen Kavaleryan	2	Georgia & Ukraine 2008

WINNING COLOURS

Is there a costume colour that is more successful than others are? Basic black or white, with a shade of red/pink seems to work well. Since the introduction of colour broadcasts in 1968, these seem to be the best options:

No single colour scheme	7	Sweden 74, The Netherlands 75, UK 81, Sweden 84, Sweden 91, UK 97, Finland 06
White	6	Ireland 70, Israel 78, Ireland 87, Switzerland 88, Italy 90, Russia 08
White & Pink	5	Spain 68, UK 69, Israel 79, Belgium 86, Turkey 03
Black & White	4	Ireland 80, Germany 82, Ireland 94, Norway 95, Norway 09
Red, White & Black	4	UK 76, Yugoslavia 89, Latvia 02, Serbia 07
Pink	2	Luxembourg 83, Sweden 99
Black	2	Luxembourg 72, Denmark 00
Red	2	The Netherlands 69, Luxembourg 74
Black & Gold	2	France 69, Monaco 71
Black & Pink	1	Norway 85
Black & Red	1	Ireland 93
Black, Red & Grey	1	Estonia 01
Blue	1	Spain 69
Orange	1	France 77
Green	1	Ireland 92
Silver	1	Israel 98
Brown	1	Ukraine 04
Gold	1	Greece 05

It's interesting to note that both France Gall and Sandie Shaw also opted for pink in the monochrome era of the contest.

CONSECUTIVE CONTEST APPEARANCES BY ARTISTS

Only singers who have been members of groups or who were given credit for a performance are included. Uncredited appearances as backing singers are excluded.

Lys Assia	4	Switzerland **56** (x2), 57, 58
Corry Brokken	3	Netherlands 56, **57**, 58
Udo Jürgens	3	Austria 64, 65, **66**
Margot Hielscher	2	Germany 57, 58
Domenico Modugno	2	Italy 58, 59
Nora Brockstedt	2	Norway 60, 61
Ronnie Carroll	2	United Kingdom 62, 63
Raphael	2	Spain 66, 67
Katja Ebstein	2	Germany 70, 71
The Family Four	2	Sweden 71, 72
Anne Karine Strøm~	2	Norway 73, 74
Marty Bremm*	2	Austria 80, 81
Jahn Teigen+	2	Norway 82, 83
Hot Eyes	2	Denmark 84, 85
Tony Wegas	2	Austria 92, 93
Marja-Liis Ilus#	2	Estonia 96, 97
Şebnem Paker^	2	Turkey 96, 97

No Name represented Serbia & Montenegro in 2005 and were selected to represent them again in 2006 but the nation withdrew from the competition.

Wins in bold

~ 73 with The Bendik Singers, 74 solo

* 80 with Blue Danube, 81 solo

+ 82 with Anita Skorgan, 83 solo

96 with Ivo Linna, 97 solo

^ 96 solo, 97 with Grup Etnic

COMPETING LANGUAGES

Final only. Semi-finals & qualifying rounds excluded

Albanian	1	Albania
Arabic	1	Morocco
Armenian/English	1	Armenia
Breton	1	France
Bulgarian	1	Bulgaria
Danish	28	Denmark
Dutch	38	The Netherlands
English	263	Albania, Armenia, Austria, Azerbaijan, Belarus, Belgium, Bosnia-Herzegovina, Croatia, Cyprus, Denmark, Estonia, Finland, Georgia, Germany, Greece, Iceland, Ireland, Latvia, Lithuania, FYR Macedonia, Malta, Moldova, The Netherlands, Norway, Poland, Romania, Russia, Slovenia, Sweden, Switzerland, Turkey, Ukraine, United Kingdom
English/Lithuanian	1	Lithuania
English/Italian/French/Spanish/Russian/Romanian	1	Romania
Estonian	6	Estonia
Finnish	31	Finland
Flemish	18	Belgium
Flemish/English	1	Belgium
French	150	France, Monaco, Belgium, Luxembourg, Switzerland
French Creole	1	France
French/English	3	France
German	86	Germany, Austria, Switzerland
German/English	6	Austria, Germany
German/French	1	Germany
German/Turkish/English/Hebrew	1	Germany
German/English/Ukrainian/Mongolian	1	Ukraine
Greek	39	Greece, Cyprus
Greek/Italian	1	Cyprus
Greek/English	1	Greece
Hebrew	22	Israel
Hebrew/English	7	Israel
Hebrew/English/Arabic	1	Israel
Hungarian	6	Hungary
Icelandic	12	Iceland
Irish	1	Ireland
Italian	47	Italy, Latvia, Switzerland
Italian/English	2	Italy
Italian/Romanian	1	Romania
Lithuanian	2	Lithuania
Luxembourgoise	2	Luxembourg
Luxembourgoise/French	1	Luxembourg
Macedonian	2	FYR Macedonia
Macedonian/English	3	FYR Macedonia
Maltese	2	Malta
Moldavian/English	2	Moldova
Norwegian	35	Norway
Polish	6	Poland
Polish/German	1	Poland
Portuguese	38	Portugal
Portuguese/English	1	Portugal
Romanian	2	Romania
Romansch	1	Switzerland
Russian	4	Russia
Serbo-Croat	47	Bosnia-Herzegovina, Croatia, Serbia, Serbia & Montenegro, Yugoslavia
Serbo-Croat/English	5	Bosnia-Herzegovina, Croatia
Serbo-Croat/French	1	Bosnia-Herzegovina
Slovakian	3	Slovakia
Slovenian	11	Slovenia, Yugoslavia
Spanish	47	Spain
Spanish/English	1	Spain
Swedish	35	Finland, Sweden
Turkish	23	Turkey
Turkish/English	4	Turkey
Ukrainian/English	2	Ukraine
Ukrainian/Russian	1	Russia

WHICH SINGERS COMPETED THE MOST OFTEN?

Only singers who have been members of groups or who were given credit for a performance are included. Uncredited appearances as backing singers are excluded.

Lys Assia	4	Switzerland 56 (x2), 57, 58
Fud Leclerc	4	Belgium 56, 58, 60, 62
Elisabeth Andreassen	4	Sweden 82*, Norway 85*, 94*, 96
Peter, Sue & Marc	4	Switzerland, 71, 76, 79*, 81
Corry Brokken	3	The Netherlands 56, 57, 58
Hanne Krogh	3	Norway 71, 85*, 91*
Domenico Modugno	3	Italy 58, 59, 66
Hot Eyes	3	Denmark 84, 85, 88
Ireen Sheer	3	Luxembourg 74, 85*, Germany 78
Anita Skorgan^	3	Norway 77, 79, 82*
Jahn Teigen	3	Norway 78, 82*, 83
Katja Ebstein	3	Germany 70, 71, 80
Stella	3	The Netherlands 70*, Belgium 77*, 82
Kirsti Sparboe	3	Norway 65, 67, 69
Romuald	3	Monaco 64, 74 Luxembourg 69
Sandra Reemer^	3	The Netherlands 72*, 76, 79*
Marie Bergman	3	Sweden 71*, 72*, 94*
Anne Karine Strøm	3	Norway 73*, 74, 76
Tommy Seebach	3	Denmark 79, 81*, 93*
Udo Jürgens	3	Austria 64, 65, 66
Anna Vissi (Vishy)	3	Greece 80, 06, Cyprus 82
Gary Lux^	3	Austria 83*, 85, 87
Carola	3	Sweden 83, 91, 06
Wind	3	Germany 85, 87, 92
Constantinos	3	Cyprus 96, 02*, 05
Chiara	3	Malta 98, 05, 09

*As part of a group or duet

^Also uncredited backing singer on other occasions

Evridiki represented Cyprus in 92 & 94 but failed to survive the 07 qualifier.

Eirikur Hauksson represented Iceland as part of Icy in 86 & Norway as part of Just 4 Fun in 91, but failed to qualify as a soloist for Iceland in 07.

SINGERS WHO REPRESENTED MULTIPLE COUNTRIES

Jean Philippe	France 59, Switzerland 62
Siw Malmkvist	Sweden 60, Germany 69
Romuald	Monaco 64, 74, Luxembourg 69
Teresa (Tereza)	Monaco 66, Yugoslavia 72
Michele Torr	Luxembourg 66, Monaco 77
Stella	Netherlands 70*, Belgium 77*, 82
Anne-Marie David	**Luxembourg 73**, France 79
Ireen Sheer	Luxembourg 74, 85*, Germany 78
Elpida	Greece 78, Cyprus 86
Anna Vissi (Vishy)	Greece 80, 06, Cyprus 82
Elisabeth Andreassen	Sweden 82*, **Norway 85***, 94*, 96
Eirikur Hauksson~	Iceland 86*, Norway 91*
Doris (Dragović)	Yugoslavia 86, Croatia 99

~Also represented Iceland in the 2007 semi final, but failed to qualify.

It should be noted that the Géraldine who sang for Switzerland in 67 is not the same Geraldine who sang for Ireland in 75. Neither are the two Michelles who sang for the Netherlands and Germany in 2001 the same person.

The Sophie who sang for Monaco in 1975 is not related to the Sophie who sang with Magaly for Luxembourg in 1980. The group Regina who represented Bosnia-Herzegovina in 2009 are no relation to Regina, the female soloist who represented Slovenia in 1996.

*As part of a group or duet

Winners in bold

WINNING COMBOS
(Counting all performers on stage)

One performer	11	56, 58, 59, 60, 61, 62, 64, 65, 66, 69 (France), 70
Two performers	4	57, 63, 69 (Netherlands), 94
Three performers	1	69 (United Kingdom)
Four performers	8	67, 68, 69 (Spain), 76, 79, 81, 87, 93
Five performers	11	71, 72, 80, 86, 88, 89, 95, 96, 98, 03, 08
Six performers	21	73, 74, 75, 77, 78, 82, 83, 84, 85, 90, 91, 92, 97, 99, 00, 01 02, 04, 05, 06, 07, 09

WINNING PERFORMERS BY TYPE OF ARTIST
Ignoring uncredited backing performers

Female Soloists	33	56, 57, 59, 60, 62, 64, 65, 67, 68, 69, 69, 69, 69, 70, 71, 72, 73, 77, 82, 83, 86, 88, 91, 92, 93, 96, 98, 99, 02, 03, 04, 05, 07
Male/Female Groups	10	74, 75, 76, 78, 79, 81, 89, 95, 97, 06
Male Soloists	8*	58, 61, 66, 80, 87, 90, 08, 09
Male Duos	3	94, 00, 01
Male Groups	1	84
Male/Female Duos	1	63
Female Duos	1	85

*Includes two wins for Johnny Logan

PERFORMED MOST WINNERS

Johnny Logan   2

Rolf Løvland was a member of the group Secret Garden who won the contest in 1995, having previously anonymously accompanied the 1985 winners Bobbysocks on stage.

George & Michel Costa have sung backing vocals on three winners for two countries (1973, 1977 & 1983) but they've never received any credit for their efforts.

WINNING LANGUAGES

English	23	67, 69*, 70, 74, 75, 76, 80, 81, 87, 92, 93, 94, 96, 97, 99, 00, 01, 02, 03, 05, 06, 08, 09
French	14	56, 58, 60, 61, 62, 65, 69*, 71, 72, 73, 77, 83, 86, 88
Dutch	3	57, 59, 69*
Hebrew	3	78, 79, 98
Spanish	2	68, 69*
German	2	66, 82
Swedish	2	84, 91
Italian	2	64, 90
Norwegian	2	85, 95
Serbo Croat	2	89, 07
Danish	1	63
English/ Ukrainian	1	04

* shared win

MOST NUMBER OF TOP MARKS RECEIVED IN ONE CONTEST
(Final only)

Norway	16/41	2009
United Kingdom	10/24	1997
Greece	10/38	2005
Germany	9/17	1982
Estonia	9/22	2001
Serbia	9/41	2007
Italy	8/15	1964
Norway	8/18	1985
Ireland	8/21	1987
Ireland	8/24	1994
Denmark	8/23	2000
Ukraine	8/35	2004
Finland	8/37	2006
Bosnia-Herzegovina	8/37	2006*
Armenia	8/42	2008*
United Kingdom	7/16	1967^
United Kingdom	7/17	1976
Ireland	7/18	1980
Ireland	7/24	1993
Ireland	7/22	1996
Serbia & Montenegro	7/35	2004*
Russia	7/37	2006*
Russia	7/42	2008
France	6/12	1960^
Luxembourg	6/15	1961^
Monaco	6/17	1971^
The Netherlands	6/18	1975
United Kingdom	6/17	1977*
Israel	6/19	1978
Israel	6/18	1979
Luxembourg	6/19	1983
France	6/21	1990*
Norway	6/22	1995
Denmark	6/22	2001*
Turkey	6/41	2009*
Greece	6/42	2008*

Did not win. ^Awarded the highest mark given by each jury.

Excludes the 1956 contest

MOST TIMES SCORED 'NUL POINTS'
(Excludes the 1956 contest)

Norway	4	63, 78, 81, 97
Austria	3	62, 88, 91
Finland	3	62, 65, 82
Spain	3	62, 65, 83
Switzerland	3	64, 67, 98
The Netherlands	2	62, 63
Belgium	2	62, 65
Germany	2	64, 65
Portugal	2	64, 97
Turkey	2	83, 87
Iceland	1	89
Italy	1	66
Lithuania	1	94
Luxembourg	1	70
Monaco	1	66
United Kingdom	1	03
Yugoslavia	1	64

THE HIGHEST-SCORING EUROVISION ENTRIES
Based on the number of points or votes scored in terms of the total available.
Excludes the 1956 contest.

Tu Te Reconnaîtras	Luxembourg	1973	1st	129/160	80.63%
Save Your Kisses For Me	United Kingdom	1976	1st	164/204	80.39%
Ein Bisschen Frieden	Germany	1982	1st	161/204	78.92%
Love Shine A Light	United Kingdom	1997	1st	227/288	78.82%
Fairytale	Norway	2009	1st	387/492	78.66%
Rock 'n' Roll Kids	Ireland	1994	1st	226/288	78.47%
Eres Tu	Spain	1973	2nd	126/160	78.13%
J'Aime La Vie	Belgium	1986	1st	164/228	77.19%
Power To All Our Friends	United Kingdom	1973	3rd	123/160	76.88%
Un Banc, Un Arbre, Une Rue	Monaco	1971	1st	128/170	75.29%
Après Toi	Luxembourg	1972	1st	128/170	75.29%
Everybody	Estonia	2001	1st	198/264	75.00%
Un, Deux, Trois	France	1976	2nd	147/204	72.06%
Fly On The Wings Of Love	Denmark	2000	1st	195/276	70.65%
Ding Dinge Dong	The Netherlands	1975	1st	152/216	70.37%
A-Ba-Ni-Bi	Israel	1978	1st	157/228	68.86%
Hold Me Now	Ireland	1987	1st	172/252	68.25%
En Un Mundo Nuevo	Spain	1971	2nd	116/170	68.24%
Diggi-Loo Diggi-Ley	Sweden	1984	1st	145/216	67.13%
Beg, Steal Or Borrow	United Kingdom	1972	2nd	114/170	67.06%
Never Ever Let You Go	Denmark	2001	2nd	177/264	67.05%
L'Oiseau Et L'Enfant	France	1977	1st	136/204	66.67%
Wild Dances	Ukraine	2004	1st	280/420	66.67%
What's Another Year?	Ireland	1980	1st	143/216	66.20%
Hard Rock Hallelujah	Finland	2006	1st	292/444	65.77%
Non Ho L'Età	Italy	1964	1st	49/75	65.33%
In Your Eyes	Ireland	1993	1st	187/288	64.93%
Let Me Be The One	United Kingdom	1975	2nd	138/216	63.89%
I Wanna	Latvia	2002	1st	176/276	63.77%
Terminal Three	Ireland	1984	2nd	137/216	63.43%
Nur Die Liebe Lässt Uns Leben	Germany	1972	3rd	107/170	62.94%
Als Het Om De Leifde Gaat	The Netherlands	1972	4th	106/170	62.35%
Si La Vie Est Cadeau	Luxembourg	1983	1st	142/228	62.28%
Take Me To Your Heaven	Sweden	1999	1st	163/264	62.94%
Lane Moje	Serbia & Montenegro	2004	2nd	263/420	62.62%
Pas Pour Moi	Switzerland	1986	2nd	140/228	62.35%
The Voice	Ireland	1993	1st	162/264	61.36%
Ey Sham	Israel	1973	4th	97/160	60.63%
Shake It	Greece	2004	3rd	252/420	60.00%
Diva	Israel	1998	1st	172/288	59.72%
Making Your Mind Up	United Kingdom	1981	1st	132/228	59.65%
7th Wonder	Malta	2002	2nd	164/276	59.42%
Rock Bottom	United Kingdom	1977	2nd	121/204	59.31%
Theater	Germany	1980	2nd	128/216	59.26%
Insieme 1992	Italy	1990	1st	149/252	59.13%
Diese Welt	Germany	1971	3rd	100/170	58.82%
Falter Im Wind	Austria	1972	5th	100/170	58.82%

TOP 20 HIGHEST SCORES REGARDLESS OF SYSTEM
(Excludes the 1956 contest)

387	Fairytale	Norway	2009
292	Hard Rock Hallelujah	Finland	2006
280	Wild Dances	Ukraine	2004
272	Believe	Russia	2008
268	Molitva	Serbia	2007
263	Lane Moje	Serbia & Montenegro	2004*
252	Shake It	Greece	2004*
248	Never Let You Go	Russia	2006*
235	Dancing Lasha Tumbai	Ukraine	2008*
230	My Number One	Greece	2005
230	Shady Lady	Ukraine	2008*
229	Lejla	Bosnia-Herzegovina	2006*
227	Love Shine A Light	United Kingdom	1997
226	Rock 'n' Roll Kids	Ireland	1994
218	Secret Combination	Greece	2008*
218	Is It True?	Iceland	2009*
207	Song #1	Russia	2007*
207	Always	Azerbaijan	2009*
199	Qele, Qele	Armenia	2008*
198	Everybody	Estonia	2001

* Did not win

LOWEST WINNING SCORES
(Excludes the 1956 contest)

18	Vivo Cantando	Spain	1969
	Boom Bang-a-Bang	United Kingdom	1969
	De Troubadour	Netherlands	1969
	Un Jour Un Enfant	France	1969
21	Een Beetje	Netherlands	1959
24	Waterloo	Sweden	1974
26	Un Premier Amour	France	1962
27	Dors Mon Amour	France	1958
29	La La La...	Spain	1968
31	Net Als Toen	Netherlands	1959
	Nous Les Amoureaux	Luxembourg	1961
	Merci Cherie	Austria	1966
32	Tom Pillibi	France	1960
	Poupée De Cire...	Luxembourg	1965
	All Kinds Of Everything	Ireland	1970
42	Dansevise	Denmark	1963
47	Puppet On A String	United Kingdom	1967
49	Non Ho L'Età	Italy	1964

LONGEST ABSENCES FROM THE CONTEST

Monaco~ (Last appeared in 1979 final)	31 years
Morocco* (Last appeared in 1980 final)	30
Yugoslavia** (Last appeared in 1992 final)	18
Luxembourg (Last appeared in 1993 final)	17
Malta (Absent 1976 – 1990)	15
Italy (Last appeared in 1997 final)	13
Denmark (Absent 1967 - 1977)	11
Slovakia~ (Absent 1998 – 2009)	11

* Only one entry. **No longer exists as a nation. All former Yugoslav constituents have entered the contest independently.
~ Has entered the semi finals.

THE MOST SUCCESSFUL EUROVISION ENTRIES BY VOTING SYSTEM
Based on the number of points or votes scored in terms of the total available, under each voting system used. Excludes the 1956 contest.

System 1: 1957-1961, 1967-1970 & 1974. 10 jurors per country with one vote each for any other song.

Net Als Toen	The Netherlands	1957	1st	31/90	34.44%
Dors Mon Amour	France	1958	1st	27/90	30.00%
Puppet On A String	United Kingdom	1967	1st	47/160	29.38%
All Kinds Of Everything	Ireland	1970	1st	32/110	29.09%
Tom Pillibi	France	1960	1st	32/120	26.67%
Giorgio	Switzerland	1958	2nd	24/90	26.67%
Knock, Knock (Who's There?)	United Kingdom	1970	2nd	26/110	23.64%
Een Beetje	The Netherlands	1959	1st	21/100	21.00%
Looking High, High, High	United Kingdom	1960	2nd	25/120	20.83%
Nous Les Amoureaux	Luxembourg	1961	1st	31/150	20.67%

Systems 2, 3 & 4: 1962-1966. Nations awarded points for their top three (or five*) preferences.

Non Ho L'Età	Italy	1964	1st	49/75	65.33%
Un Premier Amour	France	1962	1st	26/45	57.78%
Dansevise	Denmark	1963*	1st	42/75	56.00%
T'En Va Pas	Switzerland	1963*	2nd	40/75	53.33%
Uno Per Tutte	Italy	1963*	3rd	37/75	49.33%
Poupée De Cire, Poupée De Son	Luxembourg	1965	1st	32/85	37.65%
Say Wonderful Things	United Kingdom	1963*	4th	28/75	37.33%
Merci Cherie	Austria	1966	1st	31/85	36.47%
L'Amour S'En Va	Monaco	1963*	5th=	25/75	33.33%
Elle Etait Si Jolie	France	1963*	5th=	25/75	33.33%

System 5: 1971-1973. Two judges per country awarded every song but their own 1-5 votes each.

Tu Te Reconaîtras	Luxembourg	1973	1st	129/160	80.63%
Eres Tu	Spain	1973	2nd	126/160	78.13%
Power To All Our Friends	United Kingdom	1973	3rd	123/160	76.88%
Un Banc, Un Arbre, Une Rue	Monaco	1971	1st	128/170	75.29%
Aprés Toi	Luxembourg	1972	1st	128/170	75.29%
En Un Mundo Nuevo	Spain	1971	2nd	116/170	68.24%
Beg, Steal Or Borrow	United Kingdom	1972	2nd	114/170	67.06%
Nur Die Liebe Lässt Uns Leben	Germany	1972	3rd	107/170	62.94%
Als Het Om De Leifde Gaat	The Netherlands	1972	4th	106/170	62.35%
Ey Sham	Israel	1973	4th	97/160	60.63%

System 6: 1975-2006. Nations awarded points (1-8, 10 & 12) for their top ten preferences.

Save Your Kisses For Me	United Kingdom	1976	1st	164/204	80.39%
Ein Bisschen Frieden	Germany	1982	1st	161/204	78.92%
Love Shine A Light	United Kingdom	1997	1st	227/288	78.82%
Fairytale	Norway	2009	1st	387/492	78.66%
Rock 'n' Roll Kids	Ireland	1994	1st	226/288	78.47%
J'Aime La Vie	Belgium	1986	1st	164/228	77.19%
Everybody	Estonia	2001	1st	198/264	75.00%
Un, Deux, Trois	France	1976	2nd	147/204	72.06%
Fly On The Wings Of Love	Denmark	2000	1st	195/276	70.65%
Ding Dinge Dong	The Netherlands	1975	1st	152/216	70.37%

NARROWEST VICTORIES – THE SMALLEST WINNING MARGINS BY SCORES
(Excluding the 1956 contest)

| 0 points | 1991 | 1st | Sweden 146 |
| | | 2nd | France 146 |

(Sweden won by having gained 5 x 10 points to France's 2 x 10. They both received 4 x 12)

1 vote	1968	1st	Spain 29
		2nd	United Kingdom 28
1 point	1988	1st	Switzerland 137
		2nd	United Kingdom 136
2 points	1963	1st	Denmark 42
		2nd	Switzerland 40
2 points	2003	1st	Turkey 167
		2nd	Belgium 165
3 votes	1958	1st	France 27
		2nd	Switzerland 24
4 votes	1973	1st	Luxembourg 129
		2nd	Spain 125
4 points	1981	1st	United Kingdom 136
		2nd	Germany 132
5 votes	1959	1st	The Netherlands 21
		2nd	United Kingdom 16
5 votes	1969	1st	= Spain, United Kingdom, The Netherlands & France 18
		5th	Switzerland 13

NARROWEST VICTORIES – THE SMALLEST RELATIVE WINNING MARGINS
(Excluding the 1956 contest)

| 0.00% | 1991 | 1st | Sweden 146 |
| | | 2nd | France 146 |

(Sweden won by having gained 5 x 10 points to France's 2 x 10. They both received 4 x 12)

0.73%	1988	1st	Switzerland 137
		2nd	United Kingdom 136
1.20%	2003	1st	Turkey 167
		2nd	Belgium 165
2.94%	1981	1st	United Kingdom 136
		2nd	Germany 132
3.19%	1973	1st	Luxembourg 129
		2nd	Spain 125
3.45%	1968	1st	Spain 29
		2nd	United Kingdom 28
3.49%	1998	1st	Israel 172
		2nd	United Kingdom 166
4.22%	1983	1st	Luxembourg 142
		2nd	Israel 136
4.76%	1963	1st	Denmark 42
		2nd	Switzerland 40
5.11%	1989	1st	Yugoslavia 137
		2nd	United Kingdom 130

LONGEST WAIT FOR A FIRST WIN

Finland (debut 1961, first win 2006)	45 years
Greece (1974–2005)	31
Belgium (1956–1986)	30
Yugoslavia (1961–1989)	28
Turkey (1975–2003)	28
Germany (1956–1982)	26
Norway (1960–1985)	25
Sweden (1958–1974)	16
Russia (1994–2008)	14
Monaco (1959–1971)	12
United Kingdom (1957–1967)	10

RAPID WINNERS
Countries to win the contest within their first five years of competing.

Switzerland* (debut 1956, first win 1956)	0
Serbia~ (2007–2007)	0
The Netherlands (1956–1957)	1
Ukraine (2003–2004)	1
Latvia (2000–2002)	2
France (1956–1958)	2
Luxembourg (1956–1961)	5
Ireland (1965–1970)	5
Israel (1973–1978)	5

* Debut contest
~ Serbia had previously entered as part of both Yugoslavia and Serbia & Montenegro

CRUSHING VICTORIES – THE BIGGEST WINNING MARGINS BY SCORES
(Excluding the 1956 contest)

169 points	2009	1st	Norway 387
		2nd	Iceland 218
70 points	1997	1st	United Kingdom 227
		2nd	Ireland 157
61 points	1982	1st	Germany 161
		2nd	Israel 100
60 points	1994	1st	Ireland 226
		2nd	Poland 166
48 points	1996	1st	Ireland 162
		2nd	Norway 114
44 points	2006	1st	Finland 292
		2nd	Russia 248
42 points	2008	1st	Russia 272
		2nd	Ukraine 230
40 points	2000	1st	Denmark 195
		2nd	Russia 155
38 points	2005	1st	Greece 230
		2nd	Malta 192
36 points	1986	1st	Belgium 176
		2nd	Switzerland 140

CRUSHING VICTORIES – THE BIGGEST RELATIVE WINNING MARGINS
(Excluding the 1956 contest)

65.30%	1964	1st	Italy 49
		2nd	United Kingdom 17
53.19%	1967	1st	United Kingdom 47
		2nd	Ireland 22
50.00%	1962	1st	France 26
		2nd	Monaco 13
48.39%	1966	1st	Austria 31
		2nd	Sweden 16
45.16%	1957	1st	The Netherlands 31
		2nd	France 17
43.67%	2009	1st	Norway 387
		2nd	Iceland 218
37.88%	1982	1st	Germany 161
		2nd	Israel 100
30.84%	1997	1st	United Kingdom 227
		2nd	Ireland 157
29.63%	1996	1st	Ireland 162
		2nd	Norway 114
26.55%	1994	1st	Ireland 226
		2nd	Poland 166

AND STILL WAITING FOR THAT FIRST WINNER....

Portugal (Debut 1964)	46 years
Malta (1971)	39
Morocco (1980) (only competed once)	30
Cyprus (1981)	29
Iceland (1986)	24
Bosnia-Herzegovina (1993)	17
Croatia (1993)	17
Slovenia (1993)	17
Hungary (1994)	16
Lithuania (1994)	16
Poland (1994)	16
Romania (1994)	16
Slovakia (1994)	16
FYR Macedonia (1998)	12

COUNTRIES TO RECEIVE A MARK FROM EVERY OTHER IN ONE CONTEST

(Excluding the contests of 1971, 1972 and 1973 when each jury had to award a minimum of two votes to each song and 1956 where the scores and places are not known)

1957	The Netherlands	1st
1975	The Netherlands	1st
1976	United Kingdom	1st
	France	2nd
1977	France	1st
1978	France	3rd
1981	United Kingdom	1st
1982	Belgium	4th
1984	Sweden	1st
	Denmark	4th
1986	Belgium	1st
1993	Ireland	1st
1997	United Kingdom	1st
1998	United Kingdom	2nd
2001	Greece	3rd
2004	Serbia & Montenegro	2nd
	Greece	3rd
2009	Norway	1st

LONGEST GAP BETWEEN WINS

Denmark (1963 – 2000)	37 years
Switzerland (1956–1988)	32
Italy (1964–1990)	26
Israel (1979–1998)	19
United Kingdom (1981–1997)	16
Norway (1995–2009)	14
Netherlands (1959–1969)	10
Sweden (1974–1984)	10
Luxembourg (1973–1983)	10
Norway (1985–1995)	10

Yugoslavia won in 1989 before their constituent member Serbia won in 2007, a gap of 18 years

SHORTEST GAP BETWEEN WINS

Spain (1968–1969*)	1 year
Luxembourg (1972–1973)	1
Israel (1978–1979)	1
Ireland (1992–1993)	1
Ireland (1993–1994)	1
The Netherlands (1957–1959)	2 years
France (1958–1960)	2
France (1960–1962)	2
United Kingdom (1967–1969*)	2
Ireland (1994–1996)	2
Luxembourg (1961–1965)	4
United Kingdom (1976–1981)	5
Ireland (1987–1992)	5

* Shared win

STILL WAITING TO WIN AGAIN

Austria (Last won in 1966)	44 years
Spain (1969)	41
Monaco (1971)	39
The Netherlands (1975)	35
France (1977)	33
Germany (1982)	28
Luxembourg (1983)	27
Belgium (1986)	24
Switzerland (1988)	22
Yugoslavia* (1989)	21
Italy (1990)	20
Norway (1995)	15
Ireland (1996)	14
United Kingdom (1997)	13
Israel (1998)	12
Sweden (1999)	11
Denmark (2000)	10

*No longer exists as a nation.

Yugoslav constituent Serbia won in 2007.

CONSECUTIVE PLACINGS

(Excluding the 1956 contest)

1st	3	1992, 1993, 1994	Ireland
	2	1968, 1969*	Spain
	2	1972, 1973	Luxembourg
	2	1978, 1979	Israel
2nd	3	1959, 1960, 1961	United Kingdom
	2	1964, 1965	United Kingdom
	2	1980, 1981	Germany
	2	1982, 1983	Israel
	2	1988, 1989	United Kingdom
	2	1990*, 1991	France
	2	1992, 1993	United Kingdom
	2	2007, 2008	Ukraine
3rd	3	1970, 1972, 1972	Germany
	2	1967, 1968	France
	2	1978, 1979	France
	2	1988, 1989	Denmark
	2	1995, 1996	Sweden
4th	2	1962*, 1963	United Kingdom
	2	1977, 1978	Monaco
	2	1980, 1981	Switzerland
5th	2	1972, 1976	Austria (did not enter in 1973, 74, 75)
	2	1978, 1979	Ireland
6th	2	1959, 1960	Belgium
7th	3	1967, 1968, 1969	Belgium
8th	2	1978, 1979	Greece
	2	1983, 1984	France
	2	2006, 2007	Armenia
9th	2	1977, 1978	Spain
	2	1982, 1983	Austria
	2	1984, 1985	Finland
10th	2	1963, 1964	Belgium
	2	1980, 1981	Sweden
	2	1994, 1995*	United Kingdom
	2	1995*, 1996	Malta
11th	2	1968, 1969	Luxembourg
12th	2	1963, 1964	Spain
	2	1987, 1988	Sweden
13th	4	1964*, 1965, 1966, 1967	Portugal
	2	1962*, 1963*	Netherlands
	2	1982, 1983	Portugal
	2	1984, 1986	Netherlands (did not enter in 1985)
14th	2	1988, 1989	Germany
15th	2	1986, 1987	Finland
	2	1989, 1990	Netherlands
16th	3	1986, 1987, 1988	Iceland
	2	2006, 2007	Latvia
17th	2	1972, 1973	Belgium
	2	1982, 1983	Denmark
	2	2002, 2003	Greece
	2	2008, 2009	Albania
18th	2	1972, 1973	Malta
	2	1975, 1976	Norway
	2	1987, 1988	Portugal
	2	2007, 2008	Sweden
21st	2	2005, 2006	Spain
22nd	2	2006, 2007	France
Last	2	1961*, 1962*	Austria
	2	1961*, 1962*	Belgium
	2	1964*, 1965*	Germany
	2	1958*, 1960	Luxembourg (did not enter in 1959)
	2	1962*, 1963*	Netherlands
	2	1971, 1972	Malta

* Shared position

EUROVISION SCRUTINEERS

1956	Rolf Liebermann (Jury President)
1963–1965	Miroslav Vilcek
1966–1977	Clifford Brown
1978–1992	Frank Naef
1993–1995	Christian Clausen
1996	Christine Marchal-Ortiz
1997	Marie-Claire Vionnet
1998–2002	Christine Marchal-Ortiz
2003	Sarah Yuen
2004–2009	Svante Stockselius

MOST COMMON POSITION IN THE RUNNING ORDER FOR SONGS PLACED LAST

(Three or more, excluding the 1956 contest)

Pos	Count								
2nd	8	1962	1963	1968	1971	1973	1978	2001	2008
3rd	8	1960	1961	1962	1965	1995	1997	1999	2004
4th	6	1958	1959	1962	1974	2001	2007		
5th	4	1957	1963	1965	1998				
6th	4	1967	1982	1983	1991				
8th	4	1962	1970	1985	1993				
12th	4	1969	1979	1988	1992				
13th	4	1963	1964	1966	1981				
14th	4	1964	1966	1974	2002				
15th	4	1974	1986	1997	2003				
7th	3	1963	1983	2006					
16th	3	1965	1974	1994					

COUNTRIES THAT FINISHED IN EACH POSITION MOST FREQUENTLY

Pos	No.	Country	Years
1st	7	Ireland	70, 80, 87, 92, 93, 94, 96
2nd	15	United Kingdom	59, 60, 61, 64, 65, 68, 70, 72, 75, 77, 88, 89, 92, 93, 98
3rd	7	France	59, 65, 67, 68, 78, 79, 91
4th	7	France	61, 64, 70, 75, 93, 95, 01
5th	6	Sweden	68, 73, 86, 01, 03, 06
6th	4	Italy	57, 59, 72, 80
		Spain	67, 89, 97, 01
7th	5	United Kingdom	57, 79, 82, 84, 86
8th	7	Germany	59, 67, 73, 77, 86, 01, 04
9th	5	The Netherlands	58, 76, 81, 88, 92
10th	5	Austria	57, 90, 92, 96, 99
	5	Spain	72, 75, 82, 86, 04
11th	4	Cyprus	89, 92, 94, 98
12th	4	Italy	78, 88, 93
		Turkey	84, 91, 96
13th	7	The Netherlands	62, 63, 78, 84, 86, 00, 03
		Portugal	64, 65, 66, 67, 82, 83, 08
14th	5	Norway	67, 72, 74, 99, 06
15th	4	Finland	65, 86, 87, 98
16th	3	Iceland	86, 87, 88
		Norway	69, 80, 89
		Turkey	95, 99, 02
17th	3	Austria	77, 81, 94
		Belgium	72, 73, 80
		Norway	71, 84, 91
		Greece	88, 02, 03
		Switzerland	67, 87, 06
18th	4	Portugal	81, 85, 88, 89
19th	3	Spain	83, 87, 00
20th	3	Finland	88, 91, 02
21st	3	Austria	88, 97, 04
22nd	2	Iceland	87, 01
		Switzerland	97, 02
		France	06, 07
23rd	2	Finland	92, 96
		Germany	95, 08
		France	00, 05
		Spain	99, 09
24th	2	Norway	97, 04
25th			No repetitions to date
26th			No repetitions to date
Last	10	Norway	63, 69, 74, 76, 78, 81, 90, 97, 01, 04

Excludes the 1956 contest

THE CURSE OF NUMBER TWO: FINAL POSITIONS OF SONGS PERFORMED SECOND IN THE RUNNING ORDER

Year	Pos	Year	Pos	Year	Pos
1956	Unknown	1974	=4th	1992	20th
1957	=4th	1975	9th	1993	21st
1958	=Last	1976	4th	1994	=22nd
1959	5th	1977	4th	1995	14th
1960	=10th	1978	Last (nul points)	1996	8th
1961	=10th	1979	15th	1997	3rd
1962	Last (nul points)	1980	15th	1998	20th
1963	Last (nul points)	1981	=18th	1999	=12th
1964	=10th	1982	6th	2000	13th
1965	2nd	1983	9th	2001	=Last
1966	=4th	1984	10th	2002	=3rd
1967	4th	1985	9th	2003	6th
1968	=Last	1986	8th	2004	21st
1969	11th	1987	11th	2005	22nd
1970	=4th	1988	=12th	2006	20th
1971	Last	1989	=12th	2007	20th
1972	11th	1990	19th	2008	Last
1973	Last	1991	15th	2009	16th

POSITIONS IN THE RUNNING ORDER OF THE SONGS PLACED LAST

Year	Pos	Year	Pos	Year	Pos
1956	Unknown	1974	4th, 14th, 15th & 16th	1992	12th
1957	5th	1975	13th	1993	8th
1958	2nd & 4th	1976	9th	1994	16th
1959	4th	1977	13th	1995	3rd
1960	3rd	1978	2nd	1996	18th
1961	3rd & 11th	1979	12th & 18th	1997	3rd & 15th
1962	2nd, 3rd, 4th & 8th	1980	10th	1998	5th
1963	2nd, 5th, 7th & 13th	1981	13th	1999	3rd
1964	9th, 11th, 13th & 14th	1982	6th	2000	10th
1965	3rd, 5th, 8th & 16th	1983	6th & 7th	2001	2nd & 4th
1966	13th & 14th	1984	13th	2002	14th
1967	6th	1985	8th	2003	15th
1968	2nd & 9th	1986	15th	2004	3rd
1969	12th	1987	10th	2005	17th
1970	8th	1988	12th	2006	7th
1971	2nd	1989	20th	2007	4th
1972	9th	1990	9th & 22nd	2008	2nd
1973	2nd	1991	6th	2009	24th

WINNING POSITIONS IN THE DRAW

Where is it best to sing in the draw if you want to win? 17th, second from last or last seem to be the best slots for a victory.

Position	Count					
1st	3	1975	1976	1984		
2nd	None					
3rd	4	1958	1969*	1971	1994	
4th	1	2003				
5th	2	1959	1995			
6th	1	1957				
7th	1	1969*				
8th	5	1963	1969*	1974	1991	1998
9th	3	1956	1962	1966		
10th	2	1979	2004			
11th	2	1967	1973			
12th	2	1964	1970			
13th	3	1960	1985	1986		
14th	5	1961	1969*	1981	1993	2000
15th	3	1965	1968	1999		
16th	None					
17th	6	1972	1980	1992	1996	2006	2007
18th	3	1977	1978	1982		
19th	2	1990	2005			
20th	4	1983	1987	2001	2009	
21st	None					
22nd	1	1989				
23rd	1	2002				
24th	2	1997	2008			
25th	None					
26th	None					
Exactly halfway	4	1963	1966	1969*	1979	
Penultimate	4	1972	1997	2002	2008	
Two from the end	6	1961	1968	1969*	1978	1980	1987
Last	6	1960	1970	1977	1982	1983	1989

*Shared winners

MOST IMPRESSIVE DEBUTS...

Excluding the inaugural contest from 1956, the following nations placed in the first ten with their debut efforts in the final:

1st	Serbia~	2007
2nd	Poland	1994
	Serbia & Montenegro	2004
3rd	Denmark	1957
	Latvia	2000
4th	Sweden	1958
	Norway	1960
	Israel	1973
	Hungary	1994
5th	Bulgaria^	2007
6th	Ireland	1965
	Cyprus	1981
	Moldova	2005
	Belarus^	2007
7th	United Kingdom	1957
	Albania	2004
8th	Yugoslavia	1961
	Armenia	2006
	Azerbaijan	2008
9th	Spain	1961
	Russia	1994
10th	Finland*	1961

* Shared position. ^Countries had previously failed to reach the final from the qualifying rounds. ~Serbia previously entered both as part of Yugoslavia and Serbia & Montenegro

...AND LEAST IMPRESSIVE

Did Not Qualify	Estonia	1993
	Hungary	1993
	Romania	1993
	Slovakia	1993
	FYR Macedonia	1996
	Andorra~	2004
	Belarus	2004
	Bulgaria	2005
	Czech Republic~	2007
	Montenegro~	2007
	San Marino~	2008

IN THE FINAL

Last with 0 points	Portugal	1964*
	Lithuania	1994
Last	Austria	1957
	Monaco	1959
	Malta	1971
	Turkey	1975
2nd Last	Morocco	1980
	Estonia	1994
3rd Last	Slovenia	1993

* Shared position
~Yet to appear in the Eurovision final

WINNING SINGERS NOT NATIVES OF THE COUNTRY THEY REPRESENTED

Jean-Claude Pascal	France	Luxembourg 1961
France Gall	France	Luxembourg 1965
Frida Boccara	Morocco	France 1969
Dana	United Kingdom	Ireland 1970
Sèverine	France	Monaco 1971
Vicky Leandros	Greece	Luxembourg 1972
Anne-Marie David	France	Luxembourg 1973
Frida Lyngstad (*Abba*)	Norway	Sweden 1974
Getty Kaspers (*Teach-in*)	Austria	The Netherlands 1975
Marie Myriam	Congo	France 1977
Johnny Logan*	Australia	Ireland 1980
Mike Nolan (*Bucks Fizz*)	Ireland	UK 1981
Corinne Hermès	France	Luxembourg 1983
Elisabeth Andreassen (*Bobbysocks*)	Sweden	Norway 1985
Céline Dion	Canada	Switzerland 1988
Linda Martin	United Kingdom	Ireland 1992
Fionnuala Sherry (*Secret Garden*)	Ireland	Norway 1995
Katrina Leskanich (*Katrina & The Waves*)	U.S.A.	United Kingdom 1997
Vince de la Cruz (*Katrina & The Waves*)	U.S.A.	United Kingdom 1997
Dave Benton (*Tanel Padar & Dave Benton*)	Aruba	Estonia 2001
Helena Paparizou	Sweden	Greece 2005
Alexander Rybak	Belarus	Norway 2009

*Became an Irish citizen before his 1987 victory

MULTIPLE APPEARANCES BY PRESENTERS

Corry Brokken	5	*1956, 1957, 1959,* **1976,** 1997*
Katie Boyle	5	**1960, 1963, 1968, 1974** 1998^
Gigliola Cinquetti	3	*1964, 1974,* **1991**
Åse Kleveland	3	*1966,* 1980^, **1986**
Yardena Arazi	3	*1976,* **1979,** *1988*
Marie N	2	*2002,* **2003,** 2005*
Sakis Rouvas	3	*2004,* **2006,** *2009*
Terry Wogan	2	**1998,** 1999^ (plus various cameos as commentator)
Jacqueline Joubert	2	**1959, 1961**
Lill Lindfors	2	*1966,* **1985**
Daniel Pe'er	2	**1979,** 1995*
Toto Cutugno	2	*1990,* **1991**
Helga Vlahović	2	**1990,** 1994* (plus various years as unseen announcer)
Dafna Dakel	2	**1992,** *1999*
Carrie Crowley	2	**1997,** 1998^
Yigal Ravid	2	1998*, **1999**
Renars Kaupers	2	*2000,* 2001*, **2003**
Kattis Ahlström	2	**2000,** 2003*
Željko Joksimović	2	*2004,* **2008**
Jaana Pelkonen	2	**2007,** 2008*
Alsou	2	**2000,** *2009*

Bold: As main presenter
Italic: As performing artist
* Results announcer
^ Guest contributor

CONSECUTIVE RUNS OF DIFFERENT WINNING NATIONS

14	1995–2008	Norway, Ireland, United Kingdom, Israel, Sweden, Denmark, Estonia, Latvia, Turkey, Ukraine, Greece, Finland, Serbia, Russia
14	1996–2009	Ireland, United Kingdom, Israel, Sweden, Denmark, Estonia, Latvia, Turkey, Ukraine, Greece, Finland, Serbia, Russia, Norway
11	1981–1991	United Kingdom, Germany, Luxembourg, Sweden, Norway, Belgium, Ireland, Switzerland, Yugoslavia, Italy, Sweden
8	1979–1986	Israel, Ireland, United Kingdom, Germany, Luxembourg, Sweden, Norway, Belgium
7	1962–1968	France, Denmark, Italy, Luxembourg, Austria, United Kingdom, Spain
6	1973–1978	Luxembourg, Sweden, The Netherlands, United Kingdom, France, Israel

CONSECUTIVE RUNS OF FIRST TIME WINNING NATIONS

8	2001–2008	Estonia, Latvia, Turkey, Ukraine, Greece, Finland, Serbia, Russia
3	1956–1958	Switzerland, The Netherlands, France
3	1966–1968	Austria, United Kingdom, Spain

LONGEST INTERVALS FOR APPEARANCES BY COMPETING SINGERS

1982–2006	Anna Vissi (Vishy)	24 years
1972–1994	Marie Bergman (of The Family Four)	22
1961–1981	Jean-Claude Pascal	20
1969–1988	Tommy Körberg	19
1977–1992	Mia Martini	15
1991–2006	Carola	15
1971–1985	Hanne Krogh (of Bobbysocks)	14
1979–1993	Katri Helena	14
1970–1983	Guy Bonnet	13
1986–1999	Doris (Dragović)	13
1972–1984	Mary Roos	12
1981–1993	Tommy Seebach (with his band)	12
1962–1973	Marion Rung	11
1966–1977	Michèle Torr	11
1969–1980	Paola (del Medico)	11

WORST RESULTS FOR THE HOST NATION

=Last of 10	1958	The Netherlands in Hilversum
22nd of 23	1992	Sweden in Malmö
24th of 26	2004	Latvia in Riga
14th of 17	1967	Austria in Vienna
20th of 24	2005	Ukraine in Kyiv
17th of 25	2007	Finland in Helsinki
9th of 16	1964	Denmark in Copenhagen
11th of 18	1971	Ireland in Dublin
=10th of 18	1966	Luxembourg in Luxembourg
12th of 20	1986	Norway in Bergen
14th of 23	1995	Ireland in Dublin

BEST RESULTS FOR THE HOST NATION

1st	1956	Switzerland in Lugano
	1973	Luxembourg in Luxembourg
	1979	Israel in Jerusalem
	1993	Ireland in Millstreet
	1994	Ireland in Dublin
=1st	1969	Spain in Madrid
2nd	1960	United Kingdom in London
	1968	United Kingdom in London
	1972	United Kingdom in Edinburgh
	1977	United Kingdom in London
	1996	Norway in Oslo
	1997	Ireland in Dublin
	1998	United Kingdom in Birmingham
	2001	Denmark in Copenhagen
3rd	1959	France in Cannes
	1962	Luxembourg in Luxembourg
	1978	France in Paris
	1985	Sweden in Gothenburg
=3rd	2002	Estonia in Tallinn

THE DISQUALIFIED, WITHDRAWN & REPLACED ENTRIES

Spain 1963	Nubes De Colores	Jose Guardiola
Italy 1967	Non Pensare A Me	Claudio Villa
Norway 1968	Jag Har Aldri Vært Så Glad I No'En Som Deg	Odd Børre
Portugal 1970	Onde Vais Rio Que Eu Canto	Sergio Borges
France 1974	La Vie A Vingt-Cinq Ans	Dani
Germany 1976	Der Star	Tony Marshall
Turkey 1979	Seviyorum	Maria Rita Epik
Greece 1982	Sarantapente Kopelles	Themis Adamantidis
Belgium 1985	Vannacht	Mireille Capelle
Greece 1986	Wagonlit	Polina
Cyprus 1988	Thimame	Yiannis Dimitriou
Austria 1990	Das Beste	Duett
Switzerland 1992	Soleil, Soleil	Géraldine Olivier
Greece 1997	An Den Agapissis, Den Tha Agapissi	Dimosthenis Stringlis
Hungary 1998	Csak Neked!	Erika Zoltan
Germany 1999	Hor Den Kinden Einfach Zu	Corinna May
Bosnia-Herzegovina 1999	Starac I More	Hari Mata Hari
Lithuania 2002	We All	B'Avarija
France 2004	Laissez-Moi Le Temps	Jonatan Cerrada
France 2006	Nous C'Est Vous	Virginie Pouchain
Serbia & Montenegro 2006	Moja Ljubav	No Name

Tunisia withdrew from the 1977 contest without having selected their entry

Withdrawn from the Semi-Finals:

Belarus 2005	Boys And Girls	Angelica Agurbash
Lebanon 2005	Quand Tout S'Enfuit	Aline Lahoud
Georgia 2009	Put-In Disco	Stefane Da 3G
Hungary 2009	If You Wanna Party	Márk Zentai
Hungary 2009	Magányos Csónak	Kátya Tompos

Replaced Performers:

France 1960	Marcel Amont
Sweden 1961	Siw Malmkvist
Spain 1968	Joan Manuel Serrat
Belgium 1971	Nicole & Hugo
Iceland 1994	Sigrun Eva Armandsdottir

SAME SONG TITLE, DIFFERENT LANGUAGE (FINALISTS ONLY)

Oração (Prayer)	Portugal 1964
Modlitba (Prayer)	Slovakia 1998
Molitva (Prayer)	Serbia 2007
Bonjour, Bonjour (Hello, Hello)	Switzerland 1969
Halo, Halo (Hello, Hello)	Yugoslavia 1982
Hallo, Hallo (Hello, Hello)	Denmark 1990
L'Imħabba (Love)	Malta 1972
Sev (Love)	Turkey 1995
Love	Lithuania 2009
Karusell (Carousel)	Norway 1965
Dönme Dolap (Carousel)	Turkey 1981
Llámame	Spain 1962
Call Me	Bosnia-Herzegovina 2005
Oração (Prayer)	Portugal 1964
Modlitba (Prayer)	Slovakia 1998
Tijd (Time)	The Netherlands 1971
Zeit (Time)	Germany 1997
L'Imħabba (Love)	Malta 1972
Sev (Love)	Turkey 1995
Sans Toi	France 1973
Without You	The Netherlands 2004
Libera (Free)	Italy 1977
Fri? (Free?)	Finland 1990
Socrates	Greece 1979
Sokrates	Iceland 1988
Mono I Agapi (Only Love)	Cyprus 1982
Samo Ljubezen (Only Love)	Slovenia 2002
Adieu	Norway 1982
Goodbye	Bosnia-Herzegovina 1997
Love Is...	United Kingdom 1985
Kärleken Är	Sweden 1998
Maria Magdalena	Austria 1993
Marija Magdalena	Croatia 1999
Dön Artik	Turkey 1999
Come Back	United Kingdom 2002
Tell Me	Iceland 2000
Dime	Spain 2003
Leila	Yugoslavia 1981
Lejla	Bosnia-Herzegovina 2006

Following Malta's "L'Imħabba", Turkey's "Sev" & Lithuania's "Love", Ireland and Portugal entered songs with the same meaning entitled "Love?" & "Amar" in 2005, but neither qualified for the final.

It could be argued that 'Prima Donna' (Russia 1997) and 'Diva' (Israel 1998) may have the same meaning. Or that 'De Mallemolen' ('The Merry-Go-Round' – The Netherlands 1977) also means a 'Carousel'. Does 'Retour' ('Return' – Switzerland 1970) also mean 'Come Back'? and is 'Le Retour' ('The Return' – Switzerland 1961) the same? Should 'Addio, Addio' ('Goodbye, Goodbye' – Italy 1962) be listed with 'Goodbye'?

Close, but no cigar! Exact translations only!

THE LONG AND THE SHORT OF IT! (Finals only)

Longest Contest:	Kyiv 2005	3 hours, 26 minutes
Longest Performance:	Italy 1957	Corde Della Mia Chitarra (5 minutes 9 seconds)
Longest Song Title:	Germany 1964	Man Gewöhnt Sich So Schnell An Das Schöne
Longest Artist Names		
Group:	Luxembourg 1985	Margo, Franck Olivier, Chris Roberts, Malcolm Roberts, Ireen Sheer & Diane Solomon
Soloist:	Iceland 1987	Halla Margrét Anadottir*
Shortest Contest:	Frankfurt 1957	1 hour, 9 minutes
Shortest Performance:	United Kingdom 1957	All (1 minute, 52 seconds)
Shortest Song Titles:	Italy 1974	Si
	Spain 1982	El
	Israel 1983	Hi
	United Kingdom 1988	Go
Shortest Artist Names		
Groups:	Iceland 1986	Icy
	Turkey 1985 & 1988	MFÖ~
	Turkey 1989	Pan
	Croatia 1993	Put
	Hungary 1997	VIP
	Croatia 1997	ENI
	F.Y.R. Macedonia 2000	XXL
	Portugal 2001	MTM
	Cyprus 2002	One
	Latvia 2003	F.L.Y.
	Hungary 2005	Nox
Soloists:	Germany 2003	Lou
	Germany 2004	Max

The shortest named contestants ever were 2B who failed to qualify for Portugal in 2005 and DQ who didn't qualify for Denmark in 2007.

*The longest named solo artist would have been Jóhanna Guðrún Jónsdóttir, representing Iceland in 2009, but she opted for the stage name Yohanna for her performance.

~Also referred to as Mazhar, Fuat & Özkan

IDENTICALLY TITLED ENTRIES (FINALISTS ONLY)

Vivre	Switzerland 1978 & France 1983
Angel	Iceland 2001 & Malta 2005
Never Let You Go	Greece 2003 & Russia 2006

Greece entered a song entitled 'Stop' in 1997 as did Slovenia in 2005, but the Slovenians failed to qualify for the final and they were not performed in the same language.

The UK competed in the 1968 final with 'Congratulations' which was also the title of Iceland's losing semi-finalist in 2006.

TOTAL NUMBER OF TIMES EACH NATION HAS RECEIVED THE 'DOUZE POINTS!' SINCE 1975 (*Final only*)

Ireland	65
United Kingdom	58
Greece	45
France	43
Norway	43
Sweden	41
Germany	40
Turkey	35
Denmark	31
Switzerland	31
Russia	30
Spain	27
Israel	26
Italy	24
Cyprus	22
Malta	21
The Netherlands	20
Belgium	19
Estonia	18
Luxembourg	16
Ukraine	16
Yugoslavia	16
Bosnia-Herzegovina	16
Romania	14
Armenia	13
Croatia	13
Iceland	13
Latvia	13
Finland	13
Serbia & Montenegro	10
Portugal	9
Moldova	6
Poland	6
Hungary	5
Monaco	4
Albania	3
Azerbaijan	3
Belarus	3
FYR Macedonia	2
Slovenia	2
Bulgaria	1
Georgia	1
Lithuania	1
Slovakia	1

'DIX VOTES!' THE COUNTRIES THAT RECEIVED THE MAXIMUM POSSIBLE 10 VOTES EACH YEAR FROM 1971-1973

1971	**Monaco (6)**, Spain (2), Portugal (1), Finland (2),
1972	United Kingdom (1), **Luxembourg (2)**
1973	Spain (3), **Luxembourg (3)**, United Kingdom (2)

Winning Nation (x)

'CINQ POINTS!' THE COUNTRIES THAT RECEIVED THE MAXIMUM 5 POINTS EACH YEAR FROM 1963-1966 (OR 3 POINTS IN 1962)

1962	Finland (1), Sweden (1), **France (5)**, Yugoslavia (2), United Kingdom (1), Luxembourg (3), Monaco (3)
1963	United Kingdom (2), Italy (3), **Denmark (5)**, Switzerland (3), France (1), Monaco (1)
1964	Luxembourg (1), Norway (1), Austria (2), France (1), United Kingdom (2), Monaco (1), **Italy (8)**
1965	The Netherlands (1), United Kingdom (4*), Ireland (1), Austria (1), Monaco (1), France (2), Denmark (2), **Luxembourg (4)**, Switzerland (1)
1966	Germany (1), Belgium (2), Luxembourg (1), Yugoslavia (1), Norway (1), Portugal (1), **Austria (4)**, Sweden (3), Spain (1), Switzerland (1), Ireland (1), United Kingdom (1)

Winning Nation (x)

* The United Kingdom received 3 x 5 and 1 x 6 points under the allowed system

TOP POSITIONS ALL TAKEN BY SONGS IN THE SAME LANGUAGE

Top 5

2008 – English	1st	Russia	Believe
	2nd	Ukraine	Shady Lady
	3rd	Greece	Secret Combination
	4th	Armenia	Qele, Qele*
	5th	Norway	Hold On, Be Strong
2009 – English	1st	Norway	Fairytale
	2nd	Iceland	Is It True?
	3rd	Azerbaijan	Always
	4th	Turkey	Düm Tek Tek*
	5th	United Kingdom	It's My Time

Top 4

2000 – English	1st	Denmark	Fly On The Wings Of Love
	2nd	Russia	Solo
	3rd	Latvia	My Star
	4th	Estonia	Once In A Lifetime
2002 – English	1st	Latvia	I Wanna
	2nd	Malta	7th Wonder
	=3rd	United Kingdom	Come Back
	=3rd	Estonia	Runaway

Top 3

1962 – French	1st	France	Un Premier Amour
	2nd	Monaco	Dis Rien
	3rd	Luxembourg	Petit Bonhomme
1986 – French	1st	Belgium	J'Aime La Vie
	2nd	Switzerland	Pas Pour Moi
	3rd	Luxembourg	L'Amour De Ma Vie
1992 – English	1st	Ireland	Why Me?
	2nd	United Kingdom	One Step Out Of Time
	3rd	Malta	Little Child
2005 – English	1st	Greece	My Number One
	2nd	Malta	Angel
	3rd	Romania	Let Me Try

*Despite the title, the song was performed in English.

BIGGEST DECLINE – FROM FIRST ONE YEAR TO LAST THE NEXT

Netherlands:	1st	1957
	Last (=)	1958

BIGGEST IMPROVEMENT – FROM LAST ONE YEAR TO FIRST THE NEXT

Belgium:	Last	1985
	1st	1986

THE BIG 4 FINISH AS THE BOTTOM 4

2005

24th/Last	Germany
23rd	France
22nd	United Kingdom
21st	Spain

THE BIG 4 FINISH AS THE TOP 4

No instances to date. Closest so far:

1970

2nd	United Kingdom
3rd	Germany
=4th	France
=4th	Spain

1968

1st	Spain
2nd	United Kingdom
3rd	France
6th	Germany

1969

=1st	Spain
=1st	United Kingdom
=1st	France
=9th	Germany

1979

2nd	Spain
3rd	France
4th	Germany
7th	United Kingdom

REVERSED RESULTS! TOP THREE FROM ONE YEAR = BOTTOM THREE THE NEXT

2002	1st	Latvia
	2nd	Malta
	=3rd	United Kingdom
2003	26th/Last	United Kingdom
	25th	Malta
	24th	Latvia

LEADING FROM START TO FINISH IN THE VOTING
(excluding 1956)

1957	The Netherlands	Net Als Toen
1964	Italy	Non Ho L'Etá
1965	Luxembourg	Poupée De Cire, Poupée De Son *(joint 1st for one round)*
1970	Ireland	All Kinds Of Everything *(joint 1st for one round)*
1972	Luxembourg	Aprés Toi
1974	Sweden	Waterloo
2000	Denmark	Fly On The Wings Of Love
2009	Norway	Fairytale

'DOUZE POINTS!' THE COUNTRIES TO RECEIVE THE MAXIMUM 12 POINTS EACH YEAR SINCE 1975 *(Finals Only)*

1975 **The Netherlands (6)**, Ireland (1), France (2), Luxembourg (1), United Kingdom (4), Finland (2), Portugal (1), Italy (1)

1976 **United Kingdom (7)**, Switzerland (1), Belgium (1), Ireland (1), Italy (1), Portugal (1), Monaco (1), France (5)

1977 Ireland (4), Monaco (2), United Kingdom (6), Greece (1), Finland (1), Belgium (1), **France (3)**

1978 Ireland (1), France (1), Spain (1), Belgium (5), The Netherlands (1), Germany (1), Monaco (1), Luxembourg (3), **Israel (6)**

1979 Denmark (2), Switzerland (1), Germany (4), **Israel (6)**, France (2), Spain (4)

1980 Turkey (1), Italy (1), Switzerland (2), Germany (3), United Kingdom (1), The Netherlands (4), **Ireland (7)**

1981 Germany (4), Denmark (1), France (4), Ireland (2), **United Kingdom (2)**, Cyprus (1), Switzerland (5), Sweden (1)

1982 United Kingdom (2), Switzerland (3), Cyprus (2), Yugoslavia (1), Israel (2), **Germany (8)**

1983 United Kingdom (1), Sweden (2), Greece (2), The Netherlands (1), Yugoslavia (5), Germany (1), Israel (2), **Luxembourg (6)**

1984 **Sweden (5)**, France (1), Spain (2), Cyprus (1), Belgium (2), Ireland (4), Denmark (2), Italy (2)

1985 Ireland (1), Spain (1), France (1), Turkey (1), Germany (1), Israel (1), Italy (3), **Norway (8)**, Sweden (2)

1986 Luxembourg (2), Yugoslavia (1), Turkey (1), Switzerland (5), Ireland (3), **Belgium (5)**, Germany (1), Sweden (2)

1987 Sweden (1), Italy (5), Greece (1), The Netherlands (1), France (1), Germany (2), Cyprus (1), **Ireland (8)**, Yugoslavia (2)

1988 Sweden (1), United Kingdom (3), The Netherlands (2), **Switzerland (3)**, Ireland (1), Denmark (3), Norway (1), Luxembourg (3), France (1), Yugoslavia (3)

1989 Italy (1), United Kingdom (5), Sweden (3), Denmark (3), Austria (3), Cyprus (1), Greece (2), **Yugoslavia (4)**

1990 Spain (1), Luxembourg (1), United Kingdom (1), Iceland (2), Switzerland (2), Germany (1), France (6), Yugoslavia (2), Ireland (2), **Italy (3)**, Austria (1)

1991 Malta (2), Switzerland (2), **Sweden (4)**, France (4), Israel (3), Spain (2), Cyprus (3), Italy (2)

1992 Israel (1), Greece (2), France (2), Malta (4), Iceland (1), Switzerland (1), Austria (1), United Kingdom (4), **Ireland (3)**, Italy (4)

1993 Switzerland (3), Greece (1), Austria (1), Portugal (2), France (2), **Ireland (7)**, Bosnia-Herzegovina (1), United Kingdom (4), The Netherlands (1), Norway (3)

1994 **Ireland (8)**, Cyprus (1), Croatia (1), Portugal (1), Malta (1), Germany (2), Slovakia (1), Greece (1), Hungary (4), Poland (5)

1995 **Norway (6)**, Spain (2), Croatia (3), United Kingdom (2), Cyprus (1), Sweden (3), Denmark (2), Israel (1), Malta (2), Greece (1)

1996 United Kingdom (2), Portugal (2), Cyprus (2), Malta (2), Austria (2), Estonia (3), The Netherlands (1), Belgium (1), **Ireland (7)**, Sweden (1)

1997 Cyprus (2), Turkey (3), Ireland (1), Italy (1), Spain (1), Estonia (1), Greece (1), Malta (1), Russia (1), France (3), **United Kingdom (10)**

1998 Croatia (2), Greece (1), **Israel (3)**, Germany (3), Malta (4), United Kingdom (4), Cyprus (1) The Netherlands (2), Sweden (1), Belgium (1), Norway (1), Estonia (1), Turkey (1)

1999 Croatia (2), Slovenia (2), Turkey (1), Denmark (1), The Netherlands (1), Iceland (3), **Sweden (5)**, Portugal (1), Ireland (1), Germany (5), Bosnia-Herzegovina (1)

2000 Romania (1), Russia (4), Iceland (2), **Denmark (8)**, Germany (3), Sweden (1), Latvia (4), Turkey (2)

2001 Portugal (1), Spain (1), France (3), **Estonia (9)**, Malta (1), Greece (2), Denmark (6)

2002 Cyprus (2), United Kingdom (1), Austria (1), Greece (1), Spain (3), Croatia (1), Estonia (2), F.Y.R. Macedonia (1), Sweden (1), France (1), Malta (3), Romania (2), **Latvia (5)**

2003 Iceland (2), Ireland (1), **Turkey (4)**, Bosnia-Herzegovina (1), Cyprus (1), Russia (5), Spain (2), Greece (1), Norway (3), Poland (1), Belgium (3), Romania (1), Sweden (1)

2004 Spain (2), France (1), Serbia & Montenegro (7), Germany (1), Albania (1), **Ukraine (8)**, Russia (1), F.Y.R. Macedonia (1), Greece (5), Cyprus (1), Turkey (4), Sweden (4)

2005 Malta (1), Romania (3), Norway (3), Turkey (2), Moldova (2), Albania (1), Cyprus (2), Israel (1), Spain (1), Serbia & Montenegro (3), Denmark (1), Ukraine (1), Croatia (2), **Greece (10)**, Russia (1), Switzerland (2), Latvia (3)

2006 Switzerland (1), Moldova (1), Spain (1), Russia (3), Romania (2), Bosnia-Herzegovina (8), Lithuania (1), Greece (2), **Finland (8)**, Ukraine (1), Croatia (1), Turkey (3), Armenia (2)

2007 Spain (1), Belarus (3), Finland (2), Hungary (1), Lithuania (1), Greece (2), Georgia (1), Sweden (2), Russia (3), **Serbia (9)**, Ukraine (5), United Kingdom (1), Romania (2), Bulgaria (1), Turkey (5), Armenia (2), Moldova (1)

2008 Armenia (8), **Russia (7)**, Greece (6), Serbia (4), Azerbaijan (2), Bosnia-Herzegovina (2), Denmark (2), Norway (2), Romania (2), Albania (1), Germany (1), Iceland (1), Latvia (1), Spain (1), Sweden (1), Turkey (1), Ukraine (1)

2009 **Norway (16)**, Turkey (6), Bosnia-Herzegovina (3), Greece (3), Iceland (3), Estonia (2), Moldova (2), Armenia (1), Azerbaijan (1), Croatia (1), Romania (1), Russia (1), Spain (1), United Kingdom (1)

Winning Nation (x)

THE INTERVAL ACTS

1956	Les Joyeux Rossignols et Les Trois Ménestrels
1957	No Interval
1958	Ceilito Lindo – The Metropole Orchestra conducted by Dolf van der Linden
1959	No Interval
1960	No Interval
1961	Rencontre á Cannes – Tessa Beaumont & Max Bozzoni
1962	Achilles Zavatta
1963	Barbro & Ola Nordström
1964	Ballet-Harlequinade
1965	Mario del Monaco
1966	Les Haricots Rouge
1967	Die Wiener Sängerknaben (The Vienna Boy's Choir)
1968	Impressions From London. Orchestra conducted by Norrie Paramour
1969	La España Diferente
1970	De Don de Lurio Dancers van Amsterdam
1971	The Shannon Castle Entertainers
1972	The Massed Pipes and Drums of The Scottish Regiments
1973	Belle Dame – Charlie Revel
1974	The Wombles
1975	The World of John Bauer
1976	The Dutch Swing College Band
1977	Mr. Acker Bilk & His Paramount Jazz Band
1978	Stéphane Grapelli, Yehudi Menuhin & Oscar Petterson
1979	The Shalom '79 Dance Troupe
1980	San Fernando – The Dutch Rhythm Steel & Showband
1981	Timedance – Planxty
1982	Yorkshire Sights. BBC Concert Orchestra conducted by Ronnie Hazlehurst
1983	Marlene Charrell – The Song Contest Ballet
1984	The Prague Theatre of Illuminated Drawing
1985	Guitars Unlimited with Swedish Evergreens
1986	Sissel Kyrkjebø & Steiner Ofsdal
1987	Ode To Joy – The RTBF Orchestra conducted by Jo Carlier
1988	Don't Go – The Hot House Flowers
1989	Guy Tell
1990	Yugoslav Changes. Orchestra conducted by Igor Kuljerić
1991	Arturo Brachetti
1992	A Century of Dance – Crazy Feet Troupe
1993	Linda Martin, Johnny Logan and The Millstreet Children & Choirs
1994	Riverdance
1995	Lumen
1996	I Am The Firestarter – Prodigy
1997	Let The Message Run Free – Boyzone
1998	Jupiter: The Bringer of Jollity
1999	Freedom Calls – Dana International, Dancers & Chorus
2000	Strangnas Drumcorps, Caroline Lundgren & Bounce
2001	Aqua
2002	Rebirth
2003	Ilgi, Brainstorm, Marie N & Raimonds Pauls
2004	Anadolu Atesi (The Fire of Anatolia)
2005	Ruslana
2006	Helena Paparizou & 4000 Years of Greek Song
2007	Apocalyptica
2008	Goran Bregović and his Wedding and Funeral Orchestra
2009	Fuerza Bruta

PRESENTER OF THE GRAND PRIX TO THE WINNERS

1956	Marcel Besançon (SSR/SRG/RTSI)
1957	Ederhard Beckmann (HR/ARD)
1958	J.V.Rengeling (NTS)
1959	Jean d'Arcy (ORTF)
1960	Teddy Scholten
1961	Tessa Beaumont
1962	Jean-Claude Pascal
1963	Stuart Hood (BBC)
1964	Svend Pedersen (DR)
1965	Mario del Monaco
1966	France Gall
1967	Udo Jürgens
1968	Sandie Shaw
1969	Massiel
1970	Lenny Kuhr
1971	Dana
1972	Séverine
1973	Vicky Leandros
1974	Sir Charles Curran (BBC)
1975	Henrik Jarhe (SR)
1976	Getty Kaspers
1977	Sir Charles Curran (BBC)
1978	Marie Myriam
1979	Izhar Cohen
1980	Marcel Besançon (EBU)
1981	Johnny Logan & Shay Healy
1982	Sir Ian Trethowan (BBC)
1983	Nicole
1984	Corinne Hermès
1985	Herreys
1986	Bobbysocks & Rolf Løvland
1987	Sandra Kim
1988	Johnny Logan
1989	Céline Dion & 'Heidi' Cindy Eschbach
1990	Goran Radman (JRT/RTZ)
1991	Alber Schard (EBU)
1992	Carola
1993	Linda Martin
1994	Niamh Kavanagh
1995	Paul Harrington & Charlie McGettigan
1996	Rolf Løvland & Fionnuala Sherry
1997	Eimear Quinn
1998	Katrina
1999	Dana International
2000	Kattis Ahlström & Anders Lundin
2001	The Olsen Brothers
2002	Tanel Padar & Dave Benton
2003	Sarah Yuen (EBU) & Mayor Gundars Bojas
2004	Sertab Erener
2005	Ruslana, President Viktor Yuschenko & Volodymyr Klytschko
2006	Helena Paparizou & Christos Panagopoulus (ERT)
2007	Santa Claus
2008	Maria Šerifović
2009	Dima Bilan & Lys Assia

CONDUCTORS OF THE WINNING SONG

1956	Fernando Paggi
1957	Dolf van der Linden
1958	Franck Pourcel
1959	Dolf van der Linden
1960	Franck Pourcel
1961	Léo Chauliac
1962	Franck Pourcel
1963	Kai Mortensen
1964	Gianfranco Monaldi
1965	Alain Goraguer
1966	Hans Hammerschmid
1967	Kenny Woodman
1968	Rafael Ibarbia
1969	Augusto Alguero (Spain)
1969	Johnny Harris (United Kingdom)
1969	Frans de Kok (The Netherlands)
1969	Franck Pourcel (France)
1970	Dolf van der Linden
1971	Jean-Claude Petit
1972	Klaus Munro
1973	Pierre Cao
1974	Sven-Olof Walldoff
1975	Harry van Hoof
1976	Alyn Ainsworth
1977	Raymond Donnez
1978	Nurit Hirsh
1979	Kobi Oshrat
1980	Noel Kelehan
1981	John Coleman
1982	Norbert Daum
1983	Michel Bernholc
1984	Curt-Eric Holmquist
1985	Terje Fjærn
1986	Jo Carlier
1987	Noel Kelehan
1988	Atilla Sereftug
1989	Nikica Kalogjera
1990	Gianni Madonini
1991	Anders Berglund
1992	Noel Kelehan
1993	Noel Kelehan
1994	Winning song performed without the orchestra
1995	Geir Langslet
1996	Noel Kelehan
1997	Don Airey
1998	Winning song performed without the orchestra

Orchestra discontinued after 1998

THE HIGHEST SINGLE VOTES GIVEN FROM 1957–1961, 1967–1970 & 1974 WHEN JURIES HAD 10 VOTES TO AWARD IN TOTAL

1958	9 votes	Given To **France**	By Denmark
1970	9 votes	Given To **Ireland**	By Belgium
1961	8 votes	Given To United Kingdom	By Norway
1957	7 votes	Given To **The Netherlands**	By Switzerland
1958	7 votes	Given To **France**	By Austria
1959	7 votes	Given To **The Netherlands**	By Italy
1961	7 votes	Given To United Kingdom	By Switzerland
1967	7 votes	Given To **United Kingdom**	By France
1967	7 votes	Given To **United Kingdom**	By Switzerland
1967	7 votes	Given To **United Kingdom**	By Norway

Winning Nation

HOST COUNTRY'S MUSICAL DIRECTORS

1956	Fernando Paggi
1957	Willy Berking
1958	Dolf van der Linden
1959	Franck Pourcel
1960	Eric Robinson
1961	Franck Pourcel
1962	Jean Roderes
1963	Eric Robinson
1964	Kai Mortensen
1965	Gianni Ferrio
1966	Jean Roderes
1967	Johannes Fehring
1968	Norrie Paramour
1969	Augusto Alguero
1970	Dolf van der Linden
1971	Colman Pearce*
1972	Malcolm Lockyer*
1973	Pierre Cao
1974	Ronnie Hazlehurst*
1975	Mats Olsson*
1976	Jan Stulen*
1977	Ronnie Hazlehurst
1978	François Rauber*
1979	Izhak Graziani*
1980	Rogier van Otterloo
1981	Noel Kelehan
1982	Ronnie Hazlehurst
1983	Dieter Reith
1984	Pierre Cao*
1985	Curt-Eric Holmquist
1986	Egil Monn-Iversen
1987	Jo Carlier*
1988	Noel Kelehan
1989	Benoit Kaufman
1990	Igor Kuljerić*
1991	Bruno Camfora
1992	Anders Berglund
1993	Noel Kelehan
1994	Noel Kelehan*
1995	Noel Kelehan
1996	Frode Thingnæs
1997	Frank McNamara*
1998	Martin Koch*

Orchestra discontinued after 1998
*Did not conduct the host nation's entry

MOST TIMES SCORED "NUL POINTS"
(Excludes the 1956 contest)

Norway	4	63, 78, 81, 97
Austria	3	62, 88, 91
Finland	3	62, 65, 82
Spain	3	62, 65, 83
Switzerland	3	64, 67, 98
The Netherlands	2	62, 63
Belgium	2	62, 65
Germany	2	64, 65
Portugal	2	64, 97
Turkey	2	83, 87
Iceland	1	89
Italy	1	66
Lithuania	1	94
Luxembourg	1	70
Monaco	1	66
United Kingdom	1	03
Yugoslavia	1	64

THE NUL POINTERS!

1962	Belgium	"Ton Nom"
1962	Spain	"Llámame"
1962	Germany	"Nur In Der Wiener Luft"
1962	Netherlands	"Katinka"
1963	Netherlands	"Een Speeldos"
1963	Norway	"Solherv"
1963	Finland	"Muistejeni Laulu"
1963	Sweden	"En Gång I Stockholm"
1964	Germany	"Man Gewöhnt Sich So Schnell An Das Schöne"
1964	Portugal	"Oração"
1964	Yugoslavia	"Život Je Sklopio Krug"
1964	Switzerland	"I Miei Pensieri"
1965	Spain	"Qué Bueno, Qué Bueno"
1965	Germany	"Paradies, Wo Bist Du?"
1965	Belgium	"Als Het Weer Lente Is"
1965	Finland	"Aurinko Laskee Länteen"
1966	Monaco	"Bien Plus Fort"
1966	Italy	"Dio, Come Te Amo"
1967	Switzerland	"Quel Cœur Vas-Tu Briser?"
1978	Norway	"Mil Etter Mil"'
1981	Norway	"Aldri I Livet"
1982	Finland	"Nuku Pommiin"
1983	Spain	"Quién Maneja Mi Barca"
1983	Turkey	"Opera"
1987	Turkey	"Şarkim Sevgi Üstüne"
1988	Austria	"Lisa, Mona Lisa"
1989	Iceland	"Það Sem Enginn Sér"
1991	Austria	"Venedig Im Regen"
1994	Lithuania	"Lopšinė Mylimai"
1997	Norway	"San Francisco"
1997	Portugal	"Antes Do Adeus"
1998	Switzerland	"Lass 'Ihn"
2003	United Kingdom	"Cry Baby"

In 2004, Switzerland's "Celebrate" scored 'nul points' in the semi-final, as did the Czech Republic's "Aven Romale" in 2009.

SEMI-FINALS

COUNTRY	SONG	PERFORMER	PLACE	SCORE	DRAW	
1993 (3 of 7 qualified)						
Slovenia	Tih Deževen Dan	1X Band	1	54	6	Qualified
Bosnia-Herzegovina	Sva Bol Svijeta	Fazla	2	52	1	Qualified
Croatia	Don't Ever Cry	Put	3	51	2	Qualified
Slovakia	Amnestia Na Neveru	Elan	4	50	7	
Estonia	Muretut Meelt Ja Südametuld	Janika Sillamaa	5	47	3	
Hungary	Arva Reggel	Andrea Szulak	6	44	4	
Romania	Nu Pleca	Dida Dragan	7	38	5	
1996 (22 of 29 qualified)						
Sweden	Den Vilda	One More Time	1	227	26	Qualified
Ireland	The Voice	Eimear Quinn	2	198	14	Qualified
United Kingdom	Ooh Aah... Just A Little Bit	Gina G	3	153	29	Qualified
Malta	In A Woman's Heart	Miriam Christine	4	138	17	Qualified
Estonia	Kaelakee Hääl	Maarja-Liis Ilus & Ivo Linna	5	106	7	Qualified
Austria	Weil's Dr Guat Got	George Nussbaumer	6	80	1	Qualified
Turkey	Besinci Mevsim	Şebnem Paker	7	69	28	Qualified
Switzerland	Mon Cœur L'Aime	Kathy Leander	8	67	27	Qualified
Netherlands	De Eerste Keer	Maxine & Franklin Brown	9	63	18	Qualified
Iceland	Sjúbidú	Anna Mjöll Olafsdottir	10	59	13	Qualified
France	Diwanit Bugale	Dan Ar Braz Et L'Héritage Des Celtes	11	55	9	Qualified
Belgium	Liefde Is Een Kaartspel	Lisa Del Bo	12 =	45	2	Qualified
Greece	Emis Forame To Himona Aniziatika	Marianna Efstratiou	12 =	45	11	Qualified
Spain	Ay, Qué Deseo!	Antonio Carbonell	14	43	25	Qualified
Cyprus	Mono Gia Mas	Constantinos	15 =	42	5	Qualified
Poland	Chcę Znać Swój Grzech	Kasia Kowalska	15 =	42	19	Qualified
Slovakia	Kým Nás Más	Marcel Palonder	17	36	23	Qualified
Portugal	O Meu Coração Não Tem Cor	Lúcia Moniz	18	32	20	Qualified
Croatia	Sveta Ljubav	Maja Blagdan	19 =	30	4	Qualified
Slovenia	Dan Najlepših Sanj	Regina	19 =	30	24	Qualified
Bosnia-Herzegovina	Za Našu Ljubav	Amila Glamočak	21	29	3	Qualified
Finland	Niin Kaunis On Taivas	Jasmine	22	28	8	Qualified
Hungary	Fortuna	Gjon Delhusa	23	26	12	
Germany	Blauer Planet (Planet of Blue)	Leon	24	24	10	
Denmark	Kun Med Dig	Dorthe Andersen & Martin Loft	25	22	6	
F.Y.R. Macedonia	Samo Ti	Kaliopi Gril	26 =	14	16	
Russia	Ja, Eto Ja	Andrej Kosinskij	26 =	14	22	
Israel	Shalom Olam	Galit Bel	28	12	15	
Romania	Ruga Pentru Pacea Lumii	Monica Anghel & Sincron	29	11	21	

SEMI-FINALS

COUNTRY	SONG	PERFORMER	PLACE	SCORE	DRAW	
2004 (10 of 22 qualified)						
Serbia & Montenegro	Lane Moje	Željko Joksimović	1	263	20	Qualified
Ukraine	Wild Dances	Ruslana	2	256	11	Qualified
Greece	Shake It	Sakis Rouvas	3	238	10	Qualified
Albania	The Image Of You	Anjeza Shahini	4	167	13	Qualified
Cyprus	Stronger Every Minute	Lisa Andreas	5	149	14	Qualified
Netherlands	Without You	Re-Union	6	146	22	Qualified
Bosnia-Herzegovina	In The Disco	Deen	7	133	21	Qualified
Malta	On Again... Off Again	Julie & Ludwig	8	74	8	Qualified
Croatia	You Are The Only One	Ivan Mikulic	9	72	18	Qualified
F.Y.R. Macedonia	Life	Tose Proeski	10	71	15	Qualified
Israel	Leha'amin (To Believe)	David D'or	11	57	5	
Estonia	Tii	Neiokõsõ	12	57	17	
Denmark	Shame On You	Tomas Thordarson	13	56	19	
Finland	Takes 2 To Tango	Jari Sillanpää	14	51	1	
Portugal	Foi Magia	Sofia Vitória	15	37	7	
Lithuania	What's Happened To Your Love?	Linas & Simona	16	26	12	
Latvia	Dziesma Par Laimi	Fomins & Kleins	17	23	4	
Andorra	Jugarem A Estimar-Nos	Marta Roure	18	12	6	
Belarus	My Galileo	Alexandra & Konstantin	19	10	2	
Monaco	Notre Planete	Märyon	20	10	9	
Slovenia	Stay Forever	Platin	21	5	16	
Switzerland	Celebrate	Piero & The Music Stars	22	0	3	
2005 (10 of 25 qualified)						
Romania	Let Me Try	Luminita Anghel & Sincron	1	235	14	Qualified
Moldova	Boonika Bate Doba	Zdob Shi Zdub	2	207	4	Qualified
Denmark	Talking To You	Jakob Sveistrup	3	185	24	Qualified
Croatia	Vukovi Umiru Sami	Boris Novković ft. Lado Members	4	169	20	Qualified
Hungary	Forogj Világ	Nox	5	167	15	Qualified
Norway	In My Dreams	Wig Wam	6	164	13	Qualified
Israel	Hasheket Shenishar (The Silence That Remains)	Shiri Maimon	7	158	7	Qualified
Switzerland	Cool Vibes	Vanilla Ninja	8	114	19	Qualified
F.Y.R. Macedonia	Make My Day	Martin Vucic	9	97	17	Qualified
Latvia	The War Is Not Over	Walters & Kazha	10	85	5	Qualified
Poland	Czarna Dziewczyna	Ivan & Delfin	11	81	25	
Slovenia	Stop	Omar Naber	12	69	23	
Belarus	Love Me Tonight	Angelica Agurbash	13	67	8	

SEMI-FINALS

COUNTRY	SONG	PERFORMER	PLACE	SCORE	DRAW	
Ireland	Love?	Donna & Joseph McCaul	14	53	22	
Netherlands	My Impossible Dream	Glennis Grace	15	53	9	
Iceland	If I Had Your Love	Selma	16	52	10	
Portugal	Amar	2B	17	51	3	
Finland	Why?	Geir Rønning	18	50	16	
Bulgaria	Lorraine	Kaffe	19	49	21	
Estonia	Let's Get Loud	Suntribe	20	31	12	
Austria	Y Así	Global Kryner	21	30	1	
Belgium	La Grand Soir	Nuno Resende	22	29	11	
Andorra	La Mirada Interior	Mari-An Van Der Wal	23	27	18	
Monaco	Tout De Moi	Lise Darly	24	22	6	
Lithuania	Little By Little	Laura & The Lovers	25	17	2	
Lebanon	*Quand Tout S' Enfuit*	*Aline Lahoud*	*WD*			

2006 (10 of 23 qualified)

COUNTRY	SONG	PERFORMER	PLACE	SCORE	DRAW	
Finland	Hard Rock Hallelujah	Lordi	1	292	16	Qualified
Bosnia-Herzegovina	Lejla	Hari Mata Hari	2	267	22	Qualified
Russia	Never Let You Go	Dima Bilan	3	217	13	Qualified
Sweden	Invincible	Carola	4	214	20	Qualified
Lithuania	We Are The Winners	LT United	5	163	18	Qualified
Armenia	Without Your Love	André	6	150	1	Qualified
Ukraine	Show Me Your Love	Tina Karol	7	146	15	Qualified
Turkey	Süper Star	Sibel Tüzün	8	91	14	Qualified
Ireland	Every Song Is A Cry For Love	Brian Kennedy	9	79	8	Qualified
F.Y.R. Macedonia	Ninanajna	Elena Risteska	10	76	11	Qualified
Poland	Follow My Heart	Ich Troje	11	70	12	
Belgium	Je t'Adore	Kate Ryan	12	69	7	
Iceland	Congratulations	Silvía Night	13	62	23	
Albania	Zjarr E Ftohtë	Luiz Ejlli	14	58	6	
Cyprus	Why Angels Cry	Annet Artani	15	57	9	
Slovenia	Mr. Nobody	Anžej Dežan	16	49	3	
Bulgaria	Let Me Cry	Mariana Popova	17	36	2	
Estonia	Through My Window	Sandra Oxenryd	18	28	21	
Portugal	Coisas De Nada	Nonstop	19	26	19	
Netherlands	Amambanda	Treble	20	22	17	
Monaco	La Coco Dance	Séverine Ferrer	21	14	10	
Belarus	Mum	Polina Smolova	22	10	5	
Andorra	Sense Tu	Jenny	23	8	4	

WD = Withdrawn

SEMI-FINALS

COUNTRY	SONG	PERFORMER	PLACE	SCORE	DRAW	
2007 (10 of 28 qualified)						
Serbia	Molitva	Maria Šerifović	1	298	15	Qualified
Hungary	Unsubstantial Blues	Magdi Rúzsa	2	224	22	Qualified
Turkey	Shake It Up Shekerim	Kenan Doğulu	3	197	26	Qualified
Belarus	Work Your Magic	Koldun	4	176	4	Qualified
Latvia	Questa Notte	Bonaparti.lv	5	168	28	Qualified
Bulgaria	Water	Elitsa Todorova & Stoyan Yankoulov	6	146	1	Qualified
Slovenia	Cvet Z Juga	Alenka Gotar	7	140	25	Qualified
Georgia	Visionary Dream	Sopho	8	123	6	Qualified
F.Y.R. Macedonia	Mojot Svet (My World)	Karolina	9	97	18	Qualified
Moldova	Fight	Natalia Barbu	10	91	9	Qualified
Portugal	Dança Comigo	Sabrina	11	88	17	
Andorra	Salvem El Món (Let's Save The World)	Anonymous	12	80	21	
Iceland	Valentine Lost	Eiríkur Hauksson	13	77	5	
Poland	Time To Party	The Jet Set	14	75	14	
Cyprus	Comme Ci, Comme Ça	Evridiki	15	65	3	
Croatia	Vjerujem U Ljubav	Dragonfly Ft. Dado Topić	16	54	13	
Albania	Hear My Plea	Frederik Ndoci	17	49	11	
Norway	Ven A Bailar Conmigo	Guri Schanke	18	48	19	
Denmark	Drama Queen	DQ	19	45	12	
Switzerland	Vampires Are Alive	DJ BoBo	20	40	8	
Netherlands	On Top Of The World	Edsilia Rombley	21	38	10	
Estonia	Partners In Crime	Gerli Padar	22	33	23	
Montenegro	'Ajde Kroči	Stevan Faddy	23	33	7	
Israel	Push The Button	Teapacks	24	17	2	
Malta	Vertigo	Olivia Lewis	25	15	20	
Belgium	Love Power	The KMG's	26	14	24	
Austria	Get A Life - Get Alive	Eric Papilaya	27	4	27	
Czech Republic	Malá Dáma	Kabát	28	1	16	
2008 Semi Final 1 (10 of 19 qualified)						
Greece	Secret Combination	Kalomira	1	156	19	Qualified
Armenia	Qele, Qele	Sirusho	2	139	14	Qualified
Russia	Believe	Dima Bilan	3	135	18	Qualified
Norway	Hold On, Be Strong	Maria Haukass Storeng	4	106	9	Qualified
Israel	The Fire In Your Eyes	Boaz	5	104	2	Qualified
Azerbaijan	Day After Day	Elnur & Samir	6	96	7	Qualified
Romania	Pe-o Margine De Lume	Nico & Vlad	7	94	17	Qualified
Finland	Missä Miehet Ratsastaa	Teräsbetoni	8	79	16	Qualified
Bosnia-Herzegovina	Pokušaj	Laka	9	72	13	Qualified

SEMI-FINALS

COUNTRY	SONG	PERFORMER	PLACE	SCORE	DRAW	
Poland	For Life	Isis Gee	10	42	10	Qualified
Slovenia	Vrag Naj Vzame	Rebeka Dremelj	11	36	8	
Moldova	A Century Of Love	Geta Burlacu	12	36	4	
Netherlands	Your Heart Belongs To Me	Hind	13	27	15	
Montenegro	Zauvijek Volim Te	Stefan Filipović	14	23	1	
Ireland	Irlande Douze Points!	Dustin The Turkey	15	22	11	
Andorra	Casanova	Gisela	16	22	12	
Belgium	O Julissi	Ishtar	17	16	6	
Estonia	Leto Svet	Kreisiraadio	18	8	3	
San Marino	Complice	Miodio	19	5	5	

2008 Semi Final 2 (10 of 19 qualified)

COUNTRY	SONG	PERFORMER	PLACE	SCORE	DRAW	
Ukraine	Shady Lady	Ani Lorak	1	152	4	Qualified
Portugal	Senhora Do Mar (Negras Águas)	Vânia Fernandes	2	120	19	Qualified
Denmark	All Night Long	Simon Matthew	3	112	13	Qualified
Croatia	Romanca	Kraljevi Ulice & 75 Cents	4	112	11	Qualified
Georgia	Peace Will Come	Diana Gurtskaya	5	107	14	Qualified
Latvia	Wolves Of The Sea	Pirates Of The Sea	6	86	10	Qualified
Turkey	Deli	Mor Ve Ötesi	7	85	3	Qualified
Iceland	This Is My Life	Euroband	8	68	1	Qualified
Albania	Zemrën E Lamë Peng	Elena Risteska	9	67	6	Qualified
F.Y.R. Macedonia	Let Me Love You	Tamara, Vrčak & Adrijan	10	64	18	
Bulgaria	DJ, Take Me Away	Deep Zone & Balthazar	11	56	12	
Sweden	Hero	Charlotte Nilsson Perrelli	12	54	2	Qualified*
Switzerland	Era Stupendo	Paolo Meneguzzi	13	47	7	
Malta	Vodka	Morena	14	38	16	
Cyprus	Femme Fatale	Evdokia Kadi	15	36	17	
Lithuania	Nomads In The Night	Jeronimas Milius	16	30	5	
Belarus	Hasta La Vista	Ruslan Alehno	17	27	9	
Czech Republic	Have Some Fun	Tereza Kerndlová	18	19	8	
Hungary	Candlelight	Csézy	19	6	15	
	*Qualified through the Jury Vote					

2009 Semi Final 1 (10 of 18 qualified)

COUNTRY	SONG	PERFORMER	PLACE	SCORE	DRAW	
Iceland	Is It True?	Yohanna	1	174	12	Qualified
Turkey	Düm Tek Tek	Hadise	2	172	9	Qualified
Bosnia-Herzegovina	Bistra Voda	Regina	3	125	18	Qualified
Sweden	La Voix	Malena Ernman	4	105	5	Qualified
Armenia	Jan Jan	Inga & Anush	5	99	6	Qualified
Malta	What If We?	Chiara	6	86	17	Qualified
Israel	There Must Be Another Way	Noa & Mira Awad	7	75	10	Qualified

SEMI-FINALS

COUNTRY	SONG	PERFORMER	PLACE	SCORE	DRAW	
Portugal	Todas As Ruas Do Amor	Flor-De-Lis	8	70	16	Qualified
Romania	The Balkan Girls	Elena	9	67	14	Qualified
F.Y.R. Macedonia	Neshto Shto Ke Ostane	Next Time	10	45	13	
Montenegro	Get Out Of My Life	Andrea Demirović	11	44	1	
Finland	Lose Control	Waldo's People	12	42	15	Qualified*
Belarus	Eyes That Never Lie	Petr Elfimov	13	25	4	
Switzerland	The Highest Heights	Lovebugs	14	15	8	
Andorra	La Teva Decisió (Get A Life)	Susanne Georgi	15	8	7	
Bulgaria	Illusion	Krassimir Avramov	16	7	11	
Belgium	Copycat	Copycat	17	1	3	
Czech Republic	Aven Romale	Gypsy.cz	18	0	2	
Georgia	Put In Disco	Stefane da 3G	WD			
	*Qualified through the Jury Vote					

2009 Semi Final 2 (10 of 19 qualified)

COUNTRY	SONG	PERFORMER	PLACE	SCORE	DRAW	
Norway	Fairytale	Alexander Rybak	1	201	6	Qualified
Azerbaijan	Always	AySel & Arash	2	180	12	Qualified
Estonia	Rändajad	Urban Symphony	3	115	18	Qualified
Greece	This Is Our Night	Sakis Rouvas	4	110	13	Qualified
Moldova	Hora Din Moldova	Nelly Ciobanu	5	106	15	Qualified
Ukraine	Be My Valentine (Anti Crisis Girl)	Svetlana Loboda	6	80	17	Qualified
Albania	Carry Me In Your Dreams	Kejsi Tola	7	73	16	Qualified
Denmark	Believe Again	Brinck	8	69	9	Qualified
Lithuania	Love	Sasha Son	9	66	14	Qualified
Serbia	Cipela	Marko Kon & Milaan Nikolić	10	60	4	
Ireland	Et Cetera	Sinéad Mulvey & Black Daisy	11	52	2	
Poland	I Don't Wanna Leave	Lidia Kopania	12	43	5	
Croatia	Lijepa Tena	Igor Cukrov Ft. Andrea	13	33	1	Qualified*
Cyprus	Firefly	Christina Metaxa	14	32	7	
Hungary	Dance With Me	Zoli Ádok	15	16	11	
Slovenia	Love Symphony	Quartissimo Ft. Martina	16	14	10	
Netherlands	Shine	De Toppers	17	11	19	
Slovakia	Let' Tmou	Kamil Mikulčík & Nela Pocisková	18	8	8	
Latvia	Probka	Intars Busulis	19	7	3	
	*Qualified through the Jury Vote					